- Please return items before closing time
  on the last date stamped to avoid charges.
- Renew books by phoning 01305 224311 or
  online www.dorsetforyou.com/libraries
- Items may be returned to any Dorset library.
- Please note that children's books issued on
  an adult card will incur overdue charges.

Dorset County Council
Library Service

DL/2372 dd05450

"Sybil Oldfield's biography of Mrs Nassau Senior is a fascinating story of an extraordinary Victorian, her frustrating but not untypical marriage, and her mould-breaking career as the first woman Civil Servant who caused fury by her suggestions for reforming the care and education of workhouse girls. She died in mid-career and sank into undeserved oblivion. The friend of Octavia Hill, Florence Nightingale and George Eliot, Jeanie Senior's achievement parallels theirs and it is high time her biography was written. It could not be in better hands: Sybil Oldfield is a literary scholar and historian who has specialized in studying the lives and work of women humanitarians. She is both a humanely imaginative feminist and an ebullient, amusing and passionate writer."

> – Barbara Hardy, Professor Emeritus, University of London,
> author of *Forms of Feeling in Victorian Fiction* and
> *George Eliot, A Critic's Biography*

"The revelation of this wise, tender and engaging portrait of Jeanie Senior is not just that she was admired by the great and good of Victorian Britain, including her brother Thomas Hughes, George Eliot, Florence Nightingale, G.F. Watts, James Stansfeld and Octavia Hill, but that now we must count her as one of them. Sybil Oldfield sensitively captures both the inner life and the public work of this gifted musician and social reformer who, in championing the unpopular cause of pauper girls, herself became a feminist. A wonderful book."

> – Seth Koven, Rutgers University, author of
> *Slumming: Sexual and Social Politics
> in Victorian London*

Jeanie, an 'Army of One'

Mrs. Nassau Senior
1828–1877
The First Woman in Whitehall

SYBIL OLDFIELD

sussex ACADEMIC PRESS

BRIGHTON • PORTLAND

2 4 6 8 10 9 7 5 3 1

First published 2008 in Great Britain by
SUSSEX ACADEMIC PRESS
PO Box 139
Eastbourne BN24 9BP

and in the United States of America by
SUSSEX ACADEMIC PRESS
920 NE 58th Ave   Suite 300
Portland, Oregon 97213-3786

British Library Cataloguing in Publication Data
A CIP catalogue record for this book is available from the British Library.

Library of Congress Cataloging-in-Publication Data
Oldfield, Sybil.
   Jeanie, an "army of one" : Mrs. Nassau Senior,
   1828–1877, the first woman in Whitehall / Sybil
   Oldfield.
     p. cm.
   Includes bibliographical references and index.
   ISBN 978-1-84519-253-2 (acid-free paper) —
   ISBN 978-1-84519-254-9 (pbk. : acid-free paper)
   1. Senior, Jeanie, 1828-1877. 2. Women social
reformers—Great Britain—History—19th century. 3. Women
radicals—Great Britain—History—19th century. 4. Women
social reformers—Great Britain—Biography. 5. Women
radicals—Great Britain—Biography. I. Title.

DA565.S46O43—2008
305.42092—dc22
[B]   2007022750

Typeset & Designed by SAP, Brighton & Eastbourne
Printed by TJ International, Padstow, Cornwall
This book is printed on acid-free paper.

Contents

List of Illustrations

Jacket/Cover illustration: John Everett Millais (1829–1896), *The Rescue* (1855) (detail shown on front, full picture on back), oil on canvas, 121.5 × 83.6 cm. Courtesy of the National Gallery of Victoria, Melbourne, Australia. Felton Bequest, 1924. Jeanie Senior modelled for the mother. See pp. 33–34, and pp. 318–319 (note 6 to Chapter Three).

Endpapers: Jeanie Hughes' Family Tree

Foreword

My mother remembers how her father told her stories about his grand-mother, Jeanie (pronounced 'Janey') Senior née Hughes, sister of Thomas Hughes, the author of *Tom Brown's Schooldays*, and my mother has passed these stories on to her children, and we to ours. Recently my daughter gave a little presentation about her great-great-great-grandmother's humanitarian work to her class at school, telling how (in the face of strong opposition) she became the first woman civil servant in this country. However, it is not so much for her deeds that we, her descendants, remember her, I think, as for her personal qualities. Jeanie Senior was one of the many women who took part in the humanitarian struggle to alleviate the suffering of her time; but she gave of her time and effort without passing judgement – that is uncon-ditionally, regardless of whether or not the recipient was deemed 'deserving' on religious, moral or other grounds. Being genuinely good she looked only for the good in others.

At the same time Jeanie Senior knew a quite remarkable number of the most eminent artistic and literary people of her day, including Tennyson, Millais, Prosper Mérimée, George Eliot and George Frederick Watts ('the English Michelangelo') and her deep and significant relationships with the last two are examined closely for the first time in this book. She also worked closely with other outstanding humanitarians, including Florence Nightingale and Octavia Hill, founder of the National Trust. That she had an extraordinary impact on all those who knew her is recorded by her friends, one of whom wrote shortly after her early death: 'She was the most fascinating woman I ever met. The beauty of her expression, the sweetness and richness of her voice (in speaking as well as singing), and the charm of her manner combined to make her unlike anyone else.' Another friend wrote: 'She had the most lovely golden wavy hair, very long, and always looking as though the sun was shining upon it. She had a very earnest face, bright complexion, and clear blue eyes which seemed to look you through.'

Given Jeanie Senior's influential social intervention in so many different fields, her close relationships with several of the most eminent and interest-ing Victorians, her own remarkable character and her beauty, it is perhaps odd that her story has not been fully told before. This was due largely to the protective feelings of Walter Senior, her only son, who arranged and preserved and guarded all her papers with loving veneration. After Walter's death in 1933, these papers were stored in trunks and were not rediscovered until 2000, when I found them in an attic. They were subsequently made available to the historian and critic Sybil Oldfield, a biographer who has specialised in resurrecting forgotten women humanitarians. I am personally grateful to Sybil for having, in my view, brought so skilfully to life the moving story of Jeanie Senior's achievements, her struggles, her disappointments and, above all, her undaunted heart.

Graham Senior-Milne,
Baron of Mordington
Norham
June 2007

Acknowledgements

My heartfelt thanks go first to the great-granddaughters of Jeanie Senior, Mrs. Pamela Milne and Mrs. Anne Collier, who very generously shared with me their rich collection of 19th century Hughes and Senior family trees, family photograph albums and family portraits, including Jeanie Senior's own sketchbooks. To Jeanie Senior's great-great-grandson, Graham Senior-Milne, I am even more indebted. No biographer could have been more over-joyed than I when he unlocked box after box of family documents for me – and suddenly I saw that in one of them, containing the hundreds of letters from Jeanie Senior to her son, 1857–1877, lay the core of her whole life-story. Graham Senior-Milne, himself an indefatigable researcher, has since added to his kindness by being of immense assistance to me in producing genealogical and biographical information about the Hughes and Senior families and in supplying me with many invaluable introductions, not to mention other important 'leads' and helpful internet website quarries. This book is not, however, an official, 'authorized biography' but my own inter-pretation of Jeanie Senior's life. I could not have written it under any other terms and am correspondingly deeply grateful to Jeanie Senior's descendants for their interest and trust. Everything I have written is rooted in the docu-ments to which they gave me unfettered access.

I must also gratefully acknowledge the help given me by Willie Hughes' great-granddaughter Octavia Hughes of Boston; Arthur Hughes, New York; Barbara Stagg, custodian of the Thos. Hughes Museum, Rugby, Tennessee; Sharon Smith, curator of Tom Brown's School Museum, Uffington; Shirley Dalton-Morris, local historian of Longcot, Berkshire; Mark Bills, curator/librarian of the Watts Gallery, Compton, Surrey; Dr. John Potter, Dept. of Music, University of York; the archivist of the British Red Cross Library, London; the biographers Ann Blainey and Gillian Darley; Muriel Oldfield, Paris, for information about Mme. Pape-Carpentier; the late Professor John Bicknell for information about Leslie and Caroline Stephen; Malcolm Pollard and Professor David Stewart for help with 19th century English art history; Victoria Osborne, the curator of pictures at Birmingham City Art Gallery; the librarians of Dr. Barnardo's Archives, Walford and the London Metropolitan Archives; and, above all Ann Morton of the National Archives at the Public Record Office, Kew and Annette Moore and her colleagues at the inter-library loans section of my own University of Sussex library. Keith Hunt of the University of Sussex Photographic Unit has been his usual expert self.

Finally I am very grateful to Professor Barbara Hardy, Professor Eileen Grimes, Helen Debenham, Rodney and Pauline Hillman, Nicholas Tucker,

Lorna Watson, Joanna Reid and Sir Roy Shaw for reading the first drafts of various chapters and encouraging me on my way. My ninety year-old mother, Sigrid Bruegel, read the earlier uncut typescript with unflagging enthusiasm and my friend Gwen Shaw went through the whole final version offering helpful suggestions. My most sympathizing first reader, chapter by chapter, has been my husband Derek Oldfield whom I tried, this time, not to take for granted.

The Research Fund of the School of Humanities, University of Sussex, has contributed to the publication of this work.

In Memory of

Pauline Robinson, 1918–1996,
My English teacher at Christchurch Girls' High School,
New Zealand.

A life-saver.

Hughes Family Tree

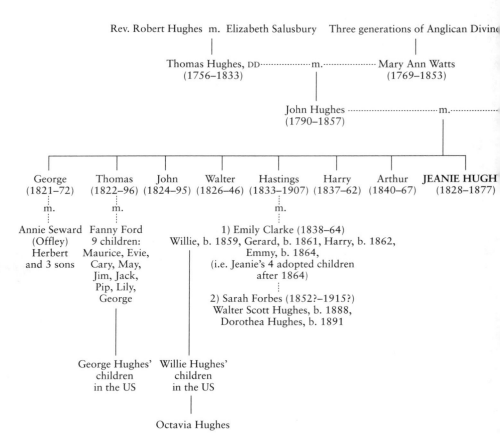

Rev. Robert Hughes m. Elizabeth Salusbury   Three generations of Anglican Divine

Thomas Hughes, DD·················· m. ···················· Mary Ann Watts
(1756–1833)   (1769–1853)

John Hughes ································ m.···············
(1790–1857)

| George
(1821–72) | Thomas
(1822–96) | John
(1824–95) | Walter
(1826–46) | Hastings
(1833–1907) | Harry
(1837–62) | Arthur
(1840–67) | **JEANIE HUGH**
(1828–1877) |

George (1821–72)
m.
Annie Seward
(Offley)
Herbert
and 3 sons

Thomas (1822–96)
m.
Fanny Ford
9 children:
Maurice, Evie,
Cary, May,
Jim, Jack,
Pip, Lily,
George

Hastings (1833–1907)
m.
1) Emily Clarke (1838–64)
Willie, b. 1859, Gerard, b. 1861, Harry, b. 1862,
Emmy, b. 1864,
(i.e. Jeanie's 4 adopted children
after 1864)

2) Sarah Forbes (1852?–1915?)
Walter Scott Hughes, b. 1888,
Dorothea Hughes, b. 1891

George Hughes'
children
in the US

Willie Hughes'
children
in the US

Octavia Hughes

Wilkinson Family Tree

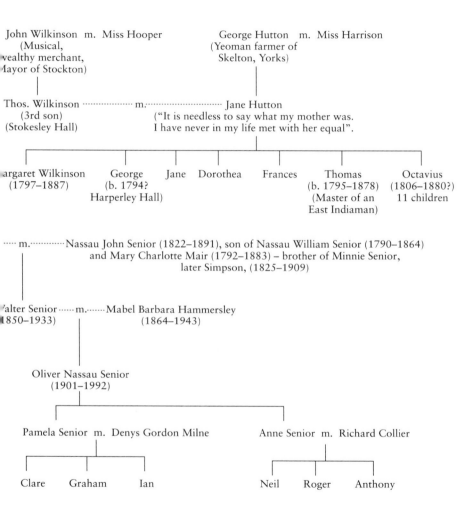

John Wilkinson m. Miss Hooper
(Musical,
wealthy merchant,
Mayor of Stockton)

George Hutton   m. Miss Harrison
(Yeoman farmer of
Skelton, Yorks)

Thos. Wilkinson ··············· m.·························· Jane Hutton
(3rd son)   ("It is needless to say what my mother was.
(Stokesley Hall)   I have never in my life met with her equal".

Margaret Wilkinson   George   Jane Dorothea   Frances   Thomas   Octavius
(1797–1887)   (b. 1794?   (b. 1795–1878)   (1806–1880?)
                                 Harperley Hall)   (Master of an   11 children
                                                                                          East Indiaman)

····· m.·············Nassau John Senior (1822–1891), son of Nassau William Senior (1790–1864)
                           and Mary Charlotte Mair (1792–1883) – brother of Minnie Senior,
                                              later Simpson, (1825–1909)

Walter Senior ······m.······Mabel Barbara Hammersley
(1850–1933)   (1864–1943)

Oliver Nassau Senior
(1901–1992)

Pamela Senior m. Denys Gordon Milne

Anne Senior m. Richard Collier

Clare   Graham   Ian

Neil   Roger   Anthony

Introduction

On 26 January 1875 *The Times* published a leader regretfully attacking a lady. The lady in question was 'Mrs. Senior', the first woman Civil Servant in Britain. Her remit, as Government Inspector of Workhouse Schools, had been to report on the effect of their education on pauper girls – the over-looked *Olive* Twists. Unfortunately Jeanie* Senior had not only threatened the closed shop of the male Civil Service by being a woman, she had also enraged the Old Guard Inspectorate by condemning many aspects of the huge 'Barrack Schools' that they themselves had established. She could not be allowed to get away with it. *The Times* accused her and her deputies of having used "dark and irresponsible" methods and of producing inaccurate, scandalous gossip about the fate of the pauper girls. "Mrs Senior must with-draw her Report" thundered the Chief Poor-Law Inspector, E. C. Tuffnell, in *The Times'* correspondence columns. She refused.

Jeanie Senior's ground-breaking appointment in Whitehall, her critical *Report* and her written defence of it, both in *The Times* and to Parliament, make her as significant a figure in 19th century British women's history as the first women university students and the first woman doctor. She is the missing link between Josephine Butler, Octavia Hill and Florence Nightingale – who saluted her as 'a noble Army of one'.

The steel in Jeanie Senior had been tempered by long years of frustrated energy and idealism. Growing up during the climacteric of Victorian domes-tic ideology, her wings had beaten against the cage as she turned this way and that trying to give her life meaning. She did her very best to find meaning in 'normal' ways – marriage, motherhood, the needs of her large extended family, respectable philanthropy. And she also sought fulfilment through the less usual routes of passion, music, radical political commitment and reli-gious questioning. But the need in her to address the needs of still more desperate others remained banked up inside her for many years. Her ardent self demanded, in George Eliot's words, a 'life beyond self'. And at last, in the 1870s, she found it. First the sick and wounded on the battlefields of the Franco-Prussian War, then the destitute little girls in British Workhouses and finally the exploited 'maids of all work', skivvying or selling themselves for a living, would find in her a rescuer.

Her Victorian contemporaries were not sure how to regard 'Mrs Nassau Senior'. Was she one of the fearsome 'Strong-minded Women' battalion, or was she an 'Angel', altogether too good for this world? In her own lifetime and for over a quarter of a century afterwards, 'Mrs. Nassau Senior' was

---

* 'Jeanie' was pronounced 'Janey'.

often bedevilled by her reputation as an angel. It did not help that she was tall, with wavy, corn-gold hair and unforgettable blue-grey eyes – and that she sang like an angel.

> I never look back on her as an ordinary woman who lived in this world. Her beauty of form and character always seemed to me as something not of this world at all . . . It was marvellous the power she had of keeping [her large household] in perfect harmony . . . . She simply threw a glamour over every one. . . .[1]

> 'surely a more beautiful life has scarcely ever been lived'. . . .[2]

> . . . 'And so this noble and brave
> Lady turned
> From glad life, luxury and
> thronging friends
> That hung on her sweet
> voice, and only yearned
> To guide her holy work to
> Useful ends.'[3]

The crescendo of unremitting hagiography came in 1905: 'Mrs. Nassau Senior used her power of attraction as a gift from God to enable her to influence and help all whom she met on her way through life.'[4] A quasi Christ-like claim was made for her: 'One can only say how she attracted every one, of whatever rank or condition, and how when she died it seemed (as was said at the time) as if a hundred people had died and as if the sun were darkened in the heavens.'[5]

How can one not feel resistant to such a fanfare of unqualified adoration? What an impossible Angel in the House 'Mrs. Nassau Senior' sounds. Virginia Woolf has said it all:

> [The Angel in the House] was intensely sympathetic. . . . She was utterly unselfish. . . . She soothed, conciliated, sacrificed herself, took the hash if there was only chicken enough for one, and in short was so constituted that she never had a wish or a mind of her own but preferred to sympathise with the wishes and minds of others. . . .

But, Virginia Woolf goes on to insist,

> This creature – . . . never had any real existence. . . . She was a dream, a phantom – . . . The Angel in the house was the ideal of

womanhood created by the imaginations of men and women . . . to lure them across a very dusty stretch [of the journey].[6]

It is my task to remove the 'angelic' mask placed so reverently (and sincerely) over Jeanie Senior. I try to reveal the much more interesting, complex, vulnerable, frustrated human being underneath who, of course, had plenty of wishes and ideas of her own, whose home-life was not miraculously harmonious and who, far from throwing a glamour over all in contact with her, actually met with ferocious disapproval, sneers, and public vilification, being called a scandal-monger and a liar. One reason for the attacks on her was precisely that she was not an Angel in the House but had left her home for an office in Whitehall. The first British woman ever to do so. A senior Civil Servant in the Treasury, alert to this alarming female precedent, immediately wrote a Memorandum stating that 'the Government must take a view.'

What could have made a beautiful, gifted Victorian woman leave the conventional safety of domestic 'Angeldom'? Why was being a wife, a mother and a lady philanthropist not enough for her? And why, if she really was so important in British women's history – 'her premature death', being, in Florence Nightingale's words, 'a national and irreparable loss' – has she been forgotten?

For over a century there did not seem to be any surviving materials, other than footnotes about her in the biographies of her contemporaries, including her famous brother Thomas Hughes, author of *Tom Brown's Schooldays*. But in December 2000 'Mrs. Nassau Senior' suddenly re-emerged in the British press. Sotheby's auctioned twenty-five letters to her from her friend George Eliot – letters deemed important enough to be placed under an export ban and bought for the nation by the British Library. That scholars' treasure trove, the Milne Collier Papers, became accessible, and was discovered to hold hundreds of letters to Jeanie Senior from famous contemporaries including G. F. Watts, Jenny Lind, Anny Thackeray, Prosper Mérimée, Cardinal Manning, many leaders of the Women's Movement and the reformers Lord Shaftesbury and Octavia Hill – as well as Florence Nightingale herself. Above all, thousands of Jeanie Senior's own startlingly outspoken, confidential 'journal letters', written 1857–1877 to her son, have survived, documenting her struggles both within her family and in the public world outside. This book tells the story of those struggles whenever possible in her own eloquent, hitherto unpublished words.

As her friend George Eliot would write in her 'Prelude' to *Middlemarch*: 'Here and there a cygnet is reared uneasily among the ducklings in the brown pond'. This particular cygnet was born Jeanie Hughes.

'You were arrayed almost single-handed,
a noble Army of one, . . . '

Florence Nightingale to Jeanie Senior,
7 December 1874

CHAPTER ONE

Tom Brown's Sister – Jeanie Hughes

'God is a wicked devil.'

(Jeanie Hughes aged about ten)

Jeanie Senior felt all her life that she had had a very happy childhood. Born 10 December 1828, the Squire's only daughter, at Uffington House, Uffington, in the Vale of the White Horse, Berkshire, she had been looked down upon by an astonishing Bronze Age tribal totem – a horse cut high into the chalk hillside – and by the great prehistoric fort known as 'Uffington Castle'. Both 'Horse' and 'Castle' were said to be five thousand years old. It must have seemed a very special birthplace.

But Jeanie Hughes' place within her family was also special, for she was the only girl in the middle of seven boys. For the first five years of her life she was the indulged youngest, her eldest brother, clever, athletic George seven years older than her, the next eldest, Tom, his devoted side-kick, nearly six years older, followed by quiet, music-loving John, and then Walter, her look-a-like and kindred spirit, exactly two years older to the day. When she was five, baby Hastings was born, when she was eight, Harry, and when she was ten, her mother's Benjamin, Arthur. Thus Jeanie Hughes could choose whether to follow after older brothers whom she hero-worshipped, or else be the responsible eldest, teaching and mothering the little boys. Her father would then tease her as 'Miss Didactic'. At other times she could play the mediator, interpreting between the two sets of young males. It was a lively, warmly affectionate family and Jeanie Senior found no difficulty in loving both her parents, as well as each of her seven brothers, wholeheartedly, all her life.

Jeanie's father, John Hughes, born in 1790, was an unusual, many-gifted man. He seemed a bluff, genial, down-to-earth English country gentleman, the 'Squire Brown' later depicted in his son Thomas' *Tom Brown's Schooldays*. But he was also a dilettante writer and something of an artist and an antiquarian. Half-Welsh, he was proud to trace his lineage on his father's side back through the family of Salusbury of Lleweni to the Welsh Princes as well as to the ancestors of the Royal House of Tudor. His father, the scholarly cleric Thomas Hughes, D.D. former tutor to the younger sons of George III, Vicar of Uffington and a Residentiary Canon of St. Paul's Cathedral, had been an indulgent parent, sending him to Westminster School and Oriel College, Oxford, happy to have his only child become a leisured gentleman with literary leanings. An outstanding classical scholar at Oxford and a very good linguist, John Hughes published *A Guide to Provence and the Rhône* illustrated by his own etchings (1819) and edited *The Boscobel Tracts relating to the escape of Charles 11 after the battle of Worcester, and his subsequent adventures* (1830). He enjoyed sketching and wood-carving, he sang and he wrote comic verse.[1] "Is there anything he cannot do?" Mary Rusell Mitford would ask in her *Recollections of a Literary Life*.

John Hughes' dominant parent, and indeed the dominant personality in the parish of Uffington, not to mention Amen Corner, St. Paul's, was not his father, the amiable Residentiary Canon, but his mother, Mrs. Mary Hughes. A fiercely energetic, highly musical woman with a wonderful singing voice, she was the 'clever, active, bustling friend'[2] of Sir Walter Scott from 1806 until his death. In his Introduction to her Letters and *Recollections of Sir Walter Scott* (1904), her last surviving grandson, Jeanie's younger brother Hastings, remembered her despotic family presence:

> We all had the utmost respect for our grandmother, in return for
> her numberless gifts to us and her untiring interest in our welfare,
> but not so much love as might have been hers had she not been so
> determined to run us (in common with the rest of the parishioners)
> without regard to our wishes and tastes.[3]

Absolutely certain of the rightness of her own sharp judgment, Mary Hughes took the closest possible interest, not to say interference, in the upbringing of her grand-children who lived next door to her own home, Uffington Vicarage, where she spent nine months of every year. She even decided upon or changed their names: Walter, she said, had to be named Walter Scott, Jane had to become Jeanie (after Scott's Jeanie Deans) and Willie, 'Hastings', after an influential admiral. She must have been an over-powering mother-in-law for her son's young wife, who was bearing six children in twelve years at nearby Uffington House.[4] Although John Hughes was a concerned, interesting and companionable father whom Jeanie could tease as well as respect and love, it was her mother who was even nearer and dearer. The first family letter to her that survives is from her mother, written to reassure her 'dearest little girl' after the last but one childbed, when the eight year-old had been sent to stay with her formidable grandmother:

> I thank you a thousand times for your nice affectionate letter and
> for your kind enquiries about me – it has pleased God to give me a
> very good confinement, and though I have had a great deal of fever

1 Three family portraits: Mrs. Hughes, Jeanie's paternal grandmother; Dr. Hughes, Jeanie's paternal grandfather; John Hughes, Jeanie's father. Courtesy of Arthur Hughes and Graham Senior-Milne.

since, and been obliged to live entirely on gruel which has made me
very weak, still I feel quite free from pain, and . . . I hope yet
before you return home to be quite strong again, that we may go
on with your lessons regularly and have many <u>delightful walks</u>
together this autumn, and perchance a run or two; will not you
<u>laugh</u>* to see Mama running? Papa hopes I shall come and fight
tough battles with him at archery, and if I am strong enough I shall
try hard to beat him; you must attend us as our arrow bearer – . . .
    . . . I am sorry to say there are only eight young chickens left out
of your fine brood, but they are doing very well; next spring when
you and I know more about poultry we must contrive to have
much earlier broods of chickens, the nights and mornings are now
too cold for the tender little things.

Then, after many details of all the other animals, and enclosing letters
from two of the older brothers at school, the mother ends with a reference
to Jeanie's early signs of musicality: 'I shall be much pleased to hear you sing
the songs you have learnt.'[5]
Jeanie's mother Margaret Hughes had been born in 1797, the second
daughter of a wealthy Yorkshireman, Thomas Wilkinson, who had married
young and gone to London to make his fortune. Starting with six silver
spoons and his wife's jointure of £200 a year, he had worked for a cousin of
his father's who was a ship owner. Ultimately he himself became the owner
of a fleet of East India sailing ships and retired to enjoy the life of a horse-
racing, greyhound-racing gentleman at Walsham-le-Willows in Suffolk and
later at Nether Hall, near Newmarket. Margaret Hughes' mother, born Jane
Hutton, had also been of Yorkshire stock (hence Jeanie's later references to
her 'Wilkinson Viking blood' when confessing to her capacity for rage), but
in her case she came not from merchant gentry but from a prosperous
country yeoman family. This Jane Wilkinson, née Hutton, had been her
daughter Margaret's beloved, exemplary woman. 'It is needless to say what
my mother was, I have never in my life met with her equal; you must ask
Col. Bonamy to speak of her, and he will tell you what she was'.[6] It is significant that she called her only daughter 'Jane' after that cherished mother
and, like her, Margaret Hughes was a real countrywoman, never happier
than when planning some new outdoor undertaking, experimenting with
garden plants and field crops or rearing animals and poultry. And she
brought up her only daughter to be as competent as herself at plain sewing,
gardening and knowledge of country remedies. She also brimmed over with
practical help to any neighbours in need. Wholly devoted to each one of her
eight children and blessed with an unquestioning faith in the loving God of

---

* Unless stated otherwise, all emphases in quotations are in the original.

the New Testament, Margaret Hughes' powers of endurance in the face of tragedy would be nothing less than heroic. She and Jeanie were not just mother and daughter but close, lifelong allies.

After her family moved from Uffington House when she was seven, Jeanie's home was Donnington Priory near Newbury. The grey Berkshire hills in the distance, the woods, the water meadows and streams would be her 'happy land' for ever and 'Dear, dear Donnnington' the blessed place of memory. 'Donnington Priory', its exterior still preserved today under a protection order, was a mid 17th century house bordering the River Lambourne on the site of an old Priory and Hospital that had been 'disestablished', i.e. seized by the Crown, under the Dissolution of the Monasteries in 1534. It was a gracious, roomy house with a five-windowed front facing south, an elegant portico, a spiral staircase and a large dining-room that boasted two great mantelpieces carved in Welsh by John Hughes with the Hughes family motto: "Y Gwir Yn Erbyn Y Byd" – "Truth against the World". A motto that Thomas, Walter and Jeanie Hughes, of all his children, would take to heart and act upon.

Donnington's glory was its garden. As well as massive trees to climb, the children had their own slow, overgrown trout-stream in the garden, a tributary of the rushing Lambourne, and so could fish and punt and wade and fall out of boats to their hearts' content. There was at least one occasion when Jeanie nearly missed drowning and had to be pulled out in time by a brother. The children's fishing-nets, as they caught their dace and chubb and roach, were all made by the quick fingers of their paternal grandmother. There was

2   Donnington Priory in the 19th Century. Courtesy of Graham Senior-Milne.

stabling for their ponies, as well as the water meadows, hills, woods and
nearby ruins to explore. The Hughes family kept their own cow which Jeanie
proudly learned to milk, their own sheep and poultry, and several much
loved dogs and puppies who were part of the family. The long summer holidays with all her older brothers home from their schools were a special,
intensely happy time and fair-haired Jeanie grew so tall and strong that her
father boasted of her at twelve and a half to his brother-in-law: 'Jane I really
think in particular, would throw most boys of her age in a trial of strength.'[7]

In the winter holidays every one would dress up and act Charades; there
was singing at the piano, listening to Scott, Jane Austen or Dickens being
read aloud as well as all the festivities of an evergreen-hung country
Christmas. On one never-forgotten December in 1838, when Jeanie was just
ten, the Hughes fireside was enchanted by a letter from the young novelist
Charles Dickens, actually addressed to five year-old Hastings. Their father
had been reading *Nicholas Nickleby* to them in monthly instalments. They
had got about halfway through when little Hastings had burst out that
Nicholas and the poor boys at Dotheboys Hall were not being given enough
of a reward and Squeers and his family enough punishment. John Hughes
said to Hastings that if he were to dictate these comments, and send a
drawing, he would write the letter down and send it to Dickens, who duly
replied to the five year-old on 12 December 1838:

> Respected Sir,
> I have given Squeers one cut on the neck and two on the head, at
> which he appeared much surprised and began to cry, which, being
> a cowardly thing, is just what I should have expected from him –
> wouldn't you?
> I have carefully done what you told me in your letter about the
> lamb and the two "sheeps" for the little boys. They have also had
> some good ale and porter, and some wine . . .[8]

Playing an essential part in that lively, warm family life were the loved and
'much attached' servants. They included the coachman 'Old Henry New', 'a
lion-like man'[9] whose magnificent physique had once led him to be a prize-
fighter and who taught all the Hughes boys to ride and wrestle and box.
Sometimes after supper he used to stagger around the dining room with
George, Tom, John and Walter all clinging on to him at once. Then there was
their father's former nurse, Mary Vann, now a handsome, dignified middle-
aged woman with endearing dimples when she talked. We 'loved her most
dearly for she fought all our battles most nobly, tho' she herself kept us in
famous tight order and we never dreamt of daring to disobey Mary however
rebellious we might have been with others.'[10] Both Jeanie's mother and
Jeanie were devoted to Jeanie's nurse, Franklin, and she to them, and finally,

there later arrived that Admirable Crichton of a gardener, Dyer, of whom much more will be heard.

There was just one shadow over Jeanie' childhood: the suffering that she witnessed in the cottages of their poverty-stricken village neighbours. She would often accompany her mother when visiting the poor, taking them food, blankets, and home-brewed medicines, or else tickets for coal; and she or her mother would then read from the New Testament to the ill and dying. To be a 'Ministering Child' was, of course, part of ordinary daily life for the well-off daughter of a kind family in the 19th century.[11] But, despite her perfectly normal appearance, with her wavy corn-gold plaits, rosy cheeks, earnest grey/blue eyes and tall, sturdy young figure, Jeanie Hughes was very far from ordinary. For there raged inside her the most radical, secret questioning, prompted by her acute awareness of others' suffering. Even though she had been taught by her parents and her grandparents that any religious doubt was an unpardonable sin, she doubted: 'Especially I could not stand the idea of Hell. . . . [When my brothers'] vacations were over I used to wander a great deal alone in the field and lanes and water meadows, and get much exercised . . . over theological matters.'[12] For how could a loving, omnipotent God permit not only terrible bodily suffering but mental torture also?

> A poor girl in the village was dying of consumption; my mother used to go constantly to read to her, and sometimes I went with her, and sometimes alone. . . . When I went to see her alone she used to get me to read to her, and generally asked for the 14th and following chapters of St. John's Gospel. [i.e. 'Let not your heart be troubled: ye believe in God, believe also in me. In my father's house are many mansions . . .'] Several times she spoke of her unworthiness and of her doubts of salvation, and when I said, "But you are so patient and good, . . . God must love you and make you happy," she used to talk . . . of her own unworthiness, *deserving* eternal flames, unless she could trust in her Saviour's blood. I used, after seeing her, to have fits of exasperation against God, and say to myself "God's a devil, God's a devil – . . . God *ought* to make [Anne] happy, and if He sends her to Hell He is very wicked and unjust" . . .[13]

Jeanie then went still further. How could it be just for the Creator to damn *any* of his Creation?

> "[If] he is Almighty why should He send any one to Hell? He could make us good if He is all-powerful, and if I were able to make everyone in the world happy and well I would do so. Even the

wicked people I would like to see happy; if they were happy perhaps they'd be good, and if I would not have any one unhappy even on earth, I must be kinder than God, for God makes people sick and poor and unhappy on earth and then He sends them to Hell for ever and ever and ever afterwards. So it seems to me that God is a wicked devil."[14]

That fierce, breathless rejection of a Hanging Judge God is surely remarkable. Intelligent, independent-minded Jeanie Hughes in the 1830s sounds already like George Eliot's young heroine Maggie Tulliver in *The Mill on the Floss* in 1860. Indeed she even anticipates Olive Schreiner's Waldo – "I hate God! . . . I love Jesus Christ, but I hate God", his unforgettable cry in *The Story of an African Farm* in 1883. Jeanie's personality would always be a rare combination of tenderness, resilient, buoyant vitality and the most implacable anger at unjust suffering.

The only personal unhappiness that she herself suffered in her Donnington years was when she was sent away from Donnington. When she was thirteen and a half she was sent to board at a ladies' seminary (Mrs. Dysott's Cliff House) in the West Country. We have her journal 'For the second half of the [school] year 1842 dedicated (with best love) . . . to her dear Mother.' And a strangely lifeless document it is, though every so often a real feeling does come across:

> Wednesday 3 August. I was so miserably melancholy, so lonely and homesick I did not know what to do! . . . If I could but have a good cry I am sure I should feel better! But I cannot! . . . I wish I could tell Mama all I feel but that would make her unhappy so I cannot.

The only good bits in her lonely life at boarding-school were reading Rollin's *Ancient History of the Grecians and Persians,* rare contacts with her best friend Fanny Ford, and piano and singing lessons. '3 September. I am at last getting over my miserable feelings a little I am happy to say. I never showed them but always appeared gay to the generality.' Her lessons seem to have been a little French, a little History, a little Geography, at least some Arithmetic, and a lot of fine sewing (i.e., 'work'), dancing lessons and music. All her life long she would be conscious of her lack of education. But it should also be pointed out that Jeanie wrote clear, vivid prose in a legible hand, was confident and competent in the handling of figures, retained a lively intellectual curiosity and read widely and seriously. For all its deficiencies, therefore, her formal education deadened neither her eagerness to learn nor her independence of mind. During Jeanie's schooldays all that really mattered to her was music and her letters from home. 'Had a letter from

Walter about Fanny in which he seems to be in love. I hope not. But I fear. . . . Heard again from Walter touching Fanny. He tries to get out of the scrape and gets deeper. . . . [In music] I got Cramer's Studies!! What an era!'[15]

Jeanie's favourite among all her brothers was the one nearest to her in age, this last-mentioned Walter. According to family tradition, Walter Hughes was 'so like her that they were always thought of as twins. They had the same happy and sweet dispositions, the same brilliantly fair colouring, and the same love of singing and music. They were constantly together whenever he was home.'[16]

Hastings, his junior by seven years, who hero-worshipped Walter, remembered him as

> the most joyous and gallant of all the brothers, – a tall, lithe figure, six foot one in his socks, broad-shouldered and thin-flanked. . . .
>
> Like Tom Brown, Walter left behind him at [Rugby] school "the name of a fellow who never bullied a little boy or turned his back on a big one". [Later on,] at Woolwich [Royal Military Academy for the Engineers] he stood out with two or three others against some abuses, winning thereby the admiration of his family and the disapproval of those of his superiors who did not wish to have the affair exposed.[17]

The most golden of all the blessed summer vacations must have been that of 1843 when, on June 24, her eldest brother George, a champion at every sport he tried, captained the Oxford boat that was reduced to seven men – but which nonetheless still triumphed at Henley over the Cambridge Eight. How the family at Donnington Priory rejoiced to greet their conquering hero when he bore the trophy oars home. Tom Hughes, George's next brother down, had witnessed the feat and wrote a ballad on the Henley Cup, especially for fourteen-year old Jeanie:

> . . . He saw the race and told the tale
> And was bored a previous time
> Till for his saucy sister
> He put it into rhyme . . .
> Now fill the cup; drink all true men
> As you dip your noses in:
> A fair field and no favour
> And may the best man win.[18]

'A fair field and no favour' became another Hughes rallying-cry and would be invoked by Jeanie many decades later when she faced the hostility of male Whitehall.

Between mid 1843 and mid 1845 much of the excitement of her young life centred on the forbidden romance between her second eldest brother Tom and her best friend Fanny Ford, most probably that same Fanny who had also attracted Walter. Tom and Fanny were forbidden to meet or even to write to one another because Tom was not regarded as a good enough 'match'; they had to depend on hearing about each other through Jeanie, Fanny's confidante. Tom and Fanny's devotion to one another was indeed well founded for they were eventually to weather a marriage of nearly fifty years. But the very intensity of the secret feelings to which she was privy, may have stirred in the younger girl a premature longing for a romance of her own. Twenty years later she would reflect: 'Often and often I remember instances when I was young when I was fool enough to imagine that I understood and experienced things (that I was not really old enough to enter into) just because people made me fancy it.'*[19]

In May 1845, Jeanie was suddenly diagnosed 'with an affection of one of her lungs', very possibly contracted through her frequent visits to the cottagers dying of TB. Her formal schooling was abruptly halted at the age of sixteen and she was taken off to Hastings by her anxious mother for a sea air and sea water cure. There her favourite Walter joined her and she soon recovered her earlier vigour. His lively Journal testifies to their close bond as they relished 'Miss Austen's "Sense and Sensibility" and "Pride and Prejudice" – capital book' – , or practised singing Gluck's "Che faro sensa Euridice' from *Orpheus*, – 'a beautiful thing'. They walked on the cliffs, or went out sea-fishing and sailing – 'sea rough, shipped lots of water . . . my sister being the more delighted the greater the swell'. And all the time they talked. 'Sunday 25 May. Tea tête-à-tête, Jeanie'.[20]

In August 1845 Walter was ordered to Clonmel in Ireland and he in his turn became dependent on family letters. He learned how Jeanie was growing rapidly into an attractive young lady, a keen rider and participant in local archery competitions At the end of December 1845 he noted in his Journal 'Jeanie has been making a tour of France and Italy with Uncle Tom. . . . [Her] mind is developing wonderfully . . . my mother has kindly sent me all her letters which are very long and equally amusing.'[21]

The whole of Jeanie's 240-page Journal of that tour with her wealthy, bachelor Wilkinson uncle has survived. It reveals a serious-minded, lively Victorian girl prone to adolescent mood swings as she devours Byron's *Childe Harold*, which her friend Fanny Ford had given her:

> I *was* melancholy today, why I cannot tell, partly by thinking of
> dear Tom and Fanny, partly because I now sometimes do feel sad I
> don't know why; I suppose because I am getting older than I was –

---

*All J.E.S.'s letters, unless otherwise indicated, are to her son Walter. Together with all her other unpublished correspondence and papers, they are held in private ownership in the Milne Collier Papers.

> I have lived many years it seems in the last two months (28
> September). I am older in mind than I was three months ago . . .
> my illness and other events . . . have made me more thoughtful, less
> giddy, I think and I hope . . . I cannot help letting out a little now
> and then in my journal – it is a kind of friend to whom I tell my
> thoughts when I am pleased and sorry. . . . (10 October)

Those four strenuous, sometimes dangerous, often extremely uncomfortable months, eaten alive by bedbugs, mosquitoes or fleas, and travelling many hundreds of miles, 'post' by horse-drawn carriage, leaving Southampton 24 September 1845 and returning to Donnington 24 January 1846, marked an epoch in Jeanie's life. Their route stretched from Falaise to Tours, Poitiers, Bordeaux, Narbonne, Montpellier, Nismes, Avignon, Vaucluse, Antibes, Nice, the Corniche, Oneglia, Genoa, Chiavari, Sarzano, Lucca, Pisa, Florence, Terni, and Rome. Then back via Leghorn, Genoa, Turin, Susa, M. Cenis, Chambéry, Lyons, Roanne, Orléans, Paris, Rouen, Dieppe, Shoreham near Brighton, London and at last HOME again to Donnington.

At first Jeanie had been desperately unwilling to leave England and her family: '[Felt] woundy cross and wished myself comfortably back again. Yes! with all dear Uncle Tom's kindness, I'd have given my ears not to have been going' (22 September). Coloured, perhaps, by her secret reluctance to go abroad in the first place, her early impressions often had something of the superior, disapproving English Miss about them, wrinkling her nose not just at the foreign dirt and stinks but at foreigners in general: 'I have been now a week in France . . . it seems to me that the women are nearly all ugly and the men small and ill made.' Her Protestant prejudice against Roman Catholics was almost comic in its self-righteous intensity, reminding one of Charlotte Bronte in *Villette:*

> How can people, with the usual degree of common reasoning sense
> . . . be Roman Catholics? They must see the impossibility of a
> human being absolving them from their sins, they must see that
> God is served by the heart, not by outward show.

And how she disapproved of a Frenchman's contemptuous verbal abuse of women, even as he tried to fondle a servant at the *table d'hôte* and how disgusted she was at the cruelty to animals that she witnessed, the whipping of horses, the beating of over-laden mules, the killing of a dog – 'It makes my blood boil'. Nine days later Jeanie was as ecstatic as she had earlier been appalled. Letters were waiting for her at Genoa:

> I nearly screamed with joy! Fan is coming at Xmas, the old man
> [Fanny's father] came round splendidly – they are to meet and I

suppose to <u>write</u> . . . I <u>never</u> felt so light hearted . . . It is no use
expatiating but I never felt more happy (25 October).[22]

She did not yet realize how his marriage would mean the partial loss to
her of her brother Tom.

Once in Italy she was given a crash course in Italian architecture and art.
Duomo after Duomo, Palazzo after Palazzo, Galleria after Galleria, ruin
after ruin, opera after opera in Pisa, Florence and Rome. By Pisa's leaning
tower 'you try to twist your head to get it upright – at least I did so instinc-
tively. Some people (for the sake of argument I suppose) uphold that the
tower was built crooked on purpose! They are noodles.' The seventeen year-
old withstood it all very well, almost surprised by her own genuine interest
in the history and art everywhere around her.

The culmination of the tour was the seven-week period spent in Rome
where Jeanie concentrated on acquiring a reading and pronunciation
knowledge of Italian and had almost daily singing lessons with a well-
known master. Her time in the Eternal City was brightened by a new
friendship with Kate, 'a most kind, charming and very pretty girl',
youngest daughter of a Lady Malcolm. They talked about books – 'both of
us went into raptures over Walter Scott – Poetry – and *Pride and Prejudice*
but quarrelled about Frederika Bremer, she liking I hating her works.' Kate
Malcolm was full of the cruelty of the Tsar of Russia (who was daily
expected to arrive in Rome) and we get a vivid picture of the two young
girls talking politics, round-eyed with shock at the revelation of tyranny.
Roman Catholics, it should be noted, could now be seen as martyrs rather
than mere dupes:

> She told me . . . that at some place in Poland the governor had
> tortured several nuns to death because they would not embrace the
> Greek Church and leave the Roman Catholic and the Emperor of
> Russia had upheld him. Three or four of the nuns escaped, one of
> the abbesses who is now in Rome, has a dreadful cut across her
> forehead inflicted by the governor. . . . The ladies of Poland, when
> their husbands were sent to work in the Siberian mines, went with
> them like good angels (honours to our sex) and live with their
> husbands in wretched little huts. They are made to work in chains,
> the chains galled their legs, a petition was presented to the Emperor
> by the wives, that they might wear worsted stockings to prevent
> this, and it was refused. If these stories are true they make one's
> blood boil, that such a devil incarnate should have defiled England
> with his presence; but one cannot believe these stories, one will not
> believe all, at least, but if I were the Pope I would see the Emperor
> 'furder furst' before he should put his foot in Rome. (25 November)

Jeanie would be unwilling to believe the worst of her fellow humans, but *enraged* when forced to believe it, all her life.

Over the four months of that tour to 'finish' her, Jeanie Hughes had grown greatly in tolerance and cultural awareness. She had become more receptive to others' otherness and more able to criticize her own Protestant English tribe as possessing less than a monopoly of goodness, beauty and truth.

At last, after fearlessly crossing the Alps in midwinter, then putting their carriage on to the new Rouen–Paris, Paris–Dieppe railroad, and enduring a stormy channel crossing, Jeanie and her uncle Tom Wilkinson arrived safely back in Shoreham Harbour. Then, on 24 January 1846, HOME at last –

> and I never in my life felt so completely happy or so full of grati-
> tude to God as I did then. . . . I am quite sure that I have laid in a
> stack of interesting reminiscences which will last me my life – and I
> am most thankful to my kind uncle for having taken me and for
> having been so kind to me – but as for being *happy* when away
> from Home and my Mother, it is *impossible*.

In 1846, her dearest Walter fell in love – after telling himself not to do so – with Charlotte Shiels, a very pretty, lively doctor's daughter in Ireland. He announced to his family that he was engaged. Whatever mixed feelings Jeanie may have had at that news, she was soon still much more distressed to learn that 'her' Walter was to be sent by the British Army right across the world to British Guiana. After a short furlough to say goodbye to his family at Donnington, at the end of 1846 the twenty year-old sailed away – for who could tell how long? And news could take months to arrive. His first letter told them he was recovering from a bout of malarial fever.

Weeks later, in January 1847, they learned that their golden lad was dead.

Jeanie Hughes collapsed, her childhood and youth over. She sat like a statue in her room, reminding her father of Mrs. Siddons, so terrible were her stillness and dignity. She could not distress her afflicted parents by sobbing out her own agony, so she held it in. Neither could she any longer dare to question God. For there was only one bearable thought: Walter had gone before her, they *would* be together again eternally, 'the tears wiped forever from their eyes'. Never again could she risk God's wrath and call him 'a wicked devil'. Instead, she made Him over in her own likeness, infinitely compassionate, refusing to judge, promising us recompense in over measure for all our earthly suffering.

At the end of that January 1847, her mother took her to Ventnor on the Isle of Wight, hoping that once again the sea air might do wonders for her daughter. On 31st March, poor grieving Margaret Hughes, just returned home from Ventnor to Donnington Priory, began writing her a heart-rending letter which Jeanie would keep all her life:

Before I lie down in my bed dearest I must have a few words with you, tell you how my heart ached to part from you this morning, and how tonight my heart blesses you, and prays that God will keep and guard and guide one who has ever been my best treasure. You too dearest must watch over <u>that treasure,</u> and in all things take <u>thought</u> to do that which is best for <i>its</i> health and happiness, knowing that thereon <u>mine</u> depends. . . . [I am] myself quite well dearest, and not sorrowful; at least not such sorrow as to be sorrowful at. Our lost treasure is every where around me, his voice floats on the air, his form waves in the trees, his smile glows in the sunshine of this place. I had almost written it is joyous – but I mean that my noble good son is so constantly in my mind that I love everything which helps to bring him still closer to me – Indeed dearest after the first painful pang this is the spot I can ever be happiest in – and could I have the blessing of seeing you in strong health and restored to me – I would ask for nothing more. . . . I shall finish this letter tomorrow dear puss – if I write more tonight, I suppose you will <i>scold</i> – so good night, and God bless you.

First thing next morning her mother continued her letter:

April 1, six o'clock. I have slept beautifully dearest Jeannie [sic] in my clean bed at home, and my first waking thought after my prayer to God must be to you my darling; this is my birthday – my fiftieth birthday; I am growing very old – but I hope not <u>very cold</u> – indeed I feel that as long as I live I shall never grow cold as to worldly matters – but I am fearfully <u>spiritually cold</u>. [Even] this morning dearest – on my return home after my sorrow – the holy season [of Easter], the daily history of Our ever blessed Saviour's suffering for us his sinful creatures – all, all – does not produce that fervour of devotion and love which I feel it ought in me. I am very hard, and at times ready to <u>despair,</u> and <u>should</u>, but that that would be my greatest sin, as throwing doubt on the efficacy of our Salvation, so I will pray on, and strive on, and hope. And do you dearest pray for me when you pray for yourself – and may God bless your prayers.[23]

It is an extraordinarily open, truth-telling document, the mother telling her equally bereft daughter what she really felt, not what she 'ought to say'. She knew that that was the only way to reach her.

Also staying at Ventnor just at that terrible time were the Hughes' old family friends, the Nassau Seniors. Nassau William Senior, Professor of Political Economy at Oxford and Master in Chancery, had been Jeanie's

3 Jeanie at eighteen, at the time of her engagement. Courtesy of Graham Senior-Milne.

father's best friend when they were boys together at Uffington, and they had also been contemporaries at Oxford. The two Senior children, Nassau John and Minnie, the same age as Tom Hughes and John Hughes Junior, had known the more countrified, unworldly Hughes children all their lives. Now Jeanie was in Ventnor devastated by her loss and there close by, full of awkward sympathy, was the twenty-five year-old law student Nassau John. He had become more and more attracted to the blooming, golden-haired Jeanie Hughes who always listened sympathetically to his tales of being browbeaten by his over-bearing Papa. (Made to put every book away that he touched; roared at when he got into debt at Oxford as though he had committed the Sin against the Holy Ghost . . .) Perhaps she had even been an indignant witness to more than one incident of the youthful Nassau's public discomfiture. Whether it was her extreme, benumbed vulnerability just then, whether she felt a rush of pity for this extra brother, whom she believed was hardly used, whether she thought it was the one thing that might make her stricken parents happy, for whatever reason, and before she had had a chance to meet almost any other young man outside her own family, in the summer of 1847 Jeanie Hughes, not yet nineteen, promised to become Mrs. Nassau Senior.

CHAPTER TWO

Being 'Mrs. Nassau Senior', 1848–1855

The Jeanie who had been her brother Walter's 'twin' died with him, but the Jeanie who survived managed to live with energy and hopefulness. She entered into her youthful marriage, when she was not yet twenty, in August 1848 at St. Mary's Church, Shaw-cum-Donnington, full of high confidence buttressed by high seriousness. She had grown up witnessing her parents' mutual respect and support. Her mother's intelligence, constantly applied to answering the needs of others, had seemed to her quite equal in value to her father's more intellectual interests. She now looked forward to a children-filled life very like that led by her warm-hearted, busy mother. But in her case Jeanie anticipated that she would also be the supportive wife of a hard-working, idealistic barrister. For would not Nassau take a leaf out of her brother Tom's book, especially with her there to encourage him? Nassau always said he could never do enough for her and she was happily confident that she could influence him to do something greatly beneficent for the world.

It was a period of exalted views on the role of women within marriage. Already in 1835 Elizabeth Starling had collected inspiring tales of conjugal heroism, affection, integrity and presence of mind, including the reformist heroism of Elizabeth Fry, in her *Noble Deeds of Woman* or *Examples of Female Courage and Virtue*. Similarly, Sarah Lewis' *Woman's Mission*, which had gone into its tenth edition by 1842, had, in its loftily idealistic way, sought to prove 'the fundamental truth of the importance of woman's influence . . . ' (Preface). For her, 'Woman's Mission' was nothing less than the 'regeneration of the world . . . [restoring] God's image in the human soul' through the feminine influence of unworldliness and self-devotion as it reached out hopefully to inspire the conduct of husbands and sons 'in the political and social conditions of mankind' (Introduction). Sarah Lewis held that this 'Woman's Mission' of mothers and wives was to testify by daily example to the true Christian ethic of self-renunciation instead of self-inter-est, forgiveness instead of retaliation. She did not anticipate John Stuart Mill's critique of 'the exaggerated self-abnegation which is the present artifi-cial ideal of feminine character' – encouraged by self-worshipping men.[1] Simultaneously, another Sarah, Sarah Ellis, was exhorting the *Wives of England* in 1843 to withstand the temptations of worldliness, and not be obsessed by fashion, rank or possessions. Instead,

> [The] English Wife should . . . regard her position as a central one,
> and remember that from her, as the head of a family, and the
> mistress of a household, branch off in every direction trains of
> thought and tones of feeling, operating upon those more immedi-
> ately around her, but by no means ceasing there; for each of her
> domestics, each of her relatives, and each of her familiar friends,
> will in their turn become the centre of another circle, from which
> will radiate good or evil influence extending onwards . . . to the
> end of all things. (Conclusion)

In 1846 Clara Lucas Balfour (a pioneer Adult Education lecturer and
herself a struggling wife and mother) had published a chapter on 'Moral
heroism exhibited in the female character' where she had pointed out, rather
more realistically than had Sarah Lewis or Sarah Ellis, that women are 'the
sex called on to endure the greatest amount of suffering' . . . and that 'No
station in life is more important and <u>arduous</u> than that of a wife and a
mother' (my emphasis).[2] The strongest statement of Separate Spheres mater-
nalist feminism of all, however, would be published just three years after
Jeanie's marriage, in Sara Josepha Hale's monumental and still fascinating
work, her collective biography, *Woman's Record* (1853):

> The office of mother is the highest a human being can hold. On
> its faithful and intelligent performance hangs the hope of the
> world . . . Wives, mothers, women teachers, women artists, women
> doctors, and women missionaries are the great civilizers in so far as
> they help humanity to become more humane. The reader will easily
> discover that I place woman's office above man's, because moral
> influence is superior to mechanical invention, and her peculiar
> mission is to mould minds, while his deals with material things.[3]

All these lofty affirmations of the woman's 'office' within marriage, as
proclaimed by contemporary women writers, would soon be capped, of
course, by the poet Coventry Patmore's sequence of poems, *The Angel in the
House* (1856–1867).

And now Jeanie Hughes found herself 'Mrs. Nassau Senior', a 'Wife of
England' with a 'Woman's Mission'. Her first reaction was to be acutely
conscious that she was an inadequately educated country girl who had
married into an eminent metropolitan and even cosmopolitan circle. She had
to begin her new life by trying hard to be equal to all its demands. For one
thing she had to learn to understand and speak fluent French – 'I well
remember when I married and came to London having an agonising time
when trying to talk to some young Frenchmen at several balls' (19
November 1873). She had also to learn to take an intelligent interest in the

conversations at her father-in-law's dinner table between politicians, lawyers, churchmen, writers, artists and musicians, including Archbishop Whately,[4] the Marquis of Lansdowne,[5] the French statesman Thiers,[6] the writer Guizot,[7] the Italian exile Massimo d'Azeglio,[8] the sculptor Marochetti,[9] the painters Watts and Millais, and the pianist Charles Hallé. That was not hard to do because she was fascinated – 'I saw delightful society for the first time' (19 January 1877). Jeanie Senior had very quickly to try to become an asset in her new family. And, as her sister-in-law Minnie later recollected, she did very soon become 'its brightest ornament'.[10]

For although her father-in-law, Nassau William Senior, was himself tone deaf and resented music as an interruption to political conversation, he had been alerted to Jeanie's possession of a quite exceptional singing voice and had therefore arranged at once for her to have the best tuition in Europe. For two years Jeanie obeyed the demands of Jenny Lind's former teacher Manuel Garcia[11] that she do little but practise scales, breath control and his own method of voice production, if she wanted, as she said she did, to become a serious musician rather than merely a drawing room entertainer. She had a powerful, warm, clear mezzo-soprano which, trained, developed into a quite marvellous instrument. It soon became known that a Nassau William Senior dinner party would end with a magnificent recital by the young, golden-haired Mrs. Nassau John Senior:

> This day I dined with Mr. Nassau Senior, a noted writer on politi-cal economy . . . His son's wife, Mrs. Nassau Senior, junior, is pretty, very fair, with a wonderful profusion of gilt flaxen crinkle-crankled hair, and a remarkably fine voice, with which she discoursed after dinner much eloquent music.[12]

Leading musicians, writers and artists of the day were increasingly attracted to attend such Nassau Senior dinner parties: 'However lively the talk, perfect silence was sure to follow when she began to sing. She also read aloud and acted admirably; she was fond of painting and modelling, and she attracted to our house some of the most distinguished artists of the day.'[13]

There can be no doubt that the dominant presence in Jeanie's early married life was that of her father-in-law, at whose house in Hyde Park Gate the young couple lived, for financial reasons. Nassau William Senior, Oxford Professor of Political Economy, Master in Chancery, had come from a family, originating in the diaspora of Sephardic Jews from Isabelline Spain – hence 'Sen(i)or' – which had made much of its money in the 18th century in the Slave Trade and West Indian plantations.[14] Moses Aaron Senior had made successful application in 1723 for a letter patent of denization, enabling him to participate in the wholesale trade with the colonies. His son, Nassau Thomas Senior, Nassau William's grandfather, was Governor of the

'Company of Merchants Trading in Africa', and must, therefore, have been baptized a Christian, in order not to have been excluded by the Corporation Act. As well as transporting slaves to the West Indies and American plantations, he imported gold, ivory and dye-stuffs. He married the daughter of a Barbadian plantation-owner, Frances Raven, who, when she died in 1790 (and was buried in Uffington Church), bequeathed her fortune, including two estates in Barbados, together with 'horses, cattle, negroes, utensils etc.' to Nassau William's father. Nassau William himself had married Charlotte Mair, born in the West Indies, the daughter of a plantation owner who had been an agent of the Seniors' holdings there.

Now, in the late 1840s, Nassau William Senior was the respected authority behind the scenes among all the men who mattered most in English Government. How could he not intimidate his nineteen year-old daughter-in-law, given his sharp brain, his marshalling of statistics to support his 'iron law' laissez-faire economics, his myriad social contacts, the breadth of his travels and his apparently impregnable reasoning? Jeanie had as yet no understanding at all of the crucial role that her father-in-law had played in drafting the draconian (and deterrent) New English Poor Law of 1834.[15] She had, after all, been only five years old at the time. Nor had she any idea of the other role that Nassau William Senior had tried to play in opposing the Ten Hours Act for factory workers in 1838 when she had been nine[16] let alone his opposition to the establishment of trade unions. She may have been more uneasily aware of his recent rejection of all proposed outdoor relief to the starving Irish in the potato famine.[17]

Nevertheless, her father-in-law's dismissal of anything resembling aid to the destitute in times of economic crisis aroused an instinctive, if inarticulate, resistance within Jeanie Senior. She would slip out furtively to attend the radical sermons then being given by Frederick Maurice on Sunday afternoons in Lincolns Inn.[18] It was not only Maurice's social sympathies that spoke to her but also his rejection of the doctrine of everlasting punishment. At last she had found someone who shared her long-held refusal to believe in Hell, holding it to be incompatible with faith in an infinitely loving God.[19]

At the very end of her life Jeanie Senior would look back with shame at her moral cowardice at this time in not having openly championed the young Christian Socialists, who included her brother Thomas Hughes,[20] during their early struggles to pioneer workers' cooperatives. 'But I was just married, and living with the old people, . . . and I was learning to sing, and living in artist Bohemia a part of my time. ' But it was not simply that Jeanie had been distracted by all the attractions of her new Society drawing-room life:

> I was such a coward too! I should not have *dared* to say where my
> sympathies lay – Living in an atmosphere of old Whigs, who had

very little sympathy with the artyzan [sic] class, who hated
Kingsley's writings and Carlyle's [Carlyle had challenged Nassau
William Senior's 1834 Poor Law as being less efficient than if he
had simply poisoned paupers with arsenic like rats!][21] . . . and who
declared that Maurice was "utterly unintelligible and did not even
know himself what he meant" I just said nothing. I was even
ashamed of owning that, whenever I could, I crept off on Sunday
afternoons to Lincoln's Inn Chapel to hear the prophet [Frederick
Maurice] preach, and that I subscribed to his Lincolns Inn Sermons
and read and pondered them.

Eventually the whole idealistic Christian Socialist vision converted her:

I have Maurice to bless for the fact that mere amusing myself in
pleasant society and hearing music did not continue to satisfy me.
But it took a long time. And the first distinct and burning *rousing*
that I remember was the conversation of old Miss Carpenter, who
did such splendid work at Bristol, among the girls. That made me
feel that I could not amuse myself all my life.[22] (19 January 1877)

In addition to her sudden immersion in London Society, her serious study
of singing, and her secret, transgressive attendance at Maurice's sermons, in
June 1849 Jeanie Senior became pregnant. Not surprisingly she turned to her
mother, the veteran of so many births, and to her old nurse Franklin, in
deciding to have her first baby at 'dear, dear Donnington' where she felt safe
and cherished. Her son was born on 17 March 1850. She called him Walter
in memory of her beloved brother and immediately became a passionately
devoted young parent.

But where in all this was her husband? Nassau John Senior, nearly seven
years older than Jeanie, had been born 2 February 1822, the first child and
only son of his dominating father. But it was the clever and vivacious
younger sister Minnie, born 25 August 1825, who was to be the favourite,
their father's chosen intellectual and social companion. She became his secretary, amanuensis and travelling companion as well as the hostess at his
dinner parties abroad. Nassau William Senior, conveyancer, barrister, writer
on political, literary and economic affairs, constant adviser to the current
Ministry and Oxford Professor, rising at six, keeping a daily account of his
working hours, and socializing for professional reasons, had been distant
from his children when they were young. Nassau John had been brought up
with a mixture of indulgence and neglect. He had been taught at King's
College, London and by private tutors including Blanco White;[23] he would
often complain in later years that by never having been sent to Public School
he had missed out on useful 'contacts'. That Professor Nassau William

Senior had not the slightest idea as to his son's real temperament and character, and that young Nassau John would have taken care to stay as much as possible out of his father's sight, is clear from the letter that the father wrote to his eighteen year-old son when the latter went up to Oxford. Its utilitarian worldly wisdom concerning friendship, was fused with an advocacy of constant self-disciplined, self-interested abstinence:

> The time that you spend in ordinary society is lost. If you can find people of distinguished talents or high political connection, particularly if they are likely to run the same courses as yourself and they are well-conducted, agreeable men, you cannot be too intimate with them. But such intimacy is made rather by walking or skiffing together than at wine parties. Unless confined to a very few persons, and to a short period they are dangerous things; they are apt to interfere with the most valuable hours of the morning. . . . [Your] best plan would be to do as I did: make your drinking no wine a ground for not going to wine parties, or giving them. Such parties may take up unprofitably much time, . . . If you cannot avoid such parties altogether go to as few as you can, stay as little time as you can, and give as few as you can. . . .

> [Keep] a register of the working hours employed each day. They ought not to be less than six (including lectures). I trust that you prepare carefully your lectures. You will find it very advantageous to construe them over to yourself before going into the lecture room every day. Pay particular attention to composition, and, as soon as you get into the Debating Society, make a point to get up every subject and speak on it every night. Orator *fit*, [is made] you know, and he *fit* only when young. As for money, the only rule I can give is to spend nothing that you can help, and to pay ready money for everything. Particularly have no bills at boat-houses, pastry-cooks, or any such places. Habits of saving or habits of expenditure are easily acquired.[24]

Little wonder that once away from such a father's eye, young Nassau John should have concentrated on enjoying himself at Christ Church. Like Pip in *Great Expectations*, trusting to a large eventual inheritance, he became a 'Finch of the Grove', believing that the world owed a gentleman a life of leisure. Nassau John Senior had gone up to Oxford in June 1840. He had graduated BA in 1844 with a Third in Classics (in contrast to his father's First), become a student at Lincoln's Inn and was named a barrister-at-law on 23 November 1847. But he never practised. Nearly thirty years later Jeanie warned her son Walter, then starting out as a barrister in his turn, that

4   Undergraduates relaxing in college rooms, 1843, Nassau John Senior's time at Christ Church, Oxford. From *The History of the University of Oxford*, vol. vi, *The Nineteenth Century* by M. G. Brock and M. L. Curthoys.

his father had 'hurt his chances of getting on at the Bar by [his] dilettante reading. He got a bad name in his pupil days' (8 March 1874). Given that Jeanie only brought £400 a year into the marriage and that Nassau John was still unemployed and dependent on an allowance from his father, they were in no position to set up a home of their own. Some time passed before Professor Nassau William Senior finally recognized that his son would never earn any money as a barrister. Eventually, in 1852, through his connections as Master in Chancery, he procured him a 'place' as one of the 'Secretaries of Commission' to the Lord Chancellor. Nassau John filled that office reluctantly for some years, but the real business of his life, then and ever after, was sleeping, eating, smoking and reading French novels. He soon grew markedly fat.

Among the thousands of Milne Collier papers that have been preserved, there is a handwritten verse sketch by Edward Borton, a visiting relative who was a friend of the family, depicting the couple at home seven years after their marriage, when Nassau John was nearly thirty-four and Jeanie just twenty-seven:

> Scene. Kensington Gore. Time 5.30 pm Library. Mr. N.J. Senior – a stout Gentleman – apparently rather shortsighted and of florid complexion – is standing in front of the fire –
>
> NJS. "Confound those onions and that garlic too,"
> I feel quite fishy. This will never do;
> Deprived of garlic, life will be a bore,
> Bereft of onions, I shall smile no more;
> Tobacco fumes will cease to yield me joy,

And I shall sink – Oh Devil take that boy!
Walter come here, I will not have that noise,
Begone to Lowe [the old nurse] or Sarah, and your toys.
Don't near me come. Why did I take a wife
And leave my happy idle single life –
But then dear Jeanie – I can't do without her,
So I'll be gracious and won't snub and flout her.
Oh here she comes. What have you been about?"
Enter Mrs. N.J. Senior, an elegant blonde, rather striking in appear-
ance –
Jeanie: "With Teddy Borton I've been walking out."
N.J.S: "Confound that fellow. How I hate your Teddies
And your and Minny's ever dangling Freddies–
What can you in those stupid fellows find
To make you like ——"
J.E.S: "Now Nass don't be unkind
But let me like my friends. Yourself you please
Just as you choose. But have you seen my keys?"
NJS: "Those hated keys. I gave them back to you.
I want them now – for that Valencia stew
Has made me seedy and I Brandy lack
To set me right and I will drink my whack.
I'm sure that I shall find them somewhere here."
(Mr. Senior rings the bell rather sharply. Enter John)
N.J.S: "John! Ask Miss Minnie if the keys she's got,
And if so bring them hither" (Enter Walter calling) "Mammy",
NJS: "What?
Have you come back, I sent you hence away
So get you gone and with your playthings play"
JES: "Now dear old Nassau let the child remain,"
(Enter John): "Here's Mr. Borton"
NJS: "What that beast again
He's come to sponge for dinner and will stay
Whether he's asked or not – I'll cut away" . . .
Enter Mr. E. Borton, a respectable middle-aged man:
JES: "Teddy you'll stay and dine, Pray don't say No,
We're quite alone and it will be so slow
Unless you stay and talk and make us laugh; . . .

——

Same scene after dinner. Present: Mrs. and Miss [Minnie] Senior,
Mr. Senior and Mr. Borton and Fanny, Miss Senior's dog.
EB: "Let's have some music, will you, Jeanie?"
JES: "Yes

What will you have? 'I rise from dreams'[25] I guess,
Or something else, which I may know by heart –
Rossini, Haydn, Verdi or Mozart?"
NJS: "Mozart's a humbug" JES: "No! Nassau. No!
I wonder you can underrate him so.
I feel convinced you're very wrong old fellow."
NJS: "I far prefer the music of *Othello*, [by Rossini]
Rossini has some music in his brain
I never wish to hear Mozart again.
And as for Haydn and his *Agnus Dei*
His various merits I can never see. I
Abhor the very sound of his *Creation*
It bores me much and fills me with vexation."
Miss Senior: "You certainly are very hard to please,
I fear your dinner with you disagrees . . .

So there we have it – or some of it at least. A spoilt complainer of a *gourmand* husband, resentful of any attention demanded by his little boy, jealously reluctant to host his wife's or sister's friends, finding everyone and everything 'stupid' or 'a bore', even his wife's venerated Mozart or Haydn's *Creation*. And beautiful, gifted Jeanie having to jolly her ill-tempered spouse along, minute by minute coaxing 'dear old Nass' – and desperate for a visitor to liven things up – 'it will be so slow/ unless you stay and talk and make us laugh'.

How could such a total mismatch ever have taken place? One irony was that the two young people had thought they really knew each other, having been acquainted ever since they could remember. But the gender *apartheid* in education and professional employment in Victorian England meant that Jeanie could not know what Nassau John was like at his Oxford College or while supposedly reading Law at Lincoln's Inn. Had she studied with him, she would have learned within a week that however amusing and harmless he might be, Nassau John Senior was simply not a serious person. Whereas he, for his part, only knew that Jeanie Hughes was a sweet girl and darn good looking, just the sort to look after a fellow and make it her business to keep him happy. He had no idea of what she called 'the Viking' Wilkinson fire within her, the fierce idealism and the imperative need to be of *use*.

One bitter irony was that this mis-marriage had very nearly been prevented. A crucial letter from Thomas Hughes to Nassau has survived, written some time after the young couple's engagement in 1847. Jeanie was still only eighteen and clearly her parents had said she was too young to marry yet. Nassau, who had recently failed some of his law exams, must wait and qualify first for the Bar.

Dear Nassau,

I was very much distressed at the way you talked last night and must write to you about it, for I shouldn't be able to say what I want and when a dear sister's happiness is at stake it is no time to shrink from one's duty; . . .

Just call to mind the shocking way in which you swore last night when you introduced the subject [of the delay to the marriage], and the remarks you made such as "I aint used to wait for anything", "I hate all trials" etc and then ask yourself whether one who could talk in this manner is training himself up to be a fit guide and supporter to a young and innocent and religious woman –

Is such conduct manly or gentlemanly or above all Christian? Who brought this trial on you? Nobody but yourself. And who brought it on Jeannie [sic] (for whom it is ten times as hard to bear)? Why nobody but you – And now instead of cheering her and helping her to bear it cheerfully, you shirk your own burden and double hers by your repining and evil temper. . . .

I know you have never been denied anything; that you aint used to wait or sacrifice yourself in any way, . . . but you know that these things are your duty; . . .

I can do no more for you (for I am as weak as yourself) except to pray heartily that you may conquer in this trial, in which my sister's happiness on earth, and your own soul's happiness through-out eternity is at stake, but this I do from my soul –

God bless you and help you – Believe me yours affectionately,
Thos. Hughes[26]

Why was that letter never sent? Why did not Tom warn Jeanie of his doubts concerning Nassau as the right husband for her? Perhaps Nassau had come round to Tom's chambers next morning, very contrite, declaring that he could not imagine what had got into him. Of course Jeanie was much, much too good for him; would Tom forgive him and not say a word to anyone?

And so it had come about on 10 August 1848, when Jeanie was nineteen and Nassau twenty-six, that they were married and, after all the new excite-ments and stimulating encounters and challenges were no longer so exciting or so new, she began to realize just what she had done. We do not know exactly when she first became disillusioned, only that it was 'soon' after the marriage. Almost twenty years later to the day she would spell it out:

When I was young I used to long and work and try that [Nassau] should make the most of himself and his life. I soon saw that I could not help him because he would not help himself. It was a dreadful trial to me when first I realized this. My ambition for him was not a worldly, bad one; I wanted him to . . . benefit his fellow-creatures. (18 August 1868)

She would be even more outspoken fifteen months later:

> It is a terrible thing when a man has no backbone. . . . life has been very different from what I hoped, and of course one expected too much and it is very good for one not have all one wanted, but it is rather hard to bear when all one wanted was the moral improvement of the person who ought to be the nearest and dearest on Earth. (16 March 1870)

To know, for over twenty years, that you were not married to your 'nearest and dearest on Earth'. And for each one of those years to recognize that it was a life-sentence from which there was no escape . . .

But it was no doubt not very pleasant to Nassau either, to find himself married to someone who did not admire him just for being her husband, but who was, instead, a critic on the hearth. How exasperating to be saddled with a wife who sought his 'moral improvement' and who constantly tried to get him to do what he least wanted to do – a job of work. For Nassau John Senior had been most unfortunate in the historical period in which he found himself:

> Except for "God," the most popular word in the Victorian vocabulary must have been "work" . . .
> The glorification of work as a supreme virtue, with the accompanying scorn of idleness, was the commonest theme of the prophets of earnestness.[27]

Not just the Puritan Carlyle but the Catholic convert Newman preached: 'every one who breathes, high and low, educated and ignorant, young and old, man and woman, has a mission, has a work'.[28] That work was to serve God by serving one's fellow man, for only in strenuous, other-directed work was secular salvation to be found. No matter if one's father were rich and one had corresponding 'expectations', a man 'must work for his living. A principle was involved: it was the gentlemanly thing to do'.[29] One very important part of that dedication to work was self-denial and delayed self-gratification. Nassau John's own father, Nassau William Senior, had written in his *Political Economy* in 1832: 'To abstain from the enjoyment which is in our power, or to seek distant rather than immediate results, are among the most painful [and necessary] exertions of the human will.'[30] What a bore that Nassau John should have eluded his father's impossible demands on him, only to find himself married into the burning heart of Victorian social idealism. He had a wife who longed with all her soul for beneficent work and she had brothers and associates, all burning in their turn to make the world a better place and help, in Charles Kingsley's words 'Lame dogs over stiles'. No wonder that he would soon turn his back on them all, whenever possible shutting himself in his den to smoke all day.

As for Jeanie, her married life was a long way indeed from the 1840s' idealization of 'Woman's Mission' or the exhortations to the *Wives of England* that she become her husband's willing, inspirational helpmeet. For how could she be a helpmeet to someone who evaded any serious project requiring help? And how could she endure the thought that she had vowed before God to honour and obey for the whole of her life someone she could not respect? If we are tempted to think that hers must have been a very common disillusionment, should we not also remember George Eliot's injunction that we recognize 'that element of tragedy which lies in the very fact of frequency'?[31] Not to mention the novelist's observation that many, after embarking on their marital voyage, have to realize they 'are exploring an enclosed basin'?[32] George Eliot was writing about Dorothea, the heroine of *Middlemarch*, after she had become the friend of Jeanie Senior.

CHAPTER THREE

Enter Watts and Mérimée, 1852–1856

There are three ways to survive a disappointing but inescapable marriage, if one is not to drown in self-pity and exasperation: work at absorbing, meaningful occupations, find other people to love – and concentrate on the children.[1] Jeanie Senior tried all three.

The absorbing occupations that she worked at outside No. 15 Hyde Park Gate, Kensington Gore during the early 1850s were philanthropic and artistic. The Crimean War that erupted in 1854 suddenly offered her the therapy of a demanding, serious function outside the home. She could not herself, of course, volunteer to go out to Scutari to nurse the sick and wounded. Nassau John would have forbidden her to leave him and how could she desert four year-old Walter? But she could at least devote herself day and night to supporting the nurses who did go:

> For a time during the Crimean War she . . . helped Miss Stanley in sending supplies to our soldiers and their families, and when it was all over she never ceased regretting the interest which this public duty and hope of doing good on a large scale had afforded her.[2]

The other expression of Jeanie Senior's real self in these years was through art and music. She studied drawing and modelling as well as singing, thereby making many significant new friends. She met the famous sculptor Marochetti at her father-in-law's house and learned to model heads, producing her remarkable bust of Walter. Through Nassau William Senior's old friends the Grotes,[3] she met their protégée, the great singer Jenny Lind; and through her singing master Manuel Garcia she met the former opera diva Adelaide Sartoris, née Kemble.[4] Both Jenny Lind and Adelaide Sartoris would become lifelong friends. At her father-in-law's Kensington dinner table she also enjoyed laughing with Tom Taylor the comic playwright and later editor of *Punch*, as well as with Thackeray and his two young, lively, motherless daughters, Anny and Minny, who lived nearby. At the beginning of 1855 Jeanie went to the painter F. B. Barwell's studio in order to model for the figure of the mother in Millais' 'The Rescue'.[5] Millais had written to Tom Taylor about her: 'I am very anxious to get a beautiful face for what I am painting this year. I hope you will use your influence in my behalf to get

5   Bust of Walter Senior aged 6–7 years, modelled by Jeanie Senior. Courtesy of Mrs. Pamela Milne.

her to sit for me'.[6] Jeanie Senior's later vocation in the field of child-rescue had been strangely prefigured.

Most important of all was Jeanie's introduction to Sara Prinsep's artistic and literary circle at Little Holland House in the 1850s.[7] '[Everything] that was gifted, amiable or admirable in the life of Victorian England . . . came . . . on Sunday afternoons and evenings, including practically all the distinguished men and beautiful women of [the]day.'[8] Virginia Woolf's mother, young Julia Jackson, was the Prinseps' cherished niece and the writer would later evoke her mother's nostalgic memories of Little Holland House as only she could:

> I think of it as a summer afternoon world. . . . Long windows open onto the lawn. . . . Tea tables with great bowls of strawberries and cream . . . are 'presided over' by some of the [seven] lovely sisters who do not wear crinolines, but are robed in splendid Venetian

draperies; they sit enthroned, and talk with foreign emphatic gestures . . . to the eminent men . . . rulers of India, statesmen, poets, painters. . . . The sound of music also comes from those long low rooms where the great Watts pictures hang; Joachim playing the violin; also the sound of a voice reading poetry – . . . Tennyson in his wide-awake; Watts in his smock frock; . . . Garibaldi in his red shirt. . . .[9]

It is not difficult to imagine what an escape Little Holland House must have offered to Jeanie Senior as an alternative to the 'oh so slow' dinners alone with her husband. And there, at Little Holland House in the early 1850s, Jeanie first met its 'resident painter', George Frederick Watts, who, as Sara Prinsep liked to recount, had come for three days and stayed for thirty years.

Watts is still something of an enigma. The enormously gifted son of a piano-tuner, 'taken up' first by Lord and Lady Holland and then by the less grand but wealthy Prinseps, Watts nursed the most exalted artistic ambitions at the same time as the most paralysing self-doubt. What he thought his greatest work, his allegories, were his weakest; what he thought his most mundane work, his portraits, were his strength.[10] Intensely and always hopelessly attracted to vivid, beautiful women who were socially 'above' him,

6   George Frederick Watts, 1817–1904, self-portrait, 1864. Copyright © Tate, London 2007.

Watts would seem to have been incapable of total commitment of body and soul to any woman. Tortured by migraines, stomach disorders and depression, he anticipated an early death – but lived to be eighty-seven. His habitual suffering and sad idealism gave him the look of a Holman Hunt Christ; his "smile" according to Ruskin, 'very sweet; but firm, not going far'.[11]

Twelve years older than Jeanie, saddened by the recent failure of his romantic devotion to Sara Prinsep's eldest sister, Virginia Pattle, who had recently married and become Lady Somers, Watts now dedicated himself to work solely for the betterment of mankind through art, starting at dawn each day. His recent paintings of social compassion and social protest – 'Found Drowned', 'Under a Dry Arch', 'The Sempstress' and 'Evicted – the Irish famine', hung, huge and sombre around his studio in the grounds of Little Holland House. How they spoke to Jeanie, marooned as she then was in the harsh political environment of her father-in-law. Watts and Jeanie were two deeply unhappy people who responded not only to the suffering that each intuited in the other, but also to their shared desire to create a less suffering world. He was already becoming famous as an artistic genius; she was wonderful to look at and to hear sing – and she needed someone noble to worship. It helped that they both loved music and riding and the out of doors. Watts encouraged Jeanie's drawing, while she made it her business to save much of his preparatory work from being lost. She collected and preserved 'many sketches and designs, made while he was working out various ideas . . . at a time when they were littering his studio, which but for her forethought would certainly have disappeared'.[12]

Several of the artist's many letters to Jeanie were lent by her son Walter in 1910 to Watts' widow and biographer, Mary Watts and transcriptions of these are held for researchers to read in the (Watts) Compton Gallery, near Guildford. But there are scores more unpublished letters and passages in letters from Watts to Jeanie Senior that Walter Senior did not release. They are painfully revealing of his mother's emotional wretchedness and turbulence in the mid 1850s, and of Watts' inadequacy of response. They are quoted here for the first time. Since she kept all Watts' letters and Watts destroyed all hers, we have to reconstruct as best we can her part of the correspondence from his.

Already in his second letter, summer 1854, Watts asked Jeanie to model for him – consonant, that is, with propriety: 'I want to make use of you, don't be frightened, it is but to lend me an elbow . . . but you promised to lend me your hair. I will I am sure add a hand or an arm occasionally.' In his third letter, late December 1854, after sharing with her his aspiration to lead 'a brave life of earnest striving after good', Watts worried:

> Perhaps you will think me absurd to send you all this, . . . but as I know your great friendship for me, and as I have become your true

and sincere friend, it is fit you should see me as I am, even though
you should feel alarmed and take me for a Methodist Parson,
    The Signor
    Many happy Xmases! Would I could ensure them to you.

That postscript shows he knew she was unhappy.

But it was in his fourth letter, early in 1855, that Watts first expressed his
miserable anxiety about Jeanie – his obsessive fear that she could be morally
at risk. By now, nearly seven years into her marriage, Jeanie had grown so
desperate that she actually confided to Watts that her life felt empty at its
centre and that she was sometimes tempted to recklessness. Watts responded:

> I feel anxious about you seeing how much there is in your active
> nature that is unsatisfied. I was pained to hear you say that but for
> the idea of the future you would give yourself up without reserve
> to the gratification of the moment. Surely I have reason to be
> anxious about you for should an unscrupulous and vigorous intel-
> lect ever . . . persuade you that you are governed by [mere] super-
> stition, [i.e. about keeping marriage vows] it seems to me that the
> only barrier between you and right and wrong would then be
> removed. . . .
>
>   You are so right minded and so sensitive and good naturally that
> I am distressed at any discrepancy. . . . I have the greatest affection
> for you and any thing that seems to be unworthy of your excellent
> nature and unusual talents grieves me, and . . . I think it dangerous.
> . . .

Watts then made the extraordinary claim that he cared more for Jeanie
than did any of her family or friends, let alone her husband:

> . . . I doubt whether any one living has a truer affection for
> you. . . . I detect profound dissatisfaction with your condition often
> in the tone of your remarks. . . . Yours too affectionately not to
> risk being tiresome. Signor.

He detected some dangerous 'foreign influence' on her that he did not
specify.

Jeanie must then have remonstrated that she did not need his surveillance
and Watts hastily retreated:

> . . . I assure you that my remarks had no particular direction what-
> soever but I know that every woman of any personal attraction is
> the object of pursuit – from such as make it their business to go

about seeking whom they may devour . . . I do not warn you
against any particular "foreign influence" . . . but when we talk
together I will tell freely why I often feel anxious.

In his next letter he wrote:

I do fear for you . . . if I am to care much or admire with all my
heart then there must be nothing that either my feeling or my taste
condemns as vicious. There is so much in you that I sympathise
with entirely, that you must let me be vexed with you and give me
influence over you . . . , but above all things do speak openly to me
and let us discuss your reasons for being so unsatisfied as I see you
are – . . . Yours ever, Signor.

It was putting it strongly indeed to say that he feared lest she might
become 'vicious' – i.e. 'a fallen woman'.

But although Watts wanted her to tell him all that was in her sad heart,
he was not bold enough to dine with her when he knew her to be alone:

I would dine with you on Friday, but you know how prudishly I
have urged circumspection, thinking it more than usually necessary
on your part for reasons which I have given you with the liberty
which only a most sincere friend could take.

Watts was clearly not the man to carry her off on a white charger.

In his next letter he was startled that she should have been reading George
Sand and thus discovering how a spirited, frustrated woman – "I suffered
from being useless"[13] had left her unhappy marriage, taken her young child
off to a garret in Paris, dressed as a man, and earned her own living by
writing. Watts was alarmed:

. . . [There] is something about the French mind (I hope I am not
prejudiced) that I cannot admire or sympathise with: a want of
modesty, softness and depth. . . . Your nature, which though not at all
affected is fond of effect, cannot be improved by French reading. . . .

On his return from Paris, Jeanie invited him to visit her in the country, but
Watts was not sure:

I don't know that I shall come to your cottage. I should most probably find you engrossed by somebody or other and I should be
disgusted. I care too much for you to not to watch you narrowly,
. . . for I could not willingly be surpast [superseded?]

He then changed his mind about not seeing her:

> Friday
> Perhaps I may come tomorrow by the 10. train . . .

There then followed the shortest of undated notes:

> I am miserable about you, and have no heart to work. Signor

In the event he decided to go after all – but failed to arrive. After all that significant dithering, betraying both Watts' constant uneasiness about Jeanie and his own need to keep a proprietary eye on her, he spelt out what tormented him:

> . . . I do nothing by halves and if I yield to my natural sympathy for you and wish to occupy the first place in your affections it is not that I am actuated by views that can make me dangerous. Whatever my impulses might have been, I should have kept aloof from any thing beyond the merest friendship "for I desire to rest". But I have watched you with great anxiety and grieved to see how large a place in your affections remained unoccupied. This I dreaded to think might be seized upon by some one who might cause you to repent bitterly, and for this reason I have laid claim to the possession of the first place.

In the same breath that Watts was saying that he wanted to come first with Jeanie, he was also saying that he wanted this not in order to become her lover, but in order that she did not take someone else, less scrupulous than himself, as a lover. She was now moved to tell Watts that his solicitous, brotherly friendship, however affectionate, was not enough for her and that yes, there was someone else. Watts was devastated:

> I deferred answering your former letter till I should be here and because it made me very sad. I cannot hope to be that guide and watcher I had hoped to be. Much of what you told me I dreaded instinctively . . . but I had permitted myself to hope from the opinion and affection you have expressed for me, that considering the obligations of your [married] position which you cannot, which you have no right to ignore, I had permitted myself to hope that my earnest, my affectionate, my tender friendship would have been sufficient to fill up your need as your best friend, [occupy your] heart and reconcile you to the conditions of your life.
> . . . I should have been contented to watch over you as one

watches over a child, . . . but from the moment I know of [another] human influence I gasp for room. I compete not, but retire . . . . My friendship is I believe as strong as most people's love, and perhaps as jealous; and while I know that a stronger or even a rival influence exists I can never feel satisfied or happy. . . . . I found so much in you sympathetic that I was beginning to permit it to unfold under the influence of the tenderest interest, but I cannot take a second place. Perhaps you will think me very selfish, but I have suffered so much that I would rather die by my own deed than risk the slightest return of the fierce malady that shattered me, . . .

God forbid I should grieve you by any thing I say . . . From this time I shall never in any way allude to the subject of the letter you sent to me before I came here. . . . And once more let me say for God's sake, for your own sake, and for your child's, be prudent, be wise and be happy. . . .

I pray God bless you always. . . .

I will say no more and you will tell me whether you can be my friend and sister and occasional nurse and sometimes helper in art – for you might be so! or whether I must try to forget . . . that I looked to be a guide and support to poor little Jeanie!. . . .

(18 August 1856)

Clearly Watts was emotionally 'all over the place' – jealous, hurt, anxious, self-protective, needing to be close to Jeanie, yet not too close. His next letter was the most desperate, most incoherent and most nearly suicidal that Watts ever wrote to her:

. . . I have cared for you, I have watched over you, I have been deeply pained, I have thought of your future and what I could do for you in many sleepless moments. I could love you better than I love any one else now for I see in you great qualities. . . . I can never fancy you but as standing upon the verge of a precipice, and can never feel that I can arrest the frightful danger . . . . You will see that I am not fit to be a friend. I don't think I am fit to live . . .

Whatever I say to you you must never intimate to any living soul,

Jeanie was clearly very frightened by his hint at suicide – 'I don't think I am fit to live' – and therefore his next letter tried to reassure her:

. . . I don't wish to frighten you. I feel for you as one might feel for a beloved child, certainly jealous and uncomfortable and unhappy knowing you to be under an influence I regret and distrust. . . . . I have very great affection for you and shall be very anxious about you, too anxious to be always certain of how much my interest amounts to, but believe me not beyond that, unhappy –

There followed many 'last notes' before Watts finally sailed away to the Levant:

When you feel inclined to be reckless, think how deeply you would wound your affectionate friend Signor . . .

Jeanie was distressed that he should finally sail without seeing her again. He replied:

I too was very sorry to let you go away without seeing you, but I could not say good bye to you in public. . . . [My] mind is like a weathercock vibrating and whirling at every gust of feeling, . . . God bless you, . . .
    . . . I am very sorry to go away without seeing you but cannot come to see you in a crowd. I rely upon your solemn promise;
(2 October 1856) [my emphasis]

In her recent monumental biography, *G. F. Watts, The Last Great Victorian*, Veronica Franklin Gould states that Jeanie was 'Troubled by nerves and unhappily married to a coarse, burly barrister'. She writes that Jeanie became 'Watts's confidante and soulmate, adding '[Watts] was consumed by desire and concern for Jeanie. Had she been free, he would surely have married her, but he must 'fiendishly' urge circumspection. Her nervous attacks worsened . . . ' After Jeanie's death, Gould concludes: 'Watts had known and loved Jeanie with deep reciprocated affection and under-standing for twenty-six years. She had been the love of his life.'[14] Gould had to work from the censored extracts from Watts' letters that Walter Senior had copied out for Mrs. Watts in 1910, which leave much of the story unclear. From the full text of Watts' letters it is evident that it was *he* rather than she who suffered from nerves – 'from the irritated state of my nervous system my mind is like a weathercock vibrating and whirling at every gust of feeling'. He was quite unequal to rescuing Jeanie from the ordeal of her empty marriage. (And Gould is also unaware that Watts had a rival).

Who was the rival that Watts so distrusted, the 'foreign influence' that he regarded with jealousy and dread? What exactly was the 'precipice' on which he saw her standing – the threatened 'recklessness' about which he was so anxious?

≈

There is another collection of letters, dated 1854–1856, which Jeanie Senior also kept all her life – letters written to her in French from Prosper Mérimée, her elder by twenty-five years. And if Watts was one enigma, Mérimée was another. What both men had in common was their prodigious creative output. Mérimée was a phenomenally energetic polymath. Before he met Jeanie in 1854 he had been not only one of the inventors but also one of the greatest practitioners of the short story, the most famous of which was the tragic novella *Carmen* (1847).[15] He had also experimented with drama and dramatic criticism and written major works of European history. A brilliant linguist, he had taught himself Russian in order to translate some of the great Russian classics into French. And he was also a gifted amateur artist. As if that were not enough, when working as a civil servant, he had been the fearless special commissioner for sanitary measures during a cholera epidemic in Paris in 1832. Most important of all, as Inspector-General of French Historic Monuments ever since 1834, Mérimée had travelled the entire country and his survey reports had made a priceless contribution to the preservation of France's architectural and archaeological heritage. He had served in the National Guard during the 1848 Revolution and had recently been made a Chevalier of the Légion d'Honneur and appointed a senator. 'Finally, he was a master of the epistolary art'[16] leaving behind him sixteen volumes of some of the most interesting letters written in Europe in the 19th century.

What did Mérimée look like? Thin, svelte, '[at] fifty, his hair was grey, but he was erect and vigorous, with a disconcerting stare and a bitter twist to his mouth'.[17] 'He was of middle height and well-built; the upper part of his face was very handsome; the broad forehead and magnificent eyes showed intelligence and lofty aspirations';[18] Jeanie's sister-in-law, Minnie Senior, found him '[tall], rather gaunt, studiously quiet in voice and manner, stately and good-looking'.[19]

But despite his attractiveness and heroic record of achievement, Prosper Mérimée 'led a lonely life and felt certain that he was a failure, [attaching] little value to the fields in which his accomplishments were most tangible'.[20] Why? His personal life had been debauched and emotionally chaotic, producing in him cynicism and despair. He was a serial seducer of other men's wives and a compulsive frequenter of brothels. 'Moi je baise sans aimer ni être aimé et je m'ennuie' – 'As for me, I have sex without loving or being loved and it bores me'.[21]

> [His] relations with women were . . . stormy and . . . unsatisfactory . . . On the one hand, his sexual appetites were voracious and his emotional needs intense; on the other, his fear of passion and mistrust of effusiveness were so acute that he shunned [commitment].[22]

7   Prosper Mérimée, 1868, épreuve sur papier albuminé par Emile Robert. Courtesy of Bibliothèque nationale de France, cabinet des Estampes.

Mérimée had recently suffered the appalling wound to his *amour-propre* of having been dismissed by his long-term mistress. How could he ever believe in any woman again? And how could Jeanie Senior, initially, not be fascinated by such a man and tempted, in her fantasies at least, to redeem such an unhappy, saturnine, lost soul? He made a better Rochester figure than Rochester. To cap all, Mérimée dared to outrage 19th century religious and moral sensibilities by publicly denouncing the institution of marriage as sheer humbug and by being aggressively, unapologetically anti-Christian. He rejected both God and the Ten Commandments. No wonder that Watts should have been in such agonies of anxiety about his foreign rival's dangerous influence over his child/sister, 'poor little Jeanie'.

Unlike Watts, Mérimée scrupulously dated his letters so we have a precise record of his correspondence with her – or of all of it that has been permitted to survive. Many of the letters were actually published soon after Jeanie's death in the *Revue des Deux Mondes*[23] as evidence that Mérimée *was* capable of writing letters to a woman that were 'parfaitement inoffensives', in contrast to his often indecent *Lettres à une inconnue*, which had been recently published in Paris.[24] Nevertheless, the editor of the *Revue des Deux Mondes* did feel obliged to add that Madame Jeanie Senior was 'un esprit libre, sans fausse pruderie' – 'a free spirit without false prudery'. And indeed these letters to a young, beautiful, unhappily married woman in mid-Victorian England strike a startling note of daring suggestiveness amounting to an encouragement to commit adultery. They are also often very funny, and Jeanie loved to laugh.

Mérimée had been introduced to her by her father-in-law, Professor Senior, whom he had originally met in Paris in 1851, probably at the apartment of Madame Mohl.[25] His first surviving letter, in answer to one in English from Jeanie that has not survived,[26] was written from Vienna, 26 September 1854, and regaled her with his amused response to mixed naked bathing at a spa in Hungary:

> . . . In the interests of morality there was a partition between the men's section and the women's but there was an open door in this partition and it was the custom to pay visits. My guide told me "That's Hungarian liberty". The female beauties who cooked in this soup covered their faces from my sight with their hands, which struck me as very oriental.[27]

Thus from the first, Mérimée cut through his English correspondent's defences of protective reticence by insisting on focusing on public nudity. After a compliment to Jeanie's golden hair, the like of which, he said, had not been seen since Homer, Mérimée's letter ended with a very reluctant agreement to accede to Jeanie's command that he read Elizabeth Gaskell's *Ruth*, recently published in 1853. He feared it would only aggravate his 'blue devils' of depression.

It must surely be one of the more piquant episodes in literary history: the creator of Carmen (the most famous of all *femmes fatales*, promiscuous, conscienceless, sexually irresistible, a destroyer of men), now being made to read the opposite, rather more common story of a vulnerable girl, naïvely trusting and tender-hearted, abandoned when made pregnant by the 'gentleman' who had claimed to love her and protect her like a brother. Jeanie Senior was surely trying to reach through to the conscience of Mérimée, testing him, or even trying to convert him, through his response to this text. For if *Ruth* did not move him, what would?[28] How did Mérimée, the purchaser of countless young girls in brothels throughout Europe, react?

His letter of 5 March 1855 began with attack as the best means of defence, criticizing the British for their strait-laced 'prejudice' in favour of the sanctity of marriage:

> We continentals don't have as many prejudices as you and what passes in England for daring is seen as a lot simpler in France. The evil comes from your church and from even further afield. People take as a *sacrament* what should never have been more than a social convention. In Southern Europe, above all in my beloved Spain, one remedies the inconvenience of marriage by marrying twice. The first time a girl marries without knowing what she is doing. She is a little schoolgirl who accepts a man who is introduced to her – or chooses him herself because he has a moustache and dances well. Naturally she makes a mistake; but happily one never does something stupid without gaining in experience. Having acquired such experience, the ex-little schoolgirl is in a position when she is about twenty-two to find the husband who suits her. This second husband, whom one terms lover, generally lives on good terms with the first and helps him pass the time.[29]

How much did Mérimée know about Jeanie Hughes' own 'ex-little schoolgirl' engagement and subsequent disillusionment? Or was the misalliance only too obvious to everyone at Professor Nassau William Senior's dinner table, whether in Kensington or in Paris, when they saw the vital, gifted, beautiful Jeanie accompanied by her silent, corpulent husband? In any event, the recommendation of a 'second marriage' to a lover was a deliberately provocative move thus early in their correspondence. By treating adultery, not fidelity, as normal, and rightly normal, Mérimée was clearly daring Jeanie to be ready to consider defying British public opinion. Had he seduced her into an affair, it would have been merely another episode in *his* life – but it would have had quite devastating consequences for *her*. We can now understand Watts' desperate entreaties to her to promise him to be prudent, not reckless.

In that same letter, Mérimée admitted his unhappiness at his own recently ended love affair – but then went on the attack again:

> It seems to me that in England women are worse enslaved than anywhere else.
>
> I think they rarely take lovers, for fear of losing caste, but the devil does not lose anything thereby. The women are very unhappy: they know temptation but never succumb and die uncertain whether it might not have been better to succumb than to resist.[30]

If the cap fits . . .

By his third letter, 23 March 1855, Mérimée had finished *Ruth*. But his response was crass. He crudely reduced Ruth's suffering to nothing but a lack of money. He was blind – or else wilfully obtuse – to Ruth's wretchedness at having loved and believed herself loved, only to find herself used and discarded. Instead of criticizing Ruth's seducer in any way, Mérimée criticized English cant for refusing to tolerate what seemed to him a mere sexual peccadillo. A fortnight later, 10 April 1855, Mérimée teased Jeanie for having remonstrated with him in her reply:

> You find the way to say the nastiest things against my sex and against me who am its ornament. There is only one thing that charmed me in your letter, your saying that it is not necessary to be young in order to be loved. . . .

Mérimée ended by inviting Jeanie to use his Paris apartment in order to see the Universal Exhibition in Paris – he would make himself scarce, he wrote. She replied that her women friends had counselled her to refuse: it simply 'wasn't done' and in any case Mérimée, they said, had a more than dubious reputation. Had Mme. Mohl told Jeanie something of the notorious details of Mérimée's private life? Or had Minnie Senior perhaps told her sister-in-law about his invitation to ladies who visited his rooms to view his interesting collection of erotica that he kept in a secret drawer?[31] Mérimée wrote back on 8 June 1855, not best pleased:

> You made me laugh with your scruples, or rather the scruples of your women friends. I would very much like to know who are those charitable souls who have given you all this marvellous information about me and where and how they know me? [But she still has time to change her mind]. Monsieur Senior [her father-in-law] will pass on to you a book that will amuse you, although it is a little naughty – I daren't say *because* it is a little naughty.

Next he appealed for sympathy. He was very ill with neuralgia and depression.

> How could you dare to recommend me to drink brandy to make me better? And you accuse me of *satanism* – it would apply much better to you. . . . Adieu Madame; I hope you haven't said your last word about coming over here'.[32]

In her reply Jeanie must have admitted that it was her husband who had actually forbidden her to accept the offer of his apartment, at which Mérimée teasingly appealed to her pride:

Madame, I did not know your husband was a tyrant. How can you allow yourself to be dictated to and why do you not make him let you do everything that you want? You should know that those who have the misfortune to belong to my sex are not happy unless they are under some despotic government. . . .

He then went on to make his famous confession that he had once possessed the most beautiful woman in the world, 'the reine de la Chine', enclosed in a bottle. He had broken the bottle and since one does not ever find a second 'princesse de la Chine', he had gone crazy over his stupidity. Hence his misanthropy. But he was delighted that Jeanie should say she believed him to be at bottom

> '[a] *good natured man*'. I think that is true. I was never an evil being, but in growing older I try to avoid doing wrong and that is more difficult than one might suppose. . . .
> I have heard that you are a great musician. But I can hardly believe it because you seem to me to have too much *esprit* and to be too lazy for that. One has to be a little stupid to do just one thing all the time – and one only excels in the arts by being devoted totally to them, working from morning to night, never exposing oneself to fresh air or eating ices in summer [as Jeanie had done with him] . . .[33]

Mérimée's epistolary flirtation, sometimes drawing close to her, sometimes drawing back again, always appealing for her sympathetic understanding, which he rightly intuited was the way to her heart, continued in early January 1856. He had not been able to write novels he said, as Jeanie encouraged him to do, ever since personal unhappiness had struck him down. Once again he mocked the prudery in contemporary English literature, which would end, he foretold, in total banality. Then, on 16 February 1856, Mérimée wrote her his most intimately confessional letter, and in doing so he tested how far he could go with her on paper. His own immoral reputation, he claimed yet again, had come simply and solely from his not having played the hypocrite by putting on a respectable mask when young:

> . . . The other day I began a novel that I shall dedicate to you if ever I finish it . . . its title could be 'The misfortune of being candid'. It's about a man who bares his whole soul to a woman whom he loves and who takes from him all his illusions. Have your ever read Beyle [i.e. Stendal] *On Love*? It's a strange little book but full of very perceptive observations.[34] . . . Let me tell you a

personal anecdote to illustrate the question which I warn you is a
bit immoral but from which one can draw a moral.

In my youth I was the only possessor, I believed, of a remarkably
beautiful leg – a rare phenomenon for reasons it would take too
long to go into. I had only seen it in a silk stocking. I took off the
stocking. The garter had left a slightly livid red mark, explained no
doubt by the fineness of the skin, but ugly all the same. Ever after I
would see that red mark across the leg.[35]

What was the 'moral' Mérimée was preaching? 'Don't let any one see *your*
red mark'? Or 'Don't risk seeing another's'? How did Jeanie feel about his
frequent use of the verb 'possess' in relation to the women in his life? Or
about his forcing her to imagine his undressing his mistress in the erotically
charged sentence – 'I took off the stocking'? He ended by saying that he was
not sure whether he dared send the letter or not but decided to trust to
Jeanie's trust in his sincere friendship – 'le sentiment d'amitié vraie' – which
had made him write so openly to her.

Thus Jeanie Senior had two self-pitying, self-dramatizing men of genius,
neither of them her husband, declaring themselves her true friend while they
pressed for ever more emotional intimacy. On 27 April 1856, after teasing
her for not having known Donizetti's *Don Pasquale* and sung the aria "Dear
husband, don't be a tyrant", Mérimée was clearly relieved that Jeanie had
taken his last letter well, but he disagreed with her insistence that it was
always better to be truthful than not. As for the subject of ladies' garters it
was too risqué a topic – 'brûlant' – so he would say no more about it. Only
that love did not depend on the beauty of a leg. [But was not that precisely
what he had implied about the ugly garter mark?] What it did depend on was
trust.

The correspondence then petered out. Mérimée and Jeanie, for whatever
reason, found it almost impossible to meet, either when she was in Paris or
he in England. And it was becoming clear that they would never see eye to
eye, whether about literature, or emotional honesty or politics. Mérimée was
becoming increasingly cynical, a reactionary: he would take the opposite side
from Jeanie on the American Civil War, for example. And perhaps Jeanie had
learned from Mme. Mohl that Mérimée was simultaneously writing to at
least six other women at this time, including her own sister-in-law Minnie. It
is also possible that Mérimée may have overstepped the mark, either in a
letter or in one of their rare encounters, and been rebuffed. For one of his
last letters to her, dated 10 June 1862, after attacking Jeanie's admiration for
Madame Récamier (not that he thought her sexually immoral, he would
have preferred her immoral 'car je ne considère pas la chasteté comme la
vertu la plus importante'), ended with something very like a sneer at Jeanie
herself. When asking her to pray for a favourable Channel crossing for him,

he gave as his reason: 'I am sure that with your moral and orthodox views on people and things, you ought to have great authority.'[36] She would have long known that he himself was no believer in orthodox morality – or in the efficacy of prayer to a non-existent God.

At first, both Watts and Mérimée must have appeared to Jeanie Senior as fit objects for hero-worship – Watts, the Hero as Artist, Mérimée the Hero as Writer and Public Servant. But it became inescapably clear that the former was all soul and no sex, while the latter only wanted yet another *confidante* with whom he could enjoy the *frisson* of sex games on paper. Neither of these two damaged men, finally, was offering her anything more than the chance to sympathize with his own misery. But she had other people to love and anguish over and live for.

CHAPTER FOUR

Surviving Four Hard Years, 1856–1860

In November 1856 Tom and Fanny Hughes, that couple whose engagement Jeanie had so rapturously hailed in 1845, and their family of four young children, were struck down by scarlet fever. Just when their golden-haired eldest daughter, six year-old Evie, seemed to be recovering, she weakened, became light-headed and died in her father's arms. There were only two bearable thoughts: first, that the child had suffered such brain damage through her illness that she would probably not have lived to adulthood, and second, that she was now transformed into an angelic presence awaiting them in the next world.

Very soon afterwards, Jeanie's father, John Hughes, began to show unmistakeable signs of mental disturbance and depression. Indicting himself for the sin of indolence and for having failed to make the most of his many natural talents, he became the prey of irrational terrors, including a baseless fear of bankruptcy, and religious mania. His down-to-earth wife Margaret could not reach him in his bouts of despairing silence or his sudden, feverish insistence that they were all about to become beggars and he himself a damned soul. In January 1857 his wife was unable to stay with him in his lodgings, because she had to nurse a servant ill at Donnington with smallpox. It was Jeanie, of course, who then went to tend her father and report back:

> Mammy darling, you would really be happy to see Papa today. He is so *very* much better. He had a good night and eat [sic] a very hearty breakfast . . . He is quite cheerful to-day and (the best sign possible with him) he has begun *talking* again – Holding forth. – He has been talking about his past life and I have been preaching him a *most admirable* sermon . . . that all retrospect of the past was wrong, as it unfits a person for doing their duty in the *present*. . . . [He] is quite in the right way [now] to get all right, please God. I long to see you my own darling, and to see *you* looking better too . . .[1]

But John Hughes did not 'get all right'. Jeanie and her mother had the horror of watching helplessly while insanity took hold. The gifted, jolly father, once so full of ballads and family history and old tales and teasing, who had delighted in every one of his eight children, was now locked into clinical depression, finally dying in December 1857. Her father's decline and collapse remained a nightmare memory for Jeanie; she would become acutely anxious ever after if any of her brothers showed signs of incipient depressive illness.

However, not only 'in the midst of life are we in death' but also, in the midst of death we are in life. In April 1857, a few months after the loss of Evie and in the midst of John Hughes' mental deterioration, Thomas Hughes brought out his vital and enormously successful novel, *Tom Brown's Schooldays*. He had begun it exuberantly, six months before Evie fell ill, in the summer holidays of 1856, and had meant it as a message of encouragement for his promising eldest son Maurice, who would soon start at Rugby.

> His was literally the first work of fiction to present a real world of boys in the setting of a real English public school. And it is still, despite the many recent novels on the subject, the most vigorous, the most convincing, and the most deeply moving of all. . . . It influenced to some extent all later fiction about public schools . . . Much more important . . . [it] made the modern public school.[2]

What concerns us here, however, is not the literary and social legacy of *Tom Brown's Schooldays*, but its immediate impact on Thomas Hughes' sister. How did she read it? Naturally she found an immense amount to relish and endorse. For were not 'the Browns' their own Hughes family? A family not aristocratic but the salt of the English earth, a fighting, argumentative lot who nevertheless always pulled together in the last resort and sided with the underdog. That was how both Tom and Jeanie saw their Hughes-ness:

> Wherever hard knocks of any kind, visible or invisible, are going, there the Brown who is nearest must shove in his carcase . . . Then for clanship, they are as bad as Highlanders; it is amazing the belief they have in one another. With them there is nothing like the Browns . . . They can't be happy unless they are always meeting one another [and] during the whole time of their being together they luxuriate in telling one another their minds . . . and their minds are wonderfully antagonistic, and all their opinions are downright beliefs. ... [Nevertheless] they love and respect one another ten times the more after a good family arguing bout, and go back, one to his curacy, another to his chambers, and another to his regiment, freshened for work, and more than ever convinced that the Browns are the height of company. . . .
> They can't let anything alone which they think is going wrong.

> They must speak their mind about it . . . and spend their time and
> money in having a tinker at it . . . It is an impossibility to a Brown
> to leave the most disreputable dog on the other side of a stile.[3]

Tom Hughes was evoking a typical combative set-to between conservative
eldest brother George Hughes,[4] John Hughes the quiescent cleric and Tom
himself, the radical barrister/enthusiast for Christian Socialism. Perhaps
there was also a memory of their young brother Walter, the outspoken
soldier home on leave. The passage unconsciously prefigures Jeanie [Hughes]
Senior's later interventions in the public world; she too would be unable to
'let [something] alone which [she thinks] is going wrong'.

Jeanie was also deeply moved by Tom's loving description of their early
childhood's setting, the Vale of the White Horse, where their parents, alias
'Squire Brown and Madam Brown', had dealt out coal and clothes and
herbal medicines and good counsel and good cheer to their poor neighbours.
An idealized image of their family, yet it served as a good memory to nourish
the Hughes children now, in sadder times. That close identification of Tom
Hughes and 'Tom Brown', however, ends as soon as the latter goes to Rugby,
and for one simple reason. 'Tom Brown' is the eldest son in his family and
therefore faces the heroic challenge of surviving Rugby School – with its
homesickness and fights and bullying, and 'fagging' and impossible set tasks
in Classics that always needed a 'crib' – as a pioneer, relying largely upon
himself. Whereas Tom Hughes had gone to Rugby as the protected younger
brother of successful, popular George Hughes, who had instructed young
Tom on how best to survive:

> . . . Escape out of bounds before you were caught by a sixth form
> boy, was the only remedy; and, once out of bounds, there was the
> river for amusement, and the railway [with its] large gangs of
> [navies] . . . George became a skilful fisherman.[5]

Thus 'Tom Brown' fuses George and Tom Hughes, perhaps adding once
again some memories of Walter. And Jeanie, like every other reader of the
book, would have sided, in passionate indignation with the young, heroic
rapscallion Tom, against the sadistic, swaggering Flashman and his side-
kicks.

The latter part of *Tom Brown's Schooldays*, as Mack and Armytage have
pointed out, is considerably 'graver and deeper', written as it was after the
sudden death of Evie.[6] The emphasis in the second half is on the necessity for
tenderness and on the courage needed to champion the vulnerable. Genuine
'manliness' for Tom Hughes always demanded tenderness and thoughtful-
ness for others: 'The words "tender" and "tenderness" were favourites of his
. . . and the pages of his book are overflowing with feeling . . . Rugby . . . is

[shown] as a place of human relationships and moral growth'.[7] Towards the end of his story, Hughes stresses the spiritual strength of those who, seeming weak, yet possess a faith that looks through death. And Jeanie would have responded ardently to Tom Brown's determination, when he leaves Rugby, 'to be doing some real good . . . in the world'.[8]

The accumulated sadness caused by the disappointment of her marriage, the death of Evie, and her father's terrible end, must have shown on Jeanie's usually radiant face, for Watts found her altered on his return from Malta late in 1857. He had been commissioned by Margaret Hughes to paint a full-length portrait of her daughter: 'I wish any effort of mine could bring back your ancient gaiety for I am grieved to see you so much changed, but you are not changed to your friends!' The deep seriousness and tenderness in her are captured wonderfully in Watts' famous portrait. He did not yet see her grit, fire and steel as he wrote to her about what he was trying to express:

> . . . I send you [a] box [of paints] etc. . . . It is not a very grand
> present but I hope it will remind you of my picture and the
> meaning I have in making you water (in the picture) a flowering

8   Detail from Watts' portrait of Jeanie Senior, 1857, now at Wightwick Manor, Staffs. Courtesy The National Trust Photo Library.

root with so much solicitude! As I told you I intend by the flowers to typify the better sentiments, aspirations and affections, which it is sometimes difficult to keep alive or at least blooming in the crush of artificial society, but I love to think of you as cultivating these beautiful and rare flowers!

> No not rare;
> – by God's dear Grace not rare,
> In many a lonely homestead blooming strong.
> Mid haunts of men requiring watchful care
> Where in tormentous swell the passions throng
> Lest haply they, the fostering hand not nigh,
> Withered by breath should fade, too rudely bruis'd, should die!

There! . . . Invoking the Muses! But if you laugh at my poetry, you won't at my intention; . . . (23 December 1857)

That part of the letter was published both in Mary Watts' biography of 1912 and in Wilfrid Blunt's *England's Michelangelo* of 1975. But Jeanie's son Walter Senior had not permitted the widowed Mary Watts to see the end of Watts' letter, so the admonition to Jeanie that follows (and follows straight on in mid sentence after 'you won't at my intention';) is published here for the first time:

> and if ever you feel reckless as sometimes you have, after thinking of Child and Mother and Brothers, . . . you will remember how earnestly I desired your welfare and happiness and how failure in your ordeal would grieve your most affectionate friend
> The Signor.[9]

The 'ordeal' that she must not fail in by being 'reckless' was her marriage.

It is not clear when Jeanie Senior first realized that Walter would be her only child. Almost certainly she must have suffered miscarriages and possibly a stillbirth, if we remember passages from Watts's letters in the mid 1850s: 'I am very sorry indeed to find you so unwell but hope remaining still will put you all right again soon' . . . 'I am most sorry to find you have been so very ill' and 'As soon as you feel up to sitting again'. . . . A friend was quoted after her death as saying 'It was her great desire to have a daughter of her own. This was denied to her by Providence'.[10] What is indisputable is that in August 1856 Jeanie, believing she might never have another child, persuaded her husband to allow her to 'adopt' Helen Wilson, the motherless five year-old daughter of an Indian Army Officer, Colonel Wilson. Little Helen had damaged feet and was slow to learn, and Jeanie became deeply absorbed in trying to answer her needs.

But first, and always first, there was 'her Boy'. Walter was a fine-looking, demanding child, self-willed and difficult to manage. Like every 19th century parent, she had known the terror of all the potentially fatal childhood illnesses which, given her nursing, he had blessedly survived. But when Walter was not yet eight, in January 1858, he was sent away to a boarding school in Brighton to be 'prepared' for Eton. Jeanie was absolutely desolate. Twelve years later, when she had to send her youngest adoptive son Harry away to preparatory boarding school, she would write to Walter:

> The house is dreadfully quiet . . . I can't tell you how sorry I am to part with Harry. He is so very little to go to school. – I feel in a small degree the sort of yearning feeling I had when you used to go to school . . . I can't bear to think of him all alone there with strangers. (May 1870)

Whether Nassau had insisted that Walter be sent away 'for his own good' rather than attend a reputable London day-school or be tutored at home, we do not know. It is possible that Jeanie's own worryingly fragile health at this time had contributed to the decision. (She would seem to have been suffering serious internal complications from a medically mishandled miscarriage and could barely walk.) But it was devastating to see Walter's empty little bed and to miss him all day every day. It is to Walter's frequent, protracted absence from home, beginning January 1858, that we owe the long, confiding letters from his mother, which give us the inner story of her life over the next twenty years. And it was the desperation in her early letters to Walter that first alerted this author to Jeanie's emotional desert of a marriage:

> I shall think of you and miss you every hour of the day, my dear little boy; but I know that it is the best thing for you to be at school; so I shall try to be happy without you. . . . Mind that you never forget that all my happiness depends on your trying to be a good boy. (24 January) . . . [Thank] you for writing so many dear and kind letters. They are the greatest happiness I have in the world next to having you with me. . . . You say that you wish I would send you 8,000 kisses. I wish I could. (2 February) . . . I watch for the postman whenever I expect a letter from you and almost cry with happiness when I see your dear writing. (4 February 1858)

Was his mother putting an impossible burden on the boy by being so emotionally demonstrative and dependent? Or was the child reassured that he had not been rejected and abandoned, though sent away from home so young? In the event, this guaranteed flow of letters from his 'ever-loving old

Mum' ensured that Walter never had to feel alone in the world. He knew he could tell her everything that worried him in his new life and that she would do her best to help. She would try to cheer him up by sending him his paint box or a hamper or reminding him that he would soon be home for the holidays and be able to play again with little Helen or his adored elder cousin Maurice; or else she would promise to visit him so that they could talk about things. When he told her that he was being bullied, she sympathized intensely: 'It makes my heart ache sadly to think my dear child is unhappy' but all she could do was entreat him not to be cross or unkind in return (April 1858). When Walter went down with measles in May 1858 she rushed to Brighton to see him but was then forced to leave him behind in his darkened room:

> I was very unwilling to leave you yesterday, . . . God has given me but one child and so you may fancy that I am anxious about him . . . I should have been so very happy if I could have remained to nurse you in this illness, as I have nursed you in all your other illnesses; but I could not have brought you home here, and I must not leave your Papa for more than a day or two at a time if I can help it.

The conflict between Jeanie's impulse to look after her young son and her husband's insistence that her first duty was to look after *him*, had begun. Gradually she came to see that she had two dependent children – or three including Helen. On 24 May Nassau actually begged her not to visit their convalescent son – 'as the journey [was] expensive'. But although Walter's Brighton Preparatory School, 'Dr. Cary's', was a 'Crammer', a little like 'Dr. Blimber's Academy', satirized by Dickens,[11] Walter was no wilting Paul Dombey but Walter Senior – a boy with a healthily stubborn streak of self-preservation.

In that same year there came the first warning sign that Nassau John Senior's employment was at risk. On 23 February 1858 Jeanie ended her usual long warm, sympathetic letter to Walter:

> You will be sorry to hear that your Father will no longer be the Lord Chancellor's Secretary – Another gentleman, called Sir Frederic Thesiger is to be Chancellor, instead of Lord Cranworth; and he does not know your Father; so Papa will lose his place, and £400 a year.

It is a startlingly frank confidence to a boy not yet eight; nowadays parents would tend to protect children from such worrying news. However his mother's next letter, four days later, was able to reassure Walter that 'the new Lord Chancellor has been so kind as to make your Papa one of his

Secretaries, so your father will not lose £400 a year as I was afraid he would'. Nevertheless, Nassau's days in that office were numbered.

The dark thing that shadowed most of the rest of 1858 was Jeanie's mysteriously weakened health, possibly after another miscarriage. From August right through till December she reported that she had to obey doctors; it was the first mention of the celebrated Dr. Gully at Malvern[12] and the Orleanist exile Dr. Guéneau de Mussy, both of whom would be her trusted family physicians for years to come. Occasionally at Malvern she was well enough to walk but for the most part she was kept indoors and constantly told that she must lie still and rest completely; sometimes she was too weak even to sit up and write to Walter. At certain times little Helen had to be sent away to be looked after by her aunts and Jeanie was forbidden to go down to Brighton for a longed-for visit to Walter in September, because the railway journey would jolt her too badly. There was still no definite diagnosis as to what was the matter with her. But at last, by Christmas 1858, everything looked brighter once more. Helen was back with her again, now reading fluently at last, and every one was looking forward to the grand reunion at Grandma Margaret Hughes' country home Hawke House, Sunbury on Thames. The young uncles, Harry and Arthur Hughes, would be there and Walter was promised his first ever Christmas tree and a huge bowl of bubbling 'Snapdragon' from which to pull out plums.

But the New Year brought no progress in Jeanie's health. The first part of 1859 found her living at her mother's home, Hawke House, cheered by visits from her friend the former opera singer Adelaide Sartoris, née Kemble. At the beginning of May, Jeanie, still at Hawke House, had to apologize to Walter for having been remiss for once in not writing to him – 'I have been very very busy, writing letters for your Papa, who wanted to get made Secretary in the Ionian Islands; but he will not get this place, as it is promised to someone else.' In other words Nassau was now unemployed. That was the first instance of Jeanie Senior's enlistment in the task of finding her husband a good paid position by writing countless letters of recommendation and entreaty to X and Y who had influence with Z who knew the man who had in his gift some desirable 'place'.

Then, on 14 May 1859, there came another blow:

> Little Helen is not going to live with me any longer I am sorry to say. Your Father says that he had rather not have any child in the house except you during the holidays. But she will come to stay with me very often I hope – I miss her dreadfully – She is to live at Ebberton [with her aunts] always now.

Jeanie's suppressed rage over her helplessness at this arbitrary command from Nassau was implicit in her next letter to Walter, commenting on some sailors who had struggled to keep a motherless baby alive: '[All] the strongest and bravest and best men, love and protect little children . . . It is only mean and cowardly men who do not love children.' And she would make sure that eventually Helen, to whom she kept writing and who missed her adoptive home miserably, would one day return.

The plan for the summer of 1859 was that they would all be at Hawke House where his uncles would take Walter swimming in the Thames with the admired older cousin Maurice, Tom Hughes' eldest son. The details of what then happened are not known – whether Maurice was showing off, whether someone took their eyes off him for half a minute, whether there was an unexpected tidal current or the sudden large wash from a passing boat – but eleven year-old Maurice was carried in to Jeanie and his grandmother, Margaret Hughes, drowned. The incredulous shock and anguish may be imagined. Who would tell Tom, so proud of his eldest boy about to start Rugby, for whom he had written *Tom Brown's Schooldays*? How could Tom possibly break it to Maurice's mother Fanny? And what could comfort nine-year old Walter in this horror? Jeanie's only recourse, as with the earlier loss of her dearest brother Walter and of Tom's little Evie, was to remember Christ's promise to the thief on the cross.

As she herself put it in a letter to her sister-in-law, Minnie Senior, at this time: 'I do not think that anything in life is real, and heaven, the only reality, will be so soon present to all of us; so it does not much matter what happens here. We shall all be joyful, and we shall love each other perfectly there.' Nevertheless, as Minnie noted, Jeanie's 'heart suffered, and it was long before she got over the effects of this terrible blow.'[13]

Understandably, Jeanie' strength collapsed again. Once more she was completely bed-ridden, and at the end of 1859 Dr de Mussy, who had been taking constant care of her, often in his own family home, broke it to her that he thought she could be suffering from cancer of the womb. It would, most probably, have been the consequence of a botched handling of an earlier miscarriage. There was a small lump in her side perceptible now and all that could be prescribed was rest and more rest in the hope of remission. (His diagnosis would be confirmed by the eminent gynaecologist Dr. Simpson in Edinburgh over a year later, in January 1861.) Jeanie was just thirty-one. There would be no call henceforth for Watts to preach 'prudence' to her since, invalided-out as she now was, perhaps terminally ill, sexually 'reckless' she could never be.

Lying in bed, or walking alone in her mother's garden or by the seashore at yet another seaside health resort, Jeanie would worry over her young son Walter. For there was an unresolved contradiction within her. She had to believe that a child's death did not need to be mourned, for the child had been released from all earthly trouble and was now blessedly in Christ's company for evermore; on the other hand, she could not stop herself from being desperately concerned for the survival of any child in her care. Thus a month after Maurice's death she was writing to Walter about his forgotten toothbrush and socks and his mourning suit to be kept for Sunday best, once he had gone back to his Brighton Preparatory school. Was he happy with his friends? Did he want her to send him more foreign stamps? How was his schoolwork going? Was he practising his swimming? Was he managing not to follow the example of the worst boys and not start smoking, drinking and swearing? (She had not been amused when Nassau had got his nine year-old son to start smoking with him for a joke) – 'It is a nasty habit in a grown man, but it is doubly horrid in a child – so do not give way to it my darling, I entreat you' (21 September 1859).

And she had also begun to worry about Walter's future. Should he really be sent to Eton? For her friend Adelaide Sartoris had reported in the February of 1859 that the Eton boys were unpleasant snobs. Walter now wrote to his mother that he was more and more unhappy at Dr. Cary's, so please could he be moved to another school? His parents promised to move Walter in September 1860, after the holidays, to Banbury in Northampton-shire, to Dr. Browning's establishment which prepared boys for the Eton College entrance exam. But once settled there at Thorpe Mandeville, Walter was no happier. Dr. Browning soon reported that he found Walter very back-ward and that he had never been taught how to set about his work. For his part, Walter reported that he was homesick, that he was bullied, and that he had even been flogged for something he had not done – telling an alleged lie. His mother responded with a long letter from her current lodgings by the sea:

> My darling, . . . I am very *very* sorry, my boy, that you are
> unhappy. It is very hard that you should have been flogged unjustly
> darling, but, after all, it is better to be flogged unjustly, than to
> have deserved it. I have the most entire belief in your word, my
> dearest child, . . . Think of my tender love for you, my own child,
> and try to bear bravely the sorrows which you have in your new
> school.
>
> Do your best, my darling, and then . . . [if] at Christmas you tell
> me that you really are unhappy at Mr. Brownings; and that,
> although you have tried *your very best*, you cannot get on, and be
> happy there, then your father will take you away.– We promise you
> this my child.–
>
> And, my pet, you must do your best to get on with your school
> fellows – They cannot all be brutes, my little boy. There must be
> some kind-hearted boys amongst them. – I will send you a hamper
> when I get to London . . . Give away the contents generously, show
> that you are not greedy, that you do not care to keep good things

for yourself. . . . Try to cheer up . . . Tell me all that grieves you –
it will relieve you, and it is a comfort to me to know that you have
no secrets from me. (23 October 1859)

Meanwhile Nassau still had no work and all his speculative investments
had failed – every mine in which he had put money had gone bankrupt
without producing a dividend. It was then suggested (by Jeanie?) that her
younger brother Hastings might take Nassau into his wine and brandy
import business. Might not Nassau hold the fort in the City whenever
Hastings was away on business in Spain? And this Nassau agreed to do.

Jeanie's mother could, understandably, no longer bear to live at Hawke
House by the Thames in which her eldest grandson had drowned, and eventually, in September 1860, she settled on a new plan. She would move to
what was then still an almost rural spot with fields and orchards just outside
London in Clapham: 'Elm House', Lavender Hill. She could rely on her
'Robinson Crusoe' Dyer to prepare all the grounds and out-buildings,
including poultry houses and pig-styes. And there at Elm House, Margaret

9   Watts' portrait of Margaret Hughes in her fifties. Courtesy of Mrs. Anne Collier.

Hughes now suggested, Jeanie could at last make her home. It would be the first real home of her own since she had married twelve years before. How could it be financed? Mrs. Hughes would pay Jeanie and Nassau £300 a year to live there with them and on that, together with the salary from the Wine business partnership from Hastings, plus Jeanie's £400 a year, plus a continued allowance of £300 a year from Nassau's father, they would be able to manage an establishment that included Dyer, a cook, two ladies' maids, two kitchen and housemaids and a stable-boy.

In November 1860 Jeanie Senior moved into Elm House, her home for the next sixteen years. That home-making and home-coming coincided, perhaps not coincidentally, with a long period of remission in the progress of her cancer. She felt much stronger again and at last her letters to Walter began to sound happy:

> [In] 5 days now, I shall hold in my arms my big boy – How very happy I shall be, please God! . . . I hope you intend to help Dyer, . . . there is a great deal to be done . . . I hope we shall be very happy my dear boy, and read a great many books together, and have many pleasant long talks in the twilight, by the side of the fire. . . . I count the hours till Thursday. (8 December 1860)

CHAPTER FIVE

Life at Elm House: 1861–1864 – 'Come to us!'

'Elm House', on the summit of Lavender Hill, Wandsworth, was large, square and deep with several great elms in front and a garden and pasture behind. It was still surrounded by fields in 1861, but brickyards, the railway lines then being built from Clapham and speculative house building, all soon encroached. In 1893 the 'prime site' of Elm House would be sold up and transformed into the palatial *Art Nouveau* edifice of Battersea Town Hall, now Battersea Arts Centre. But for a nostalgic evocation of Jeanie's home as it had been in the Lavender Hill of the 1860s, we have this domestic interior depicted by Thackeray's daughter Anny:

> Some of us may still remember Elm House, where the Seniors lived
> at Wandsworth, and the long, low drawing-room, with its big bow-
> window opening to a garden full of gay parterres, where lawns ran
> to the distant boundary, while beyond again lay a far-away
> horizon. It was not the sea that one saw spreading before one's
> eyes, but the vast plateau of London, with its drifting vapours and
> its ripple of housetops flowing to meet the sky-line. The room itself
> was pleasant, sunny, and well-worn. There were old rugs spread on
> the stained floors . . . ; many pictures were hanging on the walls; . . .
> among the good were one or two of Watts' finest portraits, and I
> can also remember a Madonna's head with a heavy blue veil, and
> in juxtaposition a Pompeian sort of ballet girl, almost springing
> from the frame; and then, besides the pictures, there was a sense of
> music in the air, and of flowers, and of more flowers. The long
> piano was piled with music-books.[1]

Very unusually for her time and class, Jeanie Senior had absolutely no trace of superior 'caste' feeling towards her servants.[2] On the contrary, she felt more and more humbled by the hard-working enablers of her own life. The young maids she called 'child' and mothered. The winter of January 1861 was a hard one and Jeanie and her mother did what they could to alleviate the miserable hardship in their neighbourhood: 'we do what we can, . . . One poor woman had nothing in the shape of a blanket all through that cold weather' (22 January 1861). Sometimes all she could do was help bury their dead:

The poor Kings have lost one of their little ones with whooping cough and I fear another will die too. They have nothing with which to pay for the burial . . . and the parish will do nothing for them, because they are navvies . . . forced to wander about wherever there are railroads making. So I have drawn up a petition . . . to see what can be got for the poor things. . . . When one sees all the sorrow and distress there is amongst the poor, one feels a profound admiration for them – they bear so much, and complain so little. (27 April 1861)

A curse of the working conditions that then prevailed of course was the frequency of industrial injuries and the total absence of industrial compensation payments, let alone sickness or unemployment insurance for casual labourers who had no Friendly Society:

One of those navvies, [Manton] to whom I go to read, had a sad accident yesterday – a truck full of soil fell on his leg and broke it . . . I hope to go and see him in St. George's Hospital. . . . [We] are going to see that [his wife and child] want for nothing while the poor man is ill. (4 May 1861)

Jeanie Senior's life of social intervention had begun. At first it took the form of energetic personal help to individuals, very much like that of which Elizabeth Gaskell wrote in *Mary Barton* and *North and South*. For both women, every worker was a named individual, not merely one constituent of a frightening, undifferentiated mass.[3] But Jeanie had no idea how to analyse the whole, grotesquely inequitable social system.

What she did have was an overwhelming impulse to invite everyone who seemed needy to 'come to us!' – from old servants in need of a bit of spoiling to navvies wanting a game of cricket. On 11 May Hastings' wife Emily and her two little boys, Willie and Gerald, were made welcome to stay and the very next day the wife and child of the injured Manton, were invited to Elm House also. On 22 June Jeanie threw a great hay-making party for all her friends' children. But all too soon, in the midst of this vigorous new life, another terrible blow struck the family. The second to youngest of the seven Hughes brothers, Harry – a gentle, sweet-natured, determined plodder of a student, and a gifted all-round athlete, had been injured while practising rifle-shooting for his old Cambridge College, Trinity Hall, and had broken a blood vessel in his right lung. Jeanie had always had a special soft spot for Harry and longed to have him and her mother, who had rushed to him, under her roof. On 25 May Jeanie reported to Walter that Harry had now been installed at Elm House but was 'still terribly weak and pale'. It was grim work nursing the young man spitting blood; sometimes he seemed to improve, only to have another attack. The damp, cold English climate was thought dangerous for him:

> Dear Granny Hughes has almost made up her mind to go with poor dear Uncle Harry to Algiers, – . . . He was very poorly yesterday. – he began to bleed from the lung and had to come home and go to bed. . . . Dr. de Mussy . . . wants Uncle Harry to start for Algiers by the steamer of the 12 October.

Jeanie tried not to feel depressed and anxious on her own account at the prospect of losing her mother, her best friend and ally at Elm House. The sixty-four year-old Margaret Hughes now had the terrible task of accompanying her desperately ill son by land and sea to North Africa – 'Cooper [Margaret Hughes' maid] and Reynolds will go with dear Granny (28 September 1861). I shall be very anxious to hear of their arrival' (19 October 1861).

On 7 November 1861, on thick, black-edged letter paper, his mother had to break it to Walter at boarding school that 'Uncle Harry died on Tuesday last 5 November at 6 in the morning'. He was twenty-five. The sad story was not over. Once again Jeanie Senior received an eloquent, heart-breaking letter from her mother, just as she had done fifteen years before, after her 'twin' Walter's death.[4]

> My beloved child,
> I have not much to say but it is a comfort to me to write to you and I know it will comfort you to hear that I continue well, quite well; try my child to be well when I join you. I could not bear to find you ill; it is the last drop that makes the cup overflow and my cup will hardly bear another. . . . I cannot tell you my child what dear Cooper has been to me in my great agony; you could not have done more for me; in all those long hours of watching her hand was ever ready, her kindness was prompt to aid my endeavours to soothe my child, and now he is taken from my care she bestows all her love and care upon <u>me</u>: bids me to look to you and my other treasures still left, and for your sakes to bear up; and I do, and I will. . . . Oh Jeanie dear, you cannot tell my longing to be with you, to lean upon your strength, and to feel that I have yet some one left to whom I can be a comfort. (Algiers, 7 November 1861)

And once again Jeanie had to support her eleven year-old son in the face of bereavement:

> We cannot sorrow for him, dear fellow, when we think that all sorrow, and sickness, and trouble, is over for him, and that he is

with dear father and Walter and Maurice and Evie, all in the presence of God, and so happy together. No! We do not sorrow for our
dear Harry – It would be selfish sorrow. –
   . . . I try not to weep much for Uncle Harry, for fear that my
tears should cloud his happiness. (7 November 1861)

Her second source of comfort was the abiding memory of Harry's exceptional sweetness of personality.[5]

On 25 November of that same year, Jeanie told Walter that Uncle
Hastings would now soon be coming to live at Elm House for several
months, with his wife and children. 'He and Aunt Emmy will have the best
room and dressing room, and the nurse and children will be in your father's
smoking room – He smokes in the dining room now'. Was it to provide the
Seniors at Elm House with more income, or was it to cheer and distract
Grandmother Hughes? Or both?

The 'Come to us' policy continued through 1862 and 1863. By the beginning
of February 1862, Hastings and his family had left Elm House, only to
return again in the summer with a very delicate new baby, called 'Harry'
after his dead uncle. Walter's Headmaster Mr. Browning warned his mother
that Walter, on present form, had little chance of gaining admission to Eton.
She kept Rugby under Dr. Temple as her preferred alternative but encouraged Walter to 'work like a dragon, darling' if he really wanted to get into
Eton. As always she was uninhibited in her declarations of her love for him:

> I am always happy with you, and I think you always are with me,
> wherever we may be – Is it not so darling ? (15 March 1862) . . .
> Every time you come home it is a dearer happiness to me than the
> last time and every time you leave me the separation is more
> painful. You are more of a companion to me and I feel as if you
> loved me better as you grow older. (30 September 1862)

But that mutual devotion – and her own emotional dependence on the twelve
year-old boy – did not prevent her from being sharply critical of young
Walter at times. She could not bear his infection by snobbery when he
referred to working-class boys as 'cads'. She was cross with him for ringing
doorbells and then running away, since it was so thoughtless to hard-worked
servants. And again and again she had to sigh over his general laziness: 'by
nature you are very idle – but you are getting over it' (15 March 1863)

Jeanie Senior's greatest social concern in the early 1860s continued to be
with the navvies and their families lodged in shacks in Latchmere just below
Elm House. Time and again she and her mother would step into the breach:

I am sure you will be sorry to hear that one of my navvies has broken his leg very badly . . . He is very tall with curly light brown hair; his name is King. His children had the whooping cough . . . A great train got wrong on that new bridge they are making over the river, and King saw that it would tumble on and crush him in another moment, so he jumped right down from the bridge into a barge [and] broke his leg . . . I wrote to him at once to say that I would help his wife and children, so I trust that his mind will not be anxious – he is one of the best men I ever knew. (14 June 1862)

Not 'best working men', but 'best men'.

Most terribly of all, Jeanie and her mother would go to mourn with those that mourned, even when it revived unbearable memories of their own:

A poor little boy, the son of one my navvies living in Latchmere fell into that great reservoir on the way to church, and was drowned. . . . As soon as Granny Hughes heard of it she went to see the poor Father and Mother; she said it brought back that terrible day when our dear Maurice was brought home drowned – And all the grief and agony of that awful time . . . (18 July 1862)

Finally, at the end of the year, with another hard winter of unemployment ahead, 'Mother and I are going to try to establish a soup kitchen in Latchmere and to put Mrs. King to make the soup and to let the poor have it very cheap' (20 November 1862). The only historical trace today of all that mid 19th century suffering are the place names – Latchmere St, Latchmere Passage, and St. George's Hospital, Battersea.

Despite Jeanie Senior's acute responsiveness to others' suffering and her imperative need always to try to *do* something about it, cheerfulness would still keep breaking in. How she laughed at her old friend Tom Taylor's uproarious play *Our American Cousin* and 'We had great fun at Mr. Thackeray's the other night, – The play was beautifully got up . . . . They will save 'Box and Cox' for your return' (1 March 1862). She would make every opportunity to practise her singing at the piano 'piled with music books' and, as Anny Thackeray recalled: 'She would cease singing to make some old friend welcome, and [then] take to her music again as a matter of course.'[6] She seized every chance to sing in public, whether for the very poor at a 'penny gaff' concert got up by her brother Tom or, the next night, for the very rich at a reception held for le Duc et Duchesse D'Aumale (22 February 1862). She also greatly enjoyed tea and talk with her closest women friends, and very occasionally, Nassau willing, she would give her own cheerful dinner party.

Throughout the early 1860s, there was one momentous political cause in which Jeanie Senior felt involved, both morally and emotionally – the

American Civil War. It is often forgotten that the British Establishment began by supporting the slave-holding South, partly out of greater sympathy for the old-fashioned Southern 'gentlefolks' than for the brash 'Yankees', and partly out of self-interest because it looked as though the South would win. Support for the South was expressed not merely in *The Times* and in Parliament; it was also given voice at the Nassau William Senior dinner table. Standing firm against that dominant current of worldly wise 'realism' within the British governing class was Jeanie's idealistic brother Tom Hughes.

He had always been an immoveable anti-racist and anti-white-supremacist. As soon as the Civil War broke out, Tom Hughes had taken sides with the North, seeing it as a straight moral issue. In November 1861 he had declared in a lecture to the Working Men's College:

> My deepest sympathies . . . are with those who are struggling for freedom all over the world . . . of the body, of the intellect, of the spirit . . . I believe it to be the will of God that all men should be free, and that Christ came into the world to do God's will, and to break every yoke.[7]

Jeanie Senior supported Tom's efforts to swing public opinion around to the North with all her own ardent idealism. She reported to Walter on 1 February 1862 how she had heard Tom lecture on the hanged abolitionist John Brown at Clapham Town Hall. The London Emancipation Society was founded in October 1862 and in January 1863 it sponsored a huge demonstration at Exeter Hall with ten thousand people, the over-flow blocking the Strand. Hughes was one of the star speakers. He was cheered to the echo by the largely working-class audience, only to be sneered at by *The Saturday Review* as one of 'Mr. Lincoln's friends', uttering 'trash' to a 'vast cheering, howling horde of men, women and dissenting preachers'.[8]

Jeanie made her own position clearest, and with most effect, in June 1863, when she met John Murray Forbes at a dinner party given by her father-in-law, Nassau William Senior. Neither his host nor she realized that Forbes, a great railway magnate and supporter of Lincoln, was in fact on a secret mission to Britain, furnished with a million pounds from the Secretary of the US Navy to go to Liverpool and intercept the sale of two ironclad ships to the South and buy fast cruisers for the North instead.[9] Forbes had also helped raise the first black regiments in Massachusetts. Nassau William Senior, ever a protagonist of *Realpolitik*, was not at all sure that the North would win, and certainly the North had been losing so far; hence he urged a compromise settlement. One of Forbes' self-assigned tasks was to try to get a message through Nassau William Senior to the Prime Minister Lord Palmerston, informally, that there could be no doubt at all of the North's eventual victory. At this particular London dinner party:

> When the time came to go in to dinner, my father glanced about
> and, at once picking out the lady whom he wished to escort,
> stepped up to Mrs. Senior [i.e.Jeanie] and offered her his arm. As
> they were going into the dining-room she said, without any
> preface, "I must tell you, Mr. Forbes, how heartily I sympathise
> with the North." He never forgot her words, coming as they did
> from a total stranger, yet with the ring of an old friend in them.
> His heart was won. . . .[10]

Forbes himself reported of Jeanie Senior:

> [She] happened to say that her brother had just returned from
> France, and that she hoped I would see him. I then had to ask who
> her brother was, and found it was Tom Hughes. "Why," said I, "he
> is the one man I wanted to see; . . . I need hardly say that the
> remainder of my evening . . . at the dinner party was very much
> more delightful than at the beginning, as it was like finding a warm
> friend in the midst of an enemy's camp.[11]

Forbes wrote to her a day or two later to thank her for bringing him in touch
with Tom Hughes and for her own support of the Northern cause:

> Your warm sympathy touches a chord that seldom vibrates. I had
> thought . . . that I was entirely indifferent to English opinions and
> feelings, which I found so generally against us. Like the traveller in
> the fable, I can stand the pelting of the storm, but your sunshine
> draws off my cloak, . . . I tell it you that you may know how much
> good you can do to others . . . .
>
>   Most truly and gratefully yours,
>   John Forbes[12]

The most startling personal news for Jeanie in 1863 was the bombshell
that her devoted admirer and friend, the forty-six year-old, ill and depressed
George Frederick Watts, had suddenly determined to marry sixteen year-old
Ellen Terry. He was set upon educating her and thus removing her 'from the
temptation and abominations of the stage'[13] – by which he meant 'the
casting couch'. We can only guess how Jeanie Senior felt about Watts's rescue
mission. He, who only a few years earlier had entreated to be allowed to
come first with *her* – and who had assured her repeatedly that he would
always "stop short of the madness of passion", was now insisting, against all
his friends' forebodings, on marrying a very young actress. Watts wrote to
her at this time, anxious to retain her good will:

My Dear Jeanie, [they are now intimate enough friends for her to be 'Mrs. Nassau' no longer]

I shall come over one of these mornings very early to talk with you; it is necessary that so old a friend, (and I am sure [a] true one) should know something about the conditions of my life, especially as I have some reason to think you misjudge me a good deal. I am afraid my life will be full of difficulties and I cannot afford to lose my friends; if I deserve to lose them, let me do so, but I wish to be fairly judged.

The rest of 1863 at Elm House is soon told. Many more people were asked to 'come to us'. Hastings and his young family, including his wife Emily, pregnant once more, stayed with them again before they all left for Spain. Jeanie's youngest brother Arthur came while preparing to set off for a military career in India. A convalescent Minny Thackeray stayed; not to mention Dyer's old mother and Jeanie's old nurse Franklin. In July Walter tried a second time for the Eton entrance exam and failed again.

Then, in December 1863, the Hughes family sustained another terrible shock. This time the awful news came from Spain. Hastings' wife Emily had given birth to their fourth child and first girl, only to die of fever ten days later. What was Hastings to do? Predictably, his sister's immediate response was 'Come to us!' She longed to go out to collect him and his children herself, but their mother 'had so set her heart on going to her boy and his bairns' that she had to be allowed her way. There began another epic expedition by the intrepid Margaret Hughes, now aged sixty-seven, once again accompanied by her maid, Cooper.

At the end of January 1864 the two women set out in a steamship heading for India that would put them off at Gibraltar. Margaret Hughes' first black-edged letter, in mourning for Emily Hughes, was written after four days of terrible sea-sickness, but the weather had at last calmed and they were now rounding Cape Vincent. Jeanie's mother possessed a quite marvellous gift for seizing the moment as it flies; she could relish whatever was good in the present, no matter how sad the past or how uncertain the future. So there she was, sitting on deck, well covered up:

[And] oh what exquisite luxury that was; the dark blue sea below, the light blue sky above, the cheering, glorious sun, the refreshing hearty breeze. I wanted but you at my side, my darling. . . . I had your dear letter in my pocket, next best blessing to having you, it was my support and comfort in the early part of the voyage – the ordeal [of seasickness] is a fearful one, but it is worth standing. I am become so good a sailor now that I snap my fingers at the wind.

At Cadiz her son Hastings met her to take her by train to Puerto, where

> [My] dear boy put his baby into my arms and I hope felt as I did
> that the darling had still another mother on earth. . . . [Next]
> morning I reeled about a little giving cause to a stranger to suspect
> my acquaintance with the eau de vie bottle was intimate – however
> I am getting every day more sober and steady on my legs.
> (6 February 1864)

The seven-week-old baby, fed on goat's milk, needed her grandmother
constantly: the first feed was at 7.30 in the morning, the last at 10, with
Hastings taking over in the middle of the night. Soon she had to confess that
baby was managing granny, rather than the other way round. Little Harry
was not yet walking at eighteen months, and appeared to have been
neglected in all the family turmoil. The eldest, Willie, aged 5, was 'one of the
most wilful children I have ever met with' and though Margaret Hughes
knew that her daughter would have a sneaking liking for that naughty,
defiant lad, she confessed that she herself could not help preferring his more
biddable younger brother Gerard.

> I sometimes question whether I have done right in letting you offer
> to take all the dear children – for they are very unruly and very
> difficult to manage and I cannot get rid of the idea that their
> presence at Elm House may be too much for you . . . Willie
> especially. . . . (26 February)

One comfort throughout, however, was her own intense love for her 'little
lassie': 'I don't think I loved any of my own better than I love little Emmy.
But I do not think love spoils. I know it has the contrary effect upon me' (21
April 1864). Jeanie, she knew was now 'arranging the rooms of her four new
children' at Elm House, while she herself and the others in Jerez were 'all
busy as bees preparing for our flitting . . . How I count the hours till I am
with you' (25 April 1864).

Margaret Hughes, Cooper, Hastings, the four children, a nursemaid and
two goats to keep the baby alive, survived their grim, stormy, seventeen day
voyage home to England. On their arrival at Elm House:

> Mother looks very worn and weak and thin but she says that,
> except feeling tired she is quite well – . . . We can never be grateful
> enough to [Cooper] for the devotion she has shown to our family.
> She has worked like *three* ordinary servants and has never
> complained nor flagged for a moment. . . . [but] did everything for
> everybody – God bless her. (13 May 1864)

At first, predictably, the going was hard with this new, instantly extended family. The eldest boy, Willie, was indeed 'the pickle' his grandmother had described; baby Emmy almost immediately become seriously ill, terrifying both Jeanie and Margaret Hughes; little Harry was worryingly delicate; and even the good one, four year old Gerard, had his moments:

> Poor little Gerard was taken with "the black dog on his shoul-
> ders"; no one knew why . – The moment he sat to the table, he put
> his finger in his mouth, and scowled and would not eat a mouthful.
> After due warning he was packed off to bed supperless, poor little
> chap. Aunt Fan [Tom's wife] said that she would have whipped him
> at once and that that would have brought him to his senses, but I
> think bed is better than whipping – . . . I cannot bear to do
> anything which seems to me the least harsh to these poor mother-
> less little ones; I want, if I can to lead them by gentle means. (21
> May 1864)

How had Jeanie persuaded her husband, who had said 'No' to the care of little Helen, to say 'Yes' to this enormous invasion of Elm House by four children under six plus their father and nursemaid? There were several reasons that would have made it very hard for him to have said 'No'. First, his wife was so passionately certain that it was her Christian duty to mother her brother's motherless children; and for herself, unable as she was ever to have another child of her own, was it not a providential chance? Moreover Hastings was now Nassau's de facto employer and the major source of his income. It would be hard to refuse to help him out in this crisis, especially since Hastings insisted on paying them very handsomely for his family's keep and lodging. Moreover it was not at all certain how long they would all need to stay at Elm House. His mother-in-law had written while she was in Jerez that she was sure Hastings really wanted to settle in Spain the following autumn and that he would most probably take the two eldest boys back with him. Hastings' mother could then look after Hastings' other children at Elm House, if that was what she wanted to do. Finally, there was his father's terminal illness. After his father's death, as subsequent letters make clear, Nassau planned to move back with Jeanie to his widowed mother's Kensington home and live as a leisured gentleman of independent means.

CHAPTER SIX

Father and Son

Nassau William Senior died on 4 June 1864. He left *c.* £18,000 – or £900,000 in today's money; but he did not leave his only son a penny. Still worse was the fact that his will appointed not Nassau John, who was a lawyer at least in name, to be one of his four executors, but rather his favoured child Minnie. And even the income Nassau John had been receiving from his father, £300 a year, was mentioned as something that his widowed mother did not now have to continue.[1] As a final blow, it was stipulated that after the death of the widow, the four executors would have 'absolute discretion' in assigning the residuary half of the estate that had not already gone to Minnie: in other words they could then assign it to young Walter rather than to Nassau John. Altogether, his father's will was an extraordinary act of partiality, contempt and rage.[2] Had Nassau William Senior seen it as his last chance to force his son to get down to real professional work and earn some money at last? If so, it was ineffective.

When her husband occasionally came downstairs on a Sunday by nine in the morning and proposed attending Church, Jeanie would be as surprised as she was delighted. 'Papa very active' (3 May 1864). If he agreed to talk cheerfully to some visitor or helped water the garden or just go for a walk, such an unprecedented burst of energy would be recorded by her as something quite extraordinary and A Good Sign. More often, however, she mentioned his inertia, crossness and general negativism. Behind everything was Nassau's unassuageable bitterness towards his dead father and his sister Minnie, now embarking on lavish spending for a new marital home while he and Jeanie sank into debt. He would often be embarrassingly rude when his wife had visitors: 'Uncle Tom and Col. Peirse arrived – Father would not come down. He said he hated talking and had a very amusing French novel' (14 May 1865). If Jeanie risked asking him to take part in amateur theatricals in the family, he would only '[offer] to read the Major's part and to let us act <u>at him</u>' (7 and 9 September 1865). Her husband had become the most difficult and most demanding of all the children in her care. She had to bear all the responsibility for running the household and when they could not pay tradesmen – or even some of the beloved older servants their wages – she felt downright ashamed.

How astonishing, therefore, to come across a long, cogent letter to *The Times*, 5 September 1865, on the important subject of sanitation, public health and the danger of cholera, written by Nassau.[3] It begins by alerting readers to the shocking state of the area near Lavender Hill:

10 Nassau John Senior, at forty, 1862. From Jeanie Senior's photo album. Courtesy of Mrs. Pamela Milne.

1. At the foot of the high ground called Battersea Rise there is a large open sewer, passing in its course several rows of cottages inhabited by labouring people. This sewer . . . is as black as ink and as thick as gruel.

2. On the summit of the hill is a pond . . . an obliging neighbour turned his house-drainage into it; . . .

3. There is an open ditch, nearly a quarter of a mile in length, which receives the drainage of several of the houses on Lavender-hill [sic] . . . Two medical men have assured me that it is a nest of typhoid fever. . . .

I hope to arraign the Board of Works for the Wandsworth district at the bar of public opinion in your columns.

   . . . Your obedient servant,

Nassau John Senior

The next day *The Times* devoted a long third leader to supporting
Nassau's letter ending:

> '[We] cannot wait for a fresh Act of Parliament before we take any
> further steps . . . If every one who is aware of the evil would adopt
> a similar course to Mr. Senior, and allow the Local Board and his
> neighbours no rest until a nuisance was removed, we should soon
> be in a more satisfactory condition'.

Had Nassau been sufficiently energized by fear of cholera to write to *The
Times*? No. It was Jeanie who had sent that letter, and

> [Of] course I signed it with your father's name. I chuckled to think
> how angry all the fifty old fogies who constitute the Board will be
> to have been shown up in *The Times*. I should not wonder to see
> an indignant denial from them, but I don't care how angry they
> are; it will force them to <u>do</u> something. (5 September 1865)

It was Jeanie Senior's first foray into the public domain, but 'of course', she
had had to conceal her gender to win the respect of *The Times*.

She would have to do more than write letters on this health hazard for, a
year later, on 5 October 1866, she was still so outraged by the filthy state of
the drains for the local poor, including the King family, that she reported it
to the Inspector – again under Nassau's name. The Kings' landlord was
forced to cover in an open cesspool and to get rid of his pig-styes, but he
punished the Kings by evicting them as troublemakers who had 'taken ladies
to pry about his property'. Whereupon Jeanie found them another house and
paid their rent.

It was now becoming ever clearer that they themselves were in money
trouble. They had to sell their remaining shares at a loss and, worse still, in
May 1866 there was a 'crash' in the City, a Bank 'failure', causing Hastings'
creditors to fail to pay what they owed him. He was only saved from bankruptcy by his sister, brothers and mother covering for him and Jeanie realized that she would now be unable to afford a carriage for a very long time
indeed. If only Nassau could, or would, work. Disappointed in his 'expectations', Nassau had now, at forty-three, very reluctantly, to turn his mind to
what he might be prepared to do.

He had already made it very clear that he did not like the wine business.
Jeanie knew that '[he] only half does his job . . . Uncle Hastings would not
be in any difficulty should Father leave him' (27 October 1865). So once
again she embarked on letter-writing, lobbying for Nassau John to be given
a salaried government position that might appeal to him:

21 October 1865: . . . writing all morning to Lord St. Leonards,[4] Lord Cranworth[5] and Sir Alexander Duff Gordon[6] that Father may be made Clerk of the Peace for Surrey . . . 26 October 1865: . . . My life is passed in writing . . . 8 and 12 November 1865: Father is going to try for [Sir William Spring Rice's] old place as Secretary to the Lunacy Commission – so I am off to London to look up friends who could help him. . . . The choice is entirely in the hands of Lord Shaftesbury.[7] I don't know how to get at him. . . . 29 November 1865: Lord Shaftesbury has written to Mr.Chadwick asking if Father still practises at the Bar. This looks bad for us. . . . However I shall not cease to hope till hope is over . . . 3 December 1865: The place is given to Mr. Phillips . . . poor fellow he needed the place for he has eleven children and his wife is dead and he is a very good lawyer and a good man; so we must not grudge it to him . . . 7 December 1865: Father says he shall have his name put in the law list as a Conveyancer and take a room in Lincoln's Inn . . . so that he may be eligible for any place that needs a practising barrister.

After that great burst of effort by Jeanie, nothing happened for another year. Neither a 'place' nor any conveyancing came Nassau's way. But she had too much on her hands during that time to fret only about him. For her most pressing pre-occupation in 1865 and 1866 were the serious illnesses suffered by Hastings' four children. Almost as soon as she had arrived in England, baby Emmy had gone down with inflammation of the lungs and this had been succeeded by a local scarlet fever scare. In October 1865 Hastings had gone to Spain, leaving all his children behind at Elm House with bad coughs and colds and baby Emmy teething. By the following February Hastings had returned but the children by then had bowel complaints, and, as if that were not bad enough, on 14 February 1866 the first of the four children went down with whooping cough. The day of 24 February is worth quoting in full:

Poor baby has been very bad all day, . . . her teeth are bothering her as well as the whooping cough . . . we must be very careful that she does not get croup. . . . Poor Willie coughs till he cries, and gets in a rage too, which makes him worse, and then he is sick; and in two minutes he is as jolly as ever . . . Sunday morning: Baby is better today tho' she had a bad night . . . [The boys] are awful hard to manage, and Harry has a will of iron . . . – [he told the new governess] 'I wish you were dead, and gone to hell' . I can't think where he heard anything about hell . . .

Tuesday evening: Baby has been very ailing indeed . . . Mussy fears that the child may have some slow inflammation of the brain.

> She is very stupid and dull sometimes and that is a bad sign. . . .
> Wednesday: Baby is perhaps a shade better, but still very
> poorly . . . I've seen no one, being quite shut up with the bairns.

No wonder that on 4 March she wrote:

> I am very tired. . . . I cannot tell you what a *trump* dear Cooper
> has been all thro' this illness – she is devotion itself and baby is
> intensely fond of her . . . I am sure if she were my sister she could
> not be kinder, or a greater help. I never can repay her for all she
> has been to me in both baby's bad illnesses.

(In May 1866 Bessie Cooper and the indispensable general factotum Jesse
Dyer, married, both remaining devoted to Jeanie and her mother for life.)

Six year-old Gerard next went down with whooping cough followed by
congestion of the lungs – 'We have had a sad anxious night with poor
Gerardy – the doctor stayed from 2.30 am till 6.am' (23 March). Jeanie was
nursing the children day and night – 'I'm sitting with baby whilst Cooper is
at church and baby is going to cough – and I must hold the basin! Poor little
thing'. Croup was a terrifying childhood illness then. The most popular
medical advice threatened parents: 'If [the mother] delay to send for assistance OR IF PROPER MEDICINES BE NOT GIVEN, . . . in a day or two,
the little sufferer will be a corpse.'[8] During all that acute anxiety and exhaustion from broken sleep, Jeanie had also had to nurse her mother suffering
from eye disease followed by influenza.

Nevertheless the 'Come to us'! open-door policy at Elm House somehow
continued. An ill-used, lame horse called 'Crusader' had to be doctored, then
little Helen came back for a long visit, followed by various widowed Senior
cousins, Aunt Minnie's stepson little Charley Simpson, a certain 'motherless
little Blackett', and finally, and most significantly for the whole trajectory of
Jeanie Senior's later life, Octavia Hill. Octavia Hill had recently been
engaged as holiday tutor to Tom Hughes' children, who, he confessed 'hated
learning'. So it was his wife Fanny who, at the end of January 1866,

> brought Miss Hill with her (Miss Octavia) [to Elm House]. The
> poor little woman looks ill and tired and she is so. I've asked her to
> come out here . . . to get some fresh air and quiet. . . . . I'm afraid
> she is far from strong and over works herself terribly, I wish that
> there were more like her and then the work of life would be more
> equally shared.
> 4 February 1866: Miss Hill (Miss Octavia) came last night. She
> looks sadly ill and tired. She greatly liked a quiet Sunday out of
> Town.

That initial relationship of benefactress and beneficiary soon changed. For as soon as Octavia Hill had the energy to talk, she quickly made an ardent convert of her generous hostess and eventually a sterling colleague.

Octavia Hill, one of the outstanding reformers of the 19th century, was then twenty-eight years-old, ten years younger than the mistress of Elm House. Smaller than Jeanie, and less impressive to look at, though her eager, dark eyes would have singled her out anywhere, Octavia Hill was feeling exhausted by all her self-allotted tasks. The grand-daughter of the radical doctor Southwood Smith[9] and daughter of two progressive Owenite parents, Octavia Hill had been brought up to think for herself. Although initially a freethinker, she had been converted in adolescence by the sermons of F. D. Maurice, and like Jeanie Senior and Tom Hughes a few years earlier, she had eagerly espoused Maurice's idealistic vision of Christian Socialism, a practical Christianity that sought to bring about justice and community.[10]

Almost penniless, and needing to work for her living, Octavia Hill had recently persuaded her employer and art teacher, John Ruskin, to spend some of his inherited wealth on purchasing run down properties that she could regenerate as a model of what could and should be done with housing unfit for human habitation. He had recently bought for her the ironically named 'Paradise Place' in Marylebone known locally as 'Little Hell', where each room housed a whole family and even a corner of a room might be sub-let to a weekly lodger. All the staircases were in darkness and the banisters non-existent, having been used for firewood. Octavia Hill's excitement at the potential for transforming lives by transforming terrible housing, is eagerly communicated in a letter of April 1865 which shows how infectious her practical idealism would be to Jeanie Senior, herself a fighter against bad drains:

> Our great event . . . has been the actual purchase for 56 years of three houses full of tenants in a court close to us. . . . The houses are well built, but were in a dreadful state of dirt and neglect . . . The place swarmed with vermin; the papers, black with dirt, hung in long strips from the walls, the drains were stopped, the water supply out of order. All these things were put in order, . . . We are hoping to improve all the children's health by taking them to row on the Regent's Park water, and we are to try to get a playground for them. . . .[11]

When she saw the poverty-stricken little girls threading beads in their new playground or taught them to draw and sing, Octavia Hill felt that all the enthusiasms of her life, her love of Nature, her love of Art, and her conviction that beauty was the birthright of every human-being, had come together under her new banner: 'Housing Reform'.

Jeanie in her turn reported excitedly to Walter at school:

> Miss Hill and I had great talks about houses for the poor – Ruskin
> has bought several houses which he allows her to let to poor
> people. . . . – I asked her if Ruskin would build some houses for me
> here – She is going to ask him – Oh! How I wish that he would. I
> would so gladly collect the rents. (2 October 1866)

By inviting Octavia Hill to come in to Elm House for rest and recuperation,
Jeanie Senior would eventually get out of her own all-too-demanding home.
But in the months immediately succeeding that initial inspiring encounter,
she was once again totally immured in the domestic demands coming at her
from all sides:

> November: Baby and Harry ill with bronchitis. . . .
> 29 November: Nassau in bed with gout once again, deeply
> depressed . . . and hardly any use to Hastings.

Early in 1867 the lobbying for Nassau had to re-start.

> I wrote to Uncle Tom and N. wrote to Sir William Erle,[12] Mr.
> Booth,[13] Mr. Merivale[14] and Sir E. Head[15] to ask that Father may
> be made Secretary to the Commission on Trades Unions. [Thomas
> Hughes was one of the Commissioners]. It would not be much pay
> and only for a short time but it would get him known. I am very
> anxious about it.

That hope also came to nothing, although Tom did engage Nassau as his
personal secretary for the duration of the Commission and paid him to translate the Comte de Paris's book on English Trade Unions from French into
English.

> Now that Father has nothing to do he is going to help Uncle Tom.
> I hope that Father may get a taste for hard work. Poor old Father!
> His terrible indolence has been the ruin of his life – [that] horrid
> fault which spoils a man completely. I am very anxious, I feel it is a
> turning-point. It is his last chance . . . and if he throws this away I
> shall have no more hope. (14 February 1867)

A climax of a sort came in March/April 1867. Through the intervention
of their friends Dr. de Mussy, Mr. Cole and the Rev. Willliam Brookfield,[17]

Nassau was appointed to be one of the Jurors on the Paris Exhibition Committee. Not a post he had wanted, but still it would bring in £50 expenses for a six-week stay. He was to be Co-juror with a Lord Canterbury. The problem then was to get Nassau to accept the post. Things did not progress happily:

11 March 1867: Father has not made up his mind about Paris yet.
13 March: Father has been declaring to me this morning that he will throw up this place unless he takes me with him [to Paris]. It is quite absurd [because of the expense] but I hope he'll come to reason. . . .
4 April: Telegrams, one from Paris direct, another from the Paris Commission at the Kensington Museum, ordering Father off at once . . . Too late to go tonight but he will go tomorrow morning I fancy as he is wanted in a hurry.
5 April. Father came home, and was much bothered to find the Telegram, but he said that it did not positively order *him* to go – It only said that 'Juror or Associate Juror' was to go at once. So he went off to see Lord Canterbury his Co-juror. I thought he would be sure to start this morning. . . . [This] morning early I went to him . . . The first thing he said was that he had gout in the knee, and could not go to Paris, and that he was very glad for that he hated to go. I sent for [Dr.] Mussy to pronounce as to what he must do – in the mean time Father keeps his bed. If it were me I should start for Paris this afternoon gout and all, but Father is not made of that kind of stuff. I am very much distressed for I am afraid that it will be most inconvenient to the Commissioners that Father should not arrive, and that it will bring Father to ill repute. Lord Canterbury is at Newmarket and will not think of giving up his racing; and all the business of the Commission must be finished by the 15th of this month.
6 April: Mussy came yesterday and pronounced Father's gout to be nothing – . . . Mussy wanted him to get up at once and start [for Paris] in the evening but his advice was thrown away. So I started off to the Kensington Museum to the Paris Commission Secretary and told him that Nassau was ill, . . . He said that if Nassau left on Sunday night it would do, and that gave two whole days. . . . On my return, Father was up, but thought himself very bad; so I told him a piece of my mind, and left him to digest it, and this morning, before 9 he was down stairs "clothed and in his right mind". . . .
8 April: On Sunday morning I went with Father to Charing Cross Station to see him safely off for I was afaid of his coming home instead of going to Paris if I had left him alone!

> 12 April: In the train for Paris . . . Father can't do without me, and
> as he finds that the £50 will cover expenses he has sent for me and
> I am on my way.

All too often Nassau compensated for his total dependency on his wife by
petty tyranny and bad temper when they were alone. Whenever Walter
returned to boarding school, Nassau would jeer at Jeanie for being 'stupid
and dull and low' without her boy. Countless invitations were refused at his
insistence. If ever Jeanie did go out on her own, she would have to come back
early 'in order not to vex Father'. Nassau's petulant temper also affected the
whole household below stairs: when there was a domestic crisis over stealing
by an unidentified servant, he threatened to sack them all. Jeanie felt sick at
heart at the thought of treating unjustly those who had been so devoted over
so many years, even her Mother's 'dear Cooper' and 'old Dyer'. It was a great
relief to discover that the thief was a newly appointed nurse (18 March 1866).

Nassau's *bête noire* above all others was the English weather, and his wife
had to jolly him through that frequent irritation also. Just once, when they
were holidaying at Torquay, in May 1866, it was neither too hot nor too
cold: 'Father even was satisfied!' But a fortnight later:

> Father dreadful cross with the wind, and above all with the dust! –
> He says "Torquay is an infernal hole – and that he is sick to death
> of the brutal blue skies and the yellow old sun glaring down at
> him". . . . We went for a walk to pass the time, but it was not over
> pleasant, for the wind was high, and very cold from the East and it
> always affects Father's temper. (24 May 1866)

And so on, day after day.

But there could be moments of good humour. On 18 March 1866, for
example, Nassau agreed to be made one of the local Wandsworth Poor Law
Guardians to please Jeanie who would thereby gain admission to visit the
local Workhouse – 'It is very good of Father is it not? For he does not like
that sort of thing at all'. And once, on 17 July 1866, when they had unexpected visitors, 'Father behaved splendidly and was very good tempered and
talked'. But such reprieves were rare. The one sure balm to Nassau's spirit,
other than a gourmet dinner, was the recently introduced Turkish Bath. On
the same day when he had earlier refused to go out to dine and Jeanie had
'had to invent some horrid excuse at the last moment . . . Father was up to
town early for a Turkish Bath' (30 May 1866). Two months later: 'Father
went to take a Turkish Bath. I unpacked' (1 July 1866). When faced by the
threat of having to go to Paris as a Co-juror and hence having to go up to
London to get French currency, he had also made time for a Turkish Bath (4
April 1867).

Recommended at its introduction by a few doctors as a way of relieving rheumatism, sciatica and Nassau's malady, gout, the Turkish bath soon caused controversy on moral grounds. For such baths, it was alleged, led to indolence and destroyed manliness:

> Can the active, fox-hunting, cricketing, boating Englishman bear the same kind of treatment that benefits and gratifies the indolent, languid, luxurious Turk? [It] may be adapted to the mental and physical constitution of . . . lazy Eastern voluptuaries . . . but healthy men of business and of sense in this country will, we venture to prophesy, never consent to the dissipation of time and matter involved in the idea of a periodical Turkish bath.[18]

Suddenly, on 25 June 1867, Nassau had a chance of being made one of the Sub-Commissioners on the [Electoral] Boundaries Commission. It would only be two months' work, 'but it could be a reason for his getting something better afterwards'. He did get that temporary post but not without incurring public ridicule. For when he was at his Club, the Oxford and Cambridge Universities', he saw in the latest number of *Echoes from the Clubs* a mocking passage about 'a certain dull personage' who, having ceased to practise at the Bar for fifteen years and having never had any briefs when he was there, was 'considered as remarkably suited for the post of legal adviser on the Boundary Commission'.[19] His professional inactivity had become a by-word within his own milieu by now.

At the end of May 1868 another temporary job for Nassau looked possible. He had discovered that there were to be thirty new 'revising barristers' appointed in order to examine the post-1867 Reform Bill lists of voters and that Lord Cockburn, the Chief Justice, had the choice of some of them. Jeanie promptly invited Lord Cockburn, a noted bon viveur and music lover, to dinner. The dinner party, followed by duets sung by herself and Helen, went off splendidly and Cockburn duly promised to try to get Nassau six weeks' work. On 8 July the Chief Justice himself walked in to Elm House to ask Jeanie to sing at his dinner party that night. 'I had to sing which was very tiresome but as Cockburn had promised Father the barristership of course I could not refuse what he wished' (9 July 1868). She was literally singing for her own and Nassau's supper.

The 'revising barristership' weeks did not go smoothly. Afraid of failure as always, at first Nassau said it was impossible for him to take in the new regulations; '[It] is very true that Father has weakened his mind by reading only novels – and above all by that inordinate smoking' . . . (9 July 1868). After weeks of self pity and dilatoriness on Nassau's part, Jeanie finally gave vent to all her years of frustration and disappointment, writing to Walter, then eighteen and a half:

> [Again] yesterday, from mere weakness of character, and to avoid
> trouble, Father gave in, because he was bothered about a point that
> he said that he *knew* it was his duty to have held out on. Now that
> agonises me. I can sympathise with failure, and with mental inabil-
> ity, but it is really heartbreaking to see anyone one loves do wrong,
> *knowing* it to be wrong, merely to avoid a little bother and trouble.
> With all Father's good and loveable qualities he has made me very
> unhappy, very often, by [his] terrible want of moral sense and
> moral purpose. . . . When I was young I used to long, and work,
> and try that Father should make the most of himself and his life. I
> soon saw that I could not help him, because he would not help
> himself. It was a dreadful trial to me when first I realized this.

That phrase 'dreadful trial' was used sparingly by her; it meant the worst of her
life's experiences, including grief at someone's death. She then spelt out what
she had once hoped, pitifully, at the start of her marriage twenty years before:

> My ambition for him was not a worldly bad one – I wanted him to
> . . . benefit his fellow creatures. I have never given up trying to
> influence Father to good, for I always hope and hope, and one
> never ought to give up trying, but I have not much real hope as to
> him. (18 August 1868)

It was not only his wife who noticed Nassau's lack of backbone. *The
Saturday Review* of 5 September 1868 mocked him by name, referring to
'Mr. Senior's shilly-shallying' in the Westminster Court, 'disagreeing one day
with what he had said the previous day and finally leaving it to appeal'.

As for Jeanie Senior, how did her cumulative exasperation, anxiety and
emotional unfulfilment in her mis-marriage, affect her relationship with her
son?

Walter Senior, a fourteen year-old public schoolboy when his grandfather
died in 1864, was a big, kind-hearted, good-looking boy, easily influenced
and usually placed below average in a class of boys younger than himself. In
most ways he was an ordinary adolescent – out to survive, be popular and
enjoy himself. The least ordinary thing about him was his relationship with
his far from ordinary mother. The regimen at Rugby then was Spartan and
demanding:

> For nine weeks in mid-winter [the boys] are expected to rise at 7,
> to take their breakfast at 7.30, and present themselves in School at

12 Walter Senior as thirteen year-old schoolboy. Courtesy of Mrs. Anne Collier.

> 8. During the rest of the year they rise at 6.30, are in School at 7,
> and work for an hour before breakfast . . . Breakfast [consists]
> simply of tea or coffee and bread and butter . . . Dinner, which
> consists of meat, vegetables, pies or puddings sometimes preceded
> by soup, is served at 1.30. Tea follows dinner after a few hours;
> and at 8.30 a supper of bread and cheese or bread and milk winds
> up the day . . . All the boys, at all seasons, are expected to go to
> bed at 10 o'clock, except the Sixth Form.[20]

No wonder that the frequent dispatch to Walter of 'tuck' – a ham or cake and pies and fresh fruit, or, on his birthday, candied plums and oranges, raisins, macaroons and homemade jams, was very welcome.

Compulsory class-attendance in school amounted to 22 hours a week – 17 Classical, and only three in Mathematics and two in Modern Languages, despite Dr. Temple's efforts to widen the curriculum. In addition there was the time needed for prep. and composition for one's Classics Tutor. The boys were required to translate excerpts from classical prose and verse into English and passages from English prose and verse into Greek and Latin. Most of them failed to see the point. Walter was not a studious boy and he struggled for years to get by with the least possible exertion at what bored him to distraction. He complained to his mother about the futile monotony of the incessant Latin and Greek; she agreed but was helpless to change anything.

The male staff of British public schools believed in breaking the bond between boys and their mothers' 'apron strings' – but they were reckoning without Jeanie Senior. Walter could depend on her long chatty letters, usually a 'Journal letter', containing instalments of several days' happenings, at least once each week. Increasingly, as Walter grew older, she felt able to cover not just family news and the people she met, but comments on religion, politics, art and literature, the concerts she attended and her own singing repertoire, her worries over the four adopted little ones, her efforts to find his father paid work, as well as her response to what Walter was telling her about his life at school. Walter wrote back, almost without fail, every week; all her letters have survived but none of his. However, we can tell from her response that his letters were also lively, affectionate and amusing. 'You don't know, love, how I enjoy your letters, and how thankful I am for the open way in which you write to me' (3 December 1865). His father asked Jeanie to read aloud just the interesting bits from Walter's letters, so the boy would mark anything he did not wish Nassau to know.

Gradually, as the reader will have noticed, his mother confided in Walter more and more: 'I tell you everything that is in my mind and heart' (31 October 1865). It may seem shocking that she broke the unwritten law that one parent should never betray the weaknesses of the other to their child, but Nassau's disinclination for work and irritable temper would have been impossible to conceal for many years. Her confiding in Walter was her essential safety-valve, the consequence of being married to a cynic in whom she could never confide. Worse still, perhaps, Jeanie Senior would seem to have broken every rule in the post-Freudian maternal handbook. We are nervously aware that terrible damage may be done if unhappily married mothers make excessive, inappropriate emotional demands upon their adolescent sons. Jeanie Senior, however, was blithely pre-Freudian and her letters to Walter overflowed with un-self-censored outpourings of passionate affection:

> I feel low and child sick. Remember that you are my dearest object in life . . . (24 August 1865) . . . [How] dreadfully I miss you – I am already looking forward to Christmas. (30 August 1865) . . . I am almost ashamed at how little real interest in any subject I have not connected with you. But almost every subject is connected with you. (7 September 1865) . . . [Without] you I feel like 'half a pair of scissors' as my dear father used to say of people who felt incomplete (20 September 1865) . . . I seem to live on your letters. (September 1866) . . .

It is the unmistakeable 'true voice of feeling'.

But Jeanie Senior was no uncritical doter of a mother; rather, she was one of Walter's harshest critics. She could not bear him to be just another lazy schoolboy, one who made no pretence of even trying to work. "<u>Think</u> before answering your exam questions" (18 May 1864). "I do not much mind that you have not been moved up" (26 August 1865). But she did mind. In October 1865 she received a damning school report (always called, significantly, a 'character') on Walter. The headmaster, Dr. Temple, wrote that 'If he would but work <u>his best</u> I could treat him specially. But [Walter] makes it rather difficult to grant him any favour of any kind by hanging dead on hand.' It is not hard to imagine how that last phrase would have alarmed and depressed his mother, raising the spectre of having produced another Nassau John. 'You dearly love me my child, and I ask you for my sake to try to overcome your faults of carelessness, and indolence – I know that you will try. I know also, how very hard it is to conquer ones faults; but I only want you to do your best (4 October 1865). Jeanie then quoted back at him the Headmaster's distressing phrase, and sympathetically, yet pressingly, tried to get him to stir his stumps: 'If you really will <u>rouse</u> I am sure that Temple won't find you a dead weight – I know that with your big body and naturally indolent temperament, it is <u>awfully</u> hard to rouse; but yet I think you will do it when you think of me' (7 October 1865). A month later she was still urging him at least to try at his work, even if he never shone: 'Work steadily for my sake – a good report of you cheers me under any disappointment. In short if you are good, nothing else <u>can</u> be a disappointment, for I care for nothing else.' Her husband had then been demanding she write countless letters on his behalf about the Clerkship of Surrey, and here we see for the first time how her injunctions to Walter to get down to work were intensified by her current disappointment over Nassau. If only Walter worked, it did not matter if Nassau did not.

It must not be thought that Walter was merely a passive, unhappy punchball at the receiving end of all these injunctions. When his mother went too far he would reproach her and she would instantly retreat into contrition. The word he used, when accusing her of being too critical and too demanding, was 'savage'. Occasionally she would try to defend her position:

> If ever I seem fretful, and tiresome, unfair and exigeante, try to put yourself in my place – Remember that you are my only child and that for nearly 17 years all my happiness has centred in you . . . I solemnly assure you that whenever you do anything wrong or fail to do anything right I feel that it is *my* fault . . . And when I am "savage" with you, it is because I am in agony, real <u>agony</u>. Think of this; beloved, and remember that all Mothers . . . feel the same; . . . (14 February 1866)

But when he was just sixteen, she engaged differently with this charge:

> If I am "savage" (as you once told me I was) with your little faults, you must forgive me, on account of the intense love and solicitude that causes the savageness . . . [It] is I daresay sometimes almost an oppression to you to know how anxious I am for you, and to think that every action, word, and thought of yours, causes me either intense joy or great sorrow – but I cannot love you less and loving you as I do, it is impossible for me to be less anxious about you. I do so long for you to be happy, and that can only be ensured by your being good. (15 March 1866)

The above letter shows that she was sensitive to his psychological vulnerability in relation to her – 'it is I dare say almost an oppression to you to know how anxious I am for you . . . '. Her only defence was: 'I cannot love you less'. And she ended the birthday letter by thanking him for loving her: 'Some sons either don't care much for their mothers, or they don't show it. In you I have a love like a daughter's as well as like a son's. . . . and I bless you for it from my inmost soul. '

Through that love from and for his mother, unrepressed and unashamedly tender, Walter Senior was enabled to escape the emotional blight on young upper-class British males known as 'the taboo on tenderness'.[21] For the products of English public schools all too often went out into the world, as E. M. Forster would write in 1920:

> with well-developed bodies, fairly developed minds, and undeveloped hearts. . . . [The] Englishman . . . is afraid to feel. He has been taught at his public school that feeling is bad form. He must not express great joy or sorrow, . . . He must bottle up his emotions.[22]

Jeanie Senior's loving, intimate letters constituted the heart of Walter's otherwise bleak world. But the connection between Jeanie's frustration over Nassau and her exasperated disappointment in Walter became ever clearer, even to her:

> . . . I am full of compunction if I have been unjust to you [about schoolwork] my beloved. You see I have been worried about Father, and then I get irritable and fanciful I suppose – . . . forgive me if I've been unjust and tiresome but I'm sad and cross and am afraid that I vent it upon you. . . . Ever your loving old Mum. (11 December 1866)

On 29 November Nassau had retired to bed with gout and depression, refusing to work in Hastings' business ever again. Jeanie felt at her wits' end about him and desperate with foreboding about the family's future. Not only did her 'ordeal' with Nassau distort her relationship with Walter, but her sense that Walter's 'besetting sin' was inherited and/or copied from his father embittered her more deeply against Nassau.

Walter's failure at academic work was sometimes the least of her worries. "God keep you from bad companions!" had been her cry in his early days at Rugby. But God did not. One fear was alcohol. The Victorians generally seem to have taken a relaxed attitude to children's drinking, but Jeanie was already alert to the addictive, dependency-creating danger of alcohol and warned Walter:

> If once a young creature gets to need such stimulants as spirits, it is almost sure that he'll get into the habit of drinking more than is good for him as a man – he will, every day, take more wine than is

good either for his pocket or for his stomach – and so he lays the foundation for gout and all sorts of wretchedness. . . . (9 December 1865)

Walter's boon companion at Rugby was Algy Sartoris, aged fourteen and his junior by 18 months. A charmer, good-looking in a fallen angel way, Algy was the younger son of Jeanie's closest friend Adelaide Sartoris. Algy, like Walter, had failed to pass the Eton entrance examination and it is very probable that Rugby had then been suggested by Jeanie. But the rigours of Rugby were not at all to Algy's liking. Jeanie had been fond of Algy ever since he was a small, affectionate child, but when he started laying bets with Walter about who could wheedle most kisses from various attractive married women, she quickly became concerned about his influence:

> If I were younger and prettier, how would you like to think that two big fellows almost men, like you and Algy, were making bets about the kisses that I might give them . . . ! You would be very angry, and want to 'punch their heads' for their 'confounded impertinence, and bad taste'. – Would you not? (10 February 1866)

Her next worry was about Walter and money, including gambling, for Algy Sartoris was now locking himself into his study to play piquet for high stakes:

> For mercy's sake dear one, don't get into debt, or if you do, tell me so frankly, and I will pay at once and you will be wiser in future. You may not be in debt, – but if you are, don't let it run on; that is ruinous to your moral sense. . . . You will have to work for your living. (11 March 1866)

She must never let Walter indulge in his father's earlier delusion about having great expectations.

Another very old friend of Jeanie Senior, Jane Brookfield, also a friend of Adelaide Sartoris, then decided to send her boy, thirteen year-old Arthur, to Rugby. The anxiety of all three mothers now focused upon sex – and in particular on whether any of the boys had secretly visited Kahn's Museum in London.

What was Kahn's Museum?

> [At] Kahn's famous anatomical museum in the West End the emphasis was on a large display of exhibits, accompanied by a lecture. The latter was generally a standard piece of spermator-rhoea propaganda, the exhibits were often prurient, and the Kahn

13 Algy Sartoris at fourteen, pencil sketch by Jeanie Senior. Courtesy of Mrs. Pamela Milne.

Harley Street practice was quackery. . . . A good deal could be learnt about the clitoris at Kahn's. . . . [who also spread] the notion that women ovulate every time they have an orgasm . . . [Female] masturbation was held to cause ovulation just as readily as the stimulus of intercourse, and the evidence of ovulation in virgins was coped with – in Kahn's museum and elsewhere – by the assumption that they had masturbated, or at least were especially "amorous".[23]

However badly adolescent boys in the mid 19th century might need to redress their sexual ignorance, the voyeuristic, inaccurate 'scientific education' offered by Dr. Kahn was not the answer. His mother felt forced to spell out some unpleasant facts about VD to Walter:

It is best now to tell you that it [Dr. Kahns] is a horrid place – you must not think me indelicate my son if I speak out. There are

wicked quacks everwhere who make money out of the honest
shame of young fellows who . . . catch loathsome and dangerous
illnesses from . . . poor wretched women. . . . [Instead] of going to
an honest doctor and friend, who will cure him quickly and influence him to good . . . [a young fellow] is too apt to go to some of
the quacks, who profess to cure quickly and secretly, and who
encourage a fellow in vice in order to keep him as their patient; . . .
One of these men is Dr. Kahn and he has a museum where he
exhibits forms that work on all the worst and filthiest passions of
men, and when they get into vice they turn to men like Kahn to
cure them. . . . I don't believe you ever went to the Museum, of if
you went, I'm sure it was in ignorance and that you won't go again
and above all I'm sure you would rather cut off your hand than
take a young fellow there, now you do know. (13 February 1867)

Their acute worry over what their boys might be getting up to, threatened
the friendship between the boys' mothers. Jeanie felt caught between
Adelaide Sartoris and Jane Brookfield and did not know whether or not to
confide her suspicions of Algy. The latter finally confessed to having bullied
and extracted money with menaces from young Arthur Brookfield, who
shared his study and whom he had promised to look after 'as a Father'.
Adelaide Sartoris then blamed Jeanie for having failed to warn her about the
real seriousness of her boy's misconduct: 'She said that she was sure I loved
her and meant well by her but that her confidence had been shaken, and that
she would never be able to believe me again. . . . I felt and feel very low.'
. . . (22 February 1867).

Walter, much the oldest of the three boys, had emerged from all this more
or less in the clear, but Jeanie was not happy that Walter should have such a
close and undesirable bond with Algy. There was so much pain in the whole
episode, pain at one's impotence to intervene in children's damaging friendships and pain at the risk of losing one's own dearest friend because she
was the mother of a 'damager', that what at first sight seems an absurd,
Lilliputian *imbroglio* quickly reveals its serious nature. Victorian mothers
were called upon from all sides to be the uplifting moral influence upon their
men-folk. In reality they were helpless bystanders, however much they really
knew about the darker world of the Victorians, forced to watch in the wings
while they knew their sons were vulnerable to corruption.

The old cure for trouble, a quite different, worse trouble, then hit the Hughes
family:

Elm House, 4 June 1867.
My darling, I have sad news for you. Dear Arthur has died in India
– I have just heard it. The Colonel of the Regiment wrote to you
Uncle Tom and Aunt Fan came this morning to tell me. – I am just
off to tell my poor Mother – she is still at Walsham [the
Wilkinsons' family estate at Walsham-le-Willows] – He seems to
have died of exhaustion; . . . I don't grieve for him, but I don't dare
think of poor Mother. He and Harry and Walter are very happy
together. – It is a sad blow for us all, but we must do our best to
cheer Mother . . .

My child, you will feel it very much, for our Pup was more like
your brother than your uncle. It makes me very sad to think that
you will have this grief, and that I shan't be near you to hold you
in my arms and cry with you, but I must go to my poor old
Mother, who will be heart broken and I must stay with her and
bring her home, and devote myself to her, poor dear . . .

Father's best love, your fond old Mother.

As Tom Hughes wrote to Hastings on 4 June, after he had given him 'the
dreadful news' that had just come from India – 'Poor dear Mother – You
hardly remember the coming of the news of dear Walter's death [see above
CHAPTER 1] so like in many of the circumstances. It almost killed her and now
the youngest has followed him.' And Jeanie herself wrote:

Mother will never get over it. She has never got over the loss of her
other children. The sorrow is ever there but she even now, takes
interest in, and is thankful for what is left her and she cannot, at
her age, be very long before she joins them all. There must be a
very happy meeting in Heaven, the three brothers and the Father
and so many friends, and dear old Franklin and Henry New. – I
often think of that meeting, it prevents my being selfish and
wanting them back again so badly. (8 June 1867)

It is significant that Jeanie Senior should have included two of the loved
servants as members of the Hughes' extended family, in that Stanley Spencer-
like vision of the Resurrection as human reunion.

Dear Mother . . . sleeps badly, and then in the long watches of the
night she gets thinking of her sorrow . . . I get her as much as
possible into the garden, and we potter about together and do a
little gardening and I think that does her good – it tires her, and
then she has more chance of sleeping. – But nothing but time can
do much good. (19 June 1867)

The last thing they had to endure was the coming of Arthur's trunk, which did not arrive until November:

> They have sent his books, and watch and two or three pictures and the tiger skin that he got just before he was taken ill . . . Poor Mother can't bear the sight of the tiger skin and I don't wonder for one may almost say that it cost the dear boy his life. (28 November 1867)

The one important, positive event during that sad half of 1867 was the return of Walter's formerly adopted 'little sister', Helen, now fourteen, to Elm House. She had been so wretched at boarding school, that her father, who had remarried, agreed that she should become a paying guest and be taught by Jeanie.

> Little Helen is delightful in the house – she has been overworked at school-cram, cram. I shan't have it go on in this way now she is with me. I will have lessons enough, but also will have play enough I am determined (21 June 1867). . . . Helen will be here for the first part of your holidays (18 July 1867) . . . Col. Wilson sent £50 – my first half year for Nell; I felt intensely pleased at the cheque, all my own earning! – as proud as a peacock! . . . I shall now clear a lot of bills that have been weighing on my mind. (5 December 1867)

It was the first money that Jeanie had ever earned. She was thirty-nine.

Walter's school life continued to be inglorious but finally at the end of 1867 he got a good end-of-term report – or 'character' – at last:

> I feel so very happy, I can't tell you dearest. – As light as if I could jump up to the sky! – And I wanted a little cheering, for I've had to give up going to poor Mother [at Walsham] – Father is gouty and is in his bed, and Helen is ill too, and of course I must stay by my sick creatures. (16 December 1867)

However, Walter's last months at Rugby continued to be fraught. In March 1868 his mother was in a state of near panic, for he had been reported to Dr. Temple – soon to be Archbishop of Canterbury – for having made an irreverent remark. There was a real possibility that he would be expelled. His mother implored him to recognize that it was a serious matter, not just something that would pain her to hear about: 'For if I am to take the place of your conscience, dearest, you will never develop into a noble and high-minded man.' She begged Walter to overcome his shyness and pride and apologize sincerely to Dr. Temple:

It is a very hard thing to do I know but God will help you to do it
. . . I have so often during the last few days reproached myself for
many jokes about serious subjects that have been told either by me
or in my presence. It is so difficult when one is young to know
where to stop, where a joke degenerates into irreverence.
(19 March 1868)

Walter did convince the Headmaster that he was truly sorry, after which
his mother could indulge in the fantasy that Walter would now show Dr.
Temple his 'own dear best self' and that Temple would tell her one day that
he 'never did a wiser thing than when he trusted you and kept you on at
Rugby' (21 March 1868). It never happened but it was good to dream about.

There were to be more crises in Walter's school-life. First came the startling revelation on 1 October 1868 from Jeanie's old friend Nina Inglefield
that there was endemic homosexual activity in all English public schools and
even in boys' preparatory schools. Naïve Jeanie had not believed such a thing
possible. Interestingly, she says that had she known about it she would have
warned Walter about the danger when he was a little boy; she does not say
she would never have sent him away to boarding school. Then, at the end of
October, there came the devastating news that Walter's young cousin, fifteen
year-old Eddy Senior, a boy of whom he was fond and whom he was
supposed to mentor, had been expelled from Rugby for visiting brothels
during the vacation. 'I wonder how Edward could have been so wicked
without your seeing it coming' (25 October 1868).

Jeanie was still bitterly aware that Walter dangerously resembled his
father: 'You inherit by nature much of your father's indolent character, and
your life will have to be a fight against giving way to it' (18 August 1868).
Walter also made Jeanie very uneasy by his imitation of his father's lofty
disparagement of other people. 'I don't like you to speak of any creature as
'blackguard devils' . . . The thing is not to call our fellow creatures devils,
but to turn our energies to making them less like devils . . . (8 November).
On 21 November she was unhappy at Walter's increasingly Nassau-like tone,
when he wrote carelessly 'a fellow can't be bothered to remember his homework' or that he felt like kicking a certain sixth former. Her dread lest her
only son be turning inexorably into a replica of her husband then led to the
last and most explicit avowal she ever made to Walter about her despair over
her marriage:

My dear dear son you must look solemnly on your life as a trust
from God. – You are not given your life for ease and pleasure. God
gave it you for duty.– You have it in your own hands to turn out
(in spite of your indolent nature) a hard working, earnest man. – I
have had one great disappointment in life – I hoped that Father

would have been more like what he ought to have been with all his natural advantages. I've had to give up that hope.

All my joy is bound up in you. If you will *help me* to form in you all that is noble and manly I know that I *can* be of use to you. I do so long for your good, my own darling. – Do lay your bones into your school life this last month. (21 November 1868)

But Walter was not the only child about whom she had constant worries. 1868 had begun with the tearaway nine year-old Willie Hughes in hospital with a crushed leg after he had jumped out of a moving carriage. At one time his life was thought to be in danger and later it was feared one foot might have to be amputated. When things looked at their worst Jeanie would spend half of every day in hospital with him and then her mother, Margaret Hughes, would spend the other half-day there. Finally, on 8 March 1868 Willie, with both his legs saved, was allowed home and for the rest of the year things went more quietly with 'the bairns'. Margaret Hughes herself, however, also gave cause for concern due to her weakening eyesight and her daughter spent more and more time reading aloud to her. The older woman enjoyed shopping and paying calls, two activities Jeanie found very tedious, but she would often take her mother out to have a bit of pleasure: 'Now she has got so old [after the death of Arthur] I like to save her all fatigue and trouble when I possibly can' (18 May 1868).

But it was the other Grandmother, 'Granny Senior', who hung most heavily of all on Jeanie's mind. Would she be moving in with them or not? In 1865 it had looked as though she well might come to them, so miserable was she at her daughter Minnie's lack of care for her, not only cheating her out of her money but even grudging her enough to eat during her infrequent visits. On 5 November 1865 Walter heard from his mother:

> Father told me this morning that he wished again to offer Granny Senior to live here. . . . Of course it is a great trial, but I am sure it was our duty to offer her a home, and so we shall be able to bear it. . . . we will do our best for the poor old lady, for whom I do feel deeply sorry. [You] will help us to be kind to her? She loves you dearly tho' she is tiresome. You will always have a refuge in Granny Hughes' sitting room or my bedroom and whenever we have you at home we will manage that the poor old lady should not bore you. (8 November 1865)

For old Mrs. Senior was a Miss Bates. She did not move in with them then after all, but in September 1869 she became very ill and had to be nursed day and night by Jeanie, her own daughter Minnie refusing to help and settling in Dieppe for a month instead:

I must say that I am rather disgusted to have all the work put on me, but there is no help for it and the old lady can't be left that's certain. . . . I write amid great difficulties my darling – Granny [Senior] keeps a perpetual fire of small conversation which drives me nearly crazy, because post time is nearly here. All day I never could find a quiet half hour to write to you, and this evening I thought I'd managed so well for I amused Father for an hour and a half before dinner and got Gran a lot of papers to amuse her, so I thought I should be in peace but no! there is no rest for the wicked. (2 September 1869)

In November 1869, 79 year-old Mrs. Senior, thought by Dr. de Mussy to be dying from stomach or liver cancer, would finally move in to Elm House, together with her furniture, her servants and her dog, with consequences that will be seen.

Throughout all these crises of family life, Walter's letters to his mother were half her lifeline – 'I live on your letters for a week' (15 October 1867); the other half was writing her letters to him:

I feel as you do, darling, that it is something like talking to you to be writing to you. [My] real joy can only be through you; and in seeing you growing a worthy man, I can bear any trouble serenely, for all my earthly joy is centred in you my beloved, and in you alone. – All the rest of life is merely a dream; the reality is my love for you. (9 December 1867)

The years when Walter was at Rugby were the most highly-charged in his relationship with his mother. They were both at their most vulnerable – frustrated, lonely, often confronted with failure. It would be good for both of them to emerge into a wider world.

CHAPTER SEVEN

Politics and Society in the Late 1860s

Every life is an intermeshing of continuity and change. Jeanie Senior's fraught domestic life seemed to her to be one of sameness and perpetual recurrence while the social and political context of her life was full of dramatic changes to which she ardently, even fiercely, responded. Given all her anxious responsibilities and the constant (and conflicting) demands on her to respond to each family member, Nassau, Walter, her mother, her brother, his four children and her foster daughter Helen – who now called herself Nell – it might be thought that she had quite enough on her hands already, without concerning herself about the suffering in the world outside Elm House. But the reverse was the case.

Inside 'Mrs. Nassau Senior' there was always fiery Jeanie Hughes who, at sixteen, had so passionately attacked the cruelty of the Russian Tsar towards Polish political prisoners in Siberia, and who, as a young married woman, had so surprised and heartened John Murray Forbes with her declaration of vehement sympathy with the North in the American Civil War. All her adult life she was a close reader of reports of national and international news in several daily newspapers. That was rare in a Victorian gentlewoman, for, as Emily Davies, soon to be foundress of Girton College, Cambridge, complained in her paper 'On Secondary Education relating to Girls', Proceedings of the Social Sciences Association, 1864: 'Newspapers are scarcely supposed to be read by women at all. When *The Times* is offered to a lady, the sheet containing the advertisements and the Births, Deaths and Marriages is considerably selected.'

What was Jeanie Senior's view of her country's political role in the world in the mid 19th century? Very unusually for her class and gender in a period of complacent world domination by Britain, she was anti-Imperialist and anti-racist. At the time of the 1862 Revolution in Greece, she had written to twelve year-old Walter:

> It seems a great shame that we English persist in keeping the Ionian Islands altho' the people in them desire to shake us off and reunite themselves with Greece again.
> I do not see how we can talk as we do about oppressed people, when we are doing the same thing. – I wish that we had given up both the Ionian Islands and Gibraltar. (29 October 1862)

On 5 November 1865 his mother reported to Walter that she had heard from his young uncle Arthur in India:

> There has been a great row in the regiment – One of the very young officers was such a beast as to throw a loaf of bread at the head of a native servant, and the affair came before a magistrate, and there was a great fuss. That is how we brought on the Mutiny – and we deserved it, for the way we behaved to the natives, treating them worse than our dogs and horses. And I fear that we are very little better now, even after that terrible warning – . . . *It makes my blood boil.* (my emphasis)

Another comment on Britain and India was on 14 July 1867:

> The ball that is given on Friday at the India House is to be paid for by taxing the wretched population of India. I think it the most abominable thing I ever heard of in my life – As if we English rolling in riches could not entertain our national guests at the national cost. This sort of thing is what brings on revolution, and very justly too – one is thoroughly ashamed of one's country.

The defining political topic of the mid to late 1860s, the issue which divided the human rights radicals from the white supremacists in Britain, was not India but the 'Governor Eyre Controversy'. In October 1865 an angry demonstration against white magistrates and police over land rights and judicial verdicts in Morant Bay, Jamaica, had resulted in lethal shooting into the crowd by the white militia and then counter violence from the enraged black protesters. Eighteen whites were killed and thirty-one wounded; it is not known how many blacks died. False rumours and a panic fear that 'they are going to overrun us' led to atrocity by the rulers. Governor Eyre ordered brutal reprisals under 'martial law' for a month after the small uprising had been quelled. Four hundred and thirty-nine black Jamaicans were summarily shot or hanged, more than six hundred men and women were flogged – the favourite punishment of recent slavery days – and over a thousand black Jamaicans' homes burnt down. 'This is a picture of martial law. The soldiers enjoy it, the inhabitants here dread it. If they run [on the soldiers'] approach, they are shot for running away.'[1] Governor Eyre contrived to have his hated political opponent, George William Gordon, the mixed race member of the Jamaican House of Assembly, arrested in Kingston and manhandled on to a boat, The Wolverine; he was court-martialled 'as the instigator of all the evils' without a chance to defend himself, and publicly hanged.

When the news of this recourse to terror by a British Governor-General reached England, it outraged those radicals who had recently championed the North in the American Civil War. Jeanie's brother Thomas Hughes, a consistent anti-racist and financial supporter of America's black freedmen after the Civil War,[2] immediately placed himself on the front line in the campaign to make Governor Eyre answerable to British law. Recently elected a radical liberal MP for Lambeth, Hughes was part of the delegation on 9 December 1865 that denounced Governor-General Eyre to the Colonial Secretary. He immediately joined the Jamaica Committee set up to bring Eyre to justice. After the Royal Commission, chaired by Russell Gurney, had reported in April 1866 that the horrific brutalities by black rioters, alleged in Eyre's first dispatch, had never occurred and that Eyre's reprisals had been 'excessive', 'barbarous', 'wanton' and 'cruel',[3] Hughes, together with the other MPs on the Jamaica Committee, attempted to have a censure motion against Eyre passed in Parliament. When this failed on 31 July 1866, they resolved to bring Eyre to trial for murder.[4]

British public opinion was fiercely divided. Old friendships were sundered: Hughes was now on the opposite side from the very man who had recently nominated him as Liberal Candidate for Lambeth – John Ruskin. T. H. Huxley struggled not to break with his old friend, the physicist John Tyndall, who did not 'hold an Englishman and a Jamaica negro to be convertible terms'.[5] And neither Tom Hughes, nor his sister, could ever feel the same towards their former Christian Socialist friend, now turned Eyre-defender, Charles Kingsley:

> When Eyre, who of yore, 'mongst diggers,
> Was muscular, prudent, and just,
> Has now slaughtered some hundreds of niggers,
> Don't censure, but "take him on trust"' –
> [a reference to Kingsley's admonition to the public concerning Eyre]
> 'Lambeth Billy' (Hastings Hughes' nom de guerre), *South London Chronicle*, August 1866.[6]

The third and last unsuccessful attempt to prosecute Eyre was made in June 1868, after which only a small core of middle-class radicals, including Hughes, backed by working-class radicals, was left for the defence of black Jamaican rights.[7]

English ladies could not then, of course, be MPs or barristers or newspaper editors; their comments on the great political issues of the day had to be made in the private world of letters, tea tables and dinner parties. In one letter to Walter, Jeanie had to make young Algy Sartoris realize that his pro-Eyre opinions would not be published by radical Hastings Hughes. On 1 July 1866 Jeanie went to a concert and chose to sit by Mrs. Russell Gurney who had just come back from accompanying her husband on the Jamaica

Commission and on 12 July Mrs. Gurney was invited by Jeanie to Elm House to talk and show her sketches of Jamaica. Late in September Jeanie described to Walter how she had recently sung at a charity concert at Shere School and then dined with the Jameses:

> Mr. James[8] is a true liberal – one after my own heart . . . [He] held his own and had much the best of the argument [on Franchise Reform] – and also on the Jamaica subject. He said that Eyre had entirely lost his head, and that he had been, not only unjust and wrong, but completely illegal in his proceedings – he said that when Gordon was safe on the *Wolverine*. Eyre had no more right to constitute a court martial (which was not even a legal court martial) and to put him to death than Mr. James would have a right to put a man to death who had broken into his house (and had been taken and safely confined in the cellar) on the approbation of a court composed of Mr. James' butler, footman and gardener.

One may contrast Jeanie Senior's relief and delight in encountering a 'true liberal' on the Eyre case with Jane Carlyle's comment during a social call after the Royal Commission on Jamaica had been published that April – 'should be surprised and grieved if I found [my husband] sentimentalizing over a pack of black brutes!'[9]

The late 1860s also witnessed Thomas Hughes' tireless commitment to greater social justice, democratic representation and equality within Britain. He championed electoral reform to include the working class. He worked within Parliament and on a Parliamentary Commission to amend the current Combination Acts and institute trade union rights including the right both to strike and to build up enabling strike funds[10]. And he backed, both personally and financially, pioneering ventures in the co-operative, profit-sharing organisation of industry, retail and commerce. His ardent social idealism, often held to be naïve and quixotic, always found its most sympathetic, encouraging echo in his sister, whereas his wife Fan, according to Jeanie, was and always had been at heart, 'a regular old Tory' (28 October 1868).[11] Jeanie Senior's political radicalism was at its most outspoken on 16 October 1870: 'The only real honest and liberal party in England are the working class.'

Only two other political topics of the late 1860s need mentioning – Jeanie Senior's fundamental antipathy to war, and her response to that age-old litmus test for Britain, the treatment of Ireland. The only war to which she was at all sympathetic, and even then with some reluctance, was Garibaldi's campaign in Italy. On 28 February 1866 Jeanie declared 'I hate all guns and all shooting. And pistols and every firearm.' On 17 July 1866 she was wretched over Prussia's military triumph over Austria. A year later, on 26 October 1867, she commented on Garibaldi's march on Rome, threatened by Louis Napoleon, the Emperor of France: 'He is a noble old hero but how I do hate war and all its horrors.'

As for Ireland, whereas her old friend W. R. Greg wanted to see *habeas corpus* immediately suspended in Ireland and the imprisonment without trial of all 'agitators', in response to the latest unrest there, she regarded Irish violence as nemesis: 'It is very terrible and very sad. – It is a just retribution for our past sins against Ireland' (7 December 1869). Her political sympathies were always with those whom she perceived to be the most oppressed and against those who triumphantly abused their power over others. This meant that she had to repeat Hazlitt's bitter experience and echo his conclusion that 'in politics one is concerned not only with what takes place, but with what ought to take place and which seldom actually does so . . . at every step our prejudices are shocked, our reason taken to task, our hopes disappointed or overturned'.[12]

∼

Jeanie Senior's response to the remediable suffering outside her own circle did not limit itself to an indignant, depressed head shaking over her favourite daily paper, *The Pall Mall Gazette*. She had to find relief in some kind of intervention, which, for a lady, meant voluntary action. In the early 1860s, as was seen in CHAPTER FIVE, she had begun by giving 'hands-on' relief to those personally known to her among the unemployed in Wandsworth. But by the later 1860s she had become dissatisfied with such individual acts. She began to identify institutions that needed intervention or support and then, under Octavia Hill's lead, to try to work at the causes of social misery. The three spheres she concentrated on were the local Workhouse infirmary for the destitute aged sick, a local Industrial School for Girls, and the atrocious state of working-class housing in London.

Precisely how inadequate and heartless was the provision for the sick, aged poor in Britain after the 1834 New Poor Law has become the subject of professional academic debate.[13] Her father-in-law Nassau William Senior's basic principle of 'lesser eligibility' meant that the new Workhouse had, by definition, to be the worst possible last resort for the poor of any age. They would not have needed to go there, if they, or their families, had had the self-discipline in better days to have saved. Hence the Workhouse with its bleak discomfort, minimal and monotonous diet, imposed uniform, enforced labour, the separation of husbands from wives, and parents from children, came to be seen as a deliberate punishment for poverty. As for 'out-relief', i.e. money doles to the aged poor in their own homes, 'a large minority of old people received poor relief, but they often received very little, very late in life and grudgingly'.[14]

The first English lady to ask – and gain – admittance to visit a Workhouse had been Louisa Twining of the Twining tea and banking family (with whom the Hughes family banked) in 1853. 'What she encountered there appalled her: there were no washing facilities, the bed linen was filthy . . . and the food was inedible.'[15] After much obstruction, she founded the Workhouse Visiting Society in 1858 and, once Workhouses could no longer be 'closed institutions', some of their iniquities began to be remedied. Six years later a reluctant Frances Power Cobbe made herself visit St. Peter's Workhouse in Bristol, and later many other workhouses in London and the provinces. '[And] this is what I saw. The sick lay on wretched beds, fit only for able-bodied tramps . . . [Lodged together were] the sick, the aged, the infirm, the insane and epileptic patients and lying-in women.'[16]

Unlike Louisa Twining, who spent much time on the religious succour of the sick and aged, Frances Power Cobbe introduced easy chairs with cushions, bed rests that enabled patients to sit up and read, spectacles for those who needed them, little packets of good tea, pictures to hang on the walls, flowers and fruit in season, and, most efficacious of all, she took in a canary in a cage. She also brought in books, magazines and papers like Dickens' *Household Words*. In 1860, working with Miss Elliot in Bristol, she organized a national campaign for the humane treatment of the incurably sick within Workhouses and to that end published her 'Workhouse Sketches' in *Macmillan's Magazine*, April 1861. She urged the necessity for women to be allowed in to reform the whole system:

> Especially we want the presence of women in nearly every department of the Workhouse. . . . The care of infants, the training of young girls, the subduing of harshness by gentleness, the reclaiming of fallen women, the tender care of the suffering and dying – these are the "Rights of Women," . . . and woe be to man when he denies them![17]

In the spring of 1866, immediately after she had been spending day and night nursing Hastings' children through one infant illness after another, Jeanie wrote to Walter that she wanted 'to get into the Workhouse infirmary to see how things are done and cheer up the poor sick creatures there'. When she began to visit the old women paupers, although she did not belong to the official Ladies' Visiting Society, she combined Lousia Twining's approach with that of Frances Power Cobbe. She read to the stricken women from the Bible, and herself conducted services for those unable to walk to church or

14   'Old Age – A Study at the Westminster Union'. Engraving by Herkomer in *The Graphic*, 1881; preparatory, harsher study for his oil painting 'Eventide', Walker Art Gallery, Liverpool. Herkomer was the black and white artist most admired by Van Gogh.

chapel, thus offering them the consolation of an imminent, better Eternity; but she also took in tea and sugar and her young nephews Willie and Gerard to try and cheer the old people with a rare sight of young things. But

> . . . Oh dear! How much suffering there is in the world. . . . Many of these poor old creatures are cripples with rheumatism, broken limbs or paralysis and numbers of them quite deaf. Nothing to cheer or enliven them and no prospect in this world of any thing that makes life precious. (26 January 1867)

Jeanie found her regular Workhouse visiting each week deeply depressing; there was so little she could do. On 28 November 1867 she reported that she was very unhappy about the women's diet:

> The wards I visit are convalescent wards, and the poor things are supposed to have meat every day; and of course they ought to have meat that they can eat. Instead of which, four times a week they have beef so hard that they can't touch it, and so go without, and the mutton is sometimes so fat (breast of mutton) that they can't touch it either. – I don't know what to do in the matter, for of course I am anxious not to get them into any scrape by making complaints about them.

Nearly thirty years later, in 1895, her niece, Tom's daughter Mary Hughes, an elected Poor Law Guardian, would still have to campaign for months until local paupers were allowed to drink tea twice a day, instead of only once, in a Bedfordshire Workhouse. '[The] women fell sobbing at her feet and kissed the edge of her skirt the next time she visited them.'[18]

Jeanie Senior did pioneer one very radical approach towards 'her' elderly women paupers, she sprang them out of the Workhouse. Thirty-eight of them came to tea on Elm House lawn in the summer of 1867. 'They were very happy, poor old things, in the garden. I sang to them and then they had wine and cake and went home. . . . One poor old woman had not been out of the [ward] for four years – she said it was like Paradise' (25 July 1867). Always a great believer in the beneficial effect of 'treats', she then made it a regular tradition to invite the old women to Elm House, sometimes to tea and sometimes even to dine. She had to make sure that they had all left before Nassau was home so that they might not bother him. On 26 November 1868 she had the happiness of providing a positively Dickensian spread for her escapees:

> Only 13 could come, for so many were ill. They did enjoy them-
> selves . . . We gave them veal pie and ham, roast beef and plum
> pudding, beer and a glass of sherry, figs and almonds and raisins.
> Then they played bagatelle, and went to see the pictures in the
> house, and then we [she and Nell] sang to them and then they had
> tea, and then a bran tub, and a little present for each in it, and then
> they went home at 5.30.

But no number of treats could diminish Jeanie Senior's haunted sense that there was something terribly wrong about the whole system of British care of the destitute, the unemployable sick or the old and infirm. '[And] I don't know how to mend matters' (9 October 1868). 'Pauperism' was caused by destitution and Workhouses did nothing to institute the living wage or sickness and unemployment benefits or the old-age pension that alone could abolish destitution.

Meanwhile she was also doing her best for another cause, a local Industrial School for Girls. It was Mary Carpenter, the heroic foundress of Ragged Schools in Bristol, who had first promoted the idea of 'Industrial Schools' which would provide simple food and training for homeless, destitute, or vagrant children, picked up off the street and/or in trouble with the law, to save them from crime and prison. By the 1861 Industrial Schools Act, such schools were put under Home Office control and the Treasury awarded them grants. Boys were taught carpentry, shoemaking, and tailoring as well as general humanities and science subjects; girls were taught laundry work and cooking as well as the 3Rs and music.[19] F. D. Maurice had become involved with one such Industrial School for girls near where Jeanie Senior lived and she decided to support it in 1867, although she found being on the committee 'a very foolish, needless bore' (1 April 1867). That December she went to the school to give the girls a singing lesson and was delighted to report to Walter another 'treat': 'There is to be a Christmas tree for the girls, but it is a great secret from them, that their surprise may be perfect'. On 20 October 1869 she reported that she 'saw all the girls looking very flourishing and happy'. When not bemoaning the tedious committee meetings, she delighted in praising the girls' prowess at cooking and laundry-work at 'her' Industrial School. She also checked up on conditions in other local schools: 'I want to make a blow up re the Rev. Hall's church school without a fire for the poor little children' (22 October 1871).

Jeanie Senior's most important social intervention of all at this time was her support for Octavia Hill's experiment in housing reclamation. It will be remembered how eagerly she had responded to the younger woman's 'great talks about houses for the poor', hoping that Ruskin might build her some houses to manage nearby in Wandsworth. Ruskin did not build houses for her, however, since he had already bought five houses, then in a deplorable state with dustbins spewing garbage, blocked drains, leaky roofs and drinking water taken from a filthy waterbutt in so-called 'Freshwater Place' off Homer St. near the Edgeware Road, as well as at least one other house in Marylebone Road.[20]

At the end of January 1867 Jeanie was taken by Octavia Hill to see the 'three small houses' in Marylebone that she would 'manage'. '[It] will not be much work' she tried to assure Walter, often concerned lest she exhaust herself (28 January 1867). Each Monday without fail she would have to cross the Thames to get from Lavender Hill to Marylebone in order to collect the rents from the very impoverished, often seasonally (un)employed tenants in the divided-up houses. Octavia Hill charged four shillings a week for a room but she persuaded those tenants with large families to take two rooms at only four shillings and sixpence. No sub-letting within a room was allowed. Jeanie would then take notes of what further repairs the tenants needed, whether or not the children seemed neglected or were not being sent to school, whether a sick child needed a note for admission to hospital, and also, all too often, the tenants' complaints about their neighbours' behaviour.[21] It was vital that a housing manager's demeanour towards the tenants should not be that of an interfering 'superior' but rather that of a respectful ally who genuinely believed in the tenants' self-respect and desire for independence.

By freeing tenants from the tyranny of bad landlords, the degradation of enforced proximity to criminals, alcoholics or drug addicts and 'the heavy incubus of accumulated dirt', Octavia Hill believed that she and her deputies could give the tenants new hope and the energy *'to help themselves'*.[22] As she wrote in her essay, 'A Few Words to Volunteer Visitors among the Poor', published in *Our Common Land* (1877), the poor needed to be seen 'primarily as husbands, wives, sons, and daughters, members of households, as are ourselves, instead of . . . as a different class'. She knew that any real help for the tenants in her 'Courts' – she never used the word 'slums' – would require 'persistent patience, gentleness, hope'.[23]

Octavia Hill's pioneering reform was thus two-pronged. On the one hand, she was trying to prove that it was possible to transform desperate working-class lives by transforming their living conditions, on the other, she was simultaneously establishing the basic principles of a new women's profession, that of salaried social work. 'It all began with Octavia Hill' as Katherine Kendall has testifed in the Preface to her *Social Work Education: its Origins in Europe*.[24] But she had had to start by depending on the right sort of volunteer, like Jeanie Senior.

15 Octavia Hill in 1882.

Now that she was one of the very first social workers in Britain, Jeanie took huge pleasure in helping Octavia provide 'treats' for the tenants. She would deliver hampers of plants for a recently reclaimed 'open space' playground or to brighten the tenants' brand new window boxes. And she would often sing at a free concert or tenants' party. But her contribution to Octavia Hill's re-housing project soon became even more vital once she took over responsibility for all the accounts, thus becoming a pioneer of 'housing management finance'.[25]

Normally the worst rented rooms in Britain yielded a *rentier* slum landlord 10 per cent annual return. Octavia Hill could not hope to find investors in reclaimed, inner city housing who would be happy to have no return at all, so her tenancies would have to yield 5% annual return in order to encourage wealthy people to invest in 'social housing', as well as to cover all her maintenance costs. Clearly her whole model of exemplary housing management for the very poor would depend on meticulous accounting as much as it would on sensitive human relations. Descent into financial chaos because of innumeracy on the tenants' side and inaccuracies on that of the amateur lady rent collectors, could have ended her whole project. 'The need to make housing management a paying proposition while improving the conditions of the poor required a hard head for business with a soft heart for people.'[26] Octavia Hill herself had taken responsibility for the accounts at first but when she had a breakdown through overwork she, turned, in June 1867, to competent Jeanie Senior.

Profoundly as she admired her, however, Jeanie did not always agree with her or limit herself to doing what Octavia Hill asked. Whereas Octavia was rigidly opposed to giving money to desperate, cash-strapped families, ever, we have seen that Jeanie actually paid the rent for the family of the injured navvy King and his family, having personally re-housed them after their eviction for having reported their noxious, cholera-threatening drains to her (5 October 1866). And whereas Octavia put all her emphasis on individual help by ladies to enable the poor to help themselves, abhorring 'dependency culture' via state-intervention or official social welfare assistance of any kind – 'She was obsessive and dogmatic, inflexible and harsh'[27] – Jeanie Senior, in contrast, was not. Just as she had combined both Louisa Twining and Frances Power Cobbe's approaches in her Workhouse visiting, so now she was both an Octavia Hill facilitator of self-help and an advocate of political legislative intervention. On 24 October 1866 she wrote to Walter endorsing 'Greg's capital article in the *Pall Mall* about the need for Government Inspectors' intervention and power to force landlords to make dwellings fit to inhabit' – a sentiment she would still be expressing, about ill-ventilated and poorly drained rural cottages, in April 1873. Jeanie Senior thought it a social priority in the inner cities that 'proper dwelling should be provided', i.e. built by local councils (12 February 1873).

Already on 30 October 1866, she had written a long letter to the press (Hastings' weekly *South London Chronicle*), on the appalling housing problem in London. She had demanded the building of decent housing at affordable rents. Given that Victorian ladies were not expected to read newspapers seriously, they were even less expected to write letters to the editor. This time Jeanie Senior did not sign her letter under Nassau's name, as she had done in *The Times*, 5 September 1865, but under her own initials, J.E.S. – but still concealing her gender:

> OUR LABOURING POOR AND THEIR DWELLINGS
>
> Sir, – . . . It is a painful fact that the rents of the houses . . . are more than the working man in general can afford to pay . . . The average wages of an ordinary labourer in and near London cannot be reckoned as high as18s. a week. The railway labourer, for instance, is off work in rainy weather, and 3s. a day being the usual wage that he receives, the average in his case would be under 18s. weekly. If his rent be more than 3s. a week it must be out of all proportion to his means, . . .
>
> In London the rent of a room is, as a general rule 2s 6d a week. If the working man in order to provide decent accommodation for himself and his family inhabits two rooms, [i.e. at 5/- rather than Octavia Hill's 4/6d] it is evident that the income left for food, clothing, education, and surplus funds in case of illness, is utterly inadequate. It is very natural there should be over-crowding in the homes of the poor when, in order to avoid it, in any degree, they would have to spend nearly one third of their annual gain on rent alone. *Either rents are too high, or wages are too low* . . .
>
> The great question appears to be whether houses can be built which will afford comfortable dwellings for the labouring poor at rates that they can afford to pay and at a cost that will pay a fair interest and a moderate profit to the landlord. At present this problem is not solved, – but *it is a disgrace that things should go on as they now do.* The overcrowding, and dirty disorder that necessarily accompanies overcrowding, is a disgrace to a Christian community, – I am, Sir, yours &c. (my emphases)

Clearly she had paid close attention to the insecurity of life experienced by 'her' navvies working to build the railway lines round Clapham Junction until they became victims of some industrial accident. She was within a whisker of making the revolutionary demand for a minimum wage and price and rent controls.

Even if she did not always agree with Octavia Hill's approach, Jeanie Senior always found inspiration in her contacts with that dynamic being. On

1 April 1867 she even refused a ticket to a first night at the Opera because 'Miss Hill is coming . . . Miss Hill came about four. . . . We have been talking all evening and now it is bed-time'.

CHAPTER EIGHT

Interlude: Music and Friendships

Music

When Jeanie Senior was born, in December 1828, Beethoven had been dead for just a year and Schubert only a month. Rossini, Mendelssohn, Chopin, Schumann, Brahms, Gounod, Meyerbeer, Berlioz, Wagner, Liszt, Verdi, Smetana, Fauré and Saint-Saens were her contemporaries. She knew she was blessed to live in London when the first English performance of Bach's *St. Matthew Passion* was given, when the Handel Centenary was celebrated, when all Beethoven's piano sonatas and late Quartets were heard for the first time, and when Schubert and Schumann were still regarded as so *avant-garde* that they had the force of a revelation.[1] The second half of the 19th century has been called 'The Renaissance' in the history of the musical life of England[2] and Jeanie Senior herself played her part in that Renaissance as concert-goer, performer and teacher.

She had inherited her musical gifts from both sides of the family and that she herself was exceptionally musically gifted had been clear from childhood. As soon as she moved to her first permanent home, Elm House, in 1860, she had the excitement of being able to attend Covent Garden for Opera, the vast new Crystal Palace for symphony concerts – and the uncomfortable benches in St. James' Hall for chamber music at the 'Monday Pop'.[3]

The three outstanding performers of her day were the pianists Charles Hallé and Clara Schumann and the violinist Joseph Joachim.[4] To be able to hear all three artists, as well as singers like Adelaide Kemble Sartoris, Mario, Jenny Lind, Pauline Viardot – and to be their cherished friend . . . The most highly cultured and wealthy people of the day were able to have the very greatest performers interpret classical music just for their own and their friends' ears within their private drawing rooms. And among kindred spirits, all passionate music-lovers, such occasions could be surprisingly warm and informal as well as musically unforgettable:

> Uncle Hastings and I went to Mrs. Benzons[5] . . . There were
> Joachim and his wife, and Mme Schumann and her daughter
> and sister and Mr. and Mrs. Lehmann,[6] Dr. de Mussy and
> Mr. Moscheles a painter. . . . [From] 8 to 10 they made divine

music . . . And Mme Schumann and all the other Germans seemed so united and fond of each other it was quite delightful . . . [It] was so primitive and pleasant and we took a jolly leave of them all as they stood on the steps in their bonnets and wide-awakes going to walk home at the sensible hour of ten instead of past midnight as most parties are inclined to. (14 May 1865)

On first April, 1867 Jeanie was able to report a musical evening more wonderful still:

I went to party at the Chief Justice's (Cockburn's) calling for Katie [Collins] on the way. There we had an enchanting evening, for Hallé and Joachim played like angels. Benedict[7] was there, so they made me sing the contralto song from *St. Cecilia*[8] twice . . . Hallé told me that I sang better than ever . . . and Joachim told me that he was quite unhappy not to have known before how well I sang.

A week later Watts reported to her that Joachim, whose portrait he was then painting,

had talked to him a great deal about my singing and had told Watts that it was by far the best amateur singing he had heard in England and that he was quite unhappy to think he had known me so many years without ever hearing me sing. – Is not all that delightful praise from the great Joachim? (8 April 1867)

That bubbling, triumphant joy, when she had been recognized at last by those whose affirmation she valued above all others, occurred in the very days when she was also coping with the tragi-comic crisis of her husband's refusal to be a Co-Juror at the Paris Exhibition.

On one unforgettable evening,

Father and I dined with the Colviles,[9] . . . Edward and Adelaide Sartoris, Joachim with his brother and sister, the Mussys and [Arthur] Sullivan. . . . HE [i.e. Joachim], played divinely, a concerto of Spohr's, then Mendelssohn's great concerto; and last Bach's Chaconne, which moves me more than anything almost. He likes playing in the dark (as I like singing), so he had the further room darkened and there he stood and played in the most wonderful manner . . . He played the accompaniment of an old Scotch song of which he is very fond and made me sing it. I hate to sing after his playing: all music sounds discordant, but he wished it, so of course I did it. (4 February 1870)

≈

Every one who ever heard Jeanie Senior testified that she was an extraordinarily moving performer. '[Her] voice, as a private singer, was, I think, surpassed by no voice I ever heard';[10] 'Even my father [Sir Alexander Duff Gordon] liked Janie [sic] Senior's singing. How lovely she looked with her crinkly golden hair, her sweet face changing with every note of her beautiful clear voice.'[11]

> I heard Garcia speaking of her with affectionate admiration when he was a hundred years old . . . How clear was her voice, how it rang and vibrated! For those who loved to listen to it, her "Vado ben spesso" rings on still.[12] Sir Theodore Martin told me that he had only met Mrs. Senior once, one day when she was singing an Irish ballad to George Eliot at North Bank, "Far from the land where her young hero sleeps," which was written about Emmet. Sir Theodore said that forty years after he "could hear the notes still quite plainly." Some voices have this peculiar quality of vibrating on and on.[13]

How did Jeanie Senior sing? What did she sing? And to whom? Her voice was a warm, clear mezzo-soprano and it must have possessed tremendous power and projection because on 24 February 1871 she was asked to test the acoustic of the vast, newly-built Albert Hall before an audience of workmen and music critics. Her intensive two years of voice tuition from the famous teacher Manuel Garcia, 1848–1850, had concentrated almost exclusively at first on her breath control and voice production.[14] Anny Thackeray Ritchie testified:

> I have heard Mrs. Sartoris say that it was because of the unremitting work of years, and because of Mrs. Senior's devotion to her art with absolute and conscientious determination, that she could use her voice as she did with tender and brilliant ease.[15]

And Jeanie's sister-in-law Minnie Simpson remembered:

> She studied under Garcia as thoroughly as if she had intended to make singing her profession. He was delighted with her voice and dramatic power, . . . Had her circumstances been different she would no doubt have obtained public success. . . .[16]

'Had her circumstances been different' . . . It was considered impossible in the mid 19th century for a married lady to perform on the operatic stage. How, it was asked, could any decent woman bear to be a public spectacle of emotional abandonment? Adelaide Kemble Sartoris, like Jenny Lind, had

retired from professional opera on marriage.[17] Thus one part of what Jeanie
Senior poured into her amateur singing was all the power of a frustrated
potential professional. Another element was emotional frustration – all the
passion and ecstasy that she had never experienced found an outlet in her
music. As Anny Thackeray Ritchie recalled in her essay 'In my lady's
chamber', 'Mrs. Nassau Senior . . . used to play her own chords and accompany herself as *she poured out her full heart*' (my emphasis). 'Song was my
speech' as George Eliot's Armgart said.

Unusually for her day, Jeanie liked unfamiliar, older music; she sang
Palestrina and Marcello as well as a great deal of folk music. 'I like old things
that no one knows in England' (27 April 1870). Her repertoire included the
bitter, dramatic story of two sisters in the Scots ballad 'Binnorie', and the
tender, and erotic, English folksong 'I wandered by a brookside' – now
almost lost:

> I wandered by a brookside, I wandered by a mill
> I could not hear the water, the murmuring was still
> Nor the sound of any grasshopper or the song of any bird
> But the beating of my own heart was the only sound I heard.
>
> With silent tears fast flowing then someone stood behind
> A hand upon my shoulder, I knew the touch was kind
> He drew me near and nearer, we neither spoke one word
> But the beating of our own two hearts was the only sound I heard.

She sang the plangent ballads 'Kathleen O'Moore' and 'Barbara Allen'
and 'My mother bids me bind my hair' set by Haydn, and she also sang some
of the most sublime classical music ever composed – Handel, Gluck, Mozart,
Leonora's aria from *Fidelio*, Beethoven's powerful 'Abendlied unterm
gestirnten Himmel' ['song at evening beneath a starry sky'] and Schubert's
'Ave Maria'. The Beethoven '*Abendlied*' became a personal 'resistance hymn'
for Jeanie Senior: 'Even if storms rack the earth and the evil are crowned
with false gain, my soul can look up in hope where the stars sit enthroned.
No terror can torment it longer, no power can command it, as it soars,
radiant, up to Heaven's light.'

Among contemporary compositions she sang John Barnett's setting of the
passionate Shelley love poem 'Lines to an Indian Air' beginning 'I arise from
dreams of thee/In the first sweet sleep of night' – singing what she could
never say. One of her favourite encores, Beethoven's '*Mollys Abschied*'
[Molly's Parting], which begins 'Lebe wohl! du Mann der Lust und
Schmerzen!' [Farewell, thou man of pleasure and of pain!] was another
warm, tender song, expressing thoughts that could not be said by a married
woman in the mid 19th century except under cover of a musical offering –

16   Jeanie Senior's Resistance hymn from Beethoven's 'Abendlied unterm gestirnten Himmel',
"Wenn die Sonne nieder sinket . . .".

and in a foreign language.[18] The aria 'Ombra adorata' ['Oh beloved shade']
from Zingerelli's *Romeo e Giuletta* is one sure instance of how Jeanie
Senior's own emotional commitment to a work could transmit a profound
sense of personal conviction. It was Romeo's lament for his lost love and
expressed his aching desire to be reunited with the dead: '[The] aria, . . .
Ombra adorata, [is] as simple as the *recitative*: sustained, soulful, lifting it
above earthly pain, expressing hope for blessed fulfilment in a higher, better
world.'[19] Jeanie, who had known so many unbearable bereavements, was
one of the great interpreters of that aria.

But she also enjoyed jollier, much earthier songs: Haydn's setting of the Scottish 'The Miller's Daughter', to the tune of 'Gin a body meet a body/Comin thro' the rye', and, for an ever popular encore, she would offer the 18th century song 'Wapping Old Stairs', startlingly outspoken to Victorian ears, where Molly reproaches her roving-eyed sailor:

> When I pass'd a whole fortnight between decks with you,
> Did I e'er give a kiss Tom, to one of the crew?
> To be useful and kind, with my Thomas I stay'd
> For his trousers I wash'd and his grog too I made.

She was never happier than when given a (rare) opportunity to discover old musical scores and then to practise and refine her art under a professional singer. Two golden days stand out:

> I went soon after breakfast to call on Mrs. Rudolf Lehmann,
> who was charming. We had a regular crack about music. She is
> delightfully enthusiastic. She is going to take me tomorrow to the
> British Museum with her – she has an order to turn over the old
> music there and there are vols. and vols. of the old Masters in their
> own writing! – Fancy seeing the real writing of Handel and
> Scarlatti and Bach and Beethoven!!!! We are going to rummage
> until we find a lovely duet or two; then we shall copy it there, (for
> we must not take music away) and learn it perfectly, and then sing
> it to Jenny Lind, in the hope that she may take us in hand and give
> us some singing lessons, when she sees how earnest we are about
> it! . . . (9 November 1869) [Mrs. Rudolf Lehmann] is a real genius
> which is a very rare thing. . . . Deutsch[20] has got me a ticket for
> the reading room for six months so if ever I have time I can go
> there again, . . . we found two lovely duets that have never been
> published. And we copied more than half of them, and enjoyed
> our work very much . . . Intense quiet is expected, one may only
> speak in a low whisper. If I had time I should go there very often
> and get lots of lovely old music! [We found] lovely Handel arias.
> (13 November 1869)

A fortnight later she reported ecstatically to Walter:

> I'm just back from Jenny [Lind's] and I have had such a happy
> afternoon – Oh! My dear boy, how I do love hard work! She told
> me all sorts of things that now I can work up by myself. There

never was such a singer, I have always thought that, and now I am certain that there is no such a teacher. It is such a great help to *hear* a thing done. – and that is the only drawback in Garcia, that he can tell one but can't show one. I am sure if I could only have a year or two of work with Jenny, I should sing really well – so well that I should give myself intense pleasure. It is immensely interesting to hear her talk of art – she is *really* an artist and has an enthusiasm about her that is glorious. I wish I had time and opportunity and was ten years younger! – I suppose my education will be completed in Heaven – it certainly will be a great happiness even there to learn singing of Jenny – . . . (2 December 1869)

'If ever I have time, . . . if I had time, . . . I wish I had time . . . ' The time for her music had always to be squeezed into the time left after answering others' needs. Those two days when she was copying music manuscripts British Museum and being tutored by Jenny Lind were in the midst of yet another domestic crisis when she was having to re-arrange the whole living accommodation of Elm House in order to nurse her ill mother-in-law. 'I wish that the days had more hours, life is so much too short for what one has to do' (11 November 1869).

To whom did Jeanie Senior sing? She sang by private invitation to some of the most powerful, wealthy and artistic people in the country; she even sang before Royalty and once she had to help Mrs. Gladstone, the nervous wife of the Prime Minister, organize a concert for the Prince and Princess of Wales. But she was not always a willing performer, though few evenings were as ludicrously discomfiting as one that took place after dinner with the Thackeray daughters on 8 February 1866 in front of the Sartorises, Millais, Leighton and Marochetti, among others.

> [They] wanted music, and I was very much disinclined to sing, but I did not like to refuse; and they would wheel the piano from the back room into the front room, and I felt like a street singer with an ambulant piano; and I felt so shy with the piano in the middle of the drawing room, and a solemn circle around! I could not sing a bit well. . . .
>
> Presently more singing was wanted and as people seemed talking in the bigger room, I asked to have the piano put back in the little room, that I might not spoil the talking, but sing quietly to anyone who wanted to hear me. I had got half thro' my song when in tripped Leighton, came up to me, stooped over, and confidentially

asked me "what I was singing and who was the composer"? The comicality of it struck me so strongly that I burst out laughing, and so did everyone else – as if I could sing and answer his questions at the same time – We had a glorious laugh.

Clearly there was more than a touch of 'status incongruence'[21] in her complex position of social equal, friend, relative – and unpaid entertainer. 'I felt like a street singer.'

She was also often asked to sing at large Charity Concerts in aid of some good cause, whether fund-raising for schools for the poor – Harrow National Schools, Sheffield schools, Berkshire and Surrey schools – or for a Children's Hospital. These were not always in salubrious settings. On 2 February 1866 she rehearsed in the dusty National School Hall in Harrow – 'a little water was sprinkled and the worst of the dirt was swept away – but it still was horribly dirty'. Jeanie would also sing to the sick or dying as a personal offering of solace when begged to come. For instance in 1867 she went to Dickens' son-in-law, Charley Collins, who was dying from cancer and sang him the Handel arias he had asked for. She would also sing to George Eliot's terminally ill stepson Thorney Lewes, and, on 21 June 1868, to Miss Smith, the dying sister of her father's young first wife.

But the people she loved to sing to most of all were the poor – whether at 'penny gaffs' in Lambeth and Sheffield or at the Girls' Industrial School, or at a party for blind poor organized by Octavia Hill or for Octavia's regular tenants' concerts in Marylebone 'courts' or else to 'her' navvies in Wandsworth while they were having their morning 'snap', or to 'her' old women in the local Workhouse infirmary. It would almost certainly have been the only time in their lives that these people ever heard great music – or such a singer.

The last aspect of Jeanie Senior's music-making that deserves attention was her work as a professional voice teacher. Her motive was money. After the thunder-bolt of Nassau's father's hostile will, June 1864, their debts had begun to accumulate. By 2 October 1866 she could not even afford to visit Walter at Rugby – 'we must not spend an unnecessary penny'. When a Miss Clark 'coolly invited herself' to Elm House in order to be given a free singing lesson it was the last straw. 'Tiresome girl – I've really not time to give music lessons unless I am paid for it!!' (24 October 1866). And by the following February 'till Father gets some paid work we must not spend an unnecessary shilling'. She even sold the horse she had been doctoring in order to pay some bills and day-dreamed fruitlessly about writing a successful novel. At last, in December 1867, after she had received £50 payment for Helen's first half-year, she realized that she could put her expertise as a singer to profitable use. If she could not be a professional performer, might she not at least make money as a teacher of young women from wealthy or aristocratic families? She had already had the occasional grateful paying pupil. But she must find many more. In fact, she had been earning money ever since November 1860, by taking in her relatives as paying guests under her roof, 'taking in lodgers' as she called it;[22] but no one outside their family had needed to know that money had changed hands. Now, however, she would have to let it be known in public that she was a professional singing teacher. And to the conventional-minded of her own class that meant losing caste as a lady. Mid 19th century England excluded

> all females who [laboured] either with their fingers or with their heads, for *remuneration*, from the rank and privileges of gentle-women . . . A woman who works . . . [was] looked upon as degraded, as separated for ever from the class in which she [was] born; this false pride, and this abject fear of the loss of caste, warp and destroy [women's] energies.[23]

Jeanie Senior, however seems to have had absolutely no fear of losing caste by working for pay. Whether or not she had read Barbara Leigh Smith Bodichon's pamphlet Women and Work, written just ten years earlier in 1857, she would have endorsed its every word:

> It seems hardly worth while to say that there is a prejudice against women accepting money for their work. . . .
> [But] what every woman, no less than every man, should have to depend upon, is an ability after some fashion or other, to turn labour into money. . . .
> Most of the work of the world must be done for money. . . . To insist on work for love of Christ only, to cry up gratuitous work, is a profound and mischievous mistake. It tends to lessen the dignity of necessary labour; as if work for daily bread could not be for love of Christ too! . . .[24]

But there were some raised eyebrows within Jeanie Senior's own family. Even her brother Tom, usually so radical and so sympathetic, seemed to her to be prejudiced and critical. On 31 January 1868 he had to apologize:

> Dearest Jeanie,
> How could I have been such an oaf as to say such things as you attribute to me on Sunday last? Indeed, dear, if I said you were mad to take pupils I ought to have been flogged. . . . I do hope we may get something for Nassau before long. . . .

> I will be more careful of my tongue, dear, . . . I am, believe me,
> sure . . . you will always act from the highest possible motives and
> in such a way as to make me proud of having such a sister.[25]

Was Tom Hughes influenced by his wife Fan's horror that a lady, her own
sister-in-law, the sister of an MP, should now openly seek paid work? Or had
he called his sister 'mad' because he was afraid she would collapse from
exhaustion? Hence his 'I do hope we get something for Nassau before long'.

On 13 February 1868 Jeanie Senior had to make her position clear to her
younger, much wealthier friend Anny Thackeray:

> Annie [sic] Thackeray asked me whether I would give Gussie
> Ritchie some lessons in singing – of course I was glad to accept. If
> Gussie comes to me I shall only ask her half a guinea – if I go to
> her I shall ask for 15 shillings. Old Annie 'hardly dared' ask me for
> fear I should be offended! So I said 'do you take me for a horrid
> snob?' I am not ashamed of honestly earning money.

Four years later she would spell out her attitude yet again, writing to the
American magnate John Forbes. She told him openly: 'I am proud to say I
make some very tidy earnings with giving singing lessons, and am immensely
proud that I can contribute to the family purse. . . . Here people think it a
sin to be poor!'[26]

In 1868 Jeanie Senior took in another young paying guest to live at Elm
House, Jessie Hazelhurst, as both ordinary pupil and singing pupil for £150
a year. She was also giving regular lessons to 'Lady Belper's girl', Gussie
Ritchie, Miss O'Shaugnessy, Miss Wilson, Miss Theodosia Marshall, Miss
Effie Wedgwood and Lady Adeane, among others. It was exhausting work.
Once, just after bringing an injured, very cross, ten year-old Willie Hughes
safely home after his several weeks in hospital, she had an interesting heart
to heart talk on the subject of music teaching with Clara Schumann, who
taught Master Classes in Piano:

> She is an old dear [she was all of forty-nine to Jeanie's thirty-nine],
> so simple and nice. She told me she could only give two lessons a
> day for that she put her whole soul into her lesson-giving and was
> so tired after she had given two that she was fit for nothing more.
> (12 March 1868)

By the end of that year Jeanie Senior also felt worn out. 'I had so hoped
Father might get some work and then I need have had no more pupils – such
a relief' (10 December 1868). The one person who did encourage her to
teach was Jenny Lind, who wrote:

More than thanks for your charming, genuine letter; you are a
born artist, that is what you are. . . . I should like to know you
are earning two thousand a year by giving singing lessons in
London. . . . [Why] should you not, in the prime still of life and
strength, do . . . work which would be both honourable and profitable to yourself, and a benefit to many? (23 November 1869)[27]

Jeanie Senior did not hand over all her earnings to her husband, as theo-
retically the law still required of married women in Britain then. For it was
she who had total charge of all the worrying family finances, juggling bills,
lying in bed sleepless over debts. On 1 November 1868 she reported to
Walter: 'Father growls about the hotel expense' of her forthcoming overnight
visit to her son at Rugby, adding roundly: 'I think when I work so hard I
have earned my treat'.

It has been said, apropos of the professional diva or operatic star, evoked in
such 19th century women's literary texts as George Sand's Consuelo[28] or
George Eliot's Armgart[29] that their singing voices are presented as 'vehicles
. . . for empowering women.'[30] Victorian culture traditionally placed women
on the side of silence. But the diva, in contrast, was a woman who had

preeminently and indisputably *gained a voice*. . . . which, impor-
tantly, no man could . . . displace . . . [and so won] the attention,
admiration and respect of the world. . . . A female success in a
male realm, [she was privileged] to probe, revise and even reject the
traditional gender code.[31] (my emphasis)

How far might that also have been true of the great amateur singer and
professional voice teacher, Mrs. Nassau Senior? Did her undoubted acclaim
as she 'gained a voice' through music, so increase her confidence that, eventually, she would not only sing, but would also, dare to speak out in her own
voice at last, no longer hiding behind initials or a male alias, in the larger
political world of men? It should not be forgotten that the German word for
'Suffrage', is 'Stimmrecht' – 'the right to a voice'.

Whatever might be the later political implications of Jeanie Senior's life as
a publicly applauded singer, the therapeutic role that music played in her
private life cannot be exaggerated. There is no need to labour the tremendous contrast between all those hours when she was immersed in family
worries or else plunged into rescue work in some of the most dismal places
in London, and those other times of rich stimulus, relief and release when she
was absorbed by music. What an escape she had, once she was singing at her

piano or listening to Joachim playing Bach's Chaconne in the dark. Music was her 'better world' on earth.[32]

> 'I sang and dear Joachim accompanied me and I was very happy.' (8 March 1871).

Friendships

Jeanie Senior badly needed friends. When Nassau was not demanding that she amuse him or nurse him, he rebuffed her, even shutting his study door upon her. 'Father says that he likes best being alone!! So I leave him with his novels and his pipes' (17 May 1865). She was driven to seek alternative close relationships – with her mother, her son, her widowed younger brother Hastings. But her mother was ageing and infirm, Walter was away for most of each year and Hastings either abroad or absorbed in business worries. That left friends.

She had two kinds of men friends in the 1860s: the Watts kind and the Mérimée kind. Both went to her for sympathy but the former were depressive as well as needy, while the latter were dynamic and answered her need to hero-worship. In the first category were a Colonel Peirse, usually referred to as 'the melancholy Peirse', the elderly journalist W. R. Greg,[33] referred to as 'the faithful Greg' and the landowner and scholar Sir Edward Strachey.[34] All three would call on her, hoping to find her alone and crossly jealous when they did not. And all three talked interminably, however late the hour. It was a measure of her loneliness inside crowded Elm House that even the company of these bores was preferable to being left with Nassau's closed door.

Her dynamic men friends she would see outside Elm House. They included her charismatic singing teacher, Manuel Garcia, the exuberant poly-math, playwright and journalist Tom Taylor,[35] and her doctor, Guineau de Mussy. All three were, allegedly, notorious 'ladies' men'. And all three extended their habitual gallantry to Jeanie Senior. But she was wary of flir-tation and found Tom Taylor particularly gushing – 'he calls all the men "dear boy" and all the women "darling" (17 October 1867). She was emotionally drawn to her Dr. de Mussy, feeling deeply in his debt for his undoubted devotion as well as his professional help to her family. She also loved both the Scottish psychiatrist, Dr. (later Sir) Arthur Mitchell,[36] and his wife Margaret. 'I can't tell which of them I love and admire most' (20 April 1873). As for the maestro Joachim, she graduated from awe-struck worship of his genius to a mutually respectful, affectionate intimacy. She was one of the few people who would ask him to dine at her home and deliberately not ask him to perform.

17 From top clockwise: Dr. de Mussy, Garcia, Tom Taylor, W. R. Greg. From Jeanie Senior's photo album. Courtesy of Mrs. Pamela Milne.

Nassau does not seem to have minded his wife's men friends so long as they made no demand on him to leave his smoking room and be sociable. It was Jeanie's love for Walter and for her brothers of which he was deeply jealous. He himself was partial to girls who encouraged him to do a little flirting himself, which his wife tolerated in her turn. She welcomed any spur to sociability. On 25 June 1866: 'Father flirted with Louisa Hallé [daughter of the pianist Charles Hallé]. It was quite delightful to see him talk so much to any one.' Later he was very susceptible to the coquettish charm of a young relative: 'Conny has turned Father round her finger! He's taking her to the play, little wretch. . . . Father's already been to call on her this morning!' (24 October 1869). Some weeks later young Conny went up to see 'her dear old Nassau' and remained shut up with him (20 November 1869).

Jeanie Senior's friendships with women went much deeper. As has already been suggested, her dearest – and most glamorous – friend in the early 1860s was Adelaide Sartoris. Adelaide, niece of Sarah Siddons, and sister of the actress Fanny Kemble, had been an opera star, famous throughout Europe for her *Norma*, her *Somanambula*, her *Ana Bolena* and her *Lucia di Lammermoor*, not to mention her Susannah in the *Marriage of Figaro*. Her friends and associates had included Chopin and George Sand, as well as Adelina Patti, Rachel and Liszt.[37]

> It was not only the welcome and the atmosphere of her home that she gave us, but the romance of it all, and the interests of every kind. The very people she had known seemed to be there too; the things which had struck her, to be happening again, with the accompaniment of her brilliant comment, her vivacious and most memorable talk.[38]

Adelaide gave Jeanie both affection and a professional's affirmation of her musicianship, including many opportunities for Jeanie herself to sing to great applause. In her turn, Jeanie Senior encouraged the older woman to use her married wealth in practical, socially beneficent ways: 'Inspired by her friend Jeanie Senior, she visited the poor and sick on the [Warnford] estate, and she and May [her daughter] ran a school for poor children, giving a large portion of their time and energy to their work.'[39]

Jeanie was not uncritical of Adelaide when it came to her dealings with her problem son Algy, for Adelaide would shower excessive indulgence on him one day only to inflict bitter public reproaches on the boy the next:

> I don't think Adelaide right in saying the things she does to Algy. Did you hear her say that he could not go to Victoria, Australia

because he 'had neither moral principle nor the desire to exert himself'? I don't think a mother should say those things to her boy before people. (11 May 1867)

But then Jeanie heard herself pontificating as though she had all the answers: 'Oh dear! . . . perhaps I am as injudicious in my way as she is in hers . . . Everyone is liable to mistake sometimes.' Whatever their occasional differences on son-rearing, Jeanie Senior was still the first person Adelaide Sartoris wanted to see on returning to England from the continent[39] and Jeanie, her 'dearest and most valued friend', would be the only non-relative invited to her daughter's wedding.

An uneasy third in that friendship was the tall, beautiful, complicated Jane Brookfield, known to her friends as JOB – the mother of the Rugby school-

18 Adelaide Kemble Sartoris. From Jeanie Senior's photo album. Courtesy of Mrs. Pamela Milne.

boy bullied by Algy Sartoris. She could be in high spirits but she could also become almost suicidally depressed, tormented by jealousy of those, like Jeanie, whom she suspected of being better liked than she was. She particularly wished to come first with Joachim and with Dr. de Mussy, not to mention with the Benzons, the Lehmanns and Adelaide Sartoris herself. Mrs. Brookfield, as the beloved of Thackeray, had become the intimate, unofficial stepmother of the two Thackeray daughters, whose own mother was confined, insane, in a nursing home. Jeanie was very fond of both the Thackeray girls but she liked Anny more, sensing that the prettier Minny always managed to do what she wanted, and had the whip hand. Anny, who was ten years younger than Jeanie, had a genius for sympathy and a rippling vein of humour with which she concealed her underlying vulnerability to depression.[41] By 1864 Anny was no longer calling her 'Mrs. Nassau' but 'dearest Jeannie' [sic], saying:

> Yesterday I saw our poor JOB who seemed very sad and out of spirits and touched me by pulling 2 little notes out of her pocket – she said she carried them about like a sort of charm to cheer her and one was yours and other was mine. I think the two letters must have rubbed up very happily together in her pocket. Mine at least was very proud of the company it was keeping.[42]

When Minny Thackeray became engaged to Leslie Stephen, in December 1866 it, was to Elm House that her elder sister Anny went to cry and be comforted:

> Poor dear Annie is divided between joy to see Minnie so happy and sorrow at the wrench that the engagement is to herself – She has been father mother sister brother and friend to Minnie, and yet of course Leslie is now first in Min's heart. And tho' this is quite natural and right, still it is a trial for dear Annie who has literally *lived* for Minnie . . . (15 December 1866)

After Minnie's wedding six months later, Anny again went straight to Jeanie: 'Poor old Annie said that she behaved very well, but that she was glad to come and have a good cry with me' (21 June 1867). Then, when Jeanie and her mother were stricken by the death of young Arthur Hughes in India, also in June 1867, it was Anny who condoled with them:

> My dear dearest Jeanie. How full our hearts are for you and your dearest Mother. . . . – Only a few days ago we were speaking of you all and of Arthur – such a bright young life so kind and brave – such a dear young fellow. Who will not be sorry and sad – and

for those who know you with your tender hearts, dear mother and daughter, it seems like a trouble come to our own home to know of your pain. . . . (n.d. July 1867)[43]

Recognizing that Anny Thackeray's worst enemy as a writer was her own disorganized, compulsive restlessness, which was her way to ward off depression, Jeanie Senior would offer her the chance to work, quiet and concentrated, at Elm House. 'She is longing to write but never finds time! (27 June 1868). 'She can write well, if only she gives herself time' (24 March 1870).

Jeanie Senior's musical friendships, not only with Adelaide Sartoris but also with the Lehmanns, Benzons, Joachim, Clara Schumann, Jenny Lind Goldschmidt, and especially with Amelia, young Mrs. Rudolf Lehmann, have already been mentioned. In the world of art, her women friends included that great, fanatical photographer Julia Margaret Cameron, young Kate Collins and Marie Spartali. Jeanie had first encountered Julia Margaret Cameron in Freshwater on the Isle of Wight on 3 June 1865:

> She was dressed in a yellow linsey woolsey with purple velvet sleeves. – She is very droll, but I like her because I feel that she is good and true. But she must be a trial to live with I think, for geniuses like Mrs. Cameron cannot be punctual or tidy, and her house is in a state of disorder that would drive me mad. No wonder it is untidy for all the maids are either sitting for their photos or printing photos or packing up photos. I hope when you marry you will not have a genius . . .

Mrs. Cameron tried to photograph Jeanie. Her attempt, showing Jeanie holding up her pendant watch, was a failure, although one does get an idea of her subject's 'presence' and gentle seriousness. Julia Margaret Cameron's subsequent twenty-six page letter to Jeanie is wonderfully characteristic and ends with the tribute:

> We are not one of us likely to forget you, for once to know you is also to know how much is lost to one for a long season until opportunity unfolds the richness of good and great natures and even as the golden hair astonished and took me by storm so much more did the golden heart win us all by its true and tender sympathies . . .
> Your affectionate Julia Margaret Cameron.[44]

19 Jeanie Senior photographed by Julia Margaret Cameron, June 1865. Courtesy of Mrs. Pamela Milne.

A very different, younger artist, the alluring Kate Collins, née Dickens, aroused Jeanie's sympathetic concern, as well as Walter's calf-love. She had married the middle-aged painter Charley Collins, younger brother of Wilkie Collins, in 1860 when she was just twenty-one, in order to get away from the tense, unhappy Dickens home. Her husband soon fell incurably ill and the 'fascinating Kate Collins', who modelled for Millais and other painters, was said to console herself with lovers including the artist Val Prinsep. The respectable would not sit by her side of the room.[45] Jeanie Senior tried to help the young couple. She wrote to Walter on 26 January 1867:

> I went to see Katie – Charlie was a little better. Katie sent you her love . . . She looks very tired, poor little dear, for she gets no real rest, she only lies on chairs at night, never really goes to bed. . . . She comes out so much in this trouble. . . .

Eventually Jeanie was relieved to see Dickens' daughter beginning to find her own creative self at last: '[She] has taken up drawing quite seriously, and draws and paints for many hours regularly every day (20 November 1869).[46]

Still more beautiful, more gifted but also in a desperate situation was young Marie Spartali who soon became a protégée of Jeanie Senior. Born in

20   From top clockwise: Anny Thackeray, photographed by Julia Margaret Cameron, 1870; Jane Brookfield, aged 30, painted by Richmond; Marie Spartali. From Jeanie Senior's photo album. Courtesy of Mrs. Pamela Milne.

1843, the daughter of a wealthy Anglo-Greek family in London where her father eventually became Greek Consul, Marie Spartali had wanted to be a painter since childhood. She was taken under the wing of Ford Madox Brown as model and student and also modelled for D. G. Rossetti, for Edward Burne-Jones, and for Julia Margaret Cameron. Her looks have been compared to those of Jane Morris: 'The two marvels had many points in

common: the same lofty stature, the same long sweep of limb, the "neck like
a tower", the night-dark tresses and the eyes of mystery.'[47] Her stunning
beauty, heightened by extraordinary Renaissance clothes in mid-Victorian
England, made her the cynosure of adoring male eyes including those of
Hastings Hughes. After several unhappy entanglements, Marie Spartali
finally defied her father in 1871, enraging him by marrying the American art
critic, William Stillman, a widower with three children whose wife had
recently killed herself.[48]

   At first Jeanie Senior had responded to the Spartali sisters as just a breath-
taking spectacle:

> [The] girls looked glorious. Marie had on a white gown with cross
> bars of yellow satin and black velvet and the deepest crimson roses
> in her bosom and crimson and yellow ones in her hair and coral
> and yellow amber on her neck and arms and a fan of scarlet feath-
> ers hung to her waist . . . and [she wore] a lot of her splendid hair
> down her back. (3 July 1868)

   But Jeanie soon realized that there was a great deal more to Marie Spartali
than her self-presentation as an Italian painting come to life.[49] ['Darling]
Marie' would become one of her dearest younger friends, cherished for her
warmth of heart as well as her giftedness. She even enabled her and Stillman
meet secretly at Elm House, though she herself did not much like the
humourless Stillman – 'an awful prig [who] can have no playfulness in him'
(31 January 1872).

   By the late 1860s Jeanie Senior was increasingly involved with a quite different world than that of High Society Bohemia – the world of urgent social
intervention. And there she made very different women friends. The tremendous impact upon her of young Octavia Hill has already been described.
Another socially beneficent, though much older, friend was Jeanie's neighbour on Clapham Common. The remarkable 'Miss Thornton', born in 1797
into the circle of the philanthropic Clapham Sect Evangelicals,[50] now lived
with her niece-cum-adoptive daughter, thirty year-old Henrietta Synnot.
Both women were highly intelligent and very active in financing and running
local schools, including a free 'Ragged School', an Infant School and an inex-
pensive school for Tradesmens' Daughters, all before the 1870 Education
Act. Jeanie warmed to the older woman's benignancy and sought a more
informal closeness with her – 'Oh! do call me Jeanie dearest Miss Thornton.
I have so often wished you would. – I shall think you are angry with me if
ever you call me anything else!' (n.d., c. 1869). Henrietta Synnot was also

21   Marianne Thornton, aged 76, drawn by Richmond; Caroline Stephen aged 30, from Jeanie Senior's photo album. Courtesy of Mrs. Pamela Milne.

devoted to Jeanie, and would become her capable assistant – and demanding friend.

Different again was Caroline Stephen, born in 1834, the younger sister of Leslie and Fitzjames Stephen. Her fineness of intellect and depth of spirit were perceived by Jeanie long before they were appreciated by any one else. To her brothers she was just 'Milly', sensitive and devoted, of course, to their invalid mother, but hardly interesting, being hopelessly emotional.[51] Caroline Stephen, like other members of the Society of Friends – which she later joined – combined an inward spiritual 'seeking' with a need to serve society. Jeanie had admired her independence of spirit from the outset: 'She is very clever and most charming, the most original girl I know and quite without affectation' (8 February 1866). On 28 June 1866 Jeanie Senior reported to Walter that Caroline Stephen was now writing for *The Saturday Review*.[52] 'She is very clever as well as very nice. 'After her visit to the Sisters of Mercy in Paris, Caroline Stephen reported back to Jeanie and on 29 June 1868 Jeanie wrote: 'I had dear Cary Stephen this morning when I came back from the workhouse. She is more pleasant than ever I think. We had a delightful long talk about her book [on nursing, Service of the Poor].' It is hard to decide whether she or Octavia Hill would influence Jeanie Senior more profoundly.

What emerges from this short, incomplete overview of Jeanie Senior's friends throughout the 1860s is their diversity. She was very responsive to beauty, vitality and intelligence – but above all to warmth and seriousness – in both sexes. Many of these friends would provide critically important support for her coming work. And it was a tribute both to Jeanie Senior and to her friends, that she would turn to them in her desperation about Nassau, and that they never refused her:

> Writing all morning . . . to Sir Alexander Duff-Gordon, . . . Mrs. Prinsep wrote for us . . . visited Fanny du Quaire to get her to ask . . . went on to ask Mrs. Benzon to ask; . . . Dr. de Mussy got the French Ambassador to speak for Nass. . . . approached Mrs. Brookfield and she approached Mr. Cole. . . . Greg advises. . . .

While Kate Collins lobbied Lord Cockburn.

What also emerges is that a sure way to Jeanie's heart was her awareness of her friends' troubles. Peirse and Greg both had wretched marital lives; the Mitchells had lost their only little girl; Julia Margaret Cameron's daughter died in her sixth childbirth; both Adelaide Sartoris and Jane Brookfield knew disappointment and tension in marriage, as well as acute anxiety over their sons. Anny Thackeray's loss of her sister Minny, Kate and Charlie Collins' ordeal by cancer, Marie Spartali's conflict with her father, Octavia Hill's collapse from exhaustion, Caroline Stephen's near-incarceration with her sick, aged mother – all these situations 'spoke' to Jeanie's sympathy. She bore out Rousseau's First Maxim in Emile: 'It is not in human nature to put ourselves in the place of those who are happier than ourselves, but only in the place of those who can claim our pity.'[53] Hence it does not come as a shock, when, on 16 October 1866, she reported to Walter that Octavia Hill, whose sister had recently married George Eliot's stepson Charles Lewes,

> . . . told me how deeply poor Mrs. Lewis [sic] feels her isolation from all women, for hardly any will go near her and no nice ones will know her. Miss Hill drew so touching a picture of the sadness and repentance of Mrs. Lewis' life that I offered to go and see Mrs. Lewis if Miss Hill thought that a visit would be acceptable.

In that not very promising way began Jeanie Senior's significant relationship with George Eliot.

CHAPTER NINE

George Eliot's Dorothea?

Blonde, blue-eyed, conventionally handsome, a little matronly, Jeanie Senior was precisely *not* the sort of woman who normally aroused the novelist's interest. One remembers foolish, blonde Mrs. Tulliver and the other Dodson sisters, or blonde, light-minded Rosamond Vincy, in contrast to dark-haired Maggie Tulliver who bursts out: 'I'm determined to read no more books where the blond-haired women carry away all the happiness . . . I want to avenge Rebecca and Flora MacIvor, and Minna and all the rest of the dark unhappy ones.'[1] But the steady, earnest eyes, the beautiful speaking voice and the unmistakeable genuineness of her visitor must have won George Eliot over; she unbent towards Jeanie.

And Jeanie Senior's response to George Eliot? It was the first time in her life that she was in the same room with a woman who was notorious, a free-thinker in religion and technically 'fallen' – for she openly 'lived in sin' with a married man (who was also with them in that room). Her letter to sixteen year-old Walter at Rugby, 21 October 1866, is acutely conscious that, by calling on George Eliot, she has done something to shock many in her circle:

> Please do not notice this in any of your letters, nor tell it to anyone. I am anxious to keep it quiet that I know her, as it might pain people who can't understand my reasons for knowing her. Hers is a very sad story which I will tell you some day, and she has set the world at defiance by living with a man who cannot marry her. His wife ran away from him, but he could not get a divorce, so as to marry this lady, who is called Mrs. Lewis [sic] . . . Of course I consulted Father. He did not mind it, and as I need consult no one but him, I am glad to think that I can give the poor woman any pleasure. If I had daughters I could not do as I liked in the matter, for fear of injuring them should it come to be known; but I may do what I think right and kind, . . .

But once she had taken the decisive step and visited 'the poor woman', Jeanie Senior had no further doubts about her: 'I liked Mrs. Lewis very much. She has a very attractive face though I suppose most people would think it very plain. The expression is charming . . . ' And she ends her letter defiantly: 'I shall go and see her whenever I can, for I am much drawn to her' (21 October 1866).

Over the four years between that first meeting and November 1870, when George Eliot began writing about Dorothea Brooke, Jeanie Senior became her valued friend. At the end of May 1867 his mother reported to Walter: 'She is a very nice woman indeed, so gentle and sweet'. George Eliot 'took to' Jeanie in return, as recently discovered, unpublished letters now held in the British Library make clear.[2] Jeanie's singing, of course, was a joy to the deeply musical Leweses,[3] and her kindness and genuineness were also quickly appreciated: 'I am not given to excessive belief in "people's" love for me, but when you say anything I believe you, and that you care for us is an assurance which it is very pleasant to believe' (14 March 1868).[4]

Several letters to Jeanie from George Eliot show that she became a much-valued, supportive friend in the misery that then suddenly afflicted the Priory. On 7 May 1869 young Thornton Lewes, George Eliot's unofficial step-son, had returned to England from Natal, pitifully wasted and in terrible pain. He was suffering from undiagnosed tuberculosis of the spine and at first could only lie on the floor in agony. Jeanie Senior was acutely reminded of the desperate attempts to nurse Harry through his advanced tuberculosis eight years before. Something of her practical experience and her acquaintance with grief must have been communicated to George Eliot. 'One finds out those who have real practical sympathy in times of trouble' (26 May 1869).[5] The novelist wrote to Jeanie in pitiful detail about what they were all going through, feeling that she could confide in her:

> The Priory, June 22, 1869.
>
> My dear Mrs Senior,
> Since we saw your bright face troubles have accumulated on us. Our boy has had more frequent attacks of pain . . . .
>
> Thornie has not listened to any music for the last weeks [Jeanie had gone several times to sing to him earlier] and we feel so worn in body and spirit that we cannot enjoy even the sight of a friend. Doubtless better moments will come.[6]

A week afterwards Jeanie was no longer 'My dear Mrs. Senior' but 'My dear Friend':

> Grateful thanks! Things are a little better with our poor lad just now but we rejoice in any improvement with inward trembling lest it should be the introduction for a new relapse, as it has always been hitherto. Come on Saturday, pray, . . .
>
> We shall be cheered by the sight of you, Ever yours affectionately . . .[7]

Just a few days later, 7 July 1869, George Eliot wrote in response to Jeanie's urgent, concerned enquiry: 'Yes! We are in better spirits. The boy suffers less and Paget [the physician] is hopeful. It is good to know that your tender heart is beating in the world.'[8]

On 4 October 1869 George Eliot wrote a letter to Jeanie Senior revealing a quite different side to the relationship between the two women, one other than that of benefactress and beneficiary in time of trouble, showing that a discussion had been going on between them, we do not know for how long, about the advisability or otherwise of University education for women

> My dear Friend,
>
> . . . I have read your last letter to me several times, and bless you with all my heart for conscientiously reconsidering your opinion. That is, to my mind, the most important sign of spiritual life – to be able always to reconsider one's conclusions and go well over the process by which they have been arrived at.
>
> I have no personal knowledge of Mrs. Manning[9] and no practical connexion with the proposed college, beyond subscribing to it, and occasionally answering questions which Miss Davies[10] has put to me about the curriculum which would be desirable.

There follows George Eliot's well-known declaration that she is no simplistic 'Women's Rights' feminist. It is not usually noted that this passage occurs in the middle of a letter in which George Eliot is not arguing with a feminist, but is trying, instead, to reassure a *non*-feminist that she herself is not a feminist of the more rabid, man-hating, kind.

> I feel too deeply the difficult complications that beset every measure likely to affect the position of women and also I feel too imperfect a sympathy with many women who have put themselves forward in connexion with such measures, to give any practical adhesion to them.[11] There is no subject on which I am more inclined to hold my peace and learn, than on the "Woman Question." . . .

But there is a But.

> But on one point I have a strong conviction, and I feel bound to act on it, so far as my retired way of life [a discreet reference to her un-discreet un-legal marriage] allows of public action. And that is, that women ought to have the same fund of truth placed within their reach as men have; that their lives (i.e. the lives of men and women) ought to be passed under the hallowing influence of a common faith as to their duty and its basis. And this unity in their faith can only be produced by their having each the same store of

fundamental knowledge. It is not likely that any perfect plan for educating women can soon be found, for we are very far from having found a perfect plan for educating men. But it will not do to wait for perfection.

The force of that *credo,* declaring George Eliot's faith in the necessity for a shared, humane education for both men and women on which they could then build a shared ethic, comes from George Eliot's effort to convert her friend Jeanie Senior to one plank of the contemporary feminist platform. This is the same woman as the early Marian Evans who had written in *The Westminster Review* in 1854, 'Let the whole field of reality be laid open to woman as well as to man',[12] the same woman as the novelist who had, in 1859, created Maggie Tulliver with her 'vehement intellectual need',[13] and the same woman who had more recently written to Barbara Bodichon, 'the better Education of Women is one of the objects about which I have *no doubt'.*[14]

That long 4 October 1869 letter ends:

> I write these hasty words to show you that I valued what you said to me. But do not let any one else see this note. I have been made rather miserable lately by revelations about women,[15] and have resolved to remain silent in my sense of helplessness. I know very little about what is specially good for women – only a few things that I feel sure are good for human nature generally, and about such as these last alone, can I ever hope to write or say anything worth saying
>
> Ever yours affectionately . . .[16]

The tragedy of Thornie then took over. George Eliot shared the terrible end with Jeanie:

> Tuesday October 19, 1869
>
> Dear Friend,
>
> I have been a dumb and apparently insensible creature towards you. For the last week I have been crushed by headaches – . . . – and all the while our boy has been getting worse. We have been losing all hope that he can revive. He seems now to be sinking fast both in strength and consciousness and life at present seems only suffering. . . .
>
> Bless you for all the tender feeling you have shown both for him and for us.
>
> Ever your grateful and affectionate . . .[17]

October 20th, 1869

My dear friend,

Our boy is dead. He died last night quite peacefully. The bitterness of death is past for him, but not for me.[18]

In December of that year George Eliot wrote to her 'dear Miss Davies' of Girton College, then at Hitchin, on Jeanie Senior's behalf:

> My friend Mrs. Nassau Senior, whose name must be well known to you, is anxious to learn all about the College. She expects to be on a visit to her brother Mr. Hughes [i.e. George at Offley, near Luton] . . . about Christmas and wishes to take that opportunity of calling on Mrs. Manning – or on you if you were there.
>
> It has occurred to me that the family at the College [including the first five women students] may be dispersed by that time, so, before writing to Mrs. Senior, I think it better to trouble you with this note.
>
> Is it of any use for Mrs. Senior to call at the College about Christmas? If you can say "Yes," I am sure you will oblige me by doing all you can to prepare a pleasant reception for her, since you are the only lady connected with the College to whom I am personally known. I have a high esteem for Mrs. Senior. She is a woman who tries to put her beliefs into action and after having been prejudiced by others [Fan? Minnie?] against the College, she is anxious to found her judgment on fuller knowledge. . . .[19]

On 10 December 1869 George Eliot wrote to Jeanie:

> [You] will be wondering that I have not answered your request about the College at Hitchin.
>
> I wrote to Miss Davies . . . Last night I had a note from Miss Davies – "My friend Mrs. Austin will be here during the Christmas vacation, and will be very glad to receive Mrs. Senior and show her as much of the College as will be left when the spirit is absent."[20]

It was a characteristically tart response from Emily Davies, but not unreasonable.

Just a fortnight earlier, George Eliot had written Jeanie a short, mysterious note:

> Dear Friend,
>
> We shall rejoice to see you on Tuesday, but when you do not fulfil an expressed intention, be sure that I shall never impute it to slackness of conscience.

I could not help crying over your letter, and the consciousness that we can do nothing to relieve you of your anxieties.

Always yours affectionately . . . (4 February 1870).[21]

What could Jeanie Senior have written to make George Eliot cry? She must have been apologizing in advance for any failure on her part to keep an appointment at The Priory as promised, explaining her situation at Elm House, with its countless conflicting, responsibilities that tied her down by every hair, like a female Gulliver in Lilliput. Jeanie Senior was depressed just then by having had to part yet again with Walter, happily off to Oxford. ' . . . [It] is as drear as usual without you. It is of no use disguising the fact that the house is utterly horrid. . . . ' (1–2 February 1870). She herself had been ill with nagging pain from her tumour, their governess, 'that poor girl Miss Rogers', had also fallen ill and now had such dreadful headaches that Jeanie had to teach Hastings' two youngest children herself. And on top of all there was the illness of Nassau's mother, now also installed at Elm House, who one day would seem to be recovering but the next be at death's door.

A very different response to her friend's account of her life, and to her longing to do more with it, was expressed in a highly significant letter from George Eliot, 13 March 1870:

Dear Friend,

Bless you first of all for being a good woman, and next for being good to me. . . .

Keep a little love for me till we come back, for I shall think of you as one of the friends who make an English home dear, and enter into my life quite out of proportion to the number of times that I see them. One lives by faith in human goodness, the only guarantee that there can be any other sort of goodness in the universe. See how diffusive your one little life may be. I say that apropos of your longing for a wider existence.

Think of me often as [yours] always affectionately, M.E. Lewes.[22]

'One lives by faith in human goodness' . . . suggests that the two women may have been discussing faith in humanity and faith in something that transcends humanity – a faith to which Jeanie Senior clung, but which, of course, George Eliot did not possess. The novelist seems to be saying that everyone lives in fact by faith in *human* goodness, and that it was only through her own conviction that *Jeanie* was good that any other, wider faith – in 'goodness in the universe' could begin to be imaginable. One is reminded of the novelist's famous, later letter to Mary Ponsonby, December 1874, in which she wrote: 'the idea of God, so far as it has been a high spiritual influence, is the ideal of a goodness entirely human'.[23] It is Jeanie in whom George Eliot believes, and who gives to all those who know her the idea of something exalted in the universe at large. '[How] diffusive', then, is her apparently 'little life' while she longs vainly, as she must have confessed to George Eliot, 'for a wider existence'. Events will suggest that Jeanie Senior was not consoled by such reflections.

There is a note of George Eliot's wanting, even needing, to see Jeanie Senior in a letter dated 12 November 1870:

> Dear Friend,
>
> I have been hindered from writing to you before by ailing health and spirits. But I have all the while been wanting to see you. Can you find time to get to our corner of the universe? Your sweet face would be a welcome bit of harmony with one's struggling hope and trust in these bad times [i.e. the Franco-Prussian War].
>
> Always, yours affectionately, . . .[24]

Intermittently during those two past years, from January 1869 until November 1870, George Eliot had been struggling to write *Middlemarch*. It was not, however, *Middlemarch* as we now know it. It was a Dorothea-less *Middlemarch*. Its only characters had been the idealistic, pioneering young doctor Lydgate, the Vincy family, the Garths, the miser Featherstone, the banker Bulstrode with his concealed, quasi-criminal past – together with a few representatives of the heavy bottom-pull of petty, materialistic Midlands town-life. George Eliot's use of the words 'my hero' in her Journal, 21 September 1869, suggests that she had originally intended Dr. Lydgate to triumph. But the writing of her first version of the novel had been painfully slow. Many of the reviewers of *Middlemarch* would find its realism oppressively pessimistic, even cynical. Such a response would have had still more force had they been reviewing the Dorothea-less book that George Eliot had originally planned but which she now was finding too negative to pursue.

Then, in November 1870, George Eliot suddenly began writing with great fluency a hundred pages of a quite different piece of fiction called 'Miss Brooke' about an ardent, great-souled girl who tried to put her beliefs into action but was frustrated by suffocating circumstances and a precipitate, wrong-headed marriage. At some point in January 1871 she had the inspiration that her two novels could be fused into one great Study of Provincial Life and by March of 1871 she had put together the first eighteen chapters, together with what is now chapter twenty-three and had joined the two separate beginnings into what would become *Middlemarch*.[25]

It is my view that before November 1870 George Eliot had lost confidence in her 'hero' Lydgate's capacity to vanquish all the regressive factors, both inside himself and out, a victory essential to realizing his progressive vision. Who knew better than she did the near-impossibility of winning acceptance within the provinces for exceptional gifts and unorthodoxy? Public opinion there was just another name for *Schadenfreude*. 'To be candid, in Middlemarch phraseology, meant, to use an early opportunity of letting your friends know that you did not take a cheerful view of their capacity, their conduct, or their position'; [26] Lydgate was too 'normal' a popularity-seeking man to be capable of withstanding that particular kind of 'candid' scrutiny for very long. George Eliot, therefore, had to seek elsewhere for faith in humanity at its best: 'One lives by faith in *human* goodness'.

When she turned with relief to depicting Dorothea, who, despite her appalling mis-marriage, would never renounce her altruistic idealism but would only try to practise it more fervently, despite the resistance and the scepticism all around her, George Eliot realized that she had created a heroine rather than a hero for *Middlemarch*. The fact that its 'Prelude' and 'Finale' begin and end the book with Dorothea, establishes that it is she who is to be, and she who has been, the whole work's pivotal figure. Lydgate's similar, not quite tragic, waste of potential would save the author from the charge of a simplistic feminism which sees women as being always the victims of men and is blind to any counterpart destruction of men by women. And Dorothea's difference in situation from Lydgate would give thoughtful feminists a heroine whose story they could still invoke in the 1870s. For the contemplation of an early 19th century Saint Theresa, whose constricted life prevented her from contributing what it was in her to give, energized the reader to insist that it was English society and its too limited prescriptions for women's education and work that had to be changed.[27]

But where had George Eliot met a large-souled Saint Theresa who was, it seemed, still fated to be 'a foundress of nothing' and whose 'little life' was merely 'diffusive'? It will come as no surprise that I nominate Jeanie Senior. Of course Jeanie was not a dark-haired, sexually ignorant, eighteen year-old heiress, about to rush into marriage with an elderly pedant whom she had precipitately mistaken for Milton. Neither was she at all puritanically suspicious of beauty in art and music. Quite the reverse. Nor was her mind 'theoretic'. Nevertheless, despite all these discrepancies in the externals of situation and appearance and even in some aspects of mental life, there is, in my view, the most profound resemblance in the souls of the two women, which is eloquently bodied forth in their speech. For, as she listened to her friend talk, George Eliot, who always '[heard] her characters talking', was given nothing less than a voice that could express Dorothea's ardently beneficent soul.

Jeanie Senior's earnest, eager letters to Walter, confiding, expostulating, urging, testifying to her own values, give us the best possible sense of her intimate talk, even though we cannot actually hear the cadences of the beautiful, musical, speaking voice which George Eliot herself heard. Every so often there are quite startling anticipations of the words and views of Dorothea in these letters. On 3 November 1866, for example, less than a month after the two women had first met, Jeanie Senior reproached Walter for his indifference to the bad acts of some of his fellow Rugbeians: 'We ought to grieve over all that is wrong in the world almost as if it were a personal matter instead of isolating ourselves from the sins and sorrows of our fellow-creatures'. On 14 February 1867 she wrote to him concerning Mrs. Brookfield's anxiety over her young son Arthur: 'it is only by putting yourself in the places of people that you can fairly judge of them and of their conduct'. On 21 March 1868 she pleaded with Walter, hoping for the answer 'Yes', "You will try to show him yourself, love, your own dear best self, won't you?" Dorothea was someone else who always pushed for the answer 'Yes'.[28] Then, in her letter to Walter of 8 November 1868, there is an even more significant testimony to Jeanie's (and Dorothea's) innermost faith: their shared belief in the resurrection of the soul in this world:

> I don't like you to speak of any creatures as "blackguard devils" –
> it is wrong for all reasons. Even wicked people have been made in
> the image of God, and never entirely lose His image – and if you
> and I had been born and bred amongst vicious people we should
> have been as bad, perhaps worse than they. The thing is not to call
> our fellow creatures devils, but to turn one's energies to making
> them less like devils. When you get home and have time, you may
> do your little mite towards the amelioration of others, and then
> you will recognise in everyone, even in the most degraded, a some-
> thing that holds out hope of an improvement.

Similarly, when the Rev. Farebrother reminds Dorothea that character "may become diseased as our bodies do." – "Then it may be rescued and healed" is her ringing response.[29] And Jeanie Senior's imperative to enable 'the amelioration of others' is very close to George Eliot's own belief in meliorism, and to Dorothea's 'widening the skirts of light' (*Middlemarch*, chapter 39).

Other Dorothea-like utterances include Jeanie's passionate indignation about the subhuman housing conditions of the working poor – 'the overcrowding and dirty disorder. . . . [are] a disgrace'; her grieving over all the ugly suffering that she saw in the Workhouse Infirmary; and her own sad confession to Walter of her failed mis-marriage (to which she too had engaged herself so precipitately at eighteen, twenty years before). All she had wanted was to be married to a man who wished 'to benefit his fellow creatures' (18 August 1868), 'but . . . of course one expected too much' (16 March 1870)

Jeanie Senior's total candour, her need to believe in others' goodness and her countless attempts to be of practical help, are always expressed with extreme simplicity, both of diction and sentence structure, a transparency which makes her convincing. Time and again she uses the basic monosyllables rooted in Old English. It has been said that '[it's] the monosyllables that are the life and bedrock of the language . . . Deep feeling probably comes out in monosyllables'.[30] George Eliot herself was struck by Jeanie's authenticity and deep feeling. One remembers her tributes to Jeanie: "When you say anything I believe you". "It is good to know that your tender heart is beating in the world". And "[She] is a woman who tries to put her beliefs into action."

As for the Jeanie-like echoes in Dorothea, expressed in the heroine's similarly simple, often monosyllabic, vigorous speech, we hear them time and again: 'It is not a sin to make yourself poor in performing experiments for the good of all' (*Middlemarch*, chapter 2). (We remember Jeanie's "Here people think it a sin to be poor" in her letter to John Forbes.) When we hear Dorothea say 'Oh, I hope I should be able to get the people well housed in Lowick!' (*Middlemarch*, chapter 3) we remember Jeanie's 'Oh, how I wish Mr. Ruskin would build some houses for me!' And when Dorothea is needled by Celia, she indignantly uses Jeanie's favourite word and concept, 'fellow-creatures', in her own defence, in order to justify her project:

> "*Fad* to draw plans! Do you think I only care about my fellow-creatures' houses in that childish way?"(*Middlemarch*, chapter 4)

We shall never know how much or how little Jeanie Senior told George Eliot about her disillusionment in her marriage. But no-one, least of all a brilliantly alert novelist, could have seen the eager, earnest Jeanie by the side of portly, lethargic Nassau without perceiving their deep incompatibility of soul. For here was a woman yearning to help create a better society, yoked to a man who had not a spark of altruistic idealism in him. 'Having once embarked on your marital voyage, it is impossible not to be aware that you make no way and that the sea is not within sight – that, in fact, you are exploring an enclosed basin' (*Middlemarch*, chapter 20). That life-sentence of being chained to a spouse's unbudgeable limitations, which Dorothea recognized after six weeks and which Jeanie Senior had had to face with almost equal speed, has never been expressed better.

Like Jeanie, Dorothea was 'alive to anything that gave her an opportunity for active sympathy' (*Middlemarch*, chapter 21). Like Jeanie, Dorothea had sincere, candid eyes and 'a habit of speaking with perfect genuineness' (p. 395) expressing her 'open ardent goodwill' (*Middlemarch,* chapter 22). Like Jeanie, Dorothea 'longed for work which would be directly beneficent' (*Middlemarch*, chapter 47). Like Jeanie, Dorothea had no time for hell-fire sermons as vented by Mr. Tyke on imputed righteousness and the prophesies of the Apocalypse – 'it is surely better to pardon too much, than to condemn too much' (*Middlemarch*, chapter 50). For again like Jeanie, Dorothea had 'always been finding [her] religion since [she] was a little girl' (*Middlemarch*, chapter 39).[31] Like Jeanie, Dorothea always needed to believe the best about others: 'I believe that people are almost always better than their neighbours think they are' (*Middlemarch*, chapter 72). And like Jeanie, though without her decades of practice, Dorothea believed in applying her Christianity, trying to help wherever she saw suffering or injustice: 'What do we live for, if it is not to make life less difficult to each other?' (*Middlemarch*, chapter 22) and 'How can we live and think that any one has trouble – piercing trouble – and we could help them, and never try?' (*Middlemarch*, chapter 81). Finally, like Jeanie, Dorothea is challengingly direct in her ethical imperatives both to herself and to others: "I think we have no right to come forward to urge wider changes for good, until we have tried to alter the evils which lie under our own hands" (*Middlemarch*, chapter 39). All that Mr. Brooke, her poor cornered uncle, can reply is: "Young ladies are a little ardent, you know."

'Ardent' is the word used over and over again by George Eliot for Dorothea and 'ardent' is how those who knew her best described Jeanie Senior. George Eliot herself was to call Jeanie 'a clear-eyed ardent practical woman' in her letter to her of May 1874.[32] Octavia Hill would write, in her private elegy on Jeanie: 'She was, among my many friends, one of the noblest, purest-hearted, . . . with an ardent longing to serve, a burning generosity, which put us all to shame'.[33] Tom Hughes called his sister 'the most ardent politician amongst us all' [in the Hughes family] in his *Memoir of a Brother*, and 'an ardent co-operator'.[34] The final, clinching stylistic echo or correlative, of course, is that between George Eliot's letter to Jeanie insisting on the 'diffusive' impact of her life and her unforgettable conclusion about Dorothea – 'the effect of her being on those around her was incalculably diffusive'.

Barbara Hardy, writing about the themes and imagery in George Eliot's letters to Jeanie Senior that have echoes in the themes and imagery in *Middlemarch*, suggests that it is difficult not to ascribe much of the inspiration for the Dorothea-ness of Dorothea to George Eliot's response to her new, younger friend:

> . . . *Middlemarch* . . . needed a woman character, an untragic Maggie Tulliver with larger vision and more defined talent, to be urgently ambitious and socially frustrated . . . Jane [sic] Senior's aspiration, frustration, and ability, may have inspired Miss Brooke . . . [their] longing, powers, frustrations and virtues were very similar.[35]

Or, as Leslie Stephen had put it a century before: 'We are to be brought to sympathise with the noble aspirations of a loving and unselfish spirit, conscious that it cannot receive any full satisfaction within the commonplace conditions of this prosaic world'.[36] Certainly George Eliot was vividly aware of Jeanie Senior's frustration. She wrote on 14 December 1871: 'I always bear in mind how many strings are pulling you'.[37] The novelist needed a Dorothea in order to make the spirit of *Middlemarch* not depressingly defeated and she needed Jeanie to give her faith that the Dorotheas do exist. She herself would explicitly acknowledge her debt to Jeanie Senior on 24 January 1873: ' . . . you have entered into my more cheerful beliefs and made them stronger because of the glimpses I have had of your character and life'. For how can one continue to be a meliorist if one loses faith in humans? Or, as George Eliot would say about Dorothea's impact on Lydgate: 'The presence of a noble nature generous in its wishes, ardent in its charity, changes the lights for us' (*Middlemarch*, chapter 76). The biographer Rosemary Ashton is the first person to have published a direct reference to Jeanie Senior as a Dorothea figure: 'This Dorothea who . . . found a public role, despite opposition, . . . '[38]

But if any further corroboration were needed for this theory of influence and inspiration, there is a hitherto unpublished letter from a 19th century contemporary, the wife of Sir Arthur Mitchell and one of Jeanie's most loved friends. On 2 July 1873 Margaret Mitchell thanked Jeanie for having 'ordered' her to read *Middlemarch:*

> [It] is *the* most wonderful book!
>
> I had to gallop thro' it, but I mean to take it to the country to *study* it there.
>
> It had this great fascination for me that Dorothea is <u>you</u>, only not nearly so nice as my dearest Jeanie. She had not your fine tact which is such a blessed gift to you and enables you to take people always on their best side whereas my poor Dorothea was at the beginning very often putting her foot down in the wrong place and was even a little hard sometimes, but in her great loving heart, in her desire to benefit all the world, and in her perfect self forgetfulness she is just you. . . .[39]

In 'real life', George Eliot tried to be a good friend to Jeanie Senior. Ludicrously, but predictably, Jeanie in her desperation asked even the greatest living English novelist to help her try to get Nassau a job. On 2 January 1871 George Eliot found herself lobbying T. H. Huxley for Nassau's appointment as Chief Secretary to the Education Board. All she could vouch for was that others had told her that Nassau had 'some of the moral qualities which help to make a good public servant and fellow-worker'. His only real recommendation was that he had 'chosen an excellent wife. . . . a very good, sweet woman – Mrs. Nassau Senior'.[40] She also wrote that same day to Emily Davies:

> I am interested in [Mr. Nassau Senior] for the sake of his wife – *one of the best women I know* [my emphasis]. But the best of wives is not a good reason for a man's election to an important office, and I am far from undertaking to recommend Mr Senior to you as the fittest candidate, since I know nothing of his rivals.[41]

Nassau was not appointed.

When *Middlemarch* was published Jeanie Senior responded with naïve wonder – 'she writes better than anyone!' (4 February 1872) On 13 November 1872 she went to dine with George Eliot – 'I had a delightful talk over *Middlemarch*'. But unfortunately she goes into no more detail. On 4 December 1872 she exclaimed to Walter: '*Middlemarch* is next to Shakespeare. The last volume is splendid. Dorothea the divine. It is a grand book indeed; and she [George Eliot] is blessed amongst women for having shown us such a noble ideal woman.'[42] How telling that Jeanie should have used the invocation to Mary, Mother of God, for the woman creator of a female redeemer. Emilia Pattison, the young, beautiful, clever and dissatisfied wife of the elderly Rev. Mark Pattison, thought by some to be the original of Mr. Casaubon,[43] '[considered] herself the model of Dorothea'.[44] But anyone who considers herself the model of a heroic altruist cannot, *ipso facto*, be that model. Fittingly, Jeanie Senior, who had a far stronger claim, could see no resemblance to herself at all. (Again like Dorothea, who was 'open, ardent and not in the least self-admiring', *Middlemarch*, chapter 1.)

There is another irony. In the very months that George Eliot was writing about her great-souled heroine, who had a Theresa's 'passionate, ideal nature' but whose 'spiritual grandeur [was] ill-matched with the meanness of opportunity' (Prelude) and so was fated to be a 'foundress of nothing', Jeanie Senior was helping to found a great humanitarian organization that exists to this day.

CHAPTER TEN

War on Two Fronts

Eighteen seventy began with no intimation of catastrophe in Europe. Jeanie Senior, however, was battling with continuing crises at Elm House. First, her seventy-nine year-old mother-in-law's move into their already crowded home, at the end of 1869, had proved still more difficult and conflict-ridden than Jeanie had long dreaded. Even before the move she reported to Walter, now 'wonderfully happy at Oxford', that the two grandmothers had begun to lock horns:

> She and dear old Mother were on the point of quarrelling all the time we were there [visiting Minnie]. Mother thinks Minnie grasping [for not taking in her own mother], and is disgusted that Mrs. Senior does not seem more thankful to us for having her here, so she feels in a state of irritation, and I had to use my utmost tact to keep the peace. My darling I sometimes quite lose heart, and fear that I shall never be clever or strong enough to ensure peace between the two Mothers. (27 October 1869)

Once the move started there had been chaos. Old Mrs. Senior had sent across all her pictures, among which was 'a terrible lot of rubbish'. And almost all the rooms in Elm House had had to be changed around. Jeanie gave her mother-in-law her own bedroom for a sitting room while Nassau was re-settled in Walter's old room – which he then immediately refused to leave, claiming gout: 'I wish he would [emerge] for I have a lot of things that he could help in if he were about. The only thoroughly tidy rooms in the house are his room and Granny Hughes' two. The others are in a fearful state' (1 November 1869).

The moment that 'failing' old Mrs. Senior actually did move into Elm House, together with her servants, she suddenly seemed 'wonderfully better'. Elm House itself, however, was in a 'horrid muddle': 'I feel like the provisional Government in a time of revolution, . . . we still are quite unsettled, and very filthy with dust and disorder' (14 November 1869). It was now uncertain whether her mother-in-law really was dying of stomach (or liver) cancer as Jeanie had been told, or whether she might rally and live for years. 'I hope she may live notwithstanding and for some time, for she seems very happy, because the place is so cheerful' (1 December 1869). The beginning of 1870 saw the old lady constantly alternating between bouts of vomiting accompanied by heartburn, refusing morphine, needing to be fomented by Jeanie, and insisting on eating what she could not digest. And her dog, now also installed in Elm House, was 'vomiting everywhere' as well.

The second domestic crisis focused on Nassau, dejected after his most recent failure when he was not appointed Registrar of University College, London. His debts had now mounted to a frightening figure and for the first time his wife had been driven to beg an old friend to give Nassau not just a reference but a job. That friend was Ernst Benzon, the financial director of the huge iron and steel concern, Naylor, Benzon and Co.[1]

> Mr. Benzon has been to offer Father some work . . . It will be
> £300 a year at first, and will increase as Father learns the business.
> . . . Benzon says that the business is a most difficult one to learn . . .
> and he says too that it is tremendously hard work, but for all that,
> Father accepted at once without asking me. (13 March 1870)

The next day there was trouble. Nassau was shown over his new office where Benzon's young business associate gave him books to study, the terms of which he could not understand. He immediately panicked and wrote to Benzon that 'he could not conscientiously accept a salary when he could not do the work'. On 16 March Jeanie Senior reported: 'I think it is settled now that Father will remain with Benzon. But I have had a very miserable anxious time, and I don't think I am through it yet.' The 'very miserable . . . time' caused her to cry out with frustration:

> You see, dear, Father hates work as soon as he has any to do, and
> he has always 50 reasons for giving it up. . . . It is a terrible thing
> when a man has no backbone; and poor old Father, with many
> good qualities, is utterly without the power of bearing what is
> disagreeable, or doing a thing that he dislikes, because it is right.
> . . . He is now in a permanent state of discontent, because he has
> to go to the City to work. . . . [At] present nothing is settled, and
> all I know is that I am very low, and that Father is awful cross –
> and I can't do anything to make him better. (16 March 1870)

As always in such a situation, Nassau scapegoated Jeanie and as always she tried, without success, to appease him:

> I've told him that now he works, I will only go out twice a week, so
> that he may have me at home almost always when he returns, . . .

> I'm only too glad to do this or anything else to please him; but the worst is that nothing does please him – I wish from my soul that I could do the business, but as I can't, Father certainly ought, for it is the only way in which our debts can be paid. (16 March 1870)

That letter ended with Jeanie's confession to Walter of her deep emotional dependence on him, writing with a candour that is shocking:

> I always prize your letters doubly when I am anxious and troubled; they make me feel that there is someone who loves me enough not to wear me and disappoint me – someone who will make up for my disappointment in marriage. . . .

Gentle and kindly, Walter would support and reassure his mother – but he was not at any risk of over-committing himself to her. He would never become an anguished Paul Morel (alias D. H. Lawrence), split and tormented by his parents' painful misalliance. Instead, he was now making new friends at Oxford, receiving invitations to balls and dreaming of rowing for his College.

A month later, during the Easter Vacation, Jeanie collapsed from a sudden acute return of her chronic uterine cancer, which had long been in remission.

22 Walter Senior aged 20 at Oxford, from his photo album. Courtesy of Mrs. Pamela Milne.

Walter nursed her and she was able to report reassuringly, on his return to Oxford, that, though weak and feverish, she had no more pain. She then became intensely worried over Walter himself. He had decided on his return to Oxford, to switch from Classics – 'Greats' – to the new, as yet much less honorific, degree in Law and History known as 'Mods'.[2] She reminded him that he was 'frightfully ignorant of politics and general literature'. If he did switch, . . . [he] must read the newspapers, and learn to take an interest in what goes on: not only in the occasional Notes in the *Pall Mall*!' (29 April 1870). She feared lest this might be another sign that Walter, like his father, would always take the easy way out:

> [With] your father's example before me I can't help being anxious. He had great abilities and yet his life is wasted utterly from *indolence*. All has been spoilt by that one fault. He is miserable himself and he often makes me very miserable.

Then for the first and last time in all the thousand letters she wrote Walter, she spelled out what Nassau's lethargic self-indulgence had cost her in material terms:

> I have had to bear privations of which I have said little to anyone, and I've had in middle life to work hard and give lessons, and tire myself, all because of his hatred of work, and unwillingness to do what he disliked. He is always complaining of being poor (tho' I've never let him go without anything he wanted; he has always had clothes of Poole and shirts of Duclos, and every comfort and fancy). – But he complains of poverty making his life a burden, tho' he has never had the courage to work so as to ensure the fortune that, ere this, he might have made, . . . I don't like to hold up your father as a "warning"! But there are times when one must speak out, even painful truths, and this is one of those times. (29 April 1870)

She roused herself from that slough of indignant self-pity by responding to the needs of someone else. In this case, bees. The bees in their orchard were too cold, she feared, to be able to swarm. So 'I picked up a lot them, stupefied with cold, [and] have got them under a glass shade on the chimney piece to get them thawed'.

Jeanie Senior's other preoccupations and duties still included her weekly visits to the local girls' Industrial School, overseeing the housing condition of the very poor in Octavia Hill's Marylebone tenements and visiting 'her' old women in the Workhouse Infirmary – as well as voice teaching – sometimes three lessons in one morning. Her mother-in-law had now returned to Elm

House, after a short stay with her daughter Minnie, 'wonderfully well again', drinking champagne by the tumbler, and 'stumping around famously. 'Jeanie found 'her much more tiring than when she was ill' . . . (5 May 1870) and was becoming increasingly tense about the frequent eruptions of hostilities inside Elm House:

> I feel nervous to leave Father alone with the two old ladies . . .
> for more than 24 hours. I think if I were not here to keep the
> peace that they would all three fight until nothing was left but
> father's spectacles and Granny S.'s false teeth, As for my poor old
> Mum, she would entirely have disappeared and no trace left of her!
> (8 May 1870)

She could not leave the house, but neither could she bear to stay there, caught in the crossfire: 'Oh, darling I shall be so thankful to get you home. I get so weary with . . . the anxiety of keeping things straight – . . . at present I am feeling as if people's nasty tempers were wearing me out' (15 June 1870).

To cap all, there had been a recent crisis over Nassau at the office:

> Poor father has been thro' an awful phase of despair the last few
> days. . . . One day young Vicars was dictating a letter to Father
> and Father made a mistake – and young V. said "What a damn'd
> stupid fellow you must be." Father came home resolved to give up.
> But we had a long talk and I said that, after all words don't hurt,
> and that it was Vicars who put himself in the wrong, and that the
> most dignified thing was for Father to take no notice; and I
> implored Father to stay there until he had paid his debts, and so
> Father has promised to do so and . . . to try not to grumble.

It is easy to feel for Nassau, now faced each morning with another day of public humiliation. Jeanie was sympathetically indignant on his behalf – 'these Vicars are disgusting'. She did not even know how to spell their name. Nassau was working under Albert *Vickers*, who would become Britain's answer to Krupp.[3]

On the Continent, meanwhile, Alfred Krupp himself was being profitably productive. By the summer of 1870 the Prussian Government's contracts for Krupp's guns had doubled its orders of 1869.[4] If Emperor Louis Napoleon of France believed that he would certainly win a war against *arriviste* Prussia, Bismarck *knew* that Prussia would win against Louis Napoleon.[5] He

23   The Battle-field of Mars-la Tour, 16 August 1870: Red Cross Aides at work amongst the
Wounded. (See Ascoli, 1987, *A Day of Battle*.)

was becoming impatient. He had forced and won quarrels with Denmark
and Austria. Now all that obstructed the consolidation of German national
unity under Prussia was jealous France. For the past three years, Bismarck
and his military advisers, pre-eminently Moltke, had planned to invade; all
Bismarck needed was a righteous pretext that would isolate France in world
opinion. Early in July 1870, the French rose to the bait: their honour regarding the Hohenzollern succession demanded that a decisive lesson be inflicted
upon Prussia. Cries of 'A Berlin!' and 'Vive la guerre!' in the Paris streets
were translated into Louis Napoleon's declaration of war on 15 July 1870.
'In the dead of the summer holiday the electric telegraph and the newspaper
press brought a wholly unanticipated quarrel to a climax, and convulsed two
of the most [apparently] civilized peoples of the world with savage hatred.'[6]
The other European Powers thought France arrogant and frivolous-minded
in going to war on such flimsy grounds. They held their distance, hoping
France would be taught a swift lesson and that all would be calm once more.
Instead, unbelievable carnage took place, anticipating – and helping to cause
– World War One.

By the end of the short, eight month-long Franco-Prussian war, some
150,000 Frenchmen and more than 28,000 Germans had killed each other;
and 150,000 French and 88,488 Germans had been seriously wounded.[7]

Those ungraspable figures are a tribute to the new factory of death that industrialized warfare had become. It is simply not possible for the imagination to feel for human bereavement by the tens of thousand, although Jeanie Senior, who had lost two young soldier brothers, could imagine better than most, the lifelong mourning by individual mothers, sisters and wives. And she needed no one to teach her what it had cost in pain and worry and work to have reared each one of those dead or mutilated young men to adulthood. She, like many other British onlookers that summer in 1870, was appalled and incredulous, desperate to 'do something' – but what?

On 22 July, only a week after Louis Napoleon's declaration of war on Prussia, Lt-Colonel Loyd-Lindsay, VC, MP,[8] a Crimean War veteran, had written a prescient letter to *The Times*:

> The news which daily reaches us from abroad shows that nations can at times go mad as well as individuals . . . Unfortunately, it is far easier to destroy than to save [life], all the glory being reserved for the former, and ten times the amount of scientific resources being devoted to it. . . .

Remembering only too well 'the pain . . . of those who remain hours and days unattended to' after battle in the Crimea, Loyd-Lindsay reminded readers of *The Times* of the international 'Society for Aiding and Ameliorating the Conditions of the Sick and Wounded of Armies in Time of War' that had issued the Geneva Convention in 1864. The Articles of that Geneva Convention had included:

1. Agreed neutrality for ambulances, military hospitals and hospital personnel.
2. Helpers of the wounded to be 'respected and remain free'.
3. Care and respect for the wounded, regardless of nationality.[9]

What was now needed was for Britain to give aid 'impartially and, above all, systematically'. But although Britain had ratified the Geneva Convention in 1867, it had not yet established its own national [Red Cross] committee. Therefore Loyd-Lindsay called for the establishment of such a committee in his letter to *The Times*, adding that he personally would deposit £1,000 to a London account of the International Society as a token of his own commitment.

On 4 August, a 'meeting of the provisional committee to procure help for the sick and wounded in the war was held in Willis' rooms . . . The attendance was small.'[10] There is no evidence as to whether or not Jeanie Senior had attended that meeting on 4 August in the summer holidays. Her first allusion to the Franco-Prussian War that has survived comes in a long letter of 27 August, written to Walter after she had arrived back home from a short visit to Adelaide Sartoris. Just two days earlier, she had read *The Times'* editorial which, shocked at 'the enormous extent of the slaughter', had asked:

> [Where] was the time or where were the hands to tend the thousands of wounded who lay helpless among the dead? . . . To carry one man off the field requires the help of two, and what is to be done for bearers, or surgeons, or nurses when the patients are counted by scores of thousands?

In other words, most of the wounded lay untended to die in unimaginable pain. August 27 was also the day that *The Illustrated Times* published its first lithograph images of the war – a peasant burying party and a transport of wounded French prisoners after the battle of Woerth. The intensity and urgency of Jeanie Senior's response to these horrors are revealed in feverish, staccato sentences:

> Poor old Dr. [de Mussy] dined here – more miserable that I can describe . . . Benzon and Lehmann are sending out 2 surgeons, paying all expenses and they give in money, besides the cost of the surgeons, £25 a week; the other day they sent 20 dozen shirts besides all sorts of other things [including] surgical instruments . . . . Mussy has offered his services to the Head of the Hospital service, but as he is an Orleanist it is quite possible that his offer may be refused – The suffering from want of comforts and attendance is awful. Strong men are wanted – the work is too hard for women – but if I were free I should go, for all that, for I know I can nurse well. – I think every strong young fellow who is capable of self-sacrifice and is in earnest about his life ought to offer to go and help. I would go tomorrow if I were a free man.
>
> The misery and suffering haunt me day and night. I've had a letter from Nina Inglefield – They are turning Versailles into a great Hospital – lots of families taking in wounded. She asks me for help. I had already sent all the money I thought I had a right to spend, to the International Society [i.e. the future British Red Cross] but I have been looking out all that I can spare of my linen etc, and have just come back from leaving it at the Depot, [2 St. Martin's Place] with a quantity of provisions fit for [the] sick which I got at the Civil Service [Stores] Nina says that famine is imminent, . . . Ah! dear, dear, what a time! – and in Alsace and Lorraine the peasants are starving – I shall send off a lot more things next week. I must help if I sell the clothes off my back. . . .

It is clear from that letter that Jeanie was already in contact with the Depot of the London Headquarters of the International Society [of the Red Cross]; it is not certain whether she was already serving on its Ladies' Committee. 'If I were free I should go' to nurse the wounded, alludes, of course, to all her dependants – young, middle-aged, old and sick – tying her down in Elm House. But she was clearly putting pressure on Walter to leave Oxford and volunteer to help in the war zone. Spurred by her, he did apply to go:

> I had a letter from Mrs. Loyd-Lindsay, who had heard from Mrs. Russell Gurney of your wish to go and help. She bids me thank you from Colonel Lindsay for your "noble wish", but at present no one is asked for but surgeons, and a few men who speak French fluently or German fluently. . . . but I am thankful that you wished to go; that is the great thing.
>   I fear that there is an awful time coming – I hope you read the papers. . . . – If only the Germans would treat for peace, and ask for nothing but the payment by the French of the expenses of the war, what a noble example they would be setting to the world – But I fear that this is too good to hope for. (10 September 1870)

It was. Always on the side of the current underdog, she had at the start championed the Prussians against Louis Napoleon. But she could not stomach Moltke and Bismarck's bullying of the defeated French who, even after Sedan, would not submit to unconditional surrender.

Jeanie Senior must have started her work for the Red Cross by the end of September, if not earlier, for on 16 October she says 'Tomorrow I return to my beloved work, thank goodness – ! I long to get to it!' The paradox was that it was only the 'awful time' which gave her that 'beloved work'. Therapeutic intervention was itself therapy for her, liberating her from the wretchedness of inaction at a time of political horror – as well as from her thousand petty responsibilities and worries inside quarrelsome Elm House. As Florence Nightingale had cried in *Cassandra*, written 1852–1857:

> Why have women passion, intellect, moral activity – these three – and a place in society where no one of the three can be exercised?
> . . .
>   But if ever women come into contact with sickness, with poverty, and crime in masses, how the practical reality of life revives them![11]

Jeanie Senior was thus revived. Her letters reporting on her new work pulse with energetic devotion to the humane idealism of Red Cross commitments '[To] succour the wounded of both sides alike . . . [To recognize] in every sick and wounded soldier of every nation a subject for its solicitude. . . . [And to] relieve the physical pain, and the mental trouble of the wounded man, from the moment of his wound to the date of his restoration to his friends.'[12] The desperate urgency of the need for funds and relief goods, called '*Matériel*', was stressed by the National Committee's appeals: 'Help given immediately is everything. Two days' delay after a battle, and the help might almost as well never be sent. The first two days' help is worth that of the next ten.'[13]

The duty of the central Ladies' [Working] Committee] was to collect, acknowledge and dispatch that medical and relief '*Matériel*' as fast as possible to the battlefields and to the French and German Hospitals, in the charge of Surgeons and others sent out by the [Society's] Central Committee. The list of gruesome articles required included:

> Amputating Instruments. Bullet Extractors. Forceps and Tenacula. Bone-Nippers. Tourniquets. Subcutaneous Syringes. Splints. Opium in all forms. Morphia. Laudanum. Chloroform. ('The medicines should be distinctly labelled in Latin and English, and the Dose stated in each case') . . . .

Wanted 'Sundries' included spoons, knives and forks, soap, waterproof sheets, blankets, warm clothing, disinfectants and cholera belts, not to mention concentrated meat essences, compressed vegetables, corn flour, condensed milk – and ale, sherry and port (in pint bottles).[14]

Local committees were being formed in almost every town and district in Great Britain, and money and aid supplies poured in to 2 St. Martin's Place (now the site of the National Portrait Gallery). Much needed extra space was quickly found in neighbouring St. Martin's disused Workhouse – 'a gloomy suite of rooms, dirty and dusty but roomy'.[15] But more rooms still were needed and the large vaults under St. Martin in the Fields' Churchyard were soon taken over and filled floor to ceiling with bales of relief packages.

The Ladies' Committee controlled and managed the [gifts in kind], receiving, unpacking, sorting, repacking, acknowledging things sent, dispatching them, making known the chief requirements abroad, corresponding with local committees, and keeping statistics of all material aid received. To this were added the management of the vaults and storerooms and the direction of storekeepers and packers.[16] Eventually nearly a million pounds – fifty million pounds in our money – was raised by voluntary donations, much of it from the poor, and all needing to be accounted for. As Florence Nightingale had already on 2 August warned the executive committee, regarding its organization and administration of aid:

> Those who undertake the work of aiding the sick and wounded
> must not be sentimental enthusiasts but downright lovers of hard
> work . . . attending to and managing the thousand and one hard
> practical details which never the less plainly determine the question
> as to whether your sick and wounded shall live or die.[17]

Efficiency was absolutely crucial to the successful establishment of the
British Red Cross during these months and Jeanie Senior, always 'a downright lover of hard work', was in her energetic, practical element. Given her
recent experience of housing management (and finance) for Octavia Hill and
her earlier work for Miss Stanley in dispatching aid to the Crimea, she
would, within a very few weeks, become the indispensable, efficient director
of operations. And no one at Elm House could demur – for the life-or-death
nature of her work put her 'home duties' into perspective, at least for a
while. There was just one problem – the distraction that accompanied every
announced visit from the Ladies' Committee Royal Patron, twenty-four year-
old Princess Christian:

> This morning I noticed an unwonted air of smartness and of excite-
> ment about the ladies at St. Martin's Place, which I could not
> understand and there was an unusual attendance also – At last I
> discovered that Princess Christian was coming! – All the work
> came to a stand still in order that everything might be shown to
> and explained to her. – When I found this, I gave "notice to quit",
> saying that Princesses were not in my line, and that there were
> enough without me; as no real work was to be done, I went off to
> poor dear Lady Lothian [responsible for aiding civilian refugees
> from the war zone] where Heaven knows there is enough work,
> but all in the most fearful muddle. No organization at all – I don't
> know if ever it will get straight; at present it looks hopeless. There
> are three dear old twiddling half French ladies, who enter things in
> the wrong books, and are as muddle-headed as possible . . . . You
> can't conceive the amount of suffering and misery on all sides that
> this most wicked war is causing. (18 October 1870)

What Jeanie always liked best was to be left to get on with the job in hand,
helped by a few keen, capable women as committed as herself:

> Today (Wednesday) I have had a delightful day at St. Martin's
> Place –Very few of us there and we did a real good hard day's work
> . . . Tomorrow and Friday the Princess comes, so I have given
> notice of absence. They all say the Princess is no woman of busi-
> ness and that their time has to be spent in arranging her work for

24   Stores of the National Society for Relief of the Wounded, London; from *Illustrated Times*, 10 October 1870.

her and in showing her how to do it. – Of course I feel still more than usual what a good thing it would be if there were no royal families. (18 October 1870)[18]

On 20 October she reported that she had had a good day's work 'at my refugees' – for the Princess again was at St. Martin's Place. There was certainly a tremendous amount of work also needing to be done for the refugees. One French woman, because she was married to a German, had been turned out of Paris with her husband and they were now destitute in London. She came to beg for money to get to Liverpool where friends might help. 'This sounds very vague . . . However we have sent them off . . . . This is only one case in a hundred'.

The next day, after her work for refugees, Jeanie called on the great musician Mme. Pauline Viardot Garcia. Even she was now a refugee from the French war zone:

> She told me that she was obliged to come and sing and give lessons, because they get no income. They have house property in Paris in a part which is sure to be destroyed if shells are thrown and a farm which has been entirely devastated by the Germans. (24 October 1870)[19]

Another even older friend, Madame Mohl, had also escaped Paris and brought news that Jeanie's former flirtatious correspondent, Prosper Mérimée, the loyal servant of the Empress Eugenie, had collapsed after the fall of the Empire on 4 September and, six weeks later, had died.

Jeanie's old school-friend, Nina Inglefield, was still trapped in Versailles where she had gone to nurse her sick father. She wrote long, urgent, fact-filled letters about the situation there, which Jeanie copied and forwarded both to Princess Christian and to Florence Nightingale, so that they in turn could tell the powers that be what was most desperately needed. The Palace of Versailles was now the Royal Prussian Headquarters *cum* German Command Post as well as an improvised hospital for the German and French wounded, all too often stinking of fatal gangrene. Always the fiery radical whose 'blood had boiled' over the Russian Tsar and Governor Eyre, Jeanie Senior now hated the old King of Prussia's pious telegrams as he thanked God for his victories:

> [He] ought to have made peace at Sedan – Till then I understand his thanking God for his success, for he was fighting to defend his fatherland and to put down a tyrant who was ruining a noble people. But now his telegrams make me sick, because if he chose he could have peace, and I can't see when he is sacrificing life on all

sides that he ought to be so sure that God is approving him. . . .
(3 November 1870)

Since she now had chief responsibility for the Ladies' Working Committee of
the British Red Cross – still known as The National Society for Sick and
Wounded in War – Jeanie Senior was spending all day at St. Martin's Place
most days a week. Sometimes there would only be three of the committee
present – herself, Mrs. Loyd-Lindsay and a Miss Alexander and the work
could get 'beautifully done . . . Tomorrow Princess Christian comes, but I
can't shirk for I have to arrange everything for [her].' (3 November 1870).
The Princess turned out to be 'very jolly, and easy to get on with; but it is a
bore having her there ' and having to supply her with work that others could
have done much more quickly. The next Saturday Jeanie went to work in the
office all day entirely alone and had 'a most delightful day' – a fact perhaps
not unconnected with the return of old Mrs. Senior to Elm House the previous evening (5 November 1870) in full talking spate.

Across the channel 'this most wicked war' was becoming ever more
wicked. On one side the French guerrilla fighters, or *'francs-tireurs'* in the
provinces, with their skull and crossbones emblem, had become a byword
for savage resistance, soon to be called 'terrorism', followed by counter-
atrocities by the Prussian troops. The 'retrograde step in military morality'
of Prussian collective punishment, burning down villages that harboured
snipers, had first been reported in the *Pall Mall Gazette* on 21 September. 'As
the war dragged on . . . throughout the autumn and winter of 1870 the
terrorism of the *francs-tireurs* and the reprisals of the Germans spiralled
down to new depths of savagery.'[20]

Meanwhile Thiers' acceptance of the Prussian demand for Alsace had
been repudiated by the French radicals. Iron-fisted Bismarck, who called war
'the natural condition of mankind', declared that there was now no stable
French Government with which he could make terms. It was not his fault if
he had to keep making war on a defeated people who would not treat for
peace. The deaths from wounds continued to mount on both sides and Jeanie
Senior was constantly being asked to send out ever more surgical, i.e. ampu-
tating, instruments. 'We have already sent lots out – so there will be less
suffering. It is very dreadful to think of – I can't get accustomed to it' (16
November 1870). Her revulsion against the competition in massacre and
mutilation caused her to think of the one group in Britain that was committed to anti-militarism. 'I am rapidly turning Quaker' (17 November 1870).

By the beginning of December Jeanie Senior was mistakenly anticipating
just three weeks' more hard work at the Red Cross London office, 'winding-
up'. But there would soon be new slaughter during the long-promised French
'sortie' from beleaguered Paris and mutually acceptable Peace Terms seemed
as far away as ever. In the event, the 'Grande Sortie' proved a total débâcle,

and the German troops, disappointed of their longing to be 'home by Christmas' began the bombardment of Paris.

The first signs of co-operation between Jeanie Senior and Florence Nightingale then began. On 9 December 1870 the latter had written to her beloved niece by marriage, young, idealistic Emily Verney, who was working for the Ladies' Committee in the London Red Cross office, giving her a message 'to Mrs. Nassau Senior with my truly respectful thanks and admiration of her'.[21] On 15 December Florence Nightingale had written again to her concerning 'your friend Mrs Nassau Senior . . . Tho' I have not the honour of knowing her, I have heard so much of her'.[22] The first letter from Florence Nightingale to Jeanie Senior herself that has survived is dated 29 December 1870, and thanks her for forwarding copies of Nina Inglefield's letters from Versailles:

> Private
>
> My dear Madam,
>
> I cannot thank you enough for sending me those most interesting and invaluable letters . . . .
>
> Might I suggest to you that, when the time comes to draw up some conclusions, whether for publication or not, as to the working of the different International (Red Cross) Societies with a view to future progress, suggestions quite invaluable will be found in these letters?
>
> I have laid many in store, tho' quite deep in my own breast.
> I am so very sorry about her distress as to the French peasantry at Versailles.
> Mr. Bullock, the gentleman who was the author of what is called the "Daily News Fund" and has been working it himself in the Ardennes, is now gone to Versailles with a similar purpose – I take for granted, at your instigation.
>
> You know also of the "War Victims' Fund" (I enclose one of their papers) 86 Houndsditch E.
>
> Pray excuse a very hasty note . . .[23]

On 31 December she wrote to Jeanie Senior again:

> Returned, this beautiful and spirited and mournful letter, with very many thanks.
>
> It seems a mockery to wish her and you a Happy New Year tho' I do with all my heart and soul and strength. At least it is a relief that this terrible and dreary and bloody and wicked Old Year is over, laden with the sorrow and agony of millions, which alas, are not over. People tell me to be thankful we are "not in it". And so I

am, most deeply thankful that our country is not "in it", but that I am not in it is the bitterest regret of my life. My whole heart and soul are longing to be with those wretched sufferers of the Loire.

I am very sorry that you have an anxiety about " a child". I trust it is nothing serious. In haste

Yours overflowingly,

Florence Nightingale.[24]

The child Jeanie was anxious about was brilliant little Harry – his frightening bout of serious infectious illness (scarlet fever?) had required all the rooms at Elm House to be 'smoked' (22 January 1871) and both Grandmothers had fallen ill as well. Everything was as cheerless as it could be, with Nassau adding to the gloom by his desperation to leave his office job at Benzon/Vickers. His application for the post on the Education Commission that George Eliot herself had tried to support, was now looking very doubtful. And the 'wine trade [was] counted strongly against' him (23 January 1871) in his other persistent dream, the Clerkship of Surrey. His sister Minnie's barrister husband, Charles Simpson, was now afraid to be seen to help Nassau in any way, lest association with him injure his own chances of advancement. Jeanie was indignant but helpless. Nassau then suddenly left the Vickers office for good, in order to suggest himself as unpaid secretary to a new Commission for founding a proposed Law University. He would mix with all sorts of 'legal swells', who might be useful to him at some time in the future, he hoped. Jeanie supported him in this venture, although she could not help regretting the abrupt loss of £200 a year.

That Jeanie was still working regularly at St. Martin's Place is attested by Princess Christian's notes to her of 9, 11, 16, 30 and 31 January, and 22 February, always admiring of Mrs. Inglefield and always wishing to see her 'dear Mrs. Senior' whenever she next called in at the office. By now the situation in besieged Paris was becoming more and more desperate, above all for the working class. Whereas the rich and the bourgeois could hoard and buy food and fuel at black market prices, crowds of poor women would stand frozen in queues for hours at a time and still come away with nothing. Bread was not rationed until the very end of the siege and the scarcity of milk contributed to a terrible surge in infant deaths. One did not have to look far to understand the intensification of extreme class hatred. The ignominious and bloody failure of the last attempt at a military *sortie* on 19 January, followed by the threat of imminent civil war in the city, forced the Republican leader Favre to sue for an armistice on 27 January. He could not fight both the Germans and his enraged fellow Frenchmen at the same time.

The Franco-Prussian War was over, but the consequences of those few months August 1870–January 1871 are still with us. Without them 'the history of our times would have been very different.'[25] The Prussian victory would prove a disaster for Germany as well as for the rest of Europe in that it produced *revanchiste* hatred of Germany within France, while deluding most Germans about the invincibility of their state militarism – both contributory factors to August 1914. Although the by-standers of 1871 were spared foreseeing the full horror of the first half of the 20th century in Europe, the immediate consequences of the Franco-Prussian war were ghastly enough. Three things stunned and enraged radical Paris after the armistice. First the rural/royalist, ultra-conservative triumph in the national elections of 8 February. Secondly Moltke's implacable peace terms negotiated with Thiers on 28 February, demanding the surrender of Alsace, Lorraine, Metz and Strasbourg on top of crippling war reparations, *plus* a triumphal German march through Paris on 1 March. And finally the oppressive upper-class legislation by the National Assembly in Bordeaux, demanding immediate payment of all outstanding debts and rents.

25   Jeanie's foster-cum-adoptive daughter 'Nell' aged 20, formerly 'little Helen'. From Jeanie Senior's photo album. Courtesy of Mrs. Pamela Milne.

Was it for this that the penniless artisans of Paris and their families had starved in the food queues and shivered and bled and buried their children? Whom could they punish for what they now felt was political and social betrayal?

Jeanie Senior had continued working in 'her' Red Cross office throughout that February. On one occasion she took her dear, adoptive daughter 'Nell' (formerly Helen) to see the work going on in the office at 2 St. Martin's Place. Despite her conventional ideas about how a fashionable lady should live, Nell 'was much impressed by my snugness and comfort . . . and quite understood that far from being a fatiguing occupation it was much less tiring than the ordinary life one leads of going about to call on people by rail, and bus and cab' (3 February 1871).

Then fell an unexpected blow. Her younger brother Hastings confessed to her that he had been very nearly ruined during the banking panic/failures of 1866 and had only been saved from bankruptcy then by loans from his brothers. But now the interest on those loans was taking too much from the profits of his struggling wine import business and he could no longer afford to pay her the £600 a year for himself and his children to live as paying guests at Elm House. His sister was devastated; she must try to cut down on every possible expense in order to be able 'to keep Hastings' who was, she said, the greatest comfort she had in Walter's absence (20 February 1871). Her only chance of talking the problem over with Hastings 'in this over peopled house' was early on Sunday morning 'before Nassau comes down and the old lady is prowling about' (24 February 1871).

At this fraught time Jeanie's great solace, once again, was music. She had gloried in one of Joachim's 'divine' Monday Pop concerts and in another by Clara Schumann; she had heard Fauré sing and she had also enjoyed singing herself, under Pauline Viardot, some choruses from Gounod's *La Reine de Saba*, with Gounod accompanying them, in order to raise money for displaced French peasants.

But very soon Jeanie Senior was mesmerized once more by what was happening across the Channel. Under a deceptive 'return to normality', Paris was in fact on the verge of a class war which finally erupted on 18 March when the *Fédérés*, the majority of radicals in the Paris National Guard, refused to surrender their cannon to generals of the Regular French Army. The new head of government, Thiers, together with his generals, then fled Paris, *reculer pour mieux sauter,* and set up a National Government in

Versailles, so very recently the German Imperial HQ. The Paris radicals were paralyzed with astonishment. Instead of pursuing Thiers and defeating him – a fatal error which Lenin would not replicate – they argued over disestablishing the Church, instituting an autonomous municipal government or 'Commune' in Paris, and on repealing the hated laws on payment of debts and rents. On 28 March 1871 the Paris Commune was officially installed in the Hôtel de Ville. No one knew what the radical 'Communards' would now do, least of all the disparate, indecisive Communards themselves.[26] 'During its lifetime, the Commune had few friends beyond the ranks of its immediate supporters in Paris, and these were rendered fewer by the unchallenged falsifications . . . put out by [its enemies].'[27] Jeanie Senior, like other English onlookers, could only watch with horror and foreboding, not sure what to think or say, appalled by each new alleged atrocity, whether committed by the Communards or by the Versailles army.

At Elm House, life continued to be its usual mixture of anxiety and occasional respite. Worry over Nell's health persisted as did worry over whether Walter was studying hard enough to pass Mods. Then, when old Mrs. Senior celebrated her 81st birthday at Elm House on 15 March 1871, 'Mother did not feel well enough to come down'. The grandmothers were barely civil foes by now. However, Jeanie also had several sources of joy. She had dined with the Leweses on 8 March 'and very pleasant it was all alone with them. She is a noble and charming creature'. George Eliot must have learned a lot that evening about what a latter-day Theresa – or a grown-up Dorothea – could do in the wake of a terrible war. It was also now that Jeanie wrote to Walter that she had sung at Eton 'and dear Joc [Joachim] accompanied me – and I was very happy' (8 March 1871). Finally, Walter's twenty-first birthday on 15 March occasioned a great, pathetic, outpouring of gratitude:

> I bless God with all my heart for what you are to me, my dear dear son – I have never had a real sorrow on your account . . . The few faults you have you have always been humble about and sorry for . . . and I have the memory of such love as very few Mothers get from their sons – and the consciousness that however dull I may be, *you* at least never find me tiresome . . . .

By the end of March Jeanie Senior had at last finished all her work for the National Society and been awarded one of the first medals minted by the British Red Cross for her service. Rimmed with gold, it was dark blue with a red cross upon a white shield and said simply: 'National Red Cross Society

1871'. The British Red Cross had been born with Jeanie one of its acknowledged, indispensable co-founders. Col. Loyd-Lindsay had compiled a
substantial interim *Report* on the receipts and expenditure of the British
National [Red Cross] Society, by 31 March, including answers to a
Questionnaire, to which Nina Inglefield was the only woman contributor.
Jeanie sent a copy of Nina's long statements to Florence Nightingale for
information and comment, and received the following reply:

> I cannot thank you enough for your extreme kindness in sending
> me a copy of Mrs. Inglefield's masterly answers to "Questions".
>   I am shocked at the trouble it must have given to copy. . . .
>   What insight she has into the best, indeed the only way of
> helping her poor people back into their lives. And how dreadful it
> is to think that this brutal Commune has forced them all again into
> anxiety.
>   Oh when will it end?
>   Again thanking you for your unparalleled kindness, believe me
> ever yours gratefully, . . .[28]

Florence Nightingale's full comment on Nina Inglefield's response to the Red
Cross Questions brimmed over with characteristic political acumen.[29]

Not surprisingly, Princess Christian was also no friend of the Paris
Commune; she considered the events in Paris 'really disgraceful' in her letter
to Jeanie of 11 April 1871. 'I trust it will be a good lesson to all here who
favour republican ideas!!' she joked, little knowing to whom she wrote. 'This
brutal Commune', as Florence Nightingale had called it, hopelessly disorganized, unmilitary and even anarchic, was now under siege and artillery fire
from the Versailles' regular army from 15 April until 27 May. The end was
quite terrible. In response to arson attacks by the Commune and its killing
of eighty-three people, Thiers' forces under Marshal MacMahon massacred
between 20,000 and 25,000 men, women and even children and took
another 40,000 prisoners. The desperate Communards had no escape route,
because the Prussian Army, France's enemy just two months earlier, was now
collaborating with Thiers' troops by blocking the St. Denis gate all week and
shooting any Parisian who tried to flee the city. Bismarck did not wish the
Commune to succeed lest it trigger a workers' uprising in Berlin.

The Pall Mall Gazette (26 May 1871) alleged that Thiers' preparations for
attack and his public statements 'amounted to little less than a State licence
for massacre'. Jeanie Senior's horror at this news may be imagined as she sent
Walter one of her most important letters she ever wrote: 'It is quite impossible to say how sad it makes me. . . . [Bad] tho' the Communists are I cannot
but feel that they have been made worse by Thiers' insane conduct' (27 May
1871). It did not help that Thiers had been a close friend of her father-in-

law.[30] And now Thiers' ruthlessness, or, at the very least, his refusal to control the ruthlessness of his troops in that *'semaine sanglante'*, when disarmed prisoners were being rounded up in batches of one hundred and fifty at a time and shot against barrack or cemetery walls, had brought desolation for years to come. She continued her long, heartfelt, political letter to Walter:

> I see the death-blow to liberty . . . – for everyone will be afraid of liberal principles, and republicanism and political life in France will again be at a standstill . . . I think the Versailles people as bad as the Reds, worse indeed, for they ought to have known better. – . . . And it is impossible not to be unhappy about our own country too. So many will be unable to see the difference between honest liberalism and Red frenzy, and will forsake the ranks of true liberality . . . I have known many already who are forsaking their liberal principles because they can't separate the truth from exaggeration. It needs great moral courage and strong faith to stand by one's flag, when people say, "You see where your principles lead!" – Even dear old Mussy calls me a Communist and says it is dreadful to think that a person whom he respects and values can say a word for the villainous perpetrators of such atrocities [i.e.those of the Commune]. (27 May 1871)

One wonders how many of Jeanie Senior's lady contemporaries in England were also labelled 'Communist' then – or was she the only one to stand by her radical flag when old liberal friends like Dr. Mussy and M. Mohl called the Commune 'vermin'?

That night's *Pall Mall Gazette* reported ever worse atrocities by the suppressors of the Commune:

SUMMARY EXECUTIONS

> . . . Many women and children (the *Times* correspondent says) have been executed around the Luxembourg, having been convicted of firing on soldiers. Thirteen women . . . have been executed after being publicly disgraced in the Place Vendome. . . . Many women have been brought in prisoners. An eminent advocate . . . says he was shocked to see an officer draw his sword upon a woman . . . and inflict a deep gash upon her face and hack off part of her shoulder. Later in the day another officer was arrested for protesting against similar barbarity. Several hundred insurgents who took refuge in the Madeleine were, it is said, bayoneted in the church. Not one, it is declared, came out alive.

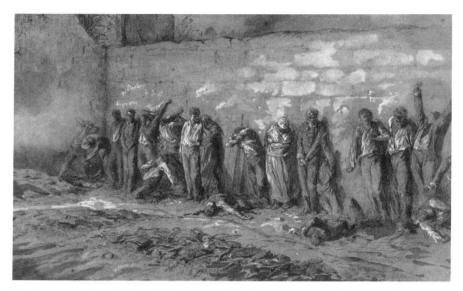

26   Mass execution of defeated Communards, Père Lachaise Cemetery, May 1871. Courtesy Bourgin, *La Guerre, 1870–1871 et La Commune* (Paris, 1971).

The Times thundered on 1 June 1871: 'The wholesale executions inflicted by the Versaillese soldiers, the triumph, the glee, the ribaldry of the "Party of Order", sicken the soul.'

Not surprisingly, as she read of this merciless infliction of massive suffering, Jeanie Senior now found herself emotionally on the side of the defeated Communards. Her vague, idealistic socialism sympathized with their craving for the basic rights of work, food and representation.[31] Nevertheless one is still not prepared for the quite astonishing moment six months later, on 4 November 1871, when she would report to Walter that Caroline Stephen had been with her for two hours,

> talking much of the Commune and the Labour question and other Social questions. She wants to get all possible information and then write a book on it. We have a plan for going to Paris together and trying to find from the Communists themselves what exactly they want and propose.

All the said Communists would have been in prison and how she and Caroline Stephen imagined that they would be granted access is hard to understand. Three weeks after writing that letter, Jeanie was devastated by the execution of the Commune's leader Rossel, tied to a post and shot at Satory.[32] 'I am very dismal because they have shot Rossel. They do all they can in that unhappy France to enlist all one's sympathies on the side of the

Communists. He was a hero and a patriot.' The next day she read all the details of the execution in *The Times* and that night she could not sleep – 'I did nothing but go over and over all the incidents of poor Rossel's execution' (29–30 November 1871). Over three years later, 25 March 1874, Jeanie would send Walter, then in Paris, £5 (£150 in our money) that he must take immediately in person to a Mlle. Broen 'for the poor Belleville women.' She had just read *The Times*' report of the maltreatment of Communard women still held in Paris prisons: 'It is really dreadful to think that revenge should be carried out to such an extent by any Government.'

And so the terrible year of 1871 came to an end. The killing had stopped at last in France but the war within Elm House had not eased, rather it had erupted ever more bitterly; Granny Senior was now openly accusing Granny Hughes of not wanting her as a member of the household:

> There was an awful jangle between the old ladies at luncheon which has quite finished me up, and I feel like a washed out rag. . . . [At] last I said they'd kill me if they went on. . . . I, who do <u>hate</u> quarrels and words ! . . . had a good cry out in the carriage alone. (4 November 1871)

No, she had not been 'clever enough and strong enough to ensure peace between the two Mothers' (27 October 1869).

The combination of the war(s) in France and the war in Elm House over-whelmed her usual resilience. She fantasized about emigrating: 'I can't help longing to be out of it all, in some nice primitive country where one could lead a simple life, amongst simple people, in fresh air, where there was food enough for every man and woman who would work' (27 May 1871). Had she talked animatedly to George Eliot of her dream in which she would 'take a great deal of land and drain it and make a little colony, where everybody should work, and all the work should be done well' – as Dorothea would put it in the fifty-fifth chapter of *Middlemarch*? It is hard, however, to imagine Nassau rolling up his sleeves to dig, and what would Jeanie do with the two old, infirm, warring grandmothers?

Fortunately she did have one source of inspiration, much nearer home, which strengthened her will to live at this bleak time – that 'splendid and brave woman', Octavia Hill (27 November 1870).

> Octavia Hill is as good and interesting as ever. It has been a great pleasure to me to have her here for one day . . . She rejoices my soul, for she is so hopeful, and no wonder for she does so much, and sees a good deal of the good fruit of her labour. (14 May 1871)

. . . The person who is like a stream of sweet water after wandering in the wilderness is Octavia Hill – She cheers me more than I can say. – She really does something, and that makes her hope and hope gives her more power to work. – I feel a miserable old stick-in-the-mud, sad and hopeless except when with her, or for a little time after seeing her. (27 May 1871)

And on 9 November 1871 she was singing once again at one of Octavia Hill's 'entertainments' for her poverty-stricken tenants.

Jeanie Senior had learned from her experience of organizing a massive relief effort by the British Red Cross in wartime that she herself was a capable Chief of Staff. That realization of her own capacities strengthened her urge to do something in peacetime also, to try to change an increasingly unjust Britain, where there was 'pauperism growing one way, and the greatest luxury the other' (27 May 1871). But she could not see what she could do or how she might do it. It would need Octavia Hill to point the way.

CHAPTER ELEVEN

The First Woman Civil Servant

The winter of 1871–2 was beset once more by the children's infectious illnesses – they had scarlet fever – and money worries; the two became interlinked, for all Jeanie's singing pupils stayed away from her for weeks on end. As soon as she had nursed all the children back to health, she returned to uninspiring normality, leavened only by each new instalment of *Middlemarch* and by music. On one notable occasion in mid-April 1872, never mentioned by Jeanie Senior herself, her social intervention actually fused with her singing. She had been supporting a young social activist, Henrietta Rowland, in giving night-time literacy classes for older children in one of the poorest, most violent districts in Whitechapel. Henrietta Rowland recalled:

> I had taken the responsibility for three evenings a week, one for boys in an underground cellar, two for girls in a small ground-floor room, in a terrible court, which had recently come into Miss Octavia's hands. The people were very rough, and many [street] fights and quarrels took place, for the settlement of which I was not infrequently called upon as umpire. One evening Mrs. Nassau Senior was in our school, when a specially noisy fight resulted in all the girls tearing out to watch or join in it.
> "What shall we do?" I asked, as she and I stood alone in the deserted heavy-aired room.
> "I will sing to them," she replied, and standing on the raised step at the doorway, the shouting angry fighting crowd just below her, she lifted up her beautiful voice and sang –
> "Angels, ever bright and fair, Take, oh! take me to your care."[1]
> The people heard, found something more interesting than the fight, and gathered round her to listen, and as she stood in the dark court with a background of flaring gas light which turned her flaxen hair into a halo, she seemed to some of us to be one of the angels of whom she sang.[2]

At the end of April Jeanie had some money over from her resumed music teaching, just enough for a short break in Paris. But once there she was not happy. The triumphalism of the victorious French upper classes over the defeated Communards was salt in a wound. She was taken to the theatre and forced to watch a comedy mocking democracy and revolution – 'and I don't think it is the right moment for that, so tho' I was amused I was pained too' (21 April 1872).

Then, on 30 April, while still in Paris, Jeanie received devastating news. Her brother George, aged 51, was dangerously ill with inflammation of the lungs. She rushed back to join her mother who had already gone to her eldest son, very ill in Liverpool. The next letter, 2 May, bore the familiar broad black edge. 'My beloved, [the] dear one has gone Home . . . I feel our loss not his gain just at present.' George Hughes was a man loved as a person rather than respected for any achievement. After Annie and George inherited Offley Place in 1867,[3] George Hughes had become an amiable sporting squire and hospitable 'head of the family'. Jeanie would tease him for his Toryism, his lack of application to his musical and other talents and his perpetual postponement of the betterment of his tenants, but she had also loved him.

She felt emotionally exhausted by her grief –

> I want to sleep on, on, on. I don't think my body is tired but all my heart and *will* seem worn. . . . I have to go about the cross for the foot of the grave this afternoon. I ever have George in my thoughts and heart, and I know that his place can never be filled. Poor Mother is sweet and good and resigned, but she looks sadly broken . . . Dyer and Bessie are so nice – so tender and sorry for us. (3–12 May 1872)

George Eliot, understanding the pull of old ties, wrote with real affection: '[You] know I count you among those who will always be dear to me' and continued:

> You are paying part of the great price for the blessing of being able to love those near to you. It is of no use to offer words under such a trial. Comfort will gradually come in your activity for others, which never leaves you long in the power of your own particular lot.[4]

The intensity of Jeanie's bereftness caused her to doubt the reality of her faith in immortality. As she remembered her four dead brothers, she confessed to Tom:

> I can't help weeping to think of all the dear boys gone before us, but I feel as if it were quite wicked to be so unhappy. I often think that though I say I believe in the Communion of Saints and eternal life, I don't really believe it, or I could not be so unhappy, or find life often so dreary as I do. (18 September 1872)[5]

In the midst of all that unhappiness yet another family disaster impinged. In early June Nassau was telegraphed for help by his widowed cousin, Emily Coleridge. The fourth of her five daughters, clever eighteen year-old Frankie, had just eloped with a clergyman's nephew, a married man whose unfortunate wife was, unbeknownst to Frankie, expecting every hour to go into labour. A few days later 'poor Frankie' had been traced and brought back, Jeanie reported to Walter:

> Your father says that her Mother *taunted* her when she saw her for half an hour; and that Frankie dreads the life her Mother will make her if they are together and I am certain that it would turn any girl into a devil to live like a toad under a harrow, more especially if her Mother played the part of the harrow. (13 June 1872)

Jeanie immediately set to thinking who might take Frankie in. The girl had moved into dingy lodgings under the name of 'Mrs. Francis' until it could be quite certain that she was not pregnant. By the beginning of September Jeanie was asking Walter to post to Frankie, still alias 'Mrs Francis', several of the Seniors' books, including a life of Mozart in French and Huc's travels in China as well as some textbooks.

> [She] wants to go on with Latin and to keep up her German. The poor child is frightfully lonely where she now is – besides being bitten by bugs at night. I spent 2 hours with the poor girl and liked much what I saw of her. She is bearing it all very bravely. (5 September 1872)

At that moment Jeanie Senior had much else besides Frankie on her mind for, just a week earlier, she had embarked on the first move in what was soon to become her ground-breaking public career.

On 16 August, under the heading 'North Surrey Schools', *The Times* had published a shocking report of Inspection by the Visiting Clapham Board of Guardians.[6] The North Surrey Schools at Hanwell and Anerley were two of the modern 'District' or 'Barrack' Schools for thousands of pauper boys and girls in the Greater Metropolitan area. The North Surrey Workhouse School District covered the London Unions (or Workhouses) of Richmond, Croydon, Lewisham and Wandsworth and Clapham. The purpose-built schools were huge models of supposed efficient reform that separated the pauper children not only from their pauper parents or other relatives but also from undesirable contact with the old, the insane, the alcoholic, the mentally handicapped, the sexually promiscuous prostitutes and the unemployable 'casuals' in their local Workhouses. But the children were thereby also separated of course from ordinary life, their incarceration preventing them in their turn from contaminating the non-pauper children and families in the world outside their 'Barracks'. The children were segregated by sex, regimented in their hundreds, their heads shaved, dressed in ill-fitting workhouse uniform, the boys being trained in shoe making, carpentry, plumbing, bricklaying, farm work or tailoring and drilled for possible service in the Army, while the girls worked unpaid in the schools' kitchens, laundries, sewing rooms and dormitories, when not attending lessons. They were intended for domestic service on leaving the school. There were no school holidays.

The Visiting Clapham Guardians reported that

> [They] were deeply impressed with the general air of discomfort prevailing in every part of the establishment, and regretted to observe the want of proper arrangements, want of ventilation, want of sufficient accommodation to separate children in different stages of disease, want of cleanliness, imperfect drainage, and the utter failure in the carrying out of what they had understood to be the resolution of the [Local Government] Board in its general management. The Visiting Guardians regretted to have occasion to report their great dissatisfaction on the state and conduct of the infirmary. . . . The children appeared neglected, those suffering from opthalmia were placed side by side with those suffering with skin diseases . . . . One girl was already in danger of losing her sight . . . . The nurses complained of not having a sufficient supply of hot water. The towels looked like . . . floor rags. . . . There was more dirt and illness than [one of the regular] Visiting Guardians had ever seen before. The children, he asserted, were underfed.

Several heated letters to *The Times* then followed. And on 27 August 1872 Jeanie Senior joined the fray – writing no longer under the male alias of her husband's name nor under the gender-neutral initials J.E.S. but at last as her public self, Jane E. Senior. 'Sir, – During a twelve years' experience in this parish I have had much experience among the poor, and can answer for there being no exaggeration as to the state of the North Surrey District Schools.'

The radical alternative to this Workhouse/District School mass incarceration of destitute children and infants was family fostering, then called 'Boarding Out'. It was practised almost universally in Scotland but was still regarded with great suspicion by Englishmen in authority as a surrender to 'out-relief'. Every form of 'out-relief' had been excoriated by Nassau's father, Nassau William Senior, architect of the New Poor Law of 1834, as merely perpetuating pauper dependency. Moreover 'boarding-out' had terrible associations with the still older abuse of the 'farming-out' of pauper babies and the exploitation of 'pauper apprentices'. However, the carefully supervised

boarding out of individual children as the responsibility of sensible, sympathetic middle-class women had recently been advocated for England in two
books: Florence Davenport Hill's *Children of the State: The Training of
Juvenile Paupers*,[7] and *The Advantages of the Boarding-out System* by Col.
C. W. Grant.[8] On 22 September 1870, Jeanie's friend Anny Thackeray had
reviewed both books for *The Cornhill* in her essay 'Little Paupers', ending:
'there are children dying and utterly wrecked for want of homes, homes sad
for want of children.' And already on 8 May 1869, Octavia Hill had written
to Florence Davenport Hill, (who was no relation of Octavia's): 'Will you
send me a copy of papers respecting boarding out? I should much like to
send them to Mrs. N. Senior. I believe the chances are better in the country,
and the plan more likely to be tried there.'[9] Jeanie Senior's self-education on
the issue that would thereafter preoccupy her, may be dated, therefore, from
1869.

Jane E. Senior's letter of 27 August was followed by attacks on her from
the Chaplains of the Barrack Schools, Mr. John Churchill Sykes and Mr.
Olinthus J. Vignoles. They turned on 'Mrs. Senior' for having found the girls
in the District Schools morally apathetic. On the contrary, they asserted,
almost all the girls were 'possessed of modesty and self-respect'. They could
attest that the 'vicious' children did not number more than four percent. For
it had been their duty as Chaplains

> to visit the children regularly, [i.e. after leaving the District Schools]
> and to enter their characters in books kept for that purpose. These
> books are open to [Mrs. Senior's] inspection, . . . although [they
> were] ready to admit with her that a large number do pass out of
> sight.

'Mrs. Senior' then re-entered the field in a long letter to *The Times* of 9
October 1872, putting the devastating question:

> What becomes of the girls who thus "pass out of sight"?
>   This is a point to which advocates of boarding-out would espe-
> cially beg attention. A girl of 16 is sent from a District School to a
> situation. She is probably unhandy; the mistress expects too much,
> and perhaps is cross and impatient. The girl runs away, or "passes
> out of sight." She has no home to go to, and no one would be
> made unhappy by her misconduct. It is well known by those who
> have studied the subject that many of these girls go on the street.

After that plainspoken shot across the reverend gentlemen's bows, she turned
her indignant attention to the deliberate joylessness of the children's regimen
while still attending a Barrack School:

About two years ago a lady living near the Anerley schools applied to the master for leave to take 250 children to the Crystal Palace. The master was most kind and courteous, but was obliged to refuse her request, as all amusements outside the walls of the institution were strictly forbidden. She then asked to be allowed to visit the sick children in the infirmary, to tell and read them stories and give them toys. This, also, the master was obliged, most unwillingly, to refuse, the Board having decided that, as the children would have to lead a hard life when they left school, they should have as few pleasures as possible while they remained there.

Jeanie Senior then made her fury at such a mean-spirited treatment of miserable infants very plain:

It is inevitable that most of the children brought up in these large schools should be turned out, as Sir Charles Trevelyan truly says, [in an earlier letter to *The Times*] listless and apparently half-idiotic.[10] What other result would be expected from such a joyless, monotonous training?

She knew how public influence worked behind the scenes in the world of men and asked Delane, the famous editor of *The Times*, to back her:

I had another letter in [the] *Times* on Tuesday – . . . When I sent it to Delane, I told him that I wanted him to back us up by a good *leader*. He wrote me a very complimentary note, saying that such a hard hitter needed no backing, and that I had routed the 2 chaplains, horse and foot, and he congratulated me on victory in what he believed was the right cause –
    I thanked him for his letter but told him that I did want backing and that no good would be done till men took up the question.–
(22 October 1872)

One of Jeanie's keenest supporters 'on the ground' was her old friend, the veteran voluntary educationist Marianne Thornton.[11]

Miss Thornton and I drove down . . . to see the N.S. [North Surrey] District Schools – I was much amused, the chairman of the Guardians had been asked over to confront us – and I think they all thought that we were going to be disagreeable.

The two women were wily enough to work their considerable disarming charm and so

[As] soon as they saw that we meant kindly they were as nice as they could be . . . But the principle [i.e.institutionalization] is wrong in my opinion – I wrote at their request in the visiting book that we . . . were pleased with what was done for the children but I put in that of course I'd rather that the children were in separate homes!! – Miss Thornton took lots of toys and I am going to send some next week. There were a terrible lot of children in hospital [the school infirmary]. (28 October 1872)

On 9 November Jeanie reported to Walter that she had just been to the German bazaar in town 'and got a lot of cheap toys for the little ones at the N.S. district schools; I shall take them [down] today'.

Two days later, on 11 November 1872, Jeanie reported to Walter the visit to Elm House that would not only alter the rest of her own life but would also be significant in British women's history:

My dear Octavia Hill came to dine and stay 2 nights. In the evening the 2 old ladies read their novels and father his paper and I talked to Octavia and had a most delightful time . . . All [the following Sunday] afternoon Octavia and I sat and talked. – No one came, so we had a most quiet uninterrupted time. Your father said he never heard anything like it. He did not think 2 people could talk so much.

What was the news that Octavia had brought with her?

. . . Octavia told me that Stansfeld [the President of the Local Government Board who was Gladstone's Cabinet Minister in charge of Poor Law matters] had offered her a room in the office at Whitehall and a good salary if she would work for him at Poor Law subjects, as he sees that women's work is needed. He wanted her to go thoroughly into all the ins and outs of Boarding-out – She says she was sorely tempted to throw over her present work and accept his offer – It would have paid her so well, and she gets no money now for her work and she would have been so interested in the work too. But she decided against taking it for she says she has to educate others to take her place in her present work among the poor, and if she left it before any one could take her place it would all go to ruin. Whereas what she now looks to is the gradual exten-sion of the system [i.e. of social housing for the very poor managed by women social workers] till it overspreads the Kingdom. – So she made the sacrifice of money and fame. (11 November 1872)

Octavia Hill now asked her friend whether she would not take up this amazing opportunity instead of her? Jeanie needed a sequence of exclamation marks to express just how intoxicated she was by the idea of herself being appointed the first woman Civil Servant in Britain. But she was also full of self-doubt:

> I only wish I knew enough of official work and were clever enough to do it instead of Octavia! I should so like it! But my education has not fitted me for it. – How nice to go to one's office daily to work at Poor Law subjects, for a good salary!

In just two days Octavia overruled all Jeanie's hesitation:

> I have told Octavia Hill that she may speak of me to Stansfeld, if she really thinks I should be equal to the work. Your father says he is sure I could do it, and is very anxious for me to apply. I feel doubtful myself whether I have intellect enough. – I know that I have love of conscientious work – but that is not enough. (13 November 1872)

Events then moved fast. On 18 November Octavia Hill wrote to her like a loving conspirator:

> My dearest Janey [sic]
>
> I had written to Stansfeld before your letter arrived . . . I told him nothing but that I think I know someone who will do . . . He is coming to the [tenants'] party on the 28th as he has long wanted to come to one and I shall introduce you to one another there if all be well. I am sure that you are the very person and if he has any sense he will feel this, we shall see. – . . .
>
> I somehow believe dear that we shall get this appointment under Stansfeld managed . . . Dear love, I am, Yours affectionately
>
> Octavia Hill.[15]

However, in the middle of the night of 22 November Jeanie was awoken by an all too familiar pain in her side, as she confided to Walter:

> – a pain I <u>do</u> have sometimes from the lump I have there. It . . . is not in the least dangerous: but it is a sign that I must keep quiet, or else I might set up some internal congestion – . . . I am going to get

up presently. . . . I <u>must</u> get quite well by the 28th as on no account
must I miss Stansfeld –

What desperation there was in her underlined 'I <u>must</u> get quite well'. That
night was a crucial, perhaps the defining, moment in her adult life. Most
other women would have taken the recurrence of the pain just then as a
warning that their health would not stand the stress of such an appointment
– it could be fatal. Jeanie, ever the optimist, told herself that her tumour was
not serious, merely benign. But should she not have recognized – and
acknowledged, both to Octavia Hill and to Stansfeld – that she might not be
strong enough for this demanding office? An assignment on which not only
the treatment of thousands of vulnerable children depended but also by
which the competence for public life of all other British women would now
be judged? Every moment of Jeanie Senior's life up to that point, however,
including all her long domestic years of frustrated energy – as well as her
brief experience of fulfilling work for the Red Cross – had determined her to
seize this chance with both hands. Should her no shoulds. She *could* not
withdraw her candidature from this once-in-a-lifetime opportunity and
dwindle yet once more into the harassed châtelaine of Elm House. Her great
voice had been confined to the private sphere; *this* would be the song she
would sing on the public stage.

On that fateful 28 November evening Jeanie Senior took a carriage to
Octavia Hill's tenants' party in poverty-stricken Maryelebone, 'as I had been
ailing last week'. A professional entertainer gave them some brilliant read-
ings from Macaulay and Dickens before she herself sang folk songs and
Handel. In the interstices she was given her quasi 'interview' with the
Cabinet Minister. It must have been an extraordinary scene:

> Stansfeld came early and stayed to the end, and we had a good deal
> of talk tho' of course it was interrupted. The awkward thing about
> it was, that I knew that he was talking to me with a certain
> purpose in view, and I suppose he knew that I knew. – But I tried
> to be natural, . . . I don't suppose that he has positively settled
> what to do as to having a woman at the office – . . . But I think I
> have a good chance of it if he decides on having a woman – For
> when he went he said that he had not had half enough talk with
> me . . . (30 November 1872)

On 3 December she learned from Octavia Hill that Stansfeld seemed
unable to believe that the sister of Tom Hughes, MP, QC, "would take hard
work and paying work", but Octavia had managed to reassure him. In the
midst of taking the children for their dental treatment, working on their
winter clothes for new schools in Scotland, and rehearsing them in their

exuberant Xmas party charades and theatricals, Jeanie received one piece of great good news. Walter had not only passed his degree but had actually gained Second Class Honours. And early in January 1873 she received Stansfeld's offer of the government appointment. She was just forty-four.

There can be no doubt as to the significance of this first appointment of a woman Civil Servant. Although a few extraordinary women – Elizabeth Fry, Mary Carpenter and Josephine Butler – had been invited to testify as witnesses to Royal Commissions on social questions, their testimony had merely been that of experienced amateurs in the field; no official notice had had to be taken of their views, let alone acted upon. But now a Cabinet Minister had gone against the advice of all his male colleagues and advisers in Whitehall and appointed a woman to have *official* responsibility for delivering a report to the Government, a report that might, very conceivably, bring about a change in legislation. Jeanie Senior had had no education after the age of sixteen; as a woman she possessed, of course, neither professional qualifications nor experience; and, unlike several other prominent women social activists, she had not held any official position in a voluntary reformist organization. She was not even eligible to vote. If an unqualified married lady could be thus appointed to report on questions relating to girls and women, why should not a whole procession of such ladies follow in her wake? Whitehall could be overrun. But it was not merely that she was a woman that caused Jeanie Senior's appointment to be received with foreboding, resentment, even indignation. She was '*that* woman' – the woman who had dared to make herself a national spokesperson recently in the correspondence columns of *The Times* as a critic of District Schools. How could she possibly be seen as an impartial judge in her new role of Government Inspector of the education of pauper girls? Was it not an extraordinarily quixotic decision to appoint her?

James Stansfeld was an extraordinary, and some would say, a quixotic man. Eight years older than Jeanie, he was the son of a Yorkshire Unitarian, a humane County Court Judge. Excluded from Oxford and Cambridge by the Test and Corporation Acts, young Stansfeld had attended University College, London in the late 1830s. He was a Shelleyan idealist then, fired to social indignation by the poverty he saw in London, and inspired to be a reformer, both by Ashley's advocacy of the Ten Hours Factory Bill in the Commons and by the Chartist agitation all around him in the 1840s. Influenced by his employer and later father-in-law, the Radical solicitor William Ashurst,[13] twenty-year old James Stansfeld soon became an ardent, lifelong convert to two other great causes – the emancipation of women and the national independence of the subject peoples of Europe. He himself was the cherished only brother of seven clever sisters (thus an exact counterpart of Jeanie, the cherished only sister of seven brothers) and in 1844 he married Caroline, one of the four feminist daughters of William Ashurst and a

27 The Rt. Hon. James
Stansfeld, MP, President of the
Local Government Board.
Courtesy the National Portrait
Gallery, London.

devoted follower of Mazzini. Thereafter Stansfeld's very promising political
career as Liberal MP for Halifax would be stopped in its tracks, time after
time, by his crusading zeal for one or other of his idealistic causes.[14] He lost
his position in the Liberal Government by his own and his wife's devotion to
Mazzini and Young Italy in 1864 and in the late 1870s he would forfeit his
re-appointment to Gladstone's Cabinet through his dogged support for
Josephine Butler's campaign to repeal the Contagious Diseases Acts.

James Stansfeld had a powerful intellect, unquestioned integrity, and what
even *The Saturday Review* called an 'indescribable charm of voice, manner
and earnestness' (13 April 1861).[15] It now becomes easier to understand
James Stansfeld's appointment of Jeanie Senior. He himself, as Gladstone's
President of the Local Government Board, had the liberal's distrust of large
institutions, and was evolving into a revisionist reformer of the draconian
1834 Poor Law.[16] He would have read Jeanie Senior's letters to *The Times*
under the heading 'District Schools' and 'Boarding Out' and recognized her
capacity for bold, trenchant argument backed by evidence, in the cause of
Britain's destitute, deserted and orphaned children. When Stansfeld actually
met Jeanie Senior for the first time and saw for himself her seriousness, her

simple directness and warmth – not at all the abrasive, humourless 'strong-minded woman' so regularly caricatured in *Punch* cartoons – he realized that she had just the qualities of humanity and sensitive intelligence that he was seeking. It was a case of 'the convergence of the twain'. Two ardent, enthu-siastic souls had met, both of them possessing an 'indescribable charm of voice, manner and earnestness.' And so 'I did the thing which they [on the Local Government Board] hated the most. I imposed a woman upon them, I made a woman a Poor Law Inspector.'[17]

CHAPTER TWELVE

The Government Inspector Goes on a Girl Hunt

Mrs. Nassau Senior was appointed 'to visit and inspect Workhouses, and Workhouse separate and District Schools for the purpose of inquiring into the operation and influence of the present system of education in those Establishments upon pauper Girls'. In an extraordinary illuminated address to James Stansfeld, 'the foremost women of our time'[1] saluted his act of faith in women:

> *On the appointment of Mrs. Nassau Senior to the office of*
> *Inspector under the Local Government Board.*
>
> Sir, – We the undersigned, believing that the Law of God is one and indivisible and equally binding upon all, that the one sole right of Humanity is the right to the free and responsible fulfilment of duty, that the duty of every human being is the gradual discovery and fulfilment of the Divine Law, that obedience to the Divine law involves the fulfilment by every human being of a threefold duty towards humanity, the fatherland and the family,
>
> That the human laws and customs which have hitherto restricted Woman to the fulfilment of the last portion of this duty only, are opposed to the design of the Almighty, who by endowing Woman with special aptitudes and faculties, complementary to the faculties and aptitudes of man, has assigned to her equally with him the duty of their full development and employment in the execution of a joint mission on earth, and acknowledging
>
> That you have been the first English Minister to recognize the great religious truths indicated above, and that by the appointment of a woman to an office of public trust and responsibility, you have taken the first step towards the practical realisation of these truths in the political system of our country,
>
> Gladly forward to you this heartfelt expression of our enduring gratitude and esteem.

> HARRIET MARTINEAU, Ambleside.[2]   ISABELLA M.S.TOD, Belfast.[3]
> KATE AMBERLEY, Ravenscroft.[4]   AMELIA E.ARNOLD.[5]
> ERNESTINE L. ROSE, New York.[6]   ELIZABETH MALLESON.[7]
> EMILIA ASHURST VENTURI.[8]   JOSEPHINE BUTLER, Liverpool.[9]

FLORENCE NIGHTINGALE, London.[10]   CATH. TAYLOR, Hampstead.
MARY CARPENTER, Bristol.[11]   ELIZ. C. WOLSTENHOLME, London.[12]
LUCY WILSON, Leeds.[13]   MENTIA TAYLOR, London.[14]

Despite the passionate religiosity of its wording (drafted by Josephine Butler?) the signatories included at least four notorious atheists, Martineau, Rose, Venturi and Wolstenholme, all of whom swallowed their non-religious principles for the sake of attesting to their feminism. The feminist *Englishwomen's Review* of April 1873 noted approvingly that it was 'the first instance of a woman being appointed as a government officer to a post that hitherto men only have been thought competent to fill, . . . a step of which the importance cannot be overestimated'.

Few people have had such a weight of significance attached to the performance of their first 'proper job'. The capacity of any woman to be a capable Civil Servant was to be judged by the success or failure of Mrs. Nassau Senior. The only analogous public testing of female intellectual competence and psychological strength in Britain was that undergone by the five women students who had dared to sit for Cambridge University examinations in 1870[15] and by the first women medical students in Edinburgh, also in 1870, who had had to outface a sheep being brought into the anatomical class by hundreds of hostile, rioting male students. If women could attend, why not a sheep?[16] Within that context of masculinist supremacism, Jeanie Senior's nervousness was equalled only by her sense of exhilaration and challenge.

On the 3rd of January Octavia Hill responded to the news of the appointment: '[Oh] Janey [sic] do try the work if you have a chance. . . . If you cannot do it no one can, and it wants doing so I hope you will try.' Two days later she wrote again, now concerned for her friend's *double* task – taking on the needs of the pauper girls while still having to see to the needs of Elm House: 'I am a little sorry in one way that it does not take you more away from home. I hoped that you might have had a few hours of rebound from the weight, and might have been stronger for home work for the daily absence.'

By 7 January Jeanie Senior had already started: 'I wrote to Stansfeld for a list of the Schools I shall have to visit. I want to see how many there are, and what order they will have to be taken in, that I may get a little idea of the extent of the work . . . '

Sensitive to the suspicion that she would be entering her investigation with her mind already made up on the subject of District Schools, she continued: 'I shall do my best to find out the *Truth*, no matter how it may go against my present belief and conviction.' Her private terror was that she might simply not be clever enough to write a Civil Service *Report* – 'I only hope I may have wits enough to do it well. I sometimes have a panic on that head'. (7 January 1873)

By 16 January she had received her first guidelines from Stansfeld. His original idea for her was a very limited survey: 'He thinks that I shall need very few journeys to the country, as the Metropolitan district will be by far the most important and will need thorough doing.' From the map of the 16 Metropolitan pauper schools, below, it can be seen that the children were deliberately moved many miles from their original place of origin in London. She happily fantasized about the spirit of co-operation that she and her male colleagues would soon enjoy:

> I have quite determined to be impartial and unprejudiced and I feel certain they will find that out and give me friendly good will and help. I have no fear of that. The only thing I doubt is whether (having no experience in such things) I shall be able to make a good *Report*. (16 January 1873)

She had asked not to be paid until her *Report* was completed and had been assessed, but Mr. Lowe, the Principal Secretary of the Poor Law Department,

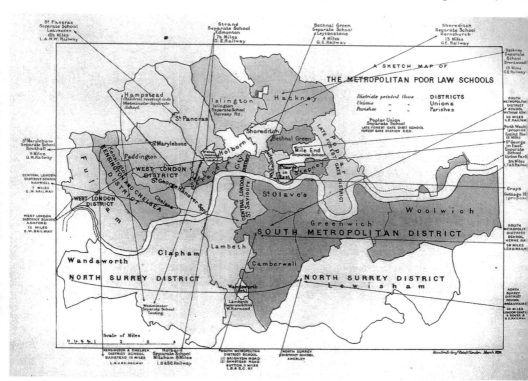

28   Sketch Map of Metropolitan Poor Law Schools, from Walter Monnington, *Our London Poor-Law Schools*, 1898, City of London. Courtesy London Metropolitan Archives

said she must be paid the same amount as all her male colleagues. She did insist, however, that her Government appointment be only temporary, pending the acceptance of her *Report*.

From the outset, she recognized that she would need to pool the intelligence and relevant experience of all her women friends and acquaintances active in social reform. As Caroline Stephen recounted:

> Mrs. Senior's first act on receiving her appointment was to call together a few female friends who had already more or less experience in work of this kind, and to form them into a sort of informal committee, with whom she could take counsel from time to time, and some of whom could help her in the inquiries she had to make.[17]

No one would be more important on that 'informal committee' than Caroline Stephen herself. Henrietta Synnot was also enrolled, especially to look at the academic side of the girls' education – 'she will be of immense help to me, with her clear head and already great experience amongst schools' (16 January). In addition, Jeanie Senior wrote to many veterans of intervention on behalf of poor children, both men and women, for their advice, including the great pioneering founder of the Ladies' Workhouse Visiting Society.[18]

> Dear Louisa,
>
> Will you give a very old friend the benefit of your advice and experience? Stansfeld has given me a job of work, and to the end of the year to do it in. I have to inquire and report on the influence of the education in district, workhouse, and separate, schools, on girls; nothing to do with boarding-out, except, of course, indirectly. No one can help me in this matter as you can. I am most proud and delighted to be given a bit of work for the nation, and, of course, I am intensely anxious to do it thoroughly and well. You have been doing splendid national work for years and years, and your advice and suggestions will be quite invaluable to me, if you'll take me in hand. I know how over-busy you are at your own work, but I'm certain you'll be glad to help me.[19]

Louisa Twining gave her blessing on 12 February 1873:

> I cannot tell you how your work interests me, and what a wonderful triumph I consider it. It is now just 20 years since I first began and went to the Poor Law Board on the subject. One sees now that all the talk and writing, so much of which seemed repetition, was

not thrown away; at several Social Science meetings where I said, "what was wanted was women Inspectors of everything" and that it has really come to pass, is to me a marvellous fact and encouragement. So much that I said seemed so perfectly hopeless at the time – much of it I always acknowledged was based on Mrs Jamesons's charming little books which I believe were the first beginnings of the movement.[20]

Florence Davenport Hill, author of *The Children of the State: the training of Juvenile Paupers* (1868), also wrote in support, and even the great rescuer and teacher of Bristol's street children, Mary Carpenter, agreed to be interviewed by Jeanie when next in London.

On 22 January Jeanie Senior reported her first encounter with the veteran Chief Inspector, C. W. Tufnell, who had both assisted her father-in-law in drafting the 1834 New Poor Law, and himself been a New Poor Law Commissioner:

At first he was stiff as a poker, and very dry; but after a bit, as I asked him questions and referred all to his opinion he quite thawed, and we parted excellent friends. I go to him for an hour's coaching on Saturday morning, and I daresay I shall get a deal of help from him, tho' he seems to me a regular old square toes!

It would be hard to say which of the two was more mistaken about the other, Tufnell about Jeanie's deference to his views or Jeanie about Tufnell's spirit of helpful friendliness towards her. Three days later she reported:

I have just been spending two hours with old Tufnell the School Inspector. I think I have convinced him that I wish to go into the enquiry with a mind like a sheet of white paper. He was really very kind and nice – of course he does not recognize the objections [to 'Barrack Schools'] that I see, and he believes that little if any improvement could be made even in the training of the girls. Now that I can't believe *yet*. (25 January 1873)

She had already started to think about how to discover the Workhouse girls' fates, once out in the world: 'Today I went in the morning to the workhouse here [i.e. Westminster Union School on Wandsworth Common] to enquire of the master how to get at the truth about the way the girls . . . turn out. I have made up my mind how to set at work to get at least some information' (22 January). And she had already had one exhilarating inspection with Henrietta Synnot:

> She is a great help to me as she thoroughly understands what I do
> not understand – the schoolwork – the 3Rs etc – and she is very
> shrewd and clear-headed [about age-related attainment levels]. . . .
> The work is very interesting but I see immense difficulties ahead.
> (25 January)

In that same letter she first outlined her plan 'to enlist a lot of amateur
workers to help get information' about the hundreds of girls who had left the
Workhouse to go into service in the preceding twelve months.

Jeanie Senior had also confessed her excitement and her trepidation to
George Eliot. The writer reassured her:

> Our joy is without misgiving, we feel sure that your work will be
> done well . . . .
>   You have only got to be a good faithful woman such as you
> have always been, and then the very thought of you will help to
> mend things. Take it as a sign of that, when I tell you that you
> have entered into my more cheerful beliefs, and made them
> stronger, because of the glimpses I have had of your character and
> life.[21]

The novelist recognized immediately that this appointment was a milestone
in women's history, and that the 'influence of one woman's life on the lot of
other women is getting greater and greater'. But then follows a hint of foreboding:

> [Two] thousand years ago Euripides made Iphigenia[22] count it a
> reason for facing her sacrifice bravely that thereby she might help
> to save Greek women (from a wrong like Helen's) in the time to
> come. There is no knife at your throat, happily.

Was there not?

For the present, Jeanie Senior was laughing with excitement and self-
mockery at her new project: 'I feel that I am rapidly becoming a bore of the
first water. I can't think of anything but my subject and find myself talking
about it perpetually. My friends will soon have to fly when I appear' (25
January). The most substantial of all the letters of encouragement in
response to her requests for help, came from Florence Nightingale:

> My dear Madam
>   I rejoice more than I can say that you have this work to do.
>   You are the person to do it.
>   And no one else.

And, tho' I would, most gladly, serve as your handmaid in it, if I could, yet I am much more glad that this work has you to do it, and that you and no one else have it to do.

The enquiry is one of the highest importance and will take a very long time to do it justice. . . . [As] you are so very good as to ask me, I will say that I should begin by the essential but least practical part, the Statistical:–

"The Passionate Statistician", as she is called in the Florence Nightingale Museum Trust Guidebook (p. 19), then proceeded to teach Jeanie Senior the ABC of statistical investigation and record:

Statistical Tables

1. Name of School: a. District   b. Separate   c. Workhouse
2. When established
3. No. of Inmates (average last year)
4. Yearly Admissions
5. Yearly Deaths and Causes of Death
6. Yearly Discharges: a. to service b. to friends [i.e. relatives] c. other causes
7. Nos. of girls for every 5 years of age – 0–5 5–10 etc.
8. No. of orphans: a. both parents dead b. father dead c. mother dead
9. No. of classes with average attendance in each
10. Branches taught in each class
11. Duration of Classes: a. hours per week b. in years.
12. Domestic training: description of and similar particulars as to time
13. No. of Teachers and salaries
14. Holidays, if any.
15. Examinations, if any –
16. How the School and Training [=] managed by Board of Guardians or School Committee (Generally some good and interested in [pauper] children, some hard-fisted or rate saving or bad).
17. Then would come your own thorough personal routing out of the School and Girls as to cleanliness, clothing, bedding, general care, etc.
18 Then, most important and most interesting of all, your own direct and indirect routing up of the moral state . . .

Amongst other points, I should go minutely into the method of placing out the girls to service and the kinds of supervision kept up over them and their situations afterwards – including (horrid blot!) the number of failures where the girls return to the Workhouse or go to the bad.

This point, its causes and remedies are of vital need, as I need not say to *you* . . .

It would be the most conceited thing in the world, if it were not the one I am most disinclined to, for me to give you hints – you who have done so much for the Boarding out in Families – the greatest step of all in favour of these poor girls who are to be our future mothers.

. . . I give you joy –

Or rather, I give Mr. Stansfeld and the girls joy.

Good speed – ever yours most truly, Florence Nightingale. (January 1873)

That letter must have been a help, if somewhat daunting.

If any additional motive were needed to spur Jeanie Senior on, it was her secret hope that this professional post of hers might help find Walter useful work in the world:

> I don't intend that all the work of your life should be spent in law which does no good to your fellow creatures. . . . I don't intend if my life is spared for a few years to let you pine away your life in chambers . . . Pauperism and all the questions arising out of it, is the great enigma now, and it must be solved. (28 January 1873)

She fantasized that Walter might realize her own and her brother Tom's radical vision:

> I trust you will walk in Uncle Tom's footsteps and do something to raise and improve the condition of the workers. They must be much better as a class than we are not to rise as one man and sweep us all away when they see how much we might do and how little we do do to make their lives more tolerable. (12 February 1873)

She was, as her old friend Dr. de Mussy recognized, 'in glorious spirits'. It was as though she were possessed by two daemons – one driving her to expose the plight of the Workhouse girls to the world, the other to show the world what she herself, and therefore Everywoman, was capable of doing. She would out-inspect every previous Inspector. As Edwin Pratt commented in retrospect: 'The amount of work she did in pursuit of her mission seems almost appalling.'[23] And her sister-in-law Minnie recalled years later: 'For some time nothing seemed to tire her.'[24]

As soon as Jeanie Senior realized that her Report must contain two parts – (1) The condition of the pauper girls currently in the schools and (2) The histories of the girls after leaving the schools, in order to gauge the impact of their education – she grasped that her pioneering social investigation had to be both quantitative and qualitative. No more vague allegations of 'unsatisfactory conditions', or mere assertions that 'many workhouse girls end up on the streets', would now do. Precise information as to diet, clothing, sanitary conditions, accurate names and numbers of all the girls coming from each institution studied, as well as the fate of as many individual girls as possible, all would now have to be uncovered, and percentages, however rough, of 'success' or 'failure' calculated, using interviews with the girls themselves, their employers and, where necessary, questionnaires. Caroline Stephen was of great use here in helping her to work out the appropriate methodology:

> Cary Stephen came at 10.30 and we had a grand set to! – Got thro' heaps of work, drew out all our forms of return and all our plans of questions, . . . She is certainly A1 of all my friends. The finest woman I know, both intellectually and morally . . . I can gather from her all sorts of information and help and strength. (15 February 1873)

Cary Stephen was tied to her home, looking after her invalid elderly mother – 'So we [she and Henrietta Synnot] shall go to see her, instead of her coming to me. I had a delightful talk with her today. She is so clever and so just and so clearheaded. I feel a little pigmy [sic] peeping out and catching crumbs of wisdom.'

The first essential, laborious step was to make accurate lists of the names of all the hundreds of girls who were then in the Workhouse Schools as well as of all those who had left during the past year so that they might be traced. A surviving undated note to Henrietta Synnot reveals something of the toil involved:

> Please let me have the Edmonton list back. . . . I am much ashamed of myself for being so stupid, but I am not sure how many lists of girls I have sent you. Have I not still to get Forest Gate, Sutton, Islington/Hornsey Rise, Leavesden, Brentwood? Ashford has sent out no girls [to domestic service] yet.

Jeanie Senior had given herself an additional remit – a personal follow-up study of at least fifty girls who had left their Workhouse District School five years earlier, in order to try to determine the long-term effect, if any, of their education. In order to end up with fifty case-studies she would have to try to trace seventy-five girls, leaving scope for non-returns. But the task proved unbelievably difficult.

> [She] found it necessary to consult, besides admission and discharge books, five enormous alphabetical registers, numerous volumes of relief lists, creed registers, service registers, and chaplains' visiting books [i.e. Register of Servants and Apprentices] . . . The time and labour necessary to extract [the required information] . . . is hardly to be realised until the experiment has been tried.[25]

As soon as Jeanie Senior had finally compiled the full list of well over six hundred girls who had left their District and Separate Schools to go into domestic service the previous year, she then engaged a team of women investigators, most of whom were unpaid, to trace the girls and discover their current situation.[26] And after turning up and cross-referencing the needed information in all those files, Jeanie Senior had additionally, over the year, to write 154 letters and call at 188 houses all over London, in order to track down the trajectory and fate of the other seventy-five girls who had left the schools five years earlier, in order to attempt her longitudinal study. As Edwin Pratt said, it is exhausting merely to contemplate.

Her remit as Inspector was to report on the girls from a woman's point of view; therefore she felt herself to be more of a Child Welfare Officer than an Education Inspector as she went over the sixteen Metropolitan District and Separate Schools, checking not just the girls' performance in the 3Rs but all she could discover about their physical and emotional well-being. As she toured one depressing 'Barrack' School after another, she became increasingly convinced that she must include in her *Report* informed observations on the alternative of fostering as opposed to the institutionalization and mass-regimentation of parentless girls. And she never stopped worrying about their aftercare once they had left their 'Barracks'. What should be done for them then?

She now made her first short tour of inspection outside London, starting in Birmingham to see Joanna Hill, sister of Florence Davenport Hill, and visiting both the Workhouse and some of Joanna Hill's own boarded-out children. Next she went on to Wolverhampton where she was 'minded' by the veteran Poor Law Inspector, Andrew Doyle. They went over Wolverhampton Workhouse and then on by train to Stafford to see another Workhouse and from there to Workhouse Schools in Stoke-on-Trent and Shrewsbury.

On her return to London, she went to Whitehall and for the first time wrote to Walter on official Poor Law Board notepaper. 'I can hear you laugh and it amuses me too! –"Mother has got her office at last!"' What must have it been like to have been the only woman to enter the front door of the grand Whitehall building and walk down its corridors, the only woman in Britain

29 Purpose-built Central London District 'Barrack' School, Hanwell (closed 1935). Courtesy London Metropolitan Archives.

who had an official, salaried, public role – other than Queen Victoria? But she did not stay put in her office. Off she went to inspect a Workhouse school in Mitcham. Next she interviewed the Parliamentary Secretary to the Home Office, requesting figures on female prisoners – she wanted to check how many of them had been brought up in 'Barrack' schools. She would also need to see a Col. Du Cane from the Home Office, head of convict prisons, and a Col. Henderson, head of police, but it was difficult to get them to make appointments convenient to her programme of inspections. 'That is the only bother in my work – I find that seeing all these men who must be seen entails such a waste of time' (1 March 1873).

Nevertheless she felt cheerful: both Hibbert and Du Cane granted the returns she wanted; her brother Hastings seemed to be emerging from one of his business cash-flow crises; the two elderly grandmothers were in better health again; and even Nassau had a brighter prospect. He was offered a Directorship on the Board of a Coal Company, not requiring him to invest any money but giving him at least £100 per annum, merely for sitting on the Board (5 March 1873). That same day she went over the huge Sutton District School (soon to have 1,500 inmates) with Tufnell – 'a world of a place but beautifully managed . . . [However] everything is so machine like, and must be so in those enormous schools'. And next day she visited Hornsey with Miss Sara Stephen:[27]

> There was a delightful Matron there, and it was satisfactory in everything but the number of bad heads, such lots of ringworm! [So she was actually inspecting each child's scalp.] On my way back, I passed my Industrial School and went in to have a look at my girls. I wish no schools had more than 25 girls! (8 March)

The following day she went even further afield with Henrietta Synnot who drove her to the Stepney Schools in Limehouse beyond East India Docks:

> I liked seeing that part of the world. There was a marine air about it and a smell of tar that I liked. We were delighted with the children and schools – not a case of opthalmia, and little ringworm and no itch [scabies] – and very nice people in charge of the children. But alas! The school is so small that it is going to be broken up and the children sent to Sutton.

She acquired a new ally, Dr. Mouat, 'a delightful old Doctor' employed by the Poor Law Board, who was going into the question of opthalmia. 'He agrees with me exactly, so I think him wondrous wise!' (12 March).[28]

A week later she recorded a memorable dinner party given by the Stansfelds. The youthful idealistic radicals Lord and Lady Amberley were there, as well as W. E. Forster of the 1870 Forster Education Act with his wife, the sister of Matthew Arnold, and the MP George Trevelyan, son of Sir Charles Trevelyan and nephew of Lord Macaulay, and several others. 'I sang to them, and had a great success tho' I only sang what I knew by heart.' She did not often claim 'a great success'. What had she sung? Almost certainly the same programme that she would perform next evening in a concert with Joachim at Eton – 'Vado ben spesso', Schubert's 'Ave Maria' and, as encores, 'Sweet and Low' and 'Wapping Old Stairs'. As Stansfeld listened to Jeanie singing Schubert, her warm, powerful mezzo-soprano pleading for motherly pity for a begging child – "O Mutter, hoer ein bittend Kind! . . . Ave Maria!" perhaps he realized for the first time just how rare a creature he had enlisted for his experiment.

She now persuaded Stansfeld not only that she should examine Boarding-out after all 'in order to say something accurate about it in my *Report*', but that she should go 'to see it in its best phase, Edinburgh and the North of England' (21 March). She planned to be off on her tour over the Easter break, beginning 7 April. Nassau was now offered another Directorship; in addition to the Coal Board and Positive Insurance, he would also be made a

Director of a Fire Assurance Co. 'without putting in a farthing'. Clearly he was a 'safe pair of hands' and, like Jeanie, he would be bringing in £400 a year. Therefore Walter must feel free to think of marrying young, his mother wrote encouragingly – just as soon as he met the right girl. Margaret Hughes, her nearly 80 year-old mother, was growing increasingly restive at Elm House, meanwhile, with Jeanie so preoccupied and so often away, while old Mrs. Senior was so often all too present. She declared that she wanted 'to buy a farm'! A cottage at Offley Place might be possible, Jeanie thought, but a *farm*?

Before she set off for the North she had two more matters to settle, one concerning the family, the other her work of Inspection. The disgraced, but thankfully not pregnant, young Frankie Coleridge had been invited to stay at Elm House and Jeanie wanted to share with the girl her brainwave concerning her future. Would Frankie be willing to work as a trainee social worker for Octavia Hill? Second was a memorable episode in her own work. She felt that she must breathe the same air that the pauper children had to breathe in bed. Therefore she travelled down to Anerley at night in order to be up before dawn next day to inspect the huge dormitories with Dr. Mouat:

> We were at the schools at 5.30 [a.m.] Such a lovely sunrise I saw! The air in the dormitories was horrid and I think old Mouat will speak so strongly about it that some better system of ventilation will be adopted. It makes me really unhappy to know that hundreds of children are sleeping all the year long in that fetid atmosphere. (5 April 1873, written in the train to Chester)

To Henrietta Synnot she wrote more tersely 'The Anerley rooms were very nasty – One or 2 awful. I think they will be put right' (9 April) .

On her journey north she travelled near Hoylake where her brother George had died almost exactly a year ago – '[I] tried not to wish him back. I don't wish him back, but life is not the same thing now' (16 April 1873). At Kendal Jeanie stayed with the Poor Law Guardian Mr. Cropper and his sister, friends of the Hills of Birmingham and saw some boarded-out children. In Cumberland she stayed with Octavia Hill's close friend, the Quaker Mary Harris and had the extra delight of having Octavia to herself there for a day and a half. 'We talked – she, I and Miss Harris – all day yesterday except when I was in church. Miss Harris is one of the most beautiful old ladies I ever saw – about 56 or 58 – a Quaker or Friend as they call them here' (14 April 1873). She visited boarded-out children there and in Broughton, accompanied by

> 2 delightful old Friends Mr and Mrs. Wilson Robinson, [also] great friends of Octavias . . . and people very much interested in

[pauperism and education]. There is something very attractive to
me about the Friends – a curious calmness about the outward man;
and a peace that emanates from the inward man, and that makes
itself felt. (16 April 1873)

That letter was written at the home of her old friends, the Mitchells,[29] at 5
East Claremont St., Edinburgh. She had immediately called nearby to see
'her boys', Gerard and Harry, having breakfast with them at 8 a.m., before
they went off to their day school. Then she had gone by cab with a Sub-
inspector to see twenty-six different children boarded out in various villages
around.

It was very interesting and on the whole very satisfactory but I
wish landlords could be compelled, when they build cottages to
make them with good ventilation and drainage . . . Luckily the
houses are not air tight, and the children live out of doors, but I
don't see why landlords should not be forced to make their
cottages fit for people to live in. (16 April 1873)

Next day she was off again immediately after breakfast, this time with Dr.
Mitchell plus two Boarding out Inspectors, to see children near Carstairs.
She would have to do more inspecting work on Friday and planned to travel
back to London with the boys on the Saturday, 20 April. But then came a
crisis – young Gerard went down with measles. First Jeanie sent Harry away
into lodgings to be out of the infection, but Harry sickened too. Harry
became very seriously ill, his bad attack of measles complicated by high fever
and acute bronchitis, making Jeanie deeply anxious, for he had always been
a very delicate child. His brilliant, lively brain could not stop working and
was preventing him from getting necessary sleep.
    Nassau now showed himself at his worst.

Your father writes to say that I must come home, for that he so
dislikes the house when I am away. So I am torn between 2 duties.
Yet I do think that, as Father is quite well and the children ill (and
one very seriously ill) that it is my duty to see them over the
danger. It is the worst part of adopting children that one loves
them almost like ones very own and yet that others don't recognize
the fact that one has a duty towards them as well as a love and
yearning. – Life is very difficult, when one has to judge between 2
courses. . . . (22 April 1873)

It was at this crisis that Jeanie Senior faced the conflict all too familiar to
working mothers: how could she possibly fulfil her responsibilities both to

her children and to her profession? She had no doubt but that her first task was to see the children safely out of danger but she still fretted that

> I find that it is almost impossible to get on with my official work – one can't do it well unless ones mind is to certain extent free. The anxiety, and the 1000 things that have to be seen to, and done, when there is sickness, make official work very difficult. I shall finish up my notes of what I have seen here and shall then give up real hard work till I get home.

She recognized that caring for her own ill or troubled children would always be the biggest problem for the professionally employed mother: 'This is the great drawback I suspect to women having work of this sort. The feminine work being the real life of a woman, she feels (rightly) that in cases of illness etc. the thing that must be put aside is the official.' Jeanie Senior then consoled herself: 'I shall soon make up tho' for lost time when the present anxiety is over – and I have eased my conscience by writing to tell Stansfeld that I have sick children and shall have to lay by his work for a week' (22 April). To Henrietta Synnot, she confessed: 'strange to say I have become, in the presence of measles, apathetic about the pauper children. It is wrong but so it is. . . . Thank you for doing some work in my absence . . . Did you get my letter about sending Miss Smedley[30] the lists? (23 April 1873)

Jeanie was especially fearful of losing Harry, the month of April being now bitterly associated for her with the death of her eldest brother:

> Even with all the interesting work that is the best help to me, still I have my heart full of tears; and I can't face the chance of Harry's being taken from me without the most dreadful agony. I try to think I am over anxious . . . but George's death seems to have weakened my power of endurance; and yet how selfish it is of me to mourn so for him when he is so blessed. (22 April)

The word 'selfish' clearly brought Nassau to mind, for her letter immediately continues: 'Try that your father shall not think himself neglected by me, because I stay. He speaks in his letter as if he were being neglected by me and that pains me so much.' On 28 April, still in Edinburgh, she wrote that Harry was nearly over the worst. Dr. Mitchell was not happy she could not stay longer to supervise the convalescence. 'But what can I do? Your father is already in a terrible state at my prolonged absence, and so there is no choice. But I shall feel very anxious I know.' She did return to Elm House and her place by the boys in Edinburgh was immediately taken by her elderly mother, Mrs. Hughes. Dr. Mitchell reassured her that the boys were doing famously but her Mother must not think of taking them off now to a

Highland Shooting Lodge! For himself, 'I cannot tell you how much I miss you. I have never met any lady with whom I so much liked to talk about the matters which have so long interested me. When are you coming North again?' (2 May). He reassured her that if she could not manage to trace many of the former Workhouse girls out in the world, she should not regard it as her failure but rather as evidence of how little was actually known of their fate. Regarding her reluctance to make an issue of the illegitimacy of many of these girls in her Report, 'I don't think you a coward. On the contrary I think you full of pluck' (12 June 1873).

On her return to London she had found a letter from the great social reformer Lord Shaftesbury offering her his support in uncovering a long neglected social sore: 'I trust that you will bring up an evil report of the District Schools – They are real nightmares on one's mind' (4 April 1873). Meanwhile Octavia Hill was reporting to her on the progress of Jeanie's protégée, the needing-to-be-rehabilitated Frankie Coleridge. In a series of hitherto unpublished letters, Octavia offered to take Frankie in to live with herself, her mother and her sisters: 'I should be very glad of her help' (30 April 1873). As for Frankie's work with Emma Cons[31] –

> She has been *every* day, and is very good and obliging, and decid-
> edly capable, but I must tell you honestly that I feel she is entirely
> uninterested – . . . I like her and shall be deeply disappointed if the
> plan of fellow-work falls through. (9 May 1873)

Octavia Hill's penultimate letter about Frankie was much more positive about the new recruit – as well as extraordinarily candid and self-critical:

> I wish I were gentler and better able to let people see what I feel; in
> one way I can conceal nothing, everyone knows what I think right
> or wrong which passes, but few know how much I care for them.
> . . . Miss Coleridge is doing quite beautifully and is becoming
> what the children here call 'one of us'. She really thinks about her
> work and has much heart in it, and what I find more rare a good
> judgment. . . . It is essential to find her a really happy home near,
> she evidently dreads fresh people knowing [i.e. that she was a 'fallen
> woman']. We are growing very fond of her. (September 1873)

Finally, on 12 October Octavia was able to write: 'Dear Miss Coleridge is turning out a real help to us. I can see how Miss Cons leans on her for much help, in a way she does not to any one on whom she cannot depend . . . Will you give her my love?'

A new character in the world of child rescue then came on the scene – Maria Rye, the messianic proponent of emigration (or 'Emancipation' as she called it) of indigent girls and women to the colonies, especially Canada.[32] Her first letters to Jeanie Senior, on paper headed 'Emigration Home for destitute little girls', vividly express the writer's passionate, 'driven', indignant personality:

> Yes the Shrewsbury Workhouse is at Atcham – and the girls there looked wretched – heads sore etc. Did I tell you that they gave me a report 20 years old about the placing of the children? . . . What can you do? . . . (3 June 1873)
>   I am starting for Canada now in about ten days. –
>   Have you been to St. George's in the East Workhouse? If not please make a point of going. You get at it by train to London Bridge and then by cab behind the Tower, in an out of the way street called 'Old Gravel Lane'. I . . . found a delightfully pompous and ignorant Board [of male Poor Law Guardians] . . . I asked how many girls brought up in their schools had ever been returned to the House as adult paupers and ruined women, to which I got the triumphant reply Only two in thirty years! Indeed, was my answer – and are you not aware that you have now within your walls twenty young women in disgrace who were once in your schools? . . .
>   I do not think we should lay much stress on the fact of there being . . . as you put it – very many places for them – because as long as people can get these little scrubs for next to nothing of course there will be plenty of people applying for them. Did I tell you of the Stoke upon Trent girls . . . that while they put the girls out at 6d a week wages [in addition to their keep] – there were girls of 15 years of age – who had been out two years – and had never even been paid that miserable sum? (16 June 1873)

Jeanie Senior was now, with the help of Menella Smedley, masterminding the tracing of 650 girls known to have left the Workhouse Schools the previous year, delegating much of the interview work to her team of trusted helpers whose completed questionnaires were then sifted by her. She, of course, had taken additional personal responsibility for the accompanying longitudinal study of fifty girls traced from three typical schools who had left to go into service five years earlier. 'However necessarily inconclusive, and possibly in some respects misleading, the results of such an inquiry might be, it seemed to be the only available means of in any degree testing the system by its results.'[33]

It may easily be imagined how such a workload, including compilation of long, annotated lists of names, a huge correspondence, and the analysis of questionnaire returns, all having to be written out by hand, most often her own hand, together with notes on visits to District Schools, Kindergartens, Reformatories, Industrial schools, Orphanages, boarded-out children and over a hundred work placements scattered throughout London, was making a superhuman demand on Jeanie Senior's whirling dervish energy. Her Edinburgh friend Dr. Mitchell grew worried: 'Do not overwork yourself. Your life is a very dear one' (30 July 1873). At the end of August her body at last rebelled, the uterine cancer no longer in remission. She suffered internal haemorrhaging, vomiting and the painful enlargement of her tumour. Utterly exhausted, she was ordered to bed.

She reported to Walter that the *belladonna* plasters the doctor had put on had relieved the pain, she had lost no more blood for some days and now felt stronger. Immediately she became impatient, wanting to get out of bed – but 'that Turk Taylor', her doctor, told her that bed rest would best reduce the size of the tumour. Dr. Mitchell was more worried than ever:

> I cannot make out what ails you, or how you can have a tumour which gives no anxiety or alarm. The story of your suffering quite depresses me, and I trust you are not making light of what is serious. . . . [You] have a power of usefulness which the world must not lose yet awhile. (14 September 1873)

By 1 October she was back at work again. 'Yesterday I went to see a girl or two in Lambeth – I could not get a Hansom so went in a growler. But it did me no harm.' 'Old Taylor' said that her tumour had much decreased in size. He wanted her to go away for a fortnight as soon as she was well enough to travel. By 4 October she declared: 'I am quite well again as long as I do only half what I could do without fatigue in times past – I feel sure I shall get back to my normal state after a fortnight's change of air.' She had 'been on a girl hunt' that very morning 'in the delightful Hansom' and was also looking after Frankie Coleridge, now on holiday at Elm House. 'It is very interesting to me to hear all her experience in the work among the poor.' To Henrietta Synnot she wrote jokingly and tenderly: 'I expect you'll find me much improved in body, and deteriorated in mind. I can't describe how idiotic I am. – I *shall* be so happy to see you dear – If you see the dear Menella give her my kind love' (8 October 1873).

At last Jeanie Senior told Stansfeld that she had been seriously ill. He did not reproach her for having concealed it from him so long, but was deeply worried, insisting she take whatever break her doctor advised. 'Do not let me have it on my conscience that I have injured you for life; I cannot help thinking that you have suffered not from the mere work, but from the burden of moral responsibility which I know you have felt so much' (18 October 1873). By 19 October she was having her prescribed 'change of air' in Paris, but alas, she had chosen just the wrong moment. Not only were the de

Mussys miserable with marital discord and illness, they were also obsessed with Monarchist politics. Jeanie was appalled to find her old friend trying to restore the Bourbons! 'I wish I had come at any other time. I can't describe how I miss and pine about my work' (23 October). The only positive professional interview that she had in Paris was with the great educationist Mme. Pape-Carpentier,[34] the Rousseauist foundress of *Ecoles Maternelles* (then called *Salles d'Asiles*):

> Yesterday I started off at 9 to see Mme Carpentier, Caroline
> Stephen's friend. We had a great talk and I was with her till past 12
> . . . I saw Mme. Carpentier's Salle d'Asile which answers to our
> ragged school, tho' it is not quite the same. It was very interesting.
> She gave me various other addresses of schools etc. This morning I
> went to one, starting very early again. It is a school managed by
> the Soeurs de Charité. (28 October 1873)

Soon after her return to England Jeanie Senior began the writing up of her *Report*. Stansfeld had told her that he wanted her to keep in close touch with him from now on:

> I thank you very much, very warmly, very seriously for your letter.
> It makes me feel all at once to know you so much better . . . I
> could hardly have taken the step I did in asking for your help, if I
> had not had something more than a mere "Statesman's" interest in
> your question.

He suggested he might visit her at home regularly to advise, 'for I have the greatest wish that your report – the first step in something very wide and important in the future [i.e the full professional participation of women as Civil Servants on all matters relating to women] – should take the place and have the influence which I trust it may'.

That letter of 5 November 1873 ended with his concern about Jeanie's medical history. 'I am very much grieved to know what a sufferer you have been and for how long. How little we know each other. I had thought you blessed with almost perfect health and very strong.' He does not say that had he known the truth he would never have appointed her. Jeanie was very strong as well as very ill, which was why her illness took so long to kill her.

Dr. Mitchell helped her with difficult questions such as the sexual vulnerability of servant girls who were 'feeble-minded'. He advised her to admit the problem – 'show it as full as possible. Then confess that there is no present way out of it'. The girls could not simply be locked up for life. He also helped with statistical tables, instructing her never to use the 'sham accuracy' of vulgar fractions when dealing with people, e.g. 26 and 60/119 but rather decimals to the first decimal point, 26.5. He reassured her that her first draft on Boarding-out was fine, he had very few queries (10 and 17 November 1873). He countered her self-doubts: 'My dear keep your heart up. You are doing the work admirably, . . . You are very sensible and very practical and your style is clear and not stilted' (12 December 1873).

Stansfeld too was very pleased by the first section of the Report she sent him. Will it do? she had asked him; to which he replied:

> This will do and well. You have only to go on.
>
> It is all very well to call yourself a Quaker and say you feel sick [at the prospect of a row], but I did not think you very quakerish or peace-at-any-pricey when you got on the subject of one of the Secretaries of the Local Government Board, and I think I know who would come rapidly worse off in a duel in that quarter!
>
> But don't misunderstand me. I don't ask you to be antagonistic or narrow, or anything but what you are, – just, generous and sympathetic. (19 November 1873)

Clearly he had been completely won over by her and his growing affection can be seen in his fantasy at the end of that year: 'I am almost tempted to wish that somebody would abuse your *Report* in the House [of Commons]; and then you might see what a champion I could be.'

CHAPTER THIRTEEN

Mrs. Senior's *Report*

'[What] is wanted in the education of the girls is more *mothering*.'

Only Jeanie Senior could have written 'Mrs. Senior's *Report*'. In her first two pages she repeatedly used the word 'I': 'I visited', 'I was not satisfied', 'I inquired personally', 'I feel indebted', 'I have had much help from women' until her declaration: 'I wished to see the question from every point of view before coming to any conclusion'. It was explicitly *her* report, written in the form of a letter to her '*you*', James Stansfeld, who had 'especially desired the judgement of a woman as to the effect on girls of the system of education at pauper schools.'[1]

The *Report* was divided into two parts, each with various subsections.

Part One

Her Report began by discussing the current three-fold classification of the child inmates of workhouse schools as (a) 'orphans', (b) 'deserted' or (c) 'casuals', and criticized the practice of including as 'casuals' the large proportion of children whose parents were chronically incapacitated by physical or mental disability. Such children, although not literally 'orphans' or 'deserted', were *de facto* permanent inmates of the workhouse schools, unlike the true 'casuals' who were put in and taken out again many times within any given year, according to the wishes of their vagrant or seasonally employed parents.

Jeanie Senior was concerned that the children of the 'casual' parents – petty criminals, beggars, tinkers, prostitutes or seasonal workers in the hop-fields and brickyards – had had to learn too much too soon about drunken violence, incest, rape and prostitution. Their brutalized language betrayed this – and would quickly corrupt the sheltered 'permanents'. She did not stigmatize the child 'casuals' themselves. She took their part, suggesting that their day-long incarceration within the high walls of the regimented schools was hateful to them; they needed 'shorter school hours and far more labour in the open air' (316). Contrary to those who doubted that any one would be willing to teach classes of children who were constantly being withdrawn from school, Jeanie Senior declared her alternative credo that there *would* be teachers anxious to '[perform] an evident duty of love towards those little vagrants who are such by no fault or will of theirs' (317). That was the first time that 'love' had ever been mentioned in an *Annual Report on Poor Law Schools*. It was also the first time that the negative term 'vagrants' had been qualified by the disarming adjective 'little'.

She was particularly concerned about the disabled girls, so many afflicted with scrofula or almost blind and therefore unemployable. Would they not be 'infinitely happier' – again a phrase never before used in a *Poor Law Report* – if boarded-out in a family where they could learn, through individual attention, to be at least a little useful and their lives thereby made brighter? She quoted one 'bright, intelligent girl [who] had lost one side of the jaw, and an eye from scrofula. I asked her if she suffered much. She answered oh no! She was quite strong and quite able to go out to service if anyone gave her a trial' (317–18). It was the first time that a pauper girl was allowed to speak for herself in a *Poor Law Report*.

Finally in her thoughts on 'classification', Jeanie Senior addressed the problem of vulnerable 'imbecile girls', unable to protect themselves from rape or seduction, who 'frequently become mothers of illegitimate children'. Here she did what Dr. Mitchell had recommended – spelled out the problem but did not pretend to have a solution. 'The mental defect . . . in the girls . . . is not such as is understood to justify the granting of certificates of insanity, and as long as there in no legal power to detain them in a place of safety, no plan seems to offer a fair prospect of success' (318).

Curriculum

What Jeanie Senior *was* positive about was her recommendation of a new 'family structure' being introduced into the huge District Schools. Not only should the large number of nursery children and girl infants be separated from the Main School, but they themselves should be split up into small groups, looked after by older girls over twelve who could be 'elder sister' or 'little mother' to individual children. That would be the best possible way of giving the little ones more individual cherishing – as well as training the older girls in the needs of young children before they tried to hold down their first work placement in a family. It was at this point that Jeanie Senior took on the question of the District School curriculum, with its narrow academic demands of the Three Rs transmitted through rote learning.

> A girl is not necessarily a better woman because she knows the height of all the mountains of Europe, and can work out a fraction in her head; but she is decidedly better fitted for the duties she will be called upon to perform in life, if she knows how to wash and tend a child, cook simple food well, and thoroughly clean a house. To do these duties really well, needs not only intelligence, but special training.

Was she saying that most girls need be taught nothing but domestic science in order to learn to be good domestic servants – and eventually wives and mothers?

> I am very anxious that it should not be supposed that I advocate a low intellectual standard of teaching, . . . or that I have any sympathy with certain popular theories about the sufficiency of cooking and needlework for the complete development of the female understanding. I am on the other side altogether, but I think that in the case of these children, the amount of positive scholastic knowledge which they acquire, is not so important as the amount of intelligence which can be developed, and of household knowledge which can be imparted to them. I believe that, . . . their wits would be very much sharpened by a greater variety of occupation, more general reading, more amusement, and more cultivation of natural sympathy. (319)

'Intelligence' as opposed to academic 'knowledge', together with 'amusement' and 'sympathy', also make their first appearance here in a *Government (Poor Law) Education Report*. 'What concerned her was whether the children were developing intelligent, active minds, which would enable them to cope with the realities of their later lives.'[2]

It was at this point that Jeanie Senior articulated her basic conclusion: the sheer size of the huge District Schools meant that the girls were 'unable to get the cherishing care and individual attention' which was of far more importance to their development 'than anything else in the world. . . . The inquiries I have made on all sides have convinced me that what is wanted in the education of the girls is more *mothering*.'[3] In support of that radical new emphasis, she again let the girls' own voices be heard: 'One will say, "We were kindly enough treated, but I felt very lonely"; another, "I was very fond of Miss A., but there were so many of us to look after that she could not be expected to make much of me." And so on.' (320).

Regarding the Infant School day, she advocated not only smaller, family grouping, but shorter hours, constant change of occupation, gentle gymnastics, the companionship of the elder girls in play 'and from the tenderest years, a systematic explanation and enforcement of the laws of health'. Much could be learned from German kindergartens and the best French *salles d'asile* – like those she had seen in Paris.[4] She ended that section of her *Report* by advocating better pay and conditions, including compulsory annual holiday leave for the staff, and half-holidays and treats for the children – who never had a break from their monotonous school routine because they had no homes to go to.

Sanitary Conditions and Diet

Jeanie Senior reported that she found the children in general in the Metropolitan District and Separate Schools to be stunted in growth, sickly, especially vulnerable to eye disease, and disquietingly apathetic, whether in the schoolroom or out in the yard. She was particularly critical of the poor sanitation in the cold, overcrowded, under-ventilated dormitories that stank of body odour, gas flues, uncovered chamber-pots, smelly boots and the girls' same woollen undergarment worn day and night for at least a week on end.

She also criticized the monotonous, unbalanced diet without green vegetables or fruit or sugar, which was so unappetizing that the children would often go hungry rather than swallow cold soup or tepid fat. Because they could not relish the monotonous food, they had no appetite and because they had no appetite, they failed to thrive. She compared the diet of these workhouse school children unfavourably with that of the poorest families in London where 'I know that tripe, and cow heel, and sausages, and occasional rashers of bacon come in to vary the cockles and red herrings' (325), not to mention the cheap fruit and vegetables sold off by costermongers from their barrows whenever there was a glut. However difficult it might be to vary the children's diet according to season, the authorities *must* act to do so. 'Every question of mere administration, ought to be subservient to the promotion of the health and vigour of the children.' For Jeanie Senior's firm position was 'that the schools were there for the children, not the children for the schools.[5]

Exercise and Play

All that Jeanie Senior remembered from her own tomboy childhood with her seven brothers, and the 'treats' and play materials that she had organized for Walter and for Hastings' motherless children, she now put to good use. Why should the workhouse girls not be re-clothed in loose bodices and jackets giving them the free use of their arms, and have drill lessons like the workhouse school boys – or even be taught to swim like them? She was appalled that the hundreds of District School girls seemed not to know *how* to play. They appeared to have 'no tradition of [children's] games' (326).[6] She herself had no doubt about the educational value of play: 'To teach them to play with intelligence and enjoyment, would be well worth the trouble, as an educational process. Playing with energy would be a step towards working with energy' (326).[7]

As for the sick children lying all day in bed in the School Infirmary, 'the life the children lead while in hospital, is beyond expression dreary'. What could be done about it? Lady volunteers should be allowed to come and break the monotony:

Even an hour's reading aloud to the children, putting new ideas into their minds, and giving them something to talk about, would be a great benefit; an occasional singing lesson, and materials for knitting or netting, might also be of great use in getting them safely through the time in hospital. (327)

What grieved her more than anything else was the 'hardening' of the pauper girls by their impersonal mass education in the 'Barrack' Schools. Time and again the children were described to her as being apathetic, sullen or even violent, by turns. She had to counter the prevalent view that 'bad temper, untruthfulness, and apathy are innate in pauper children' (328) as opposed to having been socially conditioned. In doing so she was an eternal Rousseauist, refusing to see Original Sin in any child, rather than an eternal Augustinian.[8] To prevent the 'hardening' of the girls while at school, she advocated not sermons on morality, but *much more individual attention*. She reiterated her recommendation that 'a family' grouping should be introduced into the schools, reminding her readers how 'openness of heart' – marvellous phrase – evolves naturally within every ordinary affectionate family:

> . . . [Every] mother knows how soon her own little girl develops the maternal instinct, and how good a thing it is to cultivate it. . . . A little child . . . sits on the door-step and is trusted to take care of baby at a very early age; or she is sent on an errand, or set to perform some small domestic duty.
>
> These little incidents of cottage life, contain the germs of all valuable qualities; affection, ambition, sense of usefulness, sense of responsibility, sense of membership, presence of mind. (328)

Already she could report that 'at one of the metropolitan schools where the female influence was strong and good' (328) she could see' the transformation wrought when an older trusted girl was allowed to take care of a particular tiny child. That child would be unusually bright and clean, its hair brushed or even curled, and the older girl never forgot her, . . . writing for news of 'little Sally or Polly' long after' (329). (Again this was the first time that any of the 'Children of the State' were given names in a Government Inspector's *Report*.)

It was more difficult to see how the destitute, money-less workhouse children, who worked long hours without pay within the District Schools, might be taught the meaning and value of money. The girls, once out in the world, could easily be defrauded by what looked attractive but would never last the week. 'A very intelligent girl, who had been in place some years, told me that she had not yet learnt to distinguish between a good serviceable material for a dress and a comparatively worthless one' (329). (It was a new light on

30 London Workhouse School infant girls, *c.* 1890 (note shorn heads). Courtesy Peter Higginbotham: www.workhouses.org.uk

things that a former workhouse inmate could be 'a very intelligent girl' whose experience deserved quoting.) Could not the older girls, Jeanie Senior asked, while still at school, be allowed out in turn and taken shopping, by volunteers with discretion? They so badly needed practice at everyday life.

But far too often the girls had *no* experience of personal affection, *no* understanding of everyday life, *no* learned capacity to control their aggression. Far too many of them ended in prison, in Lock Hospitals[9] or in refuges for 'the fallen', where they were then invariably described as 'the worst prisoners by far', or 'the most difficult . . . in every respect' (330). Sullen, apathetic, automatically resistant to any authority, they all seemed to 'have a hardness about them' (330). However, Jeanie Senior also discovered that, 'if a girl can be convinced that she is individually cared for, and that her misconduct causes real sorrow to the matron or lady who has had to do with her, she becomes a different creature' (330). One solution Jeanie Senior proposed was to give each pauper schoolgirl the chance to earn her own money. Why, for example, should a girl pupil not have her own little garden and sell its produce, like the workhouse boys at Eyemouth and Paxton near Berwick?[10] But she herself knew the pat reply: – '[As] it is illegal for a pauper to earn money, no payment for industrial work can be made to girls at these schools' (330). Her startling suggestion then was: Why not by-pass the rules?

> It might be allowable so far to evade the above regulation, . . . by
> raising a fund for this purpose by private subscription [i.e. the girls
> could be paid out of private monies not public rates] . . . The child
> might be given a [savings] book, in which the sums she earned
> would be noted down as they were invested, and she would receive
> the whole amount when she went to place. (330)

Having reinforced positive character development through paid, 'willing
and hopeful work', Jeanie Senior then returned to her favourite subject, the
therapeutic impact of *play*: '[Hardly] less do I value pleasures, treats, and
holidays as means of moral benefit. I am sure that joy is an immense educational power. A hearty laugh is a great help to growth and health' (330–1).
She was writing seventy-three years before Ellen Wilkinson, Labour Minister
of Education, would declare that she wanted to see 'more laughter in the
classroom'. Now Jeanie Senior really got into her stride, imagining how she
would revolutionize the whole environment and regimen of Workhouse
schools. Pages 331–332 mark a climax, the rhythm of her prose pulsing with
eager energy as she communicates her vision in simple, positive words:

> I should like to ornament the walls of the schools, and the dormi-
> tories and passages, with paintings, and scrolls, and illuminations,
> and texts, and bits of poetry, all in bright colours; the children
> would learn the texts and the poetry almost unconsciously, and the
> colours would be a delight; and I should like them to be made to
> keep themselves warm in winter by good active games.
>   In the large play rooms there are great capabilities for fun.
> Room for dancing Sir Roger de Coverley and country dances, and
> for keeping off chilblains by exercise. There is a capital game, a
> sort of Montagne Russe, that might be managed at almost every
> school; a great smoothly-planed board, placed against a rail or
> block of wood, at rather a steep incline. Children will amuse them-
> selves with this by the hour, and get all sorts of gymnastics and fun
> out of it. . . .
>   Much fun and exercise might be got out of a cart such as is used
> at the College for the Blind, at Norwood . . . . the children take it
> in turns to ride in the carriage, or in the shafts, and there is endless
> amusement in taking drives with a good team. (331–2)

What could have possessed her? 'Delight'? 'Fun'? 'Endless amusement'?
Had she forgotten that these pauper children should not have been born in
the first place? They were a burden on the rate-payers, their one duty to stop
being that burden through self-supporting toil. The sooner such children
learned that life was *not* a matter of beer and skittles the better. 'Delight'.

'Fun'. 'Endless amusement' – did she want all the children of the poor
outside the Workhouse to start queuing for admission so that they too might
dance a Sir Roger de Coverley? How could the Poor Law administrators not
be shocked by Mrs. Senior's *Report*? And how could James Stansfeld not
love her for her eager description of 'a capital game, a sort of Montagne
Russe'?

She charged on. The teachers might give out prizes and coloured beads
and different wools for knitting, and

> I should like . . . to encourage the children of all ages to learn
> poetry by heart. It seemed to me that during the long hours of
> needle-work, it might be possible to let the elder girls, in turns,
> read aloud (332). But [the] work mistresses tell me that it would be
> almost impossible to arrange this on account of the constant inter-
> ruptions that necessarily arise, in the explanations and directions
> that have to be given (332).

Stubbornly, Mrs. Senior refused to be baulked:

> But I think that though reading aloud may be impracticable, easy
> poetry might be learnt, . . . during the two or three hours needle-
> work, or written out on a black board, where the class might take
> an occasional glance, without much hindering the progress of the
> needle-work. Anything that would raise new ideas and thoughts in
> the minds of the children, would be of service to them. (332)

Her final recommendation for enlivening and enriching the curriculum was
that lessons in health, hygiene and physiology be introduced. She even used
the phrase 'the actual facts of life' (333).[11] The introduction of books for
children on elementary physiology led her to another bright idea – a circulating library for Workhouse children: 'Such books might, among others, be
supplied from a school circulating library, and the children be allowed to
read on Sundays, as a reward for good conduct and exertion during the
week' (333).

The two last points in her section on the children's life in the schools
concerned rewards and punishments. Not surprisingly Jeanie Senior
favoured the former over the latter. She did not want any of the girls to be
caned: 'Having discovered, at the outset of my inquiry, that in a school I was
visiting, caning girls was repeatedly practised, I . . . have come to the conclusion that the punishment has a demoralizing effect . . . its application only
hardens the offender' (334).

She would soon make herself responsible for the abolition of all corporal
punishment of girls in Workhouse schools.

31 Older London Workhouse School girls, c. 1890 (note shorn heads). Courtesy Peter Higginbotham: www.workhouses.org.uk

'Mrs. Senior' had now seen the girl children at the very bottom of Victorian society – the overlooked little *Olive* Twists, unwanted, neglected, stunted, dirty, smelly, pitifully unattractive with their ill-fitting drab uniforms, shorn heads, diseased eyes and skins, bored, apathetic, not knowing how to play a game or even how to enjoy a meal, drilled every day in the same strict monotonous regime – and she demanded something better for them. Her conclusion to Part One of her *Report* insisted that pauper children must be treated like any other children so as to realize their common birthright: 'All children ought by some means to be made bright, self-dependent, and capable of innocent enjoyment; and I do not see any other means but those I propose, by which these ends are likely to be attained' (334). Every child needs mothering and fun.

Part Two

What happened to the girls after they left to become servants aged fourteen or fifteen? Did they get 'a fair start in life and adequate protection'? (334). Part Two of the *Report* was still grimmer than Part One, detailing the girls' totally inadequate preparation for 'life outside', their frequent failures to hold down a job and consequent loss of hope, health, even life. The recommendations concerning the girls once they had left their Workhouse School were based on Jeanie Senior's findings in her Appendices F and G

Appendix F reported on all the (670) girls who had been sent out as servants from the 17 Metropolitan Pauper Schools 1871–1872. Its most startling finding was that out of these 670, 180 girls could not be traced at all. Just a year after they had left school they had already 'gone out of sight' – they had never been visited by any Poor Law official, and their purported employers had either moved or had failed to answer letters or had never lived at their supposed address in the first place. It was not unreasonable to make pessimistic assumptions concerning what most probably would have befallen many, if not all, such vulnerable girls so swiftly 'lost to view'. Of the 245 girls actually traced from the huge District or 'Barrack' schools (as opposed to the smaller 'Separate' schools) 24 were unemployable because of deficient eyesight, 23 had run away, two were in reformatories for having stolen, and eight were already prostitutes.

That left 182 girls recently from District Schools still 'in service' whose situation was investigated and graded by Jeanie Senior's six women volunteers (who included Henrietta Synnot and Menella Smedley) as 'Good', 'Fair', 'Unsatisfactory' or 'Bad'. 'Good' was applied to those girls who had kept their jobs and/or were praised by their employers. 'Fair' were those girls who had improved on a poorish start and were now likely to keep their current job. Only 37 per cent of the 182 coming from District Schools were described as 'good' or 'fair'. 'Unsatisfactory' included those girls who had already lost their jobs for petty pilfering or inefficiency or who had had irregular employment. Examples were 'Utterly incapable and ignorant . . . but has improved. When she came she was more like an animal than a human creature; would throw herself on the ground when it was attempted to teach her anything. Exceedingly dirty, both in person and work' (356) and 'Dishonest; untruthful; very sullen; very bad as regards housework. Very dirty in all her habits'. It needs to be remembered, of course, that to smell and be dirty had been the girls' normal state in the Barrack Schools; their underclothes not changed day or night for a week at a time and baths being run just once a week – and then with one change of water for every sixteen girls.[12] Menstruation would only make matters worse.

If 'Unsatisfactory' seems an understatement, 'Bad' describes the servant girls from Hell. 'Audacious and violent to the last degree; threatened to stab her own mother' (358); 'At times violent, on one occasion breaking a plate on the head of her fellow servant' (358); 'Mistress was afraid to keep L. her temper was so violent; she feared that she might set fire to the house' (359). The 'Unsatisfactory' and 'Bad' categories together comprised 62 per cent of the returns from the traceable girls from the District, 'Barrack' Schools, one year out in the world. The findings regarding the 245 girls from the smaller Separate Workhouse schools in Lambeth, Bethnal Green, Shoreditch, and Mile End were somewhat better. 'Good' and 'Fair' together comprised 53 per cent, 'Unsatisfactory' and 'Bad' 47 per cent.

It will immediately be asked: Were these mistresses to be trusted concerning their little skivvies? A few were definitely not trustworthy and were noted as such: 'The mistress exceedingly dirty, and hardly looked respectable' (361). Or 'Mistress spent much time in repeating scandal about her neighbours, using exceedingly coarse language' (361) Jeanie Senior was clear that some of these mistresses looked 'on their little servant as a mere drudge' (338) and that where temper or sullenness was complained of 'we have often judged that we were not justified in considering that the girl was to blame' (340). But it also had to be recognized that many of the mistresses *could* be trusted to give the basic facts about the girls as they found them. Indeed why, if they could never be trusted when giving a negative judgment, could they be trusted when their view of a girl was positive?

Jeanie Senior also had to trust the sensitivity and insight and life experience of her chief investigator, Menella Smedley, who ended *Appendix F* with her own conclusions about the forty-seven girls she herself had traced. She found them all to be literate and numerate and to have had basic religious instruction. She also found them *all* to be 'stunted in growth' and with one exception, bad-tempered to the point of violence. Compared with girls of their age from very poor families, the workhouse girls were lacking in 'life and energy . . . All, without exception, curiously apathetic in temperament, described to me as "not caring for anything", "taking no interest", "not enjoying", "seeming like old people"'. It was a pitiful, but all too credible, composite picture.

Appendix G, concerning 'Girls who left school in 1868, after not less than five years in school' had been Jeanie Senior's exclusive responsibility. It takes up thirty pages of her *Report* and consists of detailed cases notes on 51 girls and 25 slightly less detailed notes on girls who, as she eventually discovered, did not fall into the precise category she was investigating. It is not possible to quote all of *Appendix G*, although it is an invaluable, under-researched resource in the history of social investigation in Britain. Jeanie Senior's whole *Report*, especially *Appendix G*, is nothing less than the missing link in empirical sociology between Mayhew's interviews with sweated sempstresses in the 1840s,[13] and Beatrice Webb's social investigation in the late 1880s.[14] Jeanie Senior's general finding was that roughly half these girls had survived satisfactorily, but half had gone under. (And among the more or less 'satisfactory' was a girl married to a man almost certainly a pimp.) First, two examples of girls doing well:

(6) A.L.

A deserted child admitted to Workhouse in 1863 at 9 years old.

Matron says A.L was a bright good little girl, not clever, short, and not very strong. Her first place was with a kind motherly woman, who seems devoted to her. A.L. was in this place a year and a half. A.L. was a useful little servant, and an excellent girl, cheerful, good tempered and fond of children. She was not visited by relieving officer. Mrs. W., her next mistress, says that A.L. was a very good girl and a good servant. Her next place was in a large family, where the work was too hard. I promised to get her another place, and she came to see me. A nice looking girl, but very small. She was staying with a widowed sister, who is doing laundry work to keep her children. I liked A.L. so much that I recommended her to my sister-in-law, who has taken her, and is perfectly satisfied with her. But she is inconveniently small.

Jeanie Senior's 'unprofessional' personal involvement is evident – she herself promises to find the girl a better job, interviews her and then persuades her own sister-in-law [the demanding Fan] to take her on.

The next example of a currently happy ending is of a girl who told Jeanie Senior her own story:

(16) F.H.N.

An illegitimate child of a prostitute, admitted at seven years old in 1861.

. . . I saw the girl, and she told me all about herself. Her first place was with an architect, a four-storied house, and F.H.N. the only servant. She was strange at all the work, "things seemed so odd, and she got in such a fright that she broke everything she touched". So the matron of the school got her another place, but she was not happy there, and got herself the place in which I found her. She has been here more than two years, and is very happy. She gets £12 a year, and intends to stay, as she does not like change. She is cook, and said, "Bless you, I can cook anything. Master says he'd give me a kitchen maid if I'd like." I asked her if she saw her mother; she said it would never do to see her mother. She looked healthy, though very small and stunted. She was neat and clean, evidently tidied up for the afternoon, with her thimble on ready for needlework.

Jeanie Senior had gained the confidence of tiny F.H.N. The child readily confessed to all her early household breakages before proudly and (familiarly) asserting that now, "Bless you, I can cook anything."

Examples of 'Girls dropped out of sight of whom the last tidings were unsatisfactory' (363) include:

(19) M.W. a 'casual', whose mother was in and out of the
Workhouse, first admitted at the age of 5 in 1857.

M.W. belonged to a parish that joined another Union, so it was not
the duty of the chaplain to visit her. She was a strong girl, and
fairly good tempered. During her school life she was discharged 13
times, though she never appears to have been absent for long at a
time. She was taken out by her mother on these occasions. She was
at school seven years [i.e. till she was 12–13]. Mrs. B. her mistress,
found her tidy, tolerably healthy, good natured, and thinks she
would have made a good servant, but her mother used to come
constantly to the house, often drunk, and several times created
such a disturbance that the police had to be sent for, and at last
Mrs. B. could not stand it any longer, and gave M.W. warning. The
girl did not want to leave, but Mrs. B.'s patience was at an end.
The mother came to take the girl away. Mrs. B. hears that the
mother is leading an immoral life, and greatly fears that the girl is
doing the same. Mrs. B.'s would have been a comfortable place for
any girl, . . . and but for the mother, M.W. would probably have
been with her still.

Jeanie Senior is totally dependent on the testimony of Mrs. B. but uses her
own judgment to assess that Mrs. B. would have been a very reasonable
employer.

(21) R.D. admitted when both parents were to the workhouse
when she was five in 1859

. . . Her mistress, Mrs. D. a nice person, said the case was a very
sad one. The girl was a good girl enough, and the mistress determined she should not be spoiled by her bad relations, so she never
would give R.D. a day out, and she did well the first year. A
strong, nice-looking girl, very good worker, and willing; could
scrub well, and having been in the kitchen at school, could boil
potatoes, and prepare vegetables. Mrs. D. taught her and watched
her. The second year Mrs. D. discovered that R.D.'s relations had
found her out, and when sent on errands the girl would go to see
them. The mother was dead. The father, a bad man, lived in one
little room with a grown up son and a daughter, the daughter was
always about in the streets, a wretched looking girl. At the end of
two years R.D. wanted to better herself, she said, although Mrs. D.
had raised her wages. She had a few pounds in her pocket and a
box of excellent clothes. Mrs. D. got her a capital place with a
friend of hers. R.D.'s family induced her to give them her money,
and she also pawned her clothes to help them, till she was not fit to

be seen . . . After this she was found out in small pilferings and was discharged . . . She went to service at a public-house. When she had been there a short time she wrote a contrite letter to Mrs. D., her first mistress, and begged to see her. Mrs. D. let her call, and talked to her. She had hardly any decent clothes, and wanted Mrs. D. to give her or lend her something to wear, and said her sister was going to be married. The last Mrs. D. heard was that the two girls had been taking care of an empty house, and the accounts were very unsatisfactory of both . . . Mrs. D. feels sure the girl would have done well but for the relations.

Other miserable stories included (48) the orphan E.K. who had been seduced, either by her master or by one of his apprentices, at 16, and could not then be taken back, even by the workhouse school (for fear she was pregnant?). She had no relations or friends. And (50) S.T., another orphan, who was 'very quick, could turn her hand to anything, made dresses and bonnets beautifully and liked a bit of bright colour' (382). She was affectionate, and all the family liked her despite her fits of temper. But finally she ran off and was seen more than once 'going into a place of entertainment with bad girls' (383).

The most heartbreaking of all was illegitimate C.D. (14) whose mother was in the workhouse when she was admitted to the pauper school aged 9 in 1862.

Mrs. F., who was schoolmistress at the time C.D. was in school, speaks of her as a pretty, remarkably clever girl, with high notions. Mrs. F. knew she would never do in service, and wanted to keep her in school as monitress [pupil teacher], but the then matron would not let it be so, so C.D. went to service . . . From the school she went . . . to Mrs. E. She was there less than a month, as Mrs. E. could do nothing with her, she was so saucy and impertinent. On 26 June she was again admitted at workhouse and discharged on 7 July to Miss Twining's Home. The matron of the Home writes to me that C.D. was discharged thence on 2nd Feb. 1869 to service, from whence she absconded before the end of the month of trial. The next entry in workhouse book is "C.D. admitted 19 March, 1869, *destitute*," then "discharged to service" (no address) 31st March 1869. There follow six admissions and six discharges and then the final admission 31st March 1871, *ill*. Sent 22nd April 1871 to Highgate Infirmary.

Mrs. A. said that C.D. at first was a nice, quick girl, and would have made a good servant; but her mother began to visit her, and the child gradually became careless, disobedient, etc. The girl had put her wages in the savings bank, she gave her mother the book, and the mother drew out the money and spent it. . . . The admission to the workhouse on 17the April 1869 was with her mother; so the mother probably continued to influence the child for evil . . . The same old servant [at the school] and the matron of Bloomsbury Home [for Fallen Women?] told me that C.D. went on the streets, went "hopping", slept out of doors, caught cold, and died of consumption.

C.D. was eighteen and had been a gifted, spirited child.

Jeanie Senior had already had bitter knowledge of some terrible things in life – the death of children like Tom's son Maurice, drowned in the Thames, the death in childbirth of several of her women friends and relatives, the much too early deaths of her own four brothers. And, from the Franco-Prussian War and the merciless suppression of the Paris Commune, she had learned that men can be made to mass-murder strangers in cold blood. But now she had learned something worse still. From her 'Girl Hunts', she had learned what could be done to a young girl, not by hard-hearted officialdom, nor by bullying employers, but by the child's own family. Used, abused, stripped of all she had, even her clothes, her pathetic wages stolen, betrayed or pressured into 'falling' until the girl found herself prostituted, raped by strangers every night. And with little prospect but more of the same until disease and death.

> Cases of girls who would in all probability have done well, but for the bad influence exerted by their relations, recur over and over again, with sad monotony. The girls thus tempted, were often well-behaved promising children while in school, and *I am inclined to believe that the warm-hearted generous natures are just those who are the most exposed to this danger.* (my emphasis) (337)

Jeanie Senior's sympathetic imagination had leaped to identify just *why* an affection-starved girl should be especially vulnerable to pressure from new-found kith and kin who said they needed her help. To support and protect such girls, she would eventually found nothing less than a whole new voluntary organisation.[15]

There could be no comforting dream now of transforming the life of these girls. It was already too late. They could not start their own little allotment gardens or do country dancing or play Montagne Russe. Instead, the second part of Mrs. Senior's *Report* is a tough, grim-faced summary of how it might be possible to prevent the worst being done in future to *other* such friendless girls, most friendless when in the power of their 'friends'.[16]

Her recommended measures concerned (1) legal Guardianship for pauper girls, (2) Greater care in selecting a girl's first 'place' of employment, (3)

Much more careful supervision of a girl's progress once employed and (4) Provision made for her protection while unemployed.[17]

Legal guardianship

> I do not see why it should be impossible to extend some protection to the children of paupers for a few years after they leave school; say to the age of 18 or 20. . . . Something might perhaps be done in this way to protect children from oppression or ill-treatment by their employers, . . .

The allocation of a Workhouse girl's first job

> '[The] utmost trouble should be taken to find mistresses likely to train and instruct their little servants with intelligence and kindness' (337). Instead, all too often, a child was asked to do far too heavy work, and occasionally placed near an Army barracks or even a red light district. 'It requires the eye of a motherly woman to perceive the small details which go to render a situation desirable or otherwise for a young girl.' (338)

Monitoring and mentoring

Similarly, once at work, a girl's welfare needed regular monitoring by an outsider and a woman would be more effective in this than the male Chaplains, . . .

> There are many questions arising between a girl and her mistress that would never be laid before a man, and many little troubles occur in a girl's life that she would find it impossible to state to a man, . . .

How could a girl possibly be expected to tell the Workhouse School Chaplain about her heavy periods, or her fear that she might be pregnant because Master grabbed and kissed her in the hall one night?

A place of safety when unemployed

The provision for a girl's unemployment, given that she had lost not only her livelihood but also the roof over her head, was totally inadequate. All a girl could then do was starve, go on the streets or return to the Workhouse. Therefore Jeanie Senior alerted officialdom to the urgent need for a safe lodging-house or central Home (339–340).

It is important not to make Janet Horowitz Murray's mistake and regard 'Mrs. Senior's *Report*' as the view of a typical *bourgeoise*, concerned only that working-class girls make good servants.[18] Jeanie Senior *was* interested in that question, but for the sake of the girls themselves – she knew what would most probably happen to them once they lost their 'place'.

Jeanie Senior did not scapegoat the girls' mistresses for their servants' 'failure in service'. She granted that some had their faults of temper and lack of patience (340) but also stressed that she (and her fellow-investigators) had found

> many really admirable mistresses. Homely women, taking a mater-
> nal interest in the girls, . . . who understood that the little servant
> needed some pleasure and relaxation, as well as affectionate inter-
> est. Without any parade, but as bearing on other points, we have
> often heard from mistresses of a shilling given now and then to the
> girl, to be spent for her own pleasure; of little presents to her,
> subscribed for by the children; of lessons in cutting out her own
> clothes; of a new hat, because the bonnet provided in the outfit
> seemed to the girl a workhouse badge; and so on. (340)

Conclusion

The five-page Conclusion began with the unequivocal judgment:

'I was unfavourably impressed with the effect of thus massing children together in large numbers' (341). The girls from 'the splendid district schools' turned out even worse than those from the less well equipped but smaller 'separate' workhouse schools (345). In contrast, the boarded-out children she saw living in the homes of

> miners and labourers near large towns, some in Roman Catholic
> families, . . . some in an ordinary English village in
> Buckinghamshire and some in a remote country district of Scotland
> . . . looked strong and thriving and happy. . . . I received the same
> impression everywhere, in favour of the free and natural mode of
> life afforded by cottage homes. I did not see a single case of ring-
> worm or opthalmia. (341)

Her two-page *Appendix A* had found that where children were boarded-out *according to the rules issued by the Local Government Board and their continuing welfare monitored by local lady volunteers*, the children thrived:

> One very remarkable difference between the children in these [Lake
> District] homes and the children at the metropolitan school is their
> greater brightness and trustfulness of manner, and their readiness to

answer questions, and tell one all about themselves and what they are doing . . . I found signs of strong affection between foster-parents and their adopted children, . . .

Therefore Jeanie Senior made the radical recommendation that *all* pauper orphans be removed from the Metropolitan Schools forthwith and fostered. She recognized that deserted children whose parents might possibly re-surface, or children whose parents might be tempted to desert them, could not be thus boarded out. And she only favoured boarding-out under careful monitoring by local [women's] committees; the children must never be merely farmed out on the cheap by [male] Poor Law Guardians.

She was then moved to criticize the entire system of pauper relief in Britain. Far from thinking her father-in-law's brainchild, the 1834 New Poor Law,[19] to be the best social policy known to man, the tablets of which were written in stone, she declared her own counter-credo:

> The whole Poor Law system is a necessary evil, and I believe that the time will come when its provisions will be no longer necessary, when education, and improved social arrangements [i.e. the redis-tribution of wealth and welfare payments for those unable to work], will have triumphed over pauperism. The enormous build-ings that are erected for the reception of pauper children, seem to point to a belief that we are to have an ever-increasing race of paupers throughout the centuries to come. Against such a belief boarding out is a protest. (343)

In other words, children given a normal affectionate personal upbringing will be more independent, more employable, and hence much better able to fend for themselves – and their children.

Whilst she admitted that the educational advantages for boys in the metropolitan pauper schools were 'very great', she denied that these huge schools answered the needs of the *girls*. Physically they were all 'stunted in size, and a large proportion delicate in health'. They were literally, not just compassionately, termed throughout her *Report* '*little* servants'. Jeanie Senior then anticipated the criticism that her own and her women colleagues' assumption in *Appendices F* and *G* that a high proportion of vanished and 'failed girls in service' had fallen into prostitution, was based on mere hearsay. ['The] most sanguine persons cannot consider the case of such a [vanished, destitute, homeless] girl as satisfactory' (343). In order to try to prevent pauper girl servants from being driven to a life on the streets, Jeanie Senior put forward her idea of a new, state-funded, government organiza-tion, helped by a band of women volunteers, that would take responsibility for the welfare of former workhouse girls *and* young female servants generally, providing them where necessary with guardianship, a residential home for the temporarily unemployed and all the resources of a Friendly Society of their own (*Appendix H*).

She ended by summing up all the radical changes she wished to see made immediately.

She declared unequivocally that large schools were not good for girls; they needed, if family fostering were not possible, small schools which could give them individual attention. The 'casual' or vagrant children needed separate small schools focused on their particular needs as did deserted children and infants, and they all needed these smaller schools broken up into units or 'houses' of a more 'home-like character' . In her own words:

> [Orphan] children should be boarded out in cottage homes.
> . . . I should wish to break up the present schools, and to educate the deserted children apart from the casual children.
> For both classes of children I would adopt schools of a more home-like character.

~

'Jane Elizabeth Senior' had completed her outspoken, critical, humane *Report* on the education of pauper girls. 'She [had]' put her whole soul into the work',[20] advocating 'a free and natural mode of life' for all children, convinced that 'a hearty laugh [was] a great help to growth and health' and that 'All children ought by some means to be made bright, self dependent, and capable of innocent enjoyment'. To us it reads like common sense, but would the Establishment agree?

CHAPTER FOURTEEN

Reception of the *Report*

James Stansfeld accepted Jeanie Senior's *Report* and immediately asked for her appointment as Government Inspector to be made permanent. Florence Nightingale, saluted her on 5 January 1874:

> My dear "Senior" General of Female Infantry, . . .
> I am so glad to hail you inspector; Officer of a Government Office – "Senior" Officer, . . .
>   General of Infantry, tho' they are only female infants, only poor-law female Infantry.
>   I have read your papers once. . . .
>   I agree with your "conclusion" so frantically that I agree with you more than you do with yourself. That is, that Boarding out is the only way to save life and capacity in these poor children. . . .
>   Your poor little Infantry are poorly bred and poorly fed, and most, or all, more or less scrofulous. What they want of all things is: fresh air, good food, exercise, and personal kindness . . .
>   The three Rs do little to help poor law children. What is more wanted is: continued administration of the milk of human kindness, which is the appointed nutriment of Child-souls, and which no cow belonging to the R farm can yield. . . .
>   God save the General!
>   ever yours devotedly
>   Florence Nightingale.[1]

The February 1874 General Election then ousted the Liberals and installed the Tories under Disraeli, making Stansfeld no longer President of the Local Government Board and a Cabinet Minister, but an out-of-office backbencher of the Opposition. Would the Treasury still confirm his permanent appointment of Mrs. Senior? A fascinating exchange of correspondence and memoranda concerning this decision is in the National Archives. On 23 January 1874, John Lambert, Secretary to the Local Government Board, had written to the Treasury:

> . . . The Board have now the satisfaction of informing their Lordships, that Mrs. Senior has discharged the duties which were assigned to her in a very efficient manner; and they have no hesita-

tion in stating that the President's [i.e. Stansfeld's] anticipations of
the advantages likely to be derived from the services of a Lady
Inspector have been fully realized.

Their Lordships are aware that a very large proportion of the
indoor poor consists of Women and Girls, and it is obvious that
there are many circumstances in connexion with the treatment and
management of this class, which can be ascertained more readily
and effectively through the agency of one of their own sex than
that of a Male Inspector. . . .

On 27 January it was pointed out by someone in the Treasury 'that the
question of 'employing a lady in a capacity of this kind is hardly one for the
Dept. to express an opinion upon'. It was therefore sent for comment higher
up, whereupon R.R.W. Lingen, the Permanent Secretary to the Treasury,
wrote the following long private memorandum:

30 January 1874:

I would assent.

But it opens a very large question as regards inspection generally,
which is becoming one of the most serious of the civil functions of
the Government, and especially School Inspection. . . . .

The amount of unemployed women (in the middle and higher
classes) is so great that, if anything which resembles ladylike
employment is offered, we may expect the utmost pressure to
extend it. . . . [If] the Education Department once has its hand
forced on [e.g. on employing women to inspect female Training
Colleges], . . . the ladies will find plenty of reasons why they should
be employed in inspecting Day Schools also, where girls and infants
(under 6 years) are to boys as 10:5, or thereabouts.

I am far from saying that their employment on these duties
might not be right; it would also be cheaper; but it is as well to
foresee what we may be beginning.

. . . [The] attention of the Government should, I think, be called
to it.[2]

How revealing that Mrs. Senior's permanent appointment should immediately have been perceived as a hugely important precedent, with enormous
potential repercussions for the imminent widespread employment of women
inspectors in the Education Department of the Civil Service. It required
nothing less than the attention of the Government. But that Government was
about to change – and be Tory. What does not happen in history is also
history. The first (unmarried) women HMIs both of women's teacher training colleges and of day schools would not be appointed until the 1890s.

By a warrant of 18 February Mrs. Senior was officially informed that she was now not merely an inspector of pauper girls' education but of all matters concerning adult women in Workhouses as well. It was a daunting remit, and Jeanie Senior was already exhausted after her multi-faceted Inspection, and the writing up of her *Report*. Stansfeld warned her against overwork:

> What you have to do is to see and to think from what is officially a new point of view and of thought [i.e. a woman's]; so pray econo-mize yourself for the sake of your truest and highest work, and that you may remain long in it.

Her first act as a permanent Inspector was to require the Local Government Board to prohibit the infliction of corporal punishment on female children.

Now her long battle with the former Chief Inspector, E. Carleton Tufnell – 'that old square toes' – began. He had visited her at Elm House once already, early in January, when he had met both Miss Thornton and Henrietta Synnot, and had heard Jeanie read him excerpts from her unpub-lished *Report*. He had then written to her on 12 January, expressing his 'surprise' at her advocacy of boarding-out, which he, 'like all persons expe-rienced in pauper education utterly denounce [as] indefensible both in theory and practice'. He maintained that the system of huge 'Barrack' Schools, which he himself had instituted, should not be broken down but be still further enlarged and extended. On 23 March 1874 she received a very intim-idating, letter from him:

> You are probably aware that copies of your *Report* have been sent to the Inspectors for their Observations. It is however impossible to test the accuracy of your facts without knowing the schools or girls to whom you allude. . . . It is absolutely necessary that I should know the names of all the girls . . . I should like especially to have the names of schools of the 245 girls mentioned in the 4 classes as having been brought up in District Schools; . . . I also beg you will send me the names of all the girls mentioned in App[endix] B as in one of the Prisons.
>
> Also the names of all girls whom you have ascertained by evidence other than *hearsay* to have fallen, and the schools in which they were brought up . . .

Jeanie Senior at once turned to Stansfeld for advice. Clearly Chief Inspector Tufnell was now challenging her whole procedure of inquiry, and overriding the principle of confidentiality, in order to dispute her findings. Stansfeld told her to stand firm:

It is quite clear, I think, that you cannot comply with Mr Tufnell's request.

You must not break your word to those whom you have promised that their names should not appear, nor should the information they gave you be put in such a form as to implicate them.

But independently of this Mr. Tufnell's request is in my mind objectionable and quite inadmissible in its present form.

His "observations" have been invited, whereupon he writes to you as if he had been invited to test the accuracy of statement of facts – which is quite another thing; and indeed as if his function now was to sit in judgement upon your conclusions also.

You must not allow this. *He would not address a male Inspector in the same way* [my emphasis]; it is your right and your <u>duty</u> to hold your own, as an equal . . . .

You <u>must</u> now make friends, for there may be a set at you, and it may not be perfectly easy to stand alone .

Besides Longley I should advise you consulting Lambert[3] . . .

(Strictly private): I have a special reason for this. Fleming is against you and was vexed that I made you "permanent"; you <u>must</u> therefore rest on Lambert. When I talked to Sclater-Booth[4] I could <u>see</u> that Fleming had been at work. . . . (25 March 1874)

32 Jeanie Senior, aged 45 photographed by Julia Margaret Cameron, January 1874. Courtesy The RPS Collection at the National Media Museum.

There could hardly have been a more wretched situation for Britain's first woman civil servant. 'It may not be perfectly easy to stand alone' was an understatement. Tufnell reiterated his demand to be told all the girls' names on 31 March. And meanwhile, unbeknownst to her, he was writing his furious, character-assassinating, counter-blast to her *Report*, which he would lodge with Parliament in April – before her *Report* had even been published.

On 26 April, after having taken counsel with both men and women, including Caroline Stephen, Jeanie Senior gave Tufnell the names of the three Workhouse Schools from which the girls in her *Appendix G* had come – Central London, Lambeth and St. James' West. But she still would not release the names of the girls themselves, inviting him instead to come and see her and inspect all her documentation. He rejected her offer with fury and contempt:

> Dear Mrs. Senior,
>
> I cannot see the slightest good that can accrue from examining your books.
>
> Your *Report* sufficiently states the mode in which your work has been done, and it must be clear to everyone, who has had far less experience than I have in pauper education, that no fair conclusion could be arrived at by a party of ladies trying to master so complicated a question in a few months. I cannot express to you the anger your statements have excited, amongst the *experts* on this subject.
>
> *There is nothing to be done but to suppress the Report entirely,*
> . . . (my emphasis)

Hating 'rows', accustomed to being loved, even adored, and needing at least minimal respect, Jeanie Senior found this personal attack acutely painful. Still worse was her uncertainty as to what she should now do. Should she continue to withstand Tufnell's demands, ensuring that the whole body of the male Inspectorate would then refuse to implement any of her recommendations for reform, or should she publicly surrender, withdrawing her *Report* even before it had been published, in return for the Inspectors' acquiescence in some, at least, of her proposals? Her women allies urged her to stand firm at all costs. On 27 April Menella Smedley wrote:

> I am very glad you are so staunch in keeping faith but as for withdrawing an Appendix I hope Mr. Stansfeld won't let you think of anything so weak-minded. That one official should suppress his report because another official to whom he is not responsible does not like it would be a strange way of doing business – and why should there be any difference because it is <u>her</u> report?

Seventy-seven year old Marianne Thornton was even fiercer:

> Dear Jeanie,
>
> You are never going to succumb to that "doited old Carle" Tufnell!
> I would not lay down my arms at such a behest as his.
>
> [What] was the use of your appointment if you are not to tell the
> truth and the whole truth? And if Tufnell won't believe the facts, so
> much the worse for him but not for them. . . .
>
> I should like if you please to take old Tufnell with me to the few
> places I went to, and to turn the face of some of those mistresses'
> tongues on his devoted head. He would be utterly shut up. . . .
>
> So don't withdraw your report.

A letter to Henrietta Synnot has survived, 1 May 1874, revealing the
depth of Jeanie Senior's anguish at her dilemma:

> I can't help being tortured sometimes, and often at night, with the
> thought that all this quarrelling will retard any change for the
> better for the poor children – and that if I had suppressed my
> *Report* I might have gained in exchange for that concession all
> sorts of immediate advantages for the little ones . . . It is intolerable
> to me not to be in perfect peace and good will with my fellow crea-
> tures. I'm willing to fall onTufnell's neck. Why then does he want
> to claw my eyes out! We <u>both</u> want to befriend the children!!

She had lent George Eliot a copy of her *Report*, and reported her travails
with Tufnell. The novelist, who was then writing *Daniel Deronda*,
responded:

> Dear Friend
>
> I think your report is admirable for fullness, clearness, and wisdom
> of suggestion. But I can understand how the pointing out of evils
> under a system may be regarded by officials as an "attack," and
> that . . . a clear-eyed ardent practical woman may be found very
> troublesome as an inspector.[5]

She had been particularly moved by what Jeanie Senior had written about
the all-importance of warm personal relationships in the psychological development of a child:

> I enter so heartily into what you say about the superiority of that
> home education which calls out the emotions in connection with all
> the common needs of life, and creates that interest in means and
> results which is the chief part of cleverness.

George Eliot also saw that there was a profound *political* division between the radical Jeanie Senior and her angry, conservative opponents. She continued: '[You] have very firmly and clearly expressed your recognition of the whole Poor Law System as an unhappy heritage which we have to hinder as far as possible from descending to future generations. Perhaps that is part of your "attack"?' To the great women's emancipator, Barbara Bodichon, George Eliot wrote a little later, 'Do you know how our dear Mrs. Senior is tormented by the officials about her capital *Report*?'[6]

On 15 June Jeanie wrote to Tufnell, proposing he accompany her to the informants for her *Appendix G* in order that they should repeat their statements in his hearing. His reply, 16 June, was insulting and abusive:

> I cannot see the slightest advantage in looking over your books and it is too late now to make enquiries as to the correctness of your statements. All our Reports have been sent in and printed long ago, and no alteration can now be made in them.
>
> If you have any friend who is an expert in pauper education, he would certainly recommend you to ask to withdraw your *Report* altogether. I never read a *Report*, to speak candidly, so utterly unfair and mistaken from beginning to end, blaming what is good, praising what is bad, and displaying a thorough ignorance of all the conditions of pauper education. Errors of every sort bristle on every page. In fact I don't see how it was possible for a few ladies obviously quite unacquainted with the subject, to fathom all its complications after a few casual visits to schools, in which I have ascertained that not one was thoroughly examined.
>
> . . . [In] truth I never read a more unsatisfactory *Report*. . . . [Every] expert would denounce it in the strongest terms.

Are men 'experts' on the needs of girls aged three to eighteen?

Jeanie Senior replied to this onslaught with perhaps excessive forbearance in a letter that she drafted and re-drafted many times:

> Dear Mr. Tufnell,
>
> No-one can feel the shortcomings of my *Report* so keenly as I do; and pray believe that I never for a moment supposed that I had "fathomed" the question of pauper education. Mr. Stansfeld asked me to report to him my impressions as to the training and education of girls in the Metropolitan pauper Schools and after a year of enquiry I did my best to give him a fair and conscientious opinion. It is for him to withdraw my *Report* if he feels it to be "unfair and mistaken" . . .
>
> . . . I think you must recognize in me the same sort of spirit that

we all honour highly in you. I mean an earnest devotion to the
little children for whom you have done so much. I remain yours
truly, . . .

Stansfeld was furious on her behalf:

> . . . [The] enclosed [i.e. her reply to Tufnell] is really too much of
> turning the other cheek . . . .[As] far as my feeling and opinion are
> concerned, the time seems come to make a stand . . . Tufnell's
> conduct towards you has been, I consider, not only silly but insuf-
> ferably arrogant and very ungentlemanly. [undated] . . .

He continued on 18 June 1874:

> Tufnell is an insolent old fool, and you are – well, weakly Christian
> . . .

And on 20 June 1874:

> Tufnell's letters may not be unjust from his point of view, but they
> are ungentlemanly and unkind, and his point of view is intolerable,
> self-sufficient infallibility.
>   You have answered me, and I cave in. You are not weakly Xtian.
> You are intensely good and I feel the greatest respect for your
> goodness.

The bond between them was being strengthened by Tufnell's attack. But it
should not be thought that this bitter 'row', even though Jeanie experienced
it as 'torture', prevented her from engaging either with her new work as a
permanent Inspector of Workhouses – or with all her manifold family
responsibilities. At the end of April she had written to the Permanent
Secretary of the Local Government Board, John Lambert, a long letter
mapping out her proposed course of action. She agreed to delegate the visi-
tation of former pauper girls out 'in service' to local committees and
suggested that the plan be first tried in Marylebone in concert with the local
Poor Law Guardians and under the guidance and co-operation of Octavia
Hill. (In other words it would be a new task for Octavia's fledgling professional women social workers both to help 'place' and to visit the girls.) She
herself would visit all the Metropolitan Schools at least twice a year to check
on the implementation of her recommended sanitary and other changes 'and
to inspect all parts of the infants and girls' schools and the infirmaries'. In
addition she wished

to visit the Lying-in Wards and infant wards of the Metropolitan workhouses and to hold herself ready to visit any Workhouse or Workhouse School in any part of England if the Inspectors felt that the experience of a woman could be of service to them . . . on points affecting women and children.

Would Tufnell have considered only male experts on the Poor Law competent to judge pauper women's Lying-in Wards?

Jeanie Senior had by now insisted successfully that the workhouse girls be given better seating in their classrooms and a more varied diet with fruit and vegetables in season. Some practical immediate reforms, therefore, she did manage to put in hand. But the breaking down of the huge schools into small 'family' units and the fostering of all pauper orphans were quite another matter. She had announced her determination herself to help found a '[London] Home for girls between one place of service and another . . . where young servants may find a safe refuge'. But she was quickly warned that she could do no such thing in her official capacity, although she might play an *un*official consultative role, were a voluntary group to set up such a Home. Nothing daunted, she went ahead with the Refuge project, which was, in fact, already under construction. She wrote to Henrietta Synnot: 'I went to see the Home yesterday, . . . I have written to Merrett and Knowles and have offered to finish the house at my own cost' (*c*. 5 May 1874).

She had also been continuing to work hard with other activists throughout Britain who were campaigning for the extension of the 'boarding-out' of destitute orphans.[7] And at the same time she was beginning to make contact with leading feminists, anxious like herself to support vulnerable young servant girls on their own in London, writing to Henrietta Synnot, 1 May 1874: 'I am just going off to Mme. Belloc, Mrs. Knox and Mme. Bodichon to talk over future possible organization for the helping of girls in place.' By an extraordinary coincidence, some Anglican ladies were simultaneously drawing up a plan for befriending working-class girls 'in service' throughout the countryside – the future Girls' Friendly Society. Jeanie Senior, as the most prominent woman in the field, had been invited to Lambeth Palace at the beginning of May, because the Archbishop's wife, Mrs. Tait, wished her to meet the Anglican planners, including the leading progenitor of the proposed GFS, Mrs. Townsend. Jeanie Senior's initial private reaction had been that she hoped they would be able to combine forces 'but there is too strong an element of Episcopacy and priestdom to suit me completely'.

A prescient response, as matters turned out.

Yet another of her projects at this time was to assist the training of District Nurses to serve the poor in rural Britain[8] and, finally, she had also been corresponding with Louisa Hubbard,[9] concerning the desirability of employing ladies as professional workhouse administrators. But it is significant that she should write that she did not dare to come out publicly on that particular subject as yet:

> I am anxious, just at present, to keep as quiet as possible, because any public opinion I may express might do me harm at the Local Government Board, where my [permanent] appointment is not approved. *Till my report is published and abused, and fought over and forgotten, I must try to be neither heard nor seen. If I'm not very wise and judicious, my future powers of usefulness may be injured.* So please forgive me for begging you not to mention my opinion in this matter. . . . I am afraid of taking any step just at present, as there is an opposition to my appointment, and I must live it down and wear it out by disappearing from view and convincing the men that I am quite "harmless".[10] (my emphasis)

Interspersed among her official correspondence April–October 1874 are four examples of Jeanie Senior's personal involvement with individual former Workhouse girls. Most touching is the heartfelt gratitude of a young unmarried mother, Caroline Bruce:

> I am very happy and I have A Comfortable home and A Dear Mistress thank God for it I shall never forget your kindness to me and my Dear Baby I Think you have asked the Almighty to give me A home for me and my little one. I like my Place very much Dear Madam.

Needless to say, in addition to all that new professional (and voluntary) work now on her hands, there was still, of course, what Octavia Hill had called Jeanie's 'home work', the multitudinous, exhausting demands made upon her by her extended family. First, as always, came Walter. She worried over his still living at Elm House, surrounded by infirm, crotchety, old people – 'I am sure that all your laughing apparatus does not get enough used' (23 May 1874). And she also worried over his slack attitude to his pupillage in legal chambers, when he toyed with taking time off after only three weeks. Two months later, she worried that he did not seem ready to commit himself to a serious relationship with any girl, and indulged in one of her happy fantasies about his future:

> I do so wish you could fall in love with a merry stirring active girl who would routle [sic] you up well and whom you soon could marry . . . Of course darling son I do not want you to marry a girl you don't love really and truly and warmly. But I should like you seriously to remember that it is a good thing to marry young . . . I

believe that you check all thought of marriage because you believe that I should so miss you out of my home. And so I should, dear one, but in many ways I should gain far more than I should lose . . . [If] you married I should have a haven of refuge if I got tired at home. It is a claim that even your father would recognize that I should want, and ought to go to see you. I should if your wife liked me, spend most of my Sundays with you – and when I wanted harmony on a week-day, I should go off to you and your wife . . . (23 May 1874)

It was not only unemployed pauper skivvies who needed 'a haven of refuge'.

In that same letter of 23 May there is a reference to Jeanie's mother. Margaret Hughes had just taken one of those momentous, adventurous decisions so characteristic of her energetic spirit. Seeing no prospect of an end to old Mrs. Senior's presence in Elm House, she had recently bought and extended Colwell Cottage on the Isle of Wight as an alternative base for herself, for Hastings' children – and for Jeanie. The choice of Colwell may well have had Jeanie's happiness principally in mind, since, as her mother knew, it was within walking distance of Jeanie's old friends the Prinseps, G. F. Watts, Anny Thackeray, Julia Margaret Cameron and Tennyson. At all events, her mother knew that sunshine and sea air were 'really life' to her daughter.

Therefore, even though she would not be able to keep a cow there, seventy-six year-old Margaret Hughes now moved her books and pictures and furniture and Emmy and Hastings' three boys to Colwell Bay, helped by Dyer, plus his wife Bessie and their children. For the Dyer family she had also bought a cottage. And there too was Jeanie Senior in the August of 1874. She had very nearly collapsed from exhaustion in London but once at Colwell her health and strength picked up again.

And now, at long, long last, Mrs. Senior's *Report* was about to be published, very late in the day but unaltered and not flanked by any counterblasts. On 23 September she wrote: 'There will be a row and a scrimmage between me and the Inspectors, and [Workhouse] School Managers. I shall get hit about dreadfully I know, but I am girding up my loins, and I hope I shall have "a fair field and no favour".' Her fellow pioneer in radical social reform, Octavia Hill, had just written her 'one of the most beautiful and comforting letters I ever read', to prop up her moral courage as she faced the music:

My dearest Janey, [sic]

. . . I was longing for news of you . . . when the rumour reaches me that your report is really out. – What that will really mean to you of suspense, of anxiety, of attack, of doubt as to what it will be right under given circumstances to do or not to do, I can only imagine. Whatever the newspaper critics, the interested officials, the angry partisans may say, there are those who know that your work has been done with conscience, patience, singleness of eye and heart; . . . it is like good seed sown in good ground, and tho' it may seem to die for a time it will bear fruit . . . . – You and I know that it matters little if we have to be the out-of-sight piers driven deep into the marsh, on which the visible ones are carried that support the bridge; we do not mind if hereafter people forget that there are any low down at all; . . . the bridge is what we care for and not our place in it.[11]

Stansfeld had warned her, months befor, that 'everything ought to be done in the press to secure and to provoke notice' and Jeanie had alerted old friends like Tom Taylor and Anny Thackeray and newer friends and colleagues like Henrietta Synnot and Menella Smedley, as well as Octavia Hill's two brothers-in-law, C. E. Maurice and Charles Lewes, to try and review her in the periodical press. Anny Thackeray's article in *The Cornhill* stressed Jeanie's humanity and lively, sympathetic human interest: '[Mrs Senior] has not been content with merely writing a report. She has lived it, heard it speak, gone straight to the human beings concerned in her Tables.'[12]

At first the general press reaction was more unanimously in her favour than she could have dreamed possible – and it was not confined to articles by her own circle. The feminist Frances Power Cobbe in *The Echo* wrote of Mrs Senior's 'irresistible conclusions'. *The Saturday Review*, usually hostile to women's aspirations, declared on 26 September: 'One of the most interesting of the documents printed . . . is a *Report* by Mrs. Nassau Senior'. The article praised its 'freshness and completeness' and endorsed the obvious indispensability of a woman's judgment on 'the management of girls'. But why, the reviewer asked, had the *Report* been published too late to be acted upon in 1874? 'Caecilius' in *The Press and St. James' Chronicle* of 9 October praised

> intelligent investigators like Mrs. Senior, . . . whose approach is most remarkable. Everywhere in her report there is real suggestive power . . . I can imagine Mrs. Senior teaching these poor little forlorn mortals prisoners' base and rounders and warney. She evidently has grasped the idea that play is the highest form of work.

'Caecilius' took the opportunity to contrast Mrs Senior's 'simple ladylike style' with the male inspectors' 'stilted and ostentatious platitudes'. *Punch* too was unequivocal in its affirmation:

Read the *Third Annual Report of the Local Government Board*. In
the midst of that vast blue-book of 700 pages there is a bit of
motherly writing by Mrs. Nassau Senior which is delightful to
read, and cannot fail to be of immense use . . . . [Her] brief biographies of these poor little waifs are perfect in their simplicity . . .
and much more pathetic than anything in modern fiction. . . .
    Mr. Punch is delighted when a lady does what no man could
possibly do . . . Mr. Stansfeld did a wise thing when he asked Mrs.
Senior . . . kind and keen in her investigations, to undertake this
inquiry.[13]

Similarly, an anonymous writer in *The Spectator* wrote endorsing Jeanie
Senior's emphasis on the children's desperate need for more 'mothering', 'It
was a happy moment when the thought entered Mr. Stansfeld's head that he
would get a woman's view' of the question . . . '
    On the same day, 10 October, *The Civil Service Review* printed the first
of three anonymous articles devoted to respectful praise of her report:

We hope that the appointment of Mrs. Nassau Senior as Lady
Inspector of Pauper Schools will inaugurate a new era in their
management. The reforms which she advocates are so simple, so
clear, and so full of common sense, that no one who is not prejudiced in favour of a special system can fail to see their value.

The Morning Post in October/November 1874 also dedicated three articles
to quoting the *Report* and was fulsome in its praise:

The Local Government Board could have done no greater service
for the poor girls under its care than confide their distinctly feminine interests to the patient investigation, the careful comparison,
and wise counsel of the lady who has given us in this report one of
the most useful and interesting papers ever presented to Parliament.

The Scotsman, 17 November, agreed that the *Report* was 'a document of
very exceptional interest and importance'.[14] And one late accolade came in
Joanna Hill's anonymous article in *The Birmingham Daily Post*:

The report is remarkable in several ways. It is from the pen of the
first woman ever appointed one of Her Majesty's Inspectors . . .
its whole tone is candid to its opponents, anxious to do justice to
all sides and earnest in its recommendations . . . it carries conviction . . . Mr. Stansfeld performed a wise and generous action in
asking for a woman's view of the question.[15]

At last came the magisterial voice of *The Times*. First there was a long, affirming anonymous article (written by Dr. Brudenell Carter). Then the Editor of *The Times* gave his own positive verdict on Mrs. Senior in a long leading article on the same day, 4 November: 'She has discharged [her] task with admirable thoroughness and intelligence, and her *Report* is one of the most valuable contributions ever made to the solution of this problem [the education of pauper girls].'

Jeanie Senior could not complain that her work had been overlooked or unappreciated in the press.[16] Such a thoughtful, respectful, affirming reception of her *Report*, coming after all that she had suffered from Tuffnell's attempts to suppress it altogether, should have been balm to her spirit. But she was unable to rejoice because, at that very same moment, she had nearly died. As she herself said later, 'I fell down as if shot!'[17]

On 4 October she had been as vigorous as ever, writing a long, lively letter to Louisa Hubbard about the different prospects for educated ladies to do paid work in Workhouses, full of details of salaries and enthusiastic job descriptions – 'The post that *I* [double under-lining] should like better than all, would be Matron or Head nurse in the Infirmary . . . '[18] But only three or four days afterwards, after writing her usual letter to Walter, dated 6 October, she had fallen down 'as if shot'. Not only was she totally exhausted by the preceding months of hard work and nervous stress, but her uterine cancer had attacked again – the tumour had become enlarged, and she suffered a massive internal haemorrhage. At the age of forty-five she was ordered complete bed rest for at least two years as her only chance of survival.

Just three weeks later, a fierce controversy broke out in the press related to the public reception of her *Report*. It focused on her advocacy of the supervised fostering or boarding-out of all pauper orphans and was fought out very publicly in the correspondence columns of *The Times*, even more bitterly than the earlier exchange of letters in autumn 1872.[19] At the end of November an impressive deputation lobbied Sclater-Booth, President of the Local Government Board under Disraeli, asking him for some assurance that Mrs. Senior's recommendations on the boarding-out of pauper orphans would indeed be promptly implemented. Sclater-Booth's response revealed that he had already been nobbled by the Tory old guard of the Inspectorate on that vexed subject, Mrs. Senior's report:

> [He] had no wish to say anything which would appear to show
> that he was inclined to undervalue . . . Mrs. Senior's able and inter-
> esting report to the Department; but it was his duty to say that the
> statistics and the arguments drawn from them had been very
> severely criticized by those who had a much larger experience than
> Mrs. Senior in the management of schools.[20]

In its leader of 5 December 1874, headed 'A Lady Poor-Law Inspector', *The Times* pointed out that Sclater-Booth must have been referring to *unpublished* criticism of Mrs. Senior from her male colleagues, i.e. from Inspectors who resented her 'roving commission' to visit institutions where they had previously enjoyed exclusive access. In that same leader *The Times* announced with regret that Mrs. Nassau Senior had been compelled by ill-health to retire and urged on Sclater-Booth the prompt appointment of a lady successor to her – for 'the public . . . will hardly rest contented unless they can obtain, upon several points of the workhouse system [a] "woman's view"'.

We shall never know how much of all this controversy was mediated to Jeanie Senior then, or, if she were able to follow it closely, how she reacted. We do know that she was suffering mentally as well as physically from her new helplessness. George Eliot reported to Barbara Bodichon on 16 November: 'I have hired a very promising housemaid, found for me by our dear Mrs. Senior who – did you know? – is laid prostrate by illness and ordered to lay herself up for two or three years at least. She looks like a white angel in her little bed.'[21] She may have looked like an angel but she was not feeling like one. It was bitter, indeed, to have been forced, on 30 November, to resign. She confessed to Louisa Twining: 'I don't think I need tell you what it cost me to give up my work just as there seemed every chance of my being allowed to carry it out . . . [One] person more or less matters not, but I own it was a bitter trial at first.'[22]

James Stansfeld did everything in his power to console her, visiting her and writing her letters that had by now become openly and deeply affectionate. Even before she had resigned her official position she was no longer 'Mrs. Senior' to him, but his 'dear friend'.

> You leave . . . at least, with flying colours, and with pleasant memories. You have been a success; I am justified, and the cause is helped and a fruitful precedent admitted . . . .
>
>   You must rest and hope and trust; and believe as I know you do in the tender sympathizing affection of your friends . . . not least I hope,
> of your ever affectionate J. Stansfeld.

On 30 November Stansfeld wrote again, trying, very tenderly, to comfort her in her disappointment with herself:

> And now, dear, you must try to banish vain regrets. You have done your duty during your years' work, you have done your duty in resigning, and you have left behind you good work and a new light which you have thrown upon an important question and which no man could have thrown upon it, and you have left also a beautiful

example, and a pleasant memory and a precedent which must be followed and developed in future time.

It is a privilege for both you and me that we have been able together to set this example and to establish this principle and precedent. . . .

Think what it would have been had this attack come before your year's work was finished; think on that side, dear friend, rather than on the other. And will you sometimes think too – and smile – that I am rather proud of the choice which I made, and of the victory "in a canter" won by the first woman inspector appointed to do important work; though she did, unhappily, drop lame at the winning post.

Her letter of resignation, 30 November 1874, began: 'Sir, It is with deep regret that I have to inform you that the state of my health prevents me and for a long time to come will, I fear, prevent me, from undertaking any further active work.'[23]

In a thirty-two page Memorandum accompanying that sad letter of resignation, Jeanie Senior summarized first, all her proposed reforms for the humanizing of pauper girls' education and second, her plans for their protection and aid after leaving the Workhouse school system. The first topic included the employment of elder girls in the care of the infants, preferably in small infant schools; the boarding-out of orphans in cottage homes; the material improvement in the school buildings, both schoolrooms and dormitories, as well as in the children's diet; the introduction of active play and the decoration of their surroundings; the institution of savings banks where the girls could put earnings from needlework or other work; education in basic health and physiology, the introduction of day outings 'to brighten the children', the introduction of convalescent wards into the District school infirmaries where the child patients could be visited and the general upgrading of the post of workhouse officers with improved pay and paid holidays.

The second topic included introducing legal guardianship for the girls over the age of 14 up to the age of 18 or 20 and, in order to address the existing deficiencies in their after-care, to establish Committees 'consisting of the Female Inspector, the Chaplain and Matron of [each District] school, . . . a certain number of local [Poor Law] Guardians and 2 or 3 volunteer helpers'. These Committees, aided by local sub committees of lady visitors, would take on overall responsibility for tracking the girls' progress and protecting their welfare. She recommended more careful selection of their first work placement, better supervision in that placement, protection of the girls when they left their first place and found a subsequent place and better supervision in that place until they were 16. She ended that section of her long Memorandum by mentioning that a fledgling 'non-official Association for befriending young servants' had already begun its work. Her long Memorandum concluded with two poignant paragraphs:

> [This] record may save much anxious thought to some future successor in my office, and may rescue from total loss and wrack, the labor [sic] and anxious consideration which I have given to the development of my plans.
>
> I conclude with the hope that whoever succeeds to my place, may be more fortunate than I have been, in being able to continue her work till she sees her plans carried out to such effect as they are capable of.[24]

Thus Jeanie Senior assumed that she would soon have a *woman* successor – 'the female inspector in office at that time' who would 'continue *her* work till she sees her plans carried out'. But in fact she would have *no* woman successor – not in her lifetime, nor for nearly a decade after, until Miss M. H. Mason was appointed in November 1885, with a temporary remit limited to the inspection of children who were boarded-out. And, given the Civil Service 'marriage bar' for women gradually instituted by the male closed shop, there would be no *married* woman equivalent to Jeanie Senior in Whitehall until just before World War Two.[25]

This chapter began with Florence Nightingale's joy at Jeanie Senior's appointment. It has to end with her almost hysterical disappointment at the news of the resignation.

> My dear Mrs. Senior,
>
> I am so concerned at what I heard yesterday – that you had resigned Office – that I cannot help writing a word of sorrow. No personal grief has ever affected me more; (tho' I have had many and bitter; indeed, my whole life has been one of sorrows.) But I look upon your resignation as a national misfortune. No one could have done what you would have done: what you indeed have done during this brief space: against growing-up, grown up female pauperism, a worse evil than a Cholera, or a War, or Popes, or Slavery, or Indian Zamindars or than any other evil we know. Consternation is my state. How many will remain paupers whom you would have saved. You were arrayed almost singlehanded, a noble Army of one, against this evil. And who will take your place? Who will redeem our generation? The outcry of the enemy shows what a club your gentle Hercules arm has wielded: and would you leave off till you had become Apollo Victor with his bow?
>
> I only hope that ill-health is not the cause; or only a temporary cause of this great disaster.

At all events, the great principle which you have initiated
(without writing!! Or platforming about it") namely, that women
must 'inspect' women [and how well they do it!] cannot be again
laid aside.

Rather the resignation of the greatest Cabinet that ever was than
yours!

I never thanked you for your *Report*, for it was unthankable for.
I am so miserable that I can only say further how much I am, dear
Mrs. Senior,

Your faithful, and grateful servant
Florence Nightingale.
. . . I pray God that your Successor may be one tenth of you. (7
December 1874)

Jeanie felt overpowered by these Messianic claims made for her – 'Who will
redeem our generation?' Florence Nightingale had prophesied in 1857 that
'The next Christ may be a female Christ' in *Cassandra*;[26] perhaps she had
recently come to believe that Jeanie Senior was the fulfilment of that
prophecy. On learning that Jeanie had cancer, Florence Nightingale prayed,
30 December1874:

May God grant that you have perfect rest now: and perfect recovery by and by . . . we have a higher and a better hope which failure
and disappointment cannot take away, and that is that Perfect
Wisdom will some day complete His work whether we live to see it
or not. May He bless you.

Yours ever overflowingly,
Florence Nightingale

We owe the most detailed evocation of the life that Jeanie Senior was now
forced to lead, and her way of living that life, to a young woman called Sarah
Forbes, the daughter of the American rail magnate and Abolitionist John
Forbes, with whom Jeanie and her brother Tom had made fast friends in the
early 1860s.[27]

When I went to study water-colour painting in London in [winter]
1874, my father gave me an introduction to Mrs. Senior. The first
time I went to Elm House she was too ill to see me; but the second
time, I was shown upstairs to a small room, bare as a hospital
ward, though with blazing fire and open window, – no carpet, no
curtains, and a plain iron bedstead. Outlined against the pillows

was the sweetest face I have ever seen. Masses of golden hair, bright as a young child's shaded the delicate transparent features. The cheeks still had a tinge of clear colour. . . . She reminded me most of a Fra Angelico Angel, but her face was the face of one who had experienced suffering and overcome it. Weak tho' she was, . . . the glad smile, the eyes shining with welcome, the outstretched hands gave an instant sense of buoyant life. . . .

After my first visit I went often, bringing her flowers and telling her tales of my London experiences . . . Mrs. Senior used to laugh at the stories I told, until the tears ran down her cheeks; then she would draw a long breath, and say, "That did me more good than pounds of medicine." . . .[28]

We learn from Sarah Forbes' recollections of her visits to Elm House then that 'the care of [that] large household was . . . taken off her shoulders by her son. I remember her once saying of him, "He is both son and daughter to me"; . . . Mr. Senior had a den in some secluded spot'.[29] Nassau's mother, however, was much in evidence:

[Old] Madame Senior would wander in, wanting a bit of change and amusement after the tedium of her own room. She was nearly ninety and very deaf [she was in fact 84]. She would ask endless questions about the contents of her daughter-in-law's work-basket. Mrs. Senior's voice was weak, and she must have found answering hard; yet I never heard a trace of impatience in the sweet tones, and a tender, amused smile played about her mouth as she replied to each query in turn.[30]

Jeanie ended that year of mental and physical turmoil which had produced her collapse by writing a New Year's Eve letter to Walter, blessing him for his unselfish support in the recent terrible months:

I never can tell you what you are, and have been to me my darling through my illness; . . . You never will know till the next world – because words can't express feelings – . . . I trust that 1875 may see you with a delightful young wife, full of fun and life, who will stir you up to continual laughter and so delight my heart.

Unable to walk or sing or play the piano or go to hear Joachim – and nothing if not a 'doer of the word' – her active spirit was frustrated beyond expression. Weak from blood loss, in almost constant pain, often feeling too sick to eat or sleep and bedridden for the foreseeable future, Jeanie Senior would now show what she was made of.

CHAPTER FIFTEEN

Birth of a 'New Woman', 1875–1876

In her letter of 30 December 1874 to Jeanie Senior, Florence Nightingale had, with characteristic intensity, declared:

> [Any] publication of the result of your labours and of the plans you have formed is of priceless importance. All female England which is worth anything ought to be employed, officially and unofficially in carrying them out. . . .
>
> If there is the least risk of "copies enough" not being bespoken "to publish at all", pray let me 'bespeak' 20, or any larger number which may help to avert such a catastrophe.

The projected book here referred to was *Boarding Out and Pauper Schools – Especially for Girls – Being a reprint of the principal Reports on Pauper education in the Blue Book for 1873–4*, edited by Menella Smedley[1] to inform public opinion on the case for fostering destitute orphans as well as on the need to reform the education of pauper girls. A thousand copies would be published, costing one shilling and sixpence each, *if* a pre-publication sale of 500 copies could be ensured. Florence Davenport Hill had urged Menella Smedley to produce 'a powerful weapon on our side . . . I dare not of course trouble our dear Mrs. Senior in her present state with any inquiry on the subject'.[2]

Jeanie Senior could begin 1875, therefore, looking forward to a book that would forcefully juxtapose her own views on the girls' need for reforms with the complacent male inspectors' views on the education of pauper boys. But before January was over, she had to face a damning public attack on her integrity and on all her recommendations. For the *Observations on the Report of Mrs. Senior to the Local Government Board*, 'by the former Chief Inspector E. Carleton Tuffnell Esquire', which, as she knew had long been lodged with Sclater-Booth, were at last published and sent to *The Times* – even before being sent to her.

The Times immediately veered round like a weather-cock. It replaced its recent support for her in November and December, with a supercilious, reproachful leader on 26 January 1875, backing Tufnell. *The Times* leader-writer wished Tufnell's '*Observations*' had not been quite so 'conclusive' and that 'gallantry' might have allowed 'a little quarter for a lady belligerent'. But he feared that Mrs. Senior and her 'lady detectives' appeared to have been 'irresponsible' – 'too zealous' in their willingness to believe 'scandal'. '[When] all these ladies can say of a girl is that she was seen sitting on a step, or that she let her hair fall down her back . . . we must admit that the argument should not be left entirely in feminine hands'. *The Times* now opposed boarding-out altogether, alleging that a fostered or even an adopted child can never be made a true 'child of the house'. And the long article ended with the patronizing suggestion that Mrs. Senior study some oral history – she should investigate the experience of poor children apprenticed out sixty years ago at the beginning of the century, before continuing to advocate fostering.

Jeanie Senior answered *The Times* on 27 January – although she herself had still not been sent Tufnell's '*Observations*'. She rejected any 'gallant' attempt to be kind, merely because she was a woman: 'If either my method of inquiry or my logic has led me to false conclusions, I am quite ready to acknowledge my error, but till error is proved much more conclusively than Mr. Tufnell has proved it I shall fight both for my method and my conclusions.'

And fight she does:

> Before considering Mr. Tufnell's views, it is necessary to consider the position which he occupies. When a man has introduced a great improvement in administration and has for some thirty years superintended its working in detail, he must, necessarily, be the last to admit the possibility of superseding his work. . . .

She then relates how Mr. Tufnell had on several occasions refused her invitation to inspect her inquiry notes, and how he was guilty of very partial, selective quotation from her case-histories: 'The details of "girls sitting on steps" and having their "hair down their backs" are more or less trivial items of a mass of circumstantial evidence. . . . To isolate these details from the rest is the act of a singularly unjudicial mind.' As for *The Times*' recommendation that she investigate the dissimilar conditions of poor children apprenticed in the countryside sixty years ago, it 'would not throw much light on . . . the best plan of training and educating [London's] pauper girls in 1875.'

George Eliot sent Jeanie her support:

> [We] have been delighting today in your admirable letter to the *Times* which is as strong and temperate as it could well be. . . .
>
> From Mme. Bodichon and from Gertrude [Mrs. Charles Lewes, Octavia Hill's sister] I have had hints of the work going on which your labours set on foot. [i.e .the planned Metropolitan Association for Befriending Young Servants] That is something cheerful to bear

in mind when your dear pale face, as I saw it last, comes back to me with vividness – Mr. Lewes asks you to remember him, and I dare say you have plenty of time for memories in the long hours when you are obliged to rest . . .

Believe me, dear Friend, yours with deep sympathy. (26 January 1875)[3]

Stansfeld was even more fervently on her side:

Dear friend,

I was amazed at the *Times* leader this morning . . .
Your reply is perfect.

I see now what is good for you – to be insulted and hit hard and unfairly, and to feel that you must fight for a cause's sake. I know what that is too. There is an admirable firmness and clearness and conciseness and a sense and aspect of thorough possession of your subject in your letter; and I am very pleased.

He did indeed know what it was 'to feel that [he] had to fight for a cause's sake' – and to be insulted and hit unfairly in the process. For the past several months he had been the most eminent male champion of the Repeal of the Contagious Diseases Acts, and had travelled up and down Britain speaking in public for Josephine Butler's crusade. The CD Acts of 1866–1869, which aimed at a sexual cleaning up of Britain's ports and garrison towns, had annulled the civil rights of British women, subjecting them to arbitrary arrest on suspicion of being prostitutes and enforcing medical inspections and even imprisonment in 'Lock Hospitals' until pronounced 'clean'. It was an irrationally gendered piece of legislation, for no man was liable to medical inspection or imprisonment until cured of VD. Josephine Butler was the *extra*-parliamentary leader of the campaign for Repeal, while Stansfeld was its leading campaigner within Parliament.[4] In his championing of the human rights of women at the very bottom of the social pyramid, James Stansfeld was at one in spirit with Jeanie Senior. For all too many of the pauper girls for whom she was so concerned, once they lost their jobs (and roofs) as domestic servants, were prostitution fodder, vulnerable to pimps and brothel madams. 'Mrs. Senior' was concerned about how to cut down on a major source of the supply. That was the subtext of her *Report* and of her *Appendices F, G* and *H*. We have evidence that Jeanie Senior helped Josephine Butler's extra-parliamentary campaign in a letter of Stansfeld's of 4 February 1875, where he writes: 'Mrs. Butler has more than once asked me to thank you for your introductions.'

In her subsequent fierce exchange of letters with Tufnell in *The Times*, 27 January–2 February, Jeanie Senior revealed to the world that Tufnell had actually put pressure on her to 'ask to withdraw her report' before its publication. Then even *Punch* weighed in:

TUFNELL (MR.) V. SENIOR (MRS)

There is now raging between two Local Government Office Inspectors, masculine and feminine, a hot controversy – hot at least, on the gentleman's part, and provokingly cool on the lady's . . .

The masculine Inspector writes snappishly and scornfully, and *Punch* is bound to say that, in this correspondence, both in temper and argument, the lady has the best of it . . . .

Now everything turns on the evidence. If that proves untrustworthy, cadit INSPECTRESS SENIOR. But if it holds water, cadit INSPECTOR TUFNELL. Let us have no more sparring, please, but a sifting – as careful and as speedy as may be. Inspectress, even, has a right to that at the hands of Inspector. (13 February 1875)

At the end of January Jeanie Senior had at last been sent the forty pages of E. C. Tufnell's *'Observations'*. Why had the President of the Local Government Board delayed ten months before letting her see the case against her? The only possible assumption is that he – and all the male Government Inspectors working under him – had wanted to prevent her from answering back. Lying in bed, fighting her cancer, and told to have 'complete rest', Jeanie Senior read these *'Observations'* with a bitter indignation that did nothing for her recovery. Embedded in a mass of hostile anecdotes, unsubstantiated assertions, intimidating counter-statistics and horror stories about victimized boarded-out children, there erupted one personal insult after another. The whole tone of Tufnell's attack showed his assumption of moral, intellectual and gender superiority over her. Perhaps it also betrayed his sense of threat.

In the first paragraph, he declared it his 'unpleasant duty' to criticize a lady. But he had to do so because, he ventured 'to allege', she was 'irretrievably biassed', having already written 'several sensational letters' on the existing system of pauper education which he himself was satisfied was 'the best system . . . yet invented'. Even more hurtfully, he accused her, the champion and would-be rescuer of the workhouse girls, of 'stigmatising', 'condemning' and 'grossly maligning' the 'poor girls' (p. 1) on the evidence of 'the merest tittle-tattle from mostly a low class of witnesses' (p. 7). As for the hundreds of girls who could not be traced at all, he sneered ironically at Mrs. Senior's 'kind surmise' that they might have had a sorry story to tell. He, in contrast, proffered a fairytale ending for all of them – happily employed by wealthy aristocrats from whom they wished to conceal their pauper past (p. 5). He accused the fiercely truth-seeking, truth-speaking Jeanie Senior of being guilty of 'bad faith' (p. 4), 'extreme unfairness' (p. 6), 'untruthfulness' (p.10), 'glaring inaccuracy' (p. 12), 'ridiculous universal fault-finding' (p. 12), 'pure absurdity' (p. 14), 'great inconsistency' (p. 21) 'extraordinary absurdity' (p. 24) and of 'wild speculations' (p. 25). In his conclusion he declared 'how unfitted ladies are to superintend matters of this sort', i.e. – the boarding out of small children and the placement in domestic work of pauper girls (p. 19).

The first person to counter-attack these 'Observations' was Menella Smedley. She had deliberately held back her book, Boarding-Out, until she had seen Tufnell's attack in print. In the Introduction to her book, published February 1875, she makes the telling point that Tufnell's own Inspection Report of 1873 had very largely [35 pages out of 42] consisted of quotations from letters from five successful male products of his District Schools. The longest of these had been written by an unusually able boy who had received exceptional individual encouragement. Menella Smedley tartly points out that 'A man's [autobiographical] letter is only his testimonial to himself, . . .' She might also have added that Chief Inspector Tuffnell had earned his £400 of public money rather easily, since there is no word of actual inspection work done by him in his entire 1873 Report – in contrast to the unremitting, twelve month-long effort of Mrs. Senior for hers.

In her comments on Mrs. Senior's Report, Menella Smedley strongly supports the proposal to substitute small family grouping in which the oldest girls could be trained as nursery carers of the infants. But, she sadly adds: 'This wise and tender scheme, with many others of a like character, is now laid aside, as Mrs. Senior has been compelled by ill health to resign her place as Inspector' (p. 51).

Regarding Tufnell's 'Observations' on Mrs. Senior's Report, Menella Smedley's weapon is humour. She simply laughs out of court the unreal statistics of one Chaplain who purported to find almost every single former pauper school servant girl 'unexceptionably good, perfect and faultless . . . concerning whom nothing unsatisfactory is alleged' (pp. 1–2 and 23–26). Regarding Tufnell's criticism of Jeanie for not having questioned or even seen the girls who had disappeared without trace, she laughs again: '[It] would seem . . . that [Mrs. Senior] could not have satisfied her censors, unless she had employed a Medium' (p. 4). She points out that Mr. Tufnell's frequent praise of the education of pauper boys, was irrelevant to Mrs. Senior's inquiry into the education of pauper girls (pp. 10–11). Menella Smedley was especially indignant that he should have confused Mrs. Senior's warnings about a system

as if they were scandals against an individual. We cannot too often repeat that we call attention to dangers, not for the sake of denouncing girls who may, as we fear, have succumbed to them, but for the better protection of girls who have yet to encounter them. (p. 20)

In her final section dealing with Tufnell's samples of girls whose conduct, he alleged, had been unfairly condemned, she shows how in each case he had selected only the most harmless evidence and had suppressed every item of corroborative evidence that was really damaging (pp. 27–9).

But it was obviously Jeanie Senior's responsibility to answer each of Tufnell's charges against her and then to submit her reply to Parliament. She was not in the best state to do this. How could she attempt to do the research necessary for a well-substantiated rebuttal? Unable to get out of bed, she asked Walter to travel to Edinburgh to obtain her old friend Dr. Mitchell's assistance in analysing and disputing Tufnell's statistics. On 7 March Arthur Mitchell replied:

> Private
>
> Walter is a very clever fellow and has done his work admirably. He is nearly his mother's equal, which is not saying little.
>
> I return by this post the Boarding out chapter. The rest has reached you in safety long ere this I hope.
>
> I enclose some remarks on the Death rate, which you can insert as from an eminent *medical statistician* (!!), or Walter or you can father them if he likes. Do not let them cut out or curtail what you have already said . . . .

She had also tried to use Walter' help in gaining essential demographic statistics concerning pauper children's health and mortality rates in London's District Schools in 1873, 1874 and 1875 – but the officials in Whitehall stone-walled her.

> I asked the Local Government Board to allow my son to make these inquiries for me, being unable through illness to make them myself. I was told that the office could not authorise a private individual to visit district schools and workhouses for the purpose of obtaining these returns.[5]

Regarding Tufnell's allegations of past scandals in boarding-out, the sisters Joanna and Florence Davenport Hill willingly agreed to investigate every case on her behalf and report back their findings to her. On 12 March 1875 Jeanie Senior was still writing letters asking for information to help her to counter Tufnell's criticism and accusations.[5] But on 16 March she at last managed to send off her long, hand-written 'Letter addressed to the

President of the Local Government Board . . . being a Reply to the
Observations of Mr. Tufnell, . . . upon her *Report* on Pauper Schools.'

The first damaging charge was that she had come to her task with her mind
already made up, since she had already come out publicly in favour of boarding out pauper children and against large District Schools in 'several sensational letters in the newspapers' [i.e. October 1872]. She ripostes: 'If my
letters were sensational it was only because all facts which disturb our jog-
trot and humdrum acquiescence in things as they are, must be sensational'
(p. 5). She alludes to Mr. Tufnell's own total identification with the kind of
Schools that he himself had invented nearly 30 years earlier (p. 22) and asks
why the many 'useful suggestions for improvements' that he acknowledges
her *Report* made, and which, he says, were 'obvious to any intelligent
observer', had not in fact been adopted in the schools during the nearly thirty
years, when he had been in charge? (p. 6)

She points out that the subject of her *Report*'s inquiry was quite different
from any previous official investigation. No one before her had been asked
to look at the appropriateness of the education of pauper girls in relation to
their subsequent domestic employment. And no one had tried to follow up
what happened to them after the age of sixteen, two years after leaving their
pauper school. Hence no earlier opinions by chaplains or anyone else on
pauper boys, or on girls aged under 16 were relevant. She (through Dr.
Mitchell's help) shows Tuffnell's apparently damning statistics to be useless
and lists the data that he should attempt to supply if he were to offer any
serious critique (pp. 8 and 16–17). Tufnell had called her investigation using
anonymous researchers and informants 'worthless'; she supplies both the
names of her researchers[7] and their qualifications and then records how she
had repeatedly offered to show him their detailed findings, which he repeatedly refused to read. His allusion to her reliance on 'tittle-tattle of 'low class'
witnesses, she rebuts with spirit:

> I do not know what Mr. Tufnell means by saying these mistresses
> were of a low class. . . . You must take your evidence from those
> who employ [the girls] not from those who do not . . . Does
> Mr.Tufnell see his way to creating a new class of mistresses, not
> only to employ, but also to be contented with, the girls trained
> under his favourite system? . . . [The] tittle-tattle to which I have
> listened . . . is precisely the same as that to which every person is
> forced to listen, when making inquiries into the character of a
> proposed servant. (p. 6)

While he quotes a phalanx of District School Chaplains, to the effect that all the girls benefited from their moral and spiritual teaching, and that not one had 'fallen', she points out that the said Chaplains had been quite unaware that several of these same young girls had had to be readmitted to a work-house in order to give birth to illegitimate babies – a fact that she had discovered through her own constant close contact with the workhouse midwife and matron (p. 9). As for Tufnell's attempt to dismiss all her case-studies by quoting very little, and that selectively and misleadingly, e.g 'P.N. has been seen sitting on a doorstep' – she spells out that P.N. was also unemployed without a character reference, had claimed that she was married but that her husband was in Switzerland – and that she wore no wedding ring. 'There exists a class of evidence called indirect and cumulative, made up of small parcels, individually of little weight, but together of irresistible force . . . It is . . . the same kind as the [character] evidence received by a judge' (p. 7). She insists that she could not, on such evidence, 'class these poor girls otherwise than "dropped out of sight, of whom the last tidings were unsatisfactory"' (p. 7). To Tufnell they were 'poor girls' because traduced by Jeanie Senior; to her they were 'poor girls' because she feared she had not traduced them.

The largest single section of her *Reply* deals with the fierce controversy over 'boarding-out'. Her defence of the preferability of fostering to institutionalization takes in the experience of Scotland, Ireland, Germany, Switzerland, France, and America (pp. 11–12 and 18–19). Amazingly, through the assistance of her allies Joanna Hill and Florence Davenport Hill among others, she manages to take up every single instance of the alleged mistreatment of a boarded-out child in recent years in England, as listed by Tufnell, and establishes either that the case had been misrepresented or else, when true, that the abused child had had no protection from the befriending supervision of a committee of volunteer ladies such as Jeanie insisted should always be in place (pp. 13–15). 'I may add that there are not a few, but many enthusiastic ladies, who earnestly desire to look after boarded-out children' (p. 18).

Tufnell, in order to attack her advocacy of fostering destitute orphans, had invoked the original principles of the 1834 Poor Law as laid down by her father-in-law, Nassau William Senior, claiming it to have been 'the most searching inquiry ever undertaken' and its rejection of all kinds of 'out-relief' to be of unquestionable 'universal application', on analogy with the laws of gravity. Jeanie Senior laughs at him: – 'These rules [of Poor Law administration] he regards with the reverence due to a divine revelation' (p. 12). But Nassau William Senior was not God. That Tufnell himself, a former Poor Law Commissioner, had remained an 'iron-law' political economist, was evident when he opposed supplying 'all sorts of amusements' to the sick pauper children in the infirmaries, since 'there would be great danger of inducing children to make themselves ill with the view of enjoying the *otium* of the infirmary'. Here Jeanie Senior turns to the District School doctors; they, like her, found no evidence at all of children deliberately making themselves ill (pp. 19–20). And where Tufnell quotes Uriah Heep-like letters from Workhouse Old Girls: 'I now feel the advantage of the good advice I received at school, and I should like you to send me a little more to refresh my memory' (p. 16) to which he had added: 'If they [do] go the bad, the recollection of the excellent intellectual training they have received often occurs to them in after life, and brings them voluntarily to repentance', Jeanie drily responds: 'I do not myself believe in the power of intellectual training to bring anyone to repentance.' Instead, she insists: '[All] women will tell Mr. Tufnell that the recollection of home and friends has the strongest influence in keeping a girl from going to the bad' (p. 18). And children who had been fostered and adopted felt more precious than the products of his huge, impersonal schools.

Those six weeks between reading Tufnell's hostile, damaging '*Observations*' and submitting her own detailed '*Reply*' had been a terrible struggle. The signs of strain are evident in the sometimes less than clear, coherent organization of her Reply – not helped by Tufnell's less than clear and coherent attack. The ordeal would have been mentally and nervously taxing for anyone, but for her, in terrible pain, those weeks demanded teeth-clenching grit as she struggled to concentrate and keep in mental control. Was she helped by remembering her favourite, defiant Beethoven song – *Abendlied im gestirnten Himmel* [Song at evening beneath a starry sky'] – with its call to spiritual resistance in our unjust, oppressive world? (" . . . [No] terror can torment my soul longer, no power can command it, as it soars up, up to heaven's light".)

Even after she had despatched her *Reply*, there was still one more struggle to go through in this exhausting saga – her battle to get it printed by the Local Government Board and laid before the House of Commons. Just as he had delayed the original publication of her Report and the communication to her of Tufnell's *Observations*, now Sclater-Booth obstructed the publication of her rejoinder. Jeanie herself had already remonstrated with him in her covering letter of 16 March enclosing her *Reply*: 'I trust . . . that you will be of opinion that in some way I am entitled to have the same publicity given to my rejoinder as has been given to Mr. Tufnell's "*Observations*", and this on public rather than on personal grounds'.

It is clear that her *Reply* would never have been printed and presented to the House of Commons at all without the intervention of James Stansfeld. On 4 February he wrote to her that he had told the Permanent Secretary of the Local Government board, Lambert, that he proposed to move for her *Reply* being laid as a 'Return' on the Table of the House and that Lambert 'quite agreed. Don't quote this'. But he had then to keep pursuing the issue on her behalf, first asking for an interview with Sclater-Booth and later checking with Hansard the printer and with the Librarian of the House of Commons. 'Obstinate patience will do a great deal'. Just how reluctant Sclater-Booth was can be seen here:

> Dear Stansfeld,
>
> I shall be glad to consider with you when we meet how far the Senior–Tufnell controversy is to be carried on at the cost of the public, but of course I shall not object to your moving for [illegible] letter if you think it necessary.

Stansfeld said in his covering letter to Jeanie 'Of course I insisted on the return [to the House of Commons] and got it'. It was 'Ordered by The House of Commons, to be Printed, 20 April 1875'. Finally, therefore, through Stansfeld's good offices, Jeanie Senior was allowed to publish her self-defence. But Tuffnell's "*Observations*" on her *Report* are listed in the British Library Catalogue, whereas her "*Reply*" is not.[8]

This whole episode taught Jeanie Senior that her original confidence in being granted 'a fair field and no favour' in a world of male colleagues had been nothing but naïve optimism. She had been forced to face their misogyny and defensive solidarity pitted against her, a woman pioneer in social investigation. The gentlemen Inspectors and Workhouse Chaplains had a poor opinion of 'lady volunteers'; they had even less wish to see a highly paid 'lady professional' succeed. Where might it not end? Women Civil Servants, possibly even their own wives, invading every branch of life that concerned women and girls? Her appointment must be exposed as a lamentable mistake – or failing that, in the happy event of her enforced resignation, 'poor Mrs. Nassau Senior' must on no account have a woman successor replace her. Her male colleagues had shown they were not brothers – and certainly not Hughes brothers.

No wonder, then, that Jeanie Senior should now be born again, a feminist at last. She had started out conventionally enough. 'Strong-minded' women she had regarded as a joke and the issue of women's suffrage had seemed unimportant. How she had laughed when 'little Joscelin Courteney' had dressed up and guyed Miss Becker[9] 'the strong-minded lady who makes speeches about women's rights' (20 October 1869). In February 1870 she was still unconvinced about the case for women university students living in their own Cambridge College, and in June 1870 she had happily proposed playing the comic role of one of the strong-minded females in Captain Wingfield's farce '1880' for the private theatricals at Offley. 'There is a man in it who sews the buttons on his wife's *shirts* and takes care of the baby!' On

16 September 1872 she had refused to speak at a Battersea meeting for women's suffrage or even to sign her name in support – 'Of course I think all single women who pay rates have a right to vote, but I can't see that it matters much whether they do or not'. As late as April 1873 she had rejected Lady Amberley 's proposal to nominate her for a Committee to get women elected to School Boards – 'I refused, [using] the best of excuses, my pauper work; I don't at all want to be dragged into the strong-minded line!' (5 April 1873).[10]

Nevertheless, Jeanie Senior had been, in fact, a mould-breaking, practising feminist for many years. She had supported the first British woman doctor, Elizabeth Garrett Anderson; she had agreed with her brother Tom Hughes that women workers should form a great trade union for their mutual aid and protection; she had responded warmly to the 'hardworking women' social activists she met at Joanna Hill's home in Birmingham – 'I enjoyed myself much. Everyone knew and cared about some subject that interested me' (19 February 1873). She had relished the feminist Frances Power Cobbe's 'intensely amusing' *Pursuits of Women* (19 September 1874) and she had supported Elizabeth Malleson's Working Women's College in October 1874.[11] Finally, of course, she had shocked many in her own circle when she had left the ranks of respectable, leisured, Victorian ladies to give singing classes for pay and then become the first woman professional Government servant. Her subsequent *Report*, as well as the long Memorandum accompanying her letter of resignation in November 1874, had advocated the professional as well as the voluntary employment of women in British social administration in future. But Jeanie Senior's long reluctance to 'come out' and be labelled one of the derided, 'Strong-minded' brigade campaigning for equal rights for women, cannot be denied.

She had been too complacent about her own personal charm – too confident in her ability to disarm male opposition and persuade male sceptics on issues about which she had informed convictions. It had felt more dignified to champion other people rather than seem 'selfish' and class herself, with all other women, as un-enfranchised underdogs. It had taken her many years to recognize that she did not have to choose between campaigning for the interests of all her own sex including ladies and for the interests of those girls and women so much more disadvantaged. Now she realized that she would make a more effective champion of those others if she also worked for the equal citizenship of women in general.

Given her recent, bitter experience of implacable male hostility in the public world, Jeanie Senior learned fast. It was James Stansfeld who helped educate her. He himself had been a convinced feminist ever since 1840, when he had been shocked at the exclusion of women delegates from the international Anti-Slavery Convention in Birmingham.[12] When, therefore, Jeanie now complained to him that she had not received 'fair play' from her male colleagues, he answered her almost roughly:

Of course men do not look on women as entitled to fair play; there is no such thing as the sentiment of fair play – exceptions apart – where there is not recognized equality of rights. If you had heard Smollett, you would not have been sorry that I – your friend – rose and struck the beastly coward in the face (metaphorically!) I will never fail to do so; there is a limit beyond which forbearance is weakness. (10 April 1875)

Who was Smollett? On 7 April there had been a lively debate in the House of Commons on a 'Women's Disabilities Removal Bill' that proposed extending the parliamentary suffrage to unmarried women householders on the same basis as the existing municipal suffrage. Speaking against the Bill, the Conservative MP, P. B. Smollett, had insisted it was a sorry jest and a waste of parliamentary time. The social norm was for Adam to be the breadwinner and for Eve to confine herself to her domestic duties. But '[under] this Bill, elderly virgins, widows, a large class of the *demi-monde* and kept women, . . . would be admitted to the franchise.' Smollett's peroration tried to frighten his male hearers with the nightmare vision of a ridiculous future Britain in which the two sexes were equal:

If women no longer desired to be helpmates to men, if they thought that their role in this world was to compete with men and to surpass them in all the walks of life, let all the Universities in Great Britain be thrown open freely, and let young women and young men compete on equal terms for the honours of University life. They should be permitted to be called to the bar, to hold livings in the Church, to practise medicine and every other profession. They should be named as grand jurors, sit upon the bench of magistrates, and compelled to serve as petty and special jurors upon all occasions, even upon coroners' inquests. They should be not merely permitted to vote, they should be admitted to those [parliamentary] benches in the flesh. . . .[13]

[Cf. illustration overleaf from *Punch*, 6 February 1875, 'Novelty in Coiffures suitable for Ladies called to the Bar (as they soon will be, of course'.)]

Smollett's mockery did not intimidate Stansfeld, who was one of the proposers of the Bill. In response to the allegation that some of the women to be enfranchised could include prostitutes, Stansfeld agreed to disfranchise them 'on one condition, that the men who frequented the habitations of these supposed future voters should also be disfranchised'. And he insisted on the basic justice of granting the franchise to every breadwinner, regardless of sex.[14]

NOVELTY IN COIFFURES.

SUITABLE FOR LADIES CALLED TO THE BAR (AS THEY SOON WILL BE, OF COURSE).

33 *Punch*, 6 February 1875.

Over a quarter of a million signatures had already been presented on petitions to the Commons in favour of this (unsuccessful) Suffrage Bill at the beginning of the Parliamentary Session. By the end of the Session in May, 415,622 signatures had been sent in. Among them was that of Jeanie Senior. Already on 9 April 1875 she had decided to make her stand public and come over at last to the side of the 'Strong-minded' . She wrote her 'conversion letter' to Helen Blackburn, Secretary of the Central Committee for Women's Suffrage:

Dear Madam,

The Reports of the Debate on the Women's Disabilities Bill, and the leading articles in the *Times*, show so plainly that the question is not dealt with fairly either by the legislature or the press, that I feel it is a duty (holding as I do that women have a just claim to the franchise) to do my utmost to promote the success of the measure, regardless of any effect which this may possibly have on my chances of future employment under the Local Government Board, or of election to any Board of Guardians.[15]

I can do little to help on the cause, as I am confined to my bed, with small prospect of any immediate improvement in my health, but I should like to have any petitions sent me to sign, and I enclose £1 for the fund.

I am, dear madam, yours truly,

J.E. Senior.[16]

Jeanie Senior's public 'coming over' to the Women's Suffrage cause was greeted with great joy. Frances Power Cobbe wrote to her immediately: 'It is very good and nice of you to give us your countenance at this crisis! we shall all hail your accession to our Society . . . with loud cheers' (Spring 1875).[17]

The Spring of 1875 had also been turbulent for Jeanie on the family front, for it was then that her brother Hastings had proposed marriage, more than once, to her great friend Anny Thackeray. Finally, at the end of May, she rejected him. Jeanie would so have enjoyed having Anny as a sister-in-law. On 7 June she wrote to Anny, who had fled to Paris from the continued pressure to commit herself to Hastings after her initial rejection of him:[18]

I think you will like to have a line from me my dear old A. I could not imagine what made you so odd last time you came to see me. Now I understand. Of course you can't think that this could make any difference to our love for each other? My dear, I am not such an unjust fool as to love you less because you don't feel disposed to love him. But I am very, very sorry. You know how dearly I love you and what a brightness and real joy would have come into my life if I could have had you as my sister. And I am very sorry for Hastings, who has already had so much trouble in his life, and just a little sorry for you too darling (don't be vexed at my saying so!) for he is simply the noblest, and most utterly unselfish man I ever have met with in my life, and I know that if you could have promised to be his wife, you would have found the truest happiness and rest in his tender love and devoted care. . . . – I only write in the hope of sparing you a little pain and nervousness when you think of me or come to see me. Of course I shall not tell Nassau, . . .

God bless you dear – I know your kind heart is grieved to make
your friends sorry; but it can't be helped, and we shall not love you
less because you won't be one of us

June and July 1875 saw a battle between her attacks of sickening pain and
her urgent need to finalize the Constitution of the newly founded voluntary
organization for London, the Metropolitan Association for Befriending
Young Servants (hereafter MABYS). Originally she had hoped that such a
necessary London organization, providing safe residential Homes for
temporarily unemployed servant girls as well as a Labour Exchange, would
be backed and funded by the state, while using the befriending services of
women volunteers. But now she had to recognize that the Conservative
administration would never implement her proposals. She was clear that the
Association must be both secular and non-sectarian in order to reach out to
'mentor' as many vulnerable young working girls as possible. In addition she
had to confront the constant problem of fund-raising by subscription. She
was simply too ill to see to everything herself. She had to direct the work
indirectly via correspondence and visits to Elm House from Henrietta
Synnot, Menella Smedley, Caroline Stephen's cousin Miss Sara Stephen, Miss
Gassiot and a Miss Ann Townshend – among others.

Her consultant gynaecologist Spencer Wells[19] then ordered her to leave
London to be looked after at Colwell Cottage on the Isle of Wight. She wrote
to Tom: 'I have been so worried by the noise of trains, etc., since I have had
more pain than usual, that the doctor wants me to get away to some
absolutely quiet place.' And to Henrietta Synnot she wrote: 'I dare say it will
do me good – but the going is not pleasant' (6 July 1875). 'The going' – by
cab, train, ferry and another cab to her mother's cottage – she dreaded. Not
merely the physical juddering but also the public exposure as a 'spectacle'
as she was carried from wheelchair to stretcher to train. ('The thought of
seeing people I know, and being stared at as an invalid scares me quite
absurdly . . . Nassau is dreadfully nervous and frightened about it.') (12 July
1875). Nassau did not accompany her, but the long journey turned out well,
thanks to the 'love and patience of my two dearest boys [Hastings and
Walter] . . . [and was] one of the white days to remember in my life', she
wrote to Walter afterwards (20 July 1875). It was blessed to be back in the
Isle of Wight's sea air and sun. Nassau, under pressure from his mother-in-
law, did then pay a visit to Colwell Cottage, but his wife was very far from
looking forward to it; yet again she had to worry about Nassau's moods, and
whether or not the weather would be to his liking:

Father writes that he is coming tomorrow, and I'm much disgusted
to find that Mother had written to ask him. Now he'll always
believe that he was forced into it! – However I don't think he'll be

unhappy if only the weather keeps like this, and the glass is, Dyer says, going up steadily. (27 July 1875)

Stansfeld's letters cheered Jeanie rather more. Not only was he a kindred idealistic spirit, but he could also share his private feelings *and* he could make her laugh. That Stansfeld felt he could also confess his attacks of depression testified to his need for emotional intimacy with her. He had failed to visit her while she was still in London, but far from reproaching him, she had sent him her first watercolour sketch of the view from her upstairs bedroom window at Colwell Bay, looking out to sea and sky. He wrote back:

> What a sweet letter you have sent me, dear, and what a lovely sketch; really wonderful, I think. I feel quite sure that it is perfectly true, and the effect of distance beyond the water is quite charming.
>   I was indeed vexed to miss you, and conscience stricken – I ought to have come before, but you don't chide – did you ever chide anybody – but invent a pretty little excuse for me, about "business first and pleasure afterwards". . . . It is very good, and very sweet and unselfish of you, but I must not accept it. Of course I could have found time. The real truth and reason is that I have been physically and otherwise depressed too, and kept putting it off.[20] . . . Let us hope and pray that you may be stronger when you come back. . . .
>   . . . [You still] follow the old mania about kissing Tuffy [i.e. offering a kiss of peace]. I'll tell you another thing to do, quite as Christian, "smite him on one cheek and tell him to turn the other". That's more what he deserves and it would be better for him . . . .
>   I mean to mount your sketch. I am quite serious in saying how much I admire it, besides the fact of its being yours . . . (29 July 1875)

Life on the Isle of Wight that summer was a mixture of brief interludes of happiness amid long stretches of enervating, nauseous pain. Bessie Dyer insisted on tending Jeanie without pay and Jeanie's mother would gently massage her neck when the long hours of sitting or lying had made her stiffen up. 'When the tumour takes a fit of growing' Jeanie had reported to Henrietta Synnot on 10 August, 'it presses on the stomach I think . . . I have been feeling sick nearly always, . . . but I am better today'. Whenever she was well enough to go out doors, she would be helped downstairs by leaning on Walter's or Dyer's wrists. In mid-August she again lost a lot of blood (she called it 'flooding') which left her very weak – but did at least get rid of the nausea. Watts, the Prinseps and the Camerons would all send to ask if she were well enough to be visited – and sometimes she was.

She would watch the country world from her upstairs bedroom window, and see the corn harvest being brought in – '[They] were working quite late, wagons passing in the light of the rising moon, and reminding me of [pictures by] Mason and Fred Walker' (16 August 1875). Another visit from Nassau then loomed: 'Your father comes by 3.30 boat. I hope to heaven it will be fine weather – or he and I shall be miserable' (3 September). She was well enough now to be able to sit out sometimes in the garden in the sun. Across the water was her dear Adelaide Sartoris' place at Warsash; and whilst she was not sufficiently strong to go there herself of course, Walter could do so:

> I won't say that I did not wish to be with you – for I was taken
> with the most intense longing to see dear old Warsash, and wander
> about with Adelaide as of old, in happy days, before I was so ill,
> and she had had so fearful a shock and sorrow – Poor darling tell
> me about her, all you can.[21] . . . (15 September 1875)

At the end of September Jeanie was back in London. She was confined to two upstairs rooms in Elm House but could feel more in touch with the world again. She was particularly gladdened by Nell's reports of recent reforms in the local Workhouse Infirmary:

> There are great changes and improvements there since so many
> men of education have got on the Board of Guardians. The
> Infirmary is quite cheerful – ladies go and play the concertina, and
> sing. Three were performing glees yesterday and two old women
> have got prizes for "window gardening". This makes me very
> happy. I have often felt so grieved that almost the only cheering
> they got (i.e. my visits) were stopped. Now I am quite happy. . . .
> (29 September 1875)

She was also happy in Nell's happiness, preparing for marriage to the future clergyman Reggie Wynter that December, and, whenever possible, she enjoyed overlooking young Harry's homework or Emmy's music practice in her day room. But such peaceful hours did not last:

> Poor old Hastings is worrying more than ever at his debt to the
> family . . . Fan was here yesterday. She . . . seems inclined to think
> F. Steward [a solicitor who was also a relative of George Hughes'
> widow, Annie] right, in saying that . . . Hastings [is] no better than
> a swindler!!! . . .

Walter then offered to investigate the Hughes' s financial and legal situation. But it was too late. By early November Hastings had to admit both to himself and to the family that all his business dealings had failed.

Looming financial disaster was then eclipsed by a tragedy that put mere money into perspective. In mid-October Anny Thackeray had visited Jeanie, together with her sister Minny Stephen, who was seven months pregnant. On 28 November Minny gave birth to a stillborn child and died from eclampsia. Both her husband and her sister suffered indescribably; neither of them would ever be the same again. Jeanie's heart went out to them, and it was then that she wrote Caroline Stephen the letter that Leslie later called 'one of his treasures'.[22] Knowing that Leslie Stephen had lost his Christian faith, Jeanie did not mention her own yearning hope of reunion after death. Instead, she concentrated on his feelings about life on earth:

> My Carry,
>
> . . . To have seen her pine away in hopeless illness, with perhaps the bright intelligence clouded, would have been harder to him, considering his devoted unselfish love, than to lose her thus suddenly. Now his memory of her is so bright, for how happy her life was from the time he married her. And she was spared the trial of knowing of the parting or dwelling on his loss and her little Laura's. Knowing how he loved her I can divine how this must comfort him – That the bitter sorrow should be his, and not hers, will uphold him even in the worst moments.
>
> . . . It seems so sad and strange that such dear friends should be in trouble and that I can't go to them! Not that I could do any of you any good, but that it is so intense a deprivation not to be with those one loves in the crises of life . . . .
>
> And so darling, your life is shown to you now! [Caroline Stephen had written that she would dedicate herself to help Leslie and look after his and Minny's first child, three year-old handicapped Laura].
>
> I shall see but little of you in the body, dear one, I fear – But I never feel far from you, because I always think I know how it is with you. The sort of feeling I have about my dear ones gone before – only they seem still more near. Goodbye darling – God bless you, Ever your loving J. (3 December 1875)[23]

At the end of that year Jeanie suffered renewed attacks of terrible pain. Perhaps that was why she had written that she expected to see very little of Caroline Stephen in the flesh and therefore had ended her letter 'Goodbye darling'. Meanwhile, in late December 1875, Hastings Hughes was officially declared bankrupt. The Hughes family plunged financially in his wake.

CHAPTER SIXTEEN

A Bonny Fighter

Not only had the economic slump of the winter of 1875 ruined Hastings Hughes, engulfing the family's loans to him, it had also swallowed up Thomas Hughes' idealistic investment in co-operative industrial enterprises.[1] Tom went in great distress to his sister on 7 January 1876 to break the bad news. Her response was to write long, heartfelt letters in which she tried both to reassure him and to wrestle for his political soul:

> My beloved old Tom –
>
> . . . Provided the loss falls on us alone, I cannot bring myself to care one bit about it . . .
>
> [It] has long been my earnest hope that my old age may be passed in a small cottage with one maid to help me do everything. Nassau would be quite happy with me to amuse him, and he would then have no grievances as he has here. He likes to see no one, and to be as solitary as possible. For such a life as that, a very small income suffices; and we should be able to give Walter a fair allowance and to live ourselves, even if we had nothing but an allowance from Mrs. Senior of £500 or £600 a year, and not a farthing from my father's estate. And as she has £1,400 a year income we should not feel that she was pinched if left with £800 or £900 a year. . . . The more my Walter has to depend on his own exertions the better, and he owns it. So if all our money goes "it won't scare me" as the Americans say. What does scare me is, that you should fret about it. . . .
>
> . . . [In] a year I feel sure I shall be on my legs again, and if my work should be cooking and cleaning, I certainly shall not feel it a hardship . . . and heaven knows it will be less anxious and wearing than my pauper work. Darling, have faith in me as I have in you! . . .

Having to move out of Elm House into a much smaller, cheaper, rented home did not trouble her in the least. On the contrary. But she did have other acute concerns: 'The only things that could give me pain are two: First if you make difficulties about our sharing the losses . . . Second, that you should continue to be so depressed . . . '

In her second letter, Jeanie addressed what she feared was Tom' s loss of commitment to his Co-operative creed:

> I have thought a great deal dear one, about your saying that it was
> "wrong" in you to put the money in that mine; and I can't see it so
> . . . To stand by one's principles, through good report and through
> evil report, is a far higher duty than to protect our money interests
> . . . The principle of Co-operation is such an idea; and you were
> right, and not wrong to do what you could for it.

She then spelt out their shared radical vision:

> Liberty, fraternity, equality, co-operation, association, brotherly
> love, must at last come to be the guiding ideas and principles. . . .
>   My beloved I want you to be true to yourself, your highest self,
> and not to let yourself be influenced by the opinions of people in
> general on these questions.

Jeanie was afraid lest Fan, always inclined to regard her husband's politics as
his tiresome hobby, should persuade him to renounce Christian Socialism for
the sake of his family. Tom replied that he would never give up his moral
support for Co-operative Associations, but he would no longer consider
himself fit to hold any prominent office in the movement.

In that long 'political' letter, 23 January 1876, Jeanie had been able to
assure Tom of their mother's resilience in this money crisis. 'She is as brave
and true and plucky as if she were 18, instead of nearly 78, and would go
with us all to America tomorrow without one moment's hesitation or sinking
of heart. . . . Mother's pluck is not put on.'[2] When Margaret Hughes had
first learned of Hastings' imminent bankruptcy, she had written fiercely to
Jeanie, remonstrating against her children's proposal that she be spared from
sharing in the family's financial loss:

> The most painful sentence to me, in my darling Hastings' letter, is
> this: "Tom and Jeanie know the position, and whatever happens,
> they do not intend to let your income be reduced." How dare my
> children think thus of me? I have not deserved it of them. – But no,
> I am sure in their hearts they do me justice, and believe that my
> greatest happiness is to deny myself to be able to help <u>them</u>.

A mother of the Gracchi indeed.

Jeanie's deepest concern of all was that Tom might now love Hastings less,
judging him to be irresponsible and unprincipled. 'Fan told Nassau that your
feeling for Hastings has quite altered' (9 February 1876). Jeanie could understand her sister-in-law's bitterness – 'but it agonizes me that you should . . .
love him less . . . It would break his heart if he thought that you so judged him'.
Jeanie said Hastings was like Tom – both of them mistaken, and too trusting

in the goodness and honesty of your fellow creatures. Consequently
you have both lost money . . . You have done the same thing for a
principle [Co-operation] while Hastings lost between £2,000 and
£3,000 by the newspaper – why? . . . because he thought he could
make the paper of great use to you and the cause of progress and
truth.[3]

She ended with her declaration of faith in what Keats called 'the holiness of
the heart's affections':

> I care not one farthing for the things which money can give. . . .
> For I can't connect money with our real lives; but that you should
> misunderstand and misjudge Hastings . . . is the keenest pain to me
> – . . . For that is something which belongs to our real lives, our real
> selves. The diminution of respect and love for each other, through
> misunderstanding or misjudging, is the most awful and terrible
> misfortune that could fall upon me, . . . I could not enjoy anything,
> or do any work, or think of anything but the time when we should
> all be dead, and consequently in a position to judge each other
> fairly, and renew the tender love in the Kingdom where worldly
> people's judgment will be powerless to influence us.

Her 'we' was still, as ever, the Hughes family; Tom's wife Fan belonged to
'the worldly people' – as did Nassau and his sister Minnie. She tried to make
a joke of her desperation: 'Now I don't want to be forced to long for all our
deaths!' And she ended with the plea: 'Don't let us create pain for each other
by drifting apart my dear one; no earthly losses matter one straw, if we love
and trust each other and cling together, but life is worth nothing if our love
and trust is to diminish' (9 February 1876). It was her version of William
Morris's 'Fellowship is Heaven and lack of Fellowship is Hell'. Tom reassured her that he truly loved 'poor dear Hastings' as much as ever – 'Dear
Fanny (or Nassau) is quite mistaken.'

As if that family crisis were not enough, Jeanie Senior was simultaneously
facing a quite different public crisis. A fundamental problem had arisen
concerning her fledgling voluntary organization, the Metropolitan
Association for Befriending Young Servants (MABYS). A similar organization, Mrs. Townsend's Anglican Girls' Friendly Society (hereafter GFS), was
now beginning to organize not merely in country parishes as originally envis-
aged, and in provincial towns and cities, but in London also. Hence confu-
sion and a distinct danger of 'poaching' and 'Empire-building'. Jeanie Senior,

although initially she had welcomed Mrs. Townsend's scheme, born almost at the same time as the MABYS – had been disturbed from the very start by its exclusively Anglican nature.[4] Mrs. Townsend, for her part, was so concerned that the MABYS was not exclusively Anglican that she was less and less convinced that the two societies could co-operate at all. Who was Mrs. Townsend?

Mary Elizabeth Townsend, née Butler (1841–1918), was "a capable-looking rather imperious lady".[5] The daughter of an Anglo-Irish clergyman in Ireland, she had married an English Tory squire who had recently inherited a great manor house, Honington Hall, in Warwickshire. She had a genuine desire to guard working-class girls from temptation 'by associating respectable young girls together, and by training them in religious principles and domestic duty'.[6] The girls did not have to be Anglicans but most of them were, as were all their 'Lady Associates' and the whole Girls' Friendly Society was organized on the Church of England's parish and diocesan structure with wealthy ladies from the aristocracy and gentry, including the wives of several Bishops, acting as regional patrons. Queen Victoria herself would agree to become the GFS national patron in 1880. The GFS promoted self-respect and thrift as well as deference. 'The model GFS girl was expected to be devout, kindly, serious-minded, uncomplaining'[7] and above all 'pure'. According to its Clause Three, insisted on by Mrs. Townsend, every girl candidate for membership had to be vouched for as 'chaste' by a member of a class above her.[8] It would have been unthinkable for Mrs. Townsend to have done what Jeanie did – befriend Frankie Coleridge, or find a live-in 'place' for an unmarried mother like Caroline Bruce. Former workhouse girl members were segregated from the other GFS girls until they were partially amalgamated in 1900, and fully integrated only in 1922. (There was, of course, no segregation at all of ex-workhouse girls from the other girls in the MABYS.) The GFS political loyalties were to the *status quo*, from empire and monarchy down to the squire. Mrs. Townsend's *Rules and Counsels for Daily Life*, the GFS Textbook of 1884, admonished the girls to be 'pure in body and soul, [avoiding] all playing and jesting that you ought to be ashamed of, and all reading of evil in books and papers'; to be 'modest in dress and behaviour, [dressing] simply according to your station' and to be 'faithful to your employers – Obey those that are over you as an act of obedience to God.'

It is not clear how quickly Jeanie Senior had identified Mrs. Townsend's Tory, Anglican and sexual purity principles. But the collision of these two 19th century pioneers in the befriending of working-class girls was that of an irresistible force meeting an immoveable object. At first Mrs. Townsend had been delighted to name 'Mrs Nassau Senior', the national figure associated with the welfare of pauper girls, in her publicity for her new Girls' Friendly Society. And she had given Jeanie copies of her own 364-page compilation of Scripture passages and prayers, *Voices of Comfort,* for use in MABYS Homes. Jeanie had responded by reminding her that MABYS was a *secular* organization, to which Mrs. Townsend had then replied, late in 1874:

> I know that you will not like to hear what I am going to say, but I always speak my mind . . .
>
> The more I consider the matter and the working out of your scheme as it develops the more I see how utterly impossible it

MRS. HAROLD BROWNE.

THE
HISTORIC FIVE

Photo by Maull and Fox.

REV. T. V. FOSBERY.

MRS. TOWNSEND.
Foundress of the Girls' Friendly Society.

MRS. TAIT.

MRS. NASSAU, SENIOR.

34 Original supporters of the founding of The Girls' Friendly Society, from *Friendship's Highway* by May Heath-Stubbs, 1926. (Mrs. Browne was wife of the Bishop of Winchester and Mrs. Tait wife of the Archbishop of Canterbury.)

would be to combine the country organization in any way with it
[the MABYS]. I am perfectly certain that no one [from the GFS]
will join now that so many leading Roman Catholics are joining in
[MABYS], and also some, are there not, Plymouth Brethren and
Unitarians? . . . [If] you admit Roman Catholics you must certainly
admit all other denominations. If it were only Mme Belloc working
with you, as one of you, and not as a Roman Catholic, it would
not so much matter, but she and Lady G. Fullerton and Lady
Lothian together – that is quite another thing.

She proceeded:

> [You] would never get Mrs. Tait [wife of the Archbishop of
> Canterbury] and Mrs. H. Browne [wife of the Bishop of
> Winchester] to meet those Roman Catholic ladies at [your public]
> meeting – they *could not* do it, consistently with their prominent
> position; . . . [There] is such a deeply rooted distrust of the Roman
> Catholic faith in the English mind – (chiefly on account of their
> ardour in proselytising) that I feel sure we should only damage the
> cause we wish to serve by joining you.

Mrs. Townsend then went on the attack, warning Jeanie Senior patronizingly
that the very broadness of the latter's non-sectarian, secular approach might
doom her MABYS project to failure:

> Whether your work will stand on so deep and firm a basis as it
> would if it were a little less broad remains to be proved.
>   If you have so many different denominations, how will it
> be known, when you come to publish your printed lists of
> members . . . which belongs to which? . . . No Church of
> England person would like to send their girls to the care of a
> Roman Catholic or Dissenter and *vice versa*.

She only wanted to help Anglican virgins; Jeanie Senior hoped to help non-
Anglicans and non-virgins as well.
    And that was how matters had been left for a year. On 11 February 1876,
however, Jeanie felt impelled to re-open the subject of the relationship
between the two organizations. She asked Mrs. Townsend to consider how
best the two organizations might be enabled to work in harmony 'giving
each other the right hand of fellowship. I am still an invalid and unable to
leave my room, and too ill to do any work, alas'. To Joanna Hill, in
Birmingham, who was now on the National Council of the GFS, Jeanie was
rather more forthright:

> I have been getting uneasy lately at what I hear – I hoped that we
> could have formed one Society, but Mrs. Townsend could only see
> her way to making her plan a complete [i.e. exclusively] Church [of
> England] organization, and from my knowledge of the needs of my
> class of girls, I knew that my work must stand on a broader basis .
> . . I know of numbers of first-rate workers and of earnest philan-
> thropic women of different creeds whom I trusted to help in the
> work. Besides which many of the pauper girls are Roman Catholics
> and would need to be helped by R.Catholic ladies and some girls
> enter dissenting families. . . . Mrs. Townsend could not agree to
> join with us because of our <u>undenominationalism</u>!! . . .

She ended by pointing out 'It is difficult to explain why there are 2 Societies
[in London] for the same object. The explanation takes long to make, and
people seldom listen to half that is said, and only understand and remember
half of that!' In her reply of 18 March, Mrs. Townsend reiterated that the
GFS Lady Associates only worked with GFS members, and therefore
MABYS girls who were C. of E. could only be helped by such ladies if they
became GFS members – 'and these members must be virtuous girls'. There is
a clear sense that Mrs. Townsend did not want her GFS girls to get too close
to the very poor, and possibly not 'respectable' MABYS maids of all work,
many of whom were illegitimate and had come from workhouse schools. In
the event, the paper 'On the best means of befriending workhouse girls in the
provinces through the G.F.S.', June 1877, a Miss Oxenham would state that
'the G.F.S. has agreed not to attempt to do anything in the [workhouse]
unions of the Metropolitan District, or with the girls from London District
Schools, these having been undertaken by the MABYS'.

    In April 1876 Jeanie Senior managed to orchestrate, even from her
sickbed, an important national appeal for charity funding for the MABYS.
(Tom wrote: 'I am glad to see dearest that your plot is developing–'.) Henry
Austin Bruce, Lord Aberdare, the educationist who had been Gladstone's
Liberal Home Secretary, led the funding campaign in *The Times* under the
heading 'Young Servants in London':

> I make [this appeal] on behalf of a portion of our population . . .
> whose lot in life is singularly dreary, whose position is one of
> danger to themselves and to society, and who are mostly friendless
> and homeless.
>   . . . [After a passing reference to the previous year's 'Boarding-
> Out' controversy in *The Times*] I will only say of such of these
> [destitute girls] as have been brought up in our District and Pauper
> Schools, . . . that at the age of 16 – an age of all others requiring
> guidance and sympathy – . . . we wash our hands of them

"push them from the shore, and launch them into life without an oar." . . .

The need of homes especially is greatly felt. Some servants will require these homes temporarily, while out of place; some for additional training; some in cases of illness, weak health or need of rest. How frequent these last cases must be let those bear in mind the ceaseless work, the overtasked strength of many of these poor children, in places where they are alone, unprotected and uncared for, conceive, and . . . pity.[9]

Lord Aberdare ended his appeal for funds to be sent to the MABYS central office, 7 Great College St. Westminster, by attesting to the 'sense and judgement' of the ladies, 'several of whom are my intimate friends' behind 'this most Christian and charitable work'. No particular denomination of Christian was specified. His appeal was supported by Jeanie's old friend, the redoubtable Octavia Hill, who wrote strong letters both to *The Times* and *The Daily News*, instancing the need for many more volunteer women social workers to come forward to help these vulnerable girls by giving 'what is often harder to give than money – time, and thought, and heart'.[10] 'London ought to be covered with a network of visitors.'[11] Finally Lord Shaftesbury agreed to lend his priceless support to the appeal, calling the new MABYS 'a precious and indispensable service' in its combination of protection and prevention:

The industrial schools and the Metropolitan pauper schools are annually sending out many girls to various situations, exposed to all the hazards of youth, ignorance, and of ill-tempered or capricious mistresses. Many, moreover, under the pressure of the struggle for life are flowing into London in quest of employment . . . If employment is not soon found, their small means are exhausted, and they wander about homeless and friendless, exposed to every form of danger that is possible in this perilous Metropolis.[12]

Both the MABYS and the GFS would flourish, in their very different ways, for the remainder of the 19th century and well beyond.[13]

March 1876 had been a bad month for Jeanie. Whereas the previous March had seen her struggling, despite her terrible illness, to reply to Tuffnell's attack on her *Report*, this March had seen her coping not only with Mrs. Townsend, but also with the continued aftershock to the family of Hastings' bankruptcy, entailing the need to move out of Elm House and the dispersal

of many of its former residents. 'Old Mrs. Senior will live with us still, for
we have promised her a home with us as long as she lives. . . . Little Harry
. . . will remain with us and continue to attend Westminster School . . . Emmy
and Gerard already live with mother (in the Isle of Wight)'. And Hastings'
eldest, Willie Hughes, would now have to leave school to start work as a
clerk for Aylesbury Dairies, of which Nassau was a Director.[14] Possibly
caused by the strain of all this upheaval, not to mention her 'stand-off' with
Mrs. Townsend, Jeanie had suffered an acute physical relapse for most of
March. In April 1876, slowly recovering from such terrible pain that she had
needed to be mesmerized by Dr. Gully in order to be able to sleep at all,
Jeanie received a letter from Stansfeld, brimming over with tenderness and
concern for her:

> Dear and sweet friend,
>
> It's no use. I cannot call you 'dear friend' only, it is too formal and
> conventional, and I am so full of affection and grief for you, think-
> ing of your goodness and sweetness and suffering and patience.
>
> I can come and I will come at any time. When shall I come? Tell
> me the hour and the day and if in town I will come.
>
> When you are at Lindsey Row [the new apartment at 98 Cheyne
> Walk, Chelsea] I can come as often as you like; only how can I tell
> how often is good for you and for how long, and what you would
> like? . . .
>
> Will you please therefore, dear, let me say this once, that you
> have only to think and let me know what is best. . . .
>
> You have so many friends who hold you in deserved affection. I
> can't act as if you were lonely and wanted company. I shall be
> perfectly satisfied if you don't want to see me often. There! For do
> I not know that you are incapable of any but kind and loving
> thoughts.

Two days later he wrote:

> . . . I do so thoroughly agree with you about the growing capacity
> for giving and receiving affection in our older years.
>
> And fully also I agree with you about the need and value of
> sometimes being apart – and about that which alone is worth
> having a being.
>
> I fail somewhat in your serene faith; but I do my best.

He visited her frequently over the next few weeks. Anny Thackeray also
called that late Spring and wrote to Richmond Ritchie:

I took the train to Clapham and there I met Tom Taylor who
walked with me to Janie's [sic]. Seeing her did me good, for it was
all sunset and gentle, and I sat by her bed in the window. She has a
grey room full of azaleas, and all her hair shines and her face looks
like an angel's, and little Harry Hughes was deep in an arm-chair
reading *Vanity Fair*.[15]

Jeanie was then taken back to her mother's cottage to be out of the disorder and worry of the big move from Elm House to Chelsea. Walter would
oversee all that for her. The move was not helped by old Mrs. Senior: 'It was
too bad of Minnie not to ask her for these three days', Jeanie wrote to Fan,
'[She] is most dreadfully in the way I hear from Nass. and Walter, driving
everyone mad.' Back in Colwell Bay, at the end of May, 'listening to the larks
and the distant hush of waves or wind', Dyer would help Jeanie downstairs
to lie out in the garden whenever there was sun and his wife Bessie would
put her to bed at night.

Peace of mind was impossible, however, for she now worried about the
unhygienic state of their new Thames-side home, 98 Cheyne Walk, which she
herself had neither seen nor vetted. It was not an irrational fear, given the
waterborne diseases of typhoid and cholera that were still a danger in
London then:

I'm dreadfully uneasy about the drains – . . . I wish with all my
heart that I had not come away so soon – I could have made
myself so disagreeable if I had been with you all, that it would have
been less disagreeable to your father to do as I wished, than to go
into the house – At a distance I can't be actively disagreeable, so
have no power!! (2 June 1876)

She begged Walter to get their solicitor to contact the owner and discover
who was responsible for the drains and whether they, the new lease-holders,
could be permitted if necessary to pay to drain into the lower level sewer
which was safer, though more costly. 'Don't leave this to be settled by your
father, but go to Burges yourself – You know that your father's one idea is to
save himself a little bit of present trouble.' Her next letter was full of anxieties about bad drinking water for Hastings' boys, now living in poor lodgings with their bankrupt father in Bark Place – Walter *must* make sure they
had safe Apollinaris water or stone bottled Seltzer; she will pay. 'You'll have
a good laugh over my manias . . . but laugh as much as you please, only
attend to them!' (8 June 1876)

All that was possible for a 'doer' like herself to do in those long, bedridden months and years was write letters – to her friends, to her colleagues in
voluntary work, to Stansfeld and to one family member after another – from

her octogenarian, quarrelsome uncles to Hastings' young sons, now trying to 'do for themselves' in Bark Place. Most necessary of all were her private letters to Walter; but she kept up emotional appearances by also writing her daily public letter to Nassau. Walter worried lest all this letter-writing exhaust her, but she vehemently rejected his suggestion that she cut down on her private letters to him, for they were 'the greatest pleasure' she had:

> Cannot you understand that if I am longing to have a little talk with you, it is good rather than bad for me to indulge it? . . . [It] is a rest and joy to me. – And as to writing a public letter to you, I find it too tiresome! That is an effort. – If at every sentence I have to think whether it will do for the eyes of Father and Gran [Senior] I have no pleasure in writing. It is not that I have anything specially secret to say to you – . . . But it is the whole feeling of the letter that is changed if it is to be public. – I'll write once a week a public letter to you and send it to Lindsey House, . . . but I really must be allowed to write to you to chambers when I am impelled to do so; and when I do that, I can feel perfectly natural as I write. . . . I should, in any case write daily to your father with all my news – I have always done so . . . [but] I won't be bullied out of the greatest pleasure I have . . . I will write to you how and when I please,

and I won't be dictated to in the matter. If you don't like reading my effusions, burn them unread. So there! . . .

The other letter [enclosed] is a public one. Now don't try to deprive me of my comfort and joy or I shall be driven to keep a journal addressed to you – tho' you would never see it! (14 June 1876)

Walter said no more about it for the present. In her 'public' letter to Walter, she wrote: 'I suppose your father told you that Stansfeld talks of coming down to see me for a night.' What Stansfeld had written to her was: 'I *must* come and see you in that sweet spot which you describe so fascinatingly, sometime during the summer. May I?'

Jeanie had recently been engrossed in the first parts of *Daniel Deronda,* as she now told George Eliot:

> Dear friend, what I feel about Daniel it is quite impossible to tell you – The fresh delight and astonishment of each number is worth living for, if life had no other joy . . . . [And] Oh! You can't tell how delightful to me is the wonderful poetry and beauty of Mordecai [the Zionist visionary]. I don't know if others feel him as I do, but he strikes one deep hid string in my heart as powerfully as dear Klesmer [the musician] strikes another. –[16]

George Eliot replied from the Continent on 12 July 1876:

> My dear Friend
>
> I think that if I had had the choice of the friend who should write me a letter "to be forwarded" I could not have chosen more for my own pleasure than fate has chosen for me in bringing me your dear letter . . . I have quite hungered these many months for some account of you . . .
>
> Your words about my writing, dear friend, are among the gifts of life which I count the most precious to me. My dear husband read them aloud to me, and cried with happiness as he read them. . . . The words are worth the more to me because they come from you – what you say or write I have always felt to be genuine, and to come from something deeper than transient effusiveness. Especially I care for what you say about Mordecai . . .
>
> Your image will be with us often in our walks . . . and believe that the thought of you has always been a gain to me since I have known your sweet face.[17]

Jeanie's intermittent attacks of sudden pain and heavy bleeding, followed by extreme weakness, continued to afflict her. G. F. Watts' wife would write

of this period 'her friends could not but be aware that she was slipping gradually from them'[18] while Jeanie herself tried to believe that each setback was
less serious than the one before. Every so often, however, depression and
exasperation at her state would so overwhelm her that she was shocked by
the intensity of her self-pity and impatience:

> I did not write yesterday, for I was not well physically, and was
> abominably out of sorts and wicked morally, . . . I daresay it is a
> sign that I am really better, that I get such fits of impatience at not
> being quite well. – I feel very sorry for it afterwards but at the time
> the temptation seems irresistible, and I can't say how exasperated I
> feel, body and mind. – When I come to my senses, and think how
> light is my burden compared with what others are bearing uncom-
> plainingly, I am truly ashamed . . . (4 July 1876)

She would pick herself up through vicarious happiness at the thought of
Walter enjoying himself boating on the Thames or going to swell garden
parties, and she would beg him to call on Anny Thackeray and on James
Stansfeld so that she might have news of them. Finally, there was the stimulus and solace of reading: 'I was as happy as usual over *Deronda* – I delight
in the Mordecai part – I like the poetry and mysticism of it – I think the only
true things are what we <u>can't</u> see and touch. . . . I expect that Grandcourt
will murder Gwendolen – or she him!' (4 July 1876).

All domestic concerns were then utterly eclipsed by a sensational sex and
murder scandal in the British press that came horribly close home to the
Senior family. Throughout July and August 1876, the "Balham Mystery"
alias the "Bravo Case" dragged in as a suspect Jeanie Senior's own Doctor
Gully who had tried to help her ever since the late 1850s with his homeo-
pathic remedies, 'water cure' and even, most recently, mesmerism. Both he
and his daughters had become family friends. But now 68 year-old Dr. Gully
was suspected not only of having procured an abortion for Mrs. Florence
Bravo, his mistress, forty years younger than he – 'a handsome lady . . . with
large expressive blue eyes, chestnut hair tinged with gold, and . . . a graceful
figure'[19] but also of having given her a prescription for poison to kill her
(second) violent husband. Jeanie of course was instantly at her most
Dorothea-like, convinced of Dr. Gully's innocence on all charges – 'I am as
certain of his innocence as of my own' – and aghast lest he be 'hung for a
crime he never committed' (22 July 1876). Most other people were a good
deal more sceptical; she found herself having to champion Gully even against
Stansfeld.

On 3 August she told Walter, rather startlingly, that 'Gully assured me that their intercourse was innocent, and till this is proved to the contrary I shall believe old Gully'. In other words Dr. Gully had pretended to use Jeanie as his *confidante*. But under the influence of ever more damning reportage in *The Daily Telegraph*, even she began to suspect that the worst might be true. Walter asked her whether she thought Gully had been right to lie to her, Jeanie, about his affair with Mrs. Bravo in order to save the latter's reputation? His mother replied:

> Dear lad, I hardly know what to answer! – When I was younger I should unhesitatingly have said yes. Now my yes is hesitating and uncertain. I find every month that I live, that I am more and more convinced that truth is the only right and beautiful thing. . . . But I don't know. I can't judge. I have lied myself to save people's good name, and though I more and more hate and loathe all untruth, yet I think I should do the same again. (5 August 1876)

She was less hesitant in her feminist condemnation of the poisoned husband:

> Bravo because he is a man, is thought 'a capital good fellow', and is much pitied, tho' he had a mistress and child at Maidenhead and struck and abused his wife and, tho' all the money was on her side, grudged her a maid and her ponies. – A thoroughly contemptible, mean, unprincipled fellow, who well deserved his fate whether he killed himself or was killed.

One cannot but feel that Jeanie had been influenced by Grandcourt in *Daniel Deronda*. Eventually the poisoning charge against Florence Bravo was left open as 'unproven' and the allegation against Dr. Gully was also unproved, though his reputation was destroyed. It is now thought that he did procure the abortion, but did not procure the poison.[20]

Stansfeld's short visit to Colwell Bay had been almost too happy. They had talked and talked and talked 'of everything under the sun. I'm almost sorry he came, for I shall miss him so terribly when he goes' (26 July 1876). He had walked by the side of her donkey carriage, still talking as they went down to the sea or called at Tennyson's house. What did they talk about? Their hopes for their two sons, and Stansfeld and his wife's tolerance of friendships outside marriage:

> He told me that he has always had his separate interests and friends, and that he thought that was the secret of a happy ménage. He and his wife [who was devoted to Mazzini] quite understand each other, and she never grudges him his friends tho' some she

likes less than others. He has one friend whom Mrs. S. does not much like. A Jessie someone.[21] He says she is rough but thoroughly staunch and good. She [Jessie] has just written to ask him to go and see her in the mountains in Italy – he'll have meat only twice a week and eggs and Liebig's essence of beef other days! . . . He says it is very tempting; all but the Liebig's extract! (27 July)

No wonder Jeanie ended: 'I miss him much after 2 days of constant talk; he is a most delightful companion, and I love him dearly' (27 July). She must have confided in Stansfeld that she and Nassau did not have 'a marriage of true minds', for he wrote shortly after his visit 'Your mother told me that both your husband and son wanted you to stay on [at Colwell]. I observed a discreet silence! In fact Nassau would have preferred Jeanie to return to him in London, for he did not want the fag of going down to see her in the Isle of Wight. 'I told your father that I should not ask him to come to see me, and I shan't! . . . [He] told me before I left that he did not want to come here and I won't ask him. So there!!' (27 July 1876).

All that could comfort her after Stansfeld had left was to write frequently to him, telling him in ever more detail about her life and her feelings; but then she would worry lest she had 'tried his interest too much'. Stansfeld would have none of it:

> . . . You are boundlessly generous in all your judgements and all your acts. Why are you wanting in bare justice to me? There's an accusation. For you do me injustice, and you make as complete a mistake as you could make, in fearing that "it is almost trying my interest too much, to give all these details", when the truth is that you can't give me too many and that you have not given me half enough. . . . [To] speak seriously it does so happen that what I especially desire with those I love is to be made participator of their daily lives, with all their details, so that it may be as much as possible as if I were with them day by day . . .
>
> I like so much to hear of your intense happiness in having your son with you – sunshine in a shady place as Thomas Hood said.
>
> Ever dear, your affectionate . . .

Jeanie could warm herself in the knowledge that she was now included in Stansfeld's 'those I love' and that he 'especially' desired to be in as close touch with her as if he were with her 'day by day'.

That summer in Colwell was soon over. Jeanie had had many visits from Watts and the Prinseps which transported her back to the old Sunday afternoons at Holland Park. There was also the joyous prospect of having Hastings and his three boys to holiday with them at Colwell. And there was also just time for one last, very Emma Woodhouse-like, fantasy. Still griev-

ing that Anny Thackeray had not become her sister-in -law, Jeanie now had
a new inspiration about

> the right woman for Hastings – Not Octavia – but Miranda [Hill –
> Octavia's elder sister]! I don't think Octavia would give up the least
> bit of her work for any one – but I think Miranda is of a less stern
> material, and might be induced to give her heart – . . . I can't think
> why I never thought of her before . . .
>
> If he got her to marry him I should have a sister at last with
> whom I had the most entire sympathy, and for whom I should have
> a perfect affection too, and she would be so tender and good to
> Mother and the children! – She is very clever. She keeps the school
> almost entirely herself now, and is adored by the girls – and she is
> as good as good can be, and she is very nice to look at, with lovely
> green-hazel eyes, and beautiful hair and teeth; and she must be
> tough in health for she works as hard as a horse . . .
>
> My only fear is that, as Miranda has no money at all except
> what she makes by teaching, they could not muster enough
> between them to live on. – But I really intend to talk to Hastings
> about it, for I am quite serious!

The only problem was that this ideal couple had never met – but Jeanie could
soon solve that.

> – If he consents to try, I shall send by him the illuminated mottoes
> which I and the bairns have done for her "Society for promoting
> beauty"[22] and that will introduce him, and I shall get her to dine
> and meet him at Lindsey House and so on. – She is far more attrac-
> tive to a man than Octavia – because she is softer . . . [One] would
> not dare to propose to Ockie to give up her work. She would
> return such a stern indignant No! . . . But unless she [Miranda]
> continued her school I don't know how they'd get bread and meat,
> for I don't think she has a shilling of private fortune, and what
> provision could be made for possible children? There would not be
> a very large family, for Miranda must be 35 or 36 I think –
> [Hastings was 43]
>
> I know you will have a good laugh at me. But all the same, if
> you think it over, you 'll see how right I am – right for him,
> because she would make exactly the wife for him, with her simplic-
> ity and unconventionality, and right, righter, rightest for me!! Dear
> me what a comfort it would be to have a sister like that; whose
> views and aims are so completely in harmony with my own. – If
> only it is not too good to come true!! – (8 August 1876)

It was.

That summer on the Isle of Wight did finally seem to do her good. On 18 August she wrote to the young American heiress Sarah Forbes, whom, though Jeanie would never know it, Hastings Hughes *would* eventually marry, 'I am wonderfully better for this glorious sunshine and heat. I can't tell you how different I feel. I really think now, of some day being better again'.[23] Thus strengthened, attended by Hastings and Walter, she returned to London.

The moment she was known to be back in London, friends and relatives flocked to call. Stansfeld was the first to enquire after her and ask whether he might see her at once or later that same day. Next came old Uncle Tom and his new companion Wilkinson niece, for two hours, followed by Henrietta Synnot and then Tom Hughes, followed by Fan and the three girls. Jeanie loved sitting by the window whenever there was sun and watching the barges and steamers and brown-sailed lighters on the Thames. It was tempting to plan an outing on the water herself when the weather was really warm but 'your father says that he <u>hates</u> going, so it is little pleasure I should get out of the excursion. . . . I shall stay at home' (27 August). To cap all, there was heartening news about her cancer from her consultant, Spencer Wells:

> He is astonished at the change for the better in every way. The tumour has decidedly got smaller and he finds me much stronger and healthier. He is sure now he says that in a year or so I shall be really strong and able to do anything I like! Even official work, if Stansfeld is back [in Government] again. – I may make a change for the bettering my life even now –I may sit up to the piano for half an hour at a time 2 or 3 times a day, and gradually increase that allowance – and I may go out on the river, or in a carriage two or three times a week. His only reason for . . . [not saying] daily, is that he thinks I might find the 2 flights of stairs trying. He would not mind a daily outing if I were carried up. . . . He does not expect that I shall ever have another flooding, but that I shall gradually get better and better and that the tumour will get smaller and smaller till it gives me no trouble at all . . . My darling this news will make you very happy and thankful as indeed it has me . . . I don't think that death would have been so hard to face . . . as invalidism for the rest of life. (29 August 1876)

Jeanie told Stansfeld the good news. He was thrilled, but at the same time too afraid to feel completely reassured:

I am indeed delighted . . . and grateful; . . . but I confess to a little superstition about not "tempting Providence." . . . But whenever any one that I have loved has been ill – really ill – I have felt as if I might do them harm by being too sanguine or cock-a-hoop, and that if instead of avoiding anxiety on their account, I took it to myself, it might give them a better chance . . . Could you have guessed me so near insanity! (early September 1876)

Her life did indeed begin to look up. Lindsey House, built in 1674 on the site of Sir Thomas More's farm, later the London headquarters of the Moravian Brethren in the 18th century, had most recently been the home of the great engineer, Isambard Kingdom Brunel. It was now divided into beautifully situated apartments facing the river below Chelsea Bridge:

Last night was most lovely moonlight on the water; and being warmer I could sit on the balcony well wrapped up. I did enjoy it . – What a lovely situation this is! – The barges creeping silently along, across the path of the moon, and out of the mysterious half-darkness on into the half darkness again . . . Even your father had to own it, but he said constantly "and yet it really is not a pretty view – It is ugly and squalid." Is not that like him? (30 August 1876)

The stream of visitors did try Nassau's patience: 'Nassau will be quite unbearable if so many come, for he hates visitors!' Jeanie confided to Henrietta Synnot on 5 September. But for herself, feeling so much stronger at last, even a tooth-filling at the dentist was positive, involving as it did a trip in a hansom. 'I was much amused by the shops and the people in the streets. I have not seen them for 2 years' (1 September 1876). And she also had music in her life again at last. Instead of her singing to her sick friends, her musical friends now came to sing and play to her:

Mrs Watts Hughes called . . . She is a Welshwoman, a pupil of Garcia's, a lovely singer [who] no longer sings in public, but . . . her whole heart is still in music . . . She is a very nice woman, as well as fine singer and she offered to sing to me . . . She sang to me Welsh songs, most lovely and pathetic and stirring . . . [They] stir up my Welsh blood. Tell Adelaide [Sartoris]. She was very kind to [her] and will be glad to hear of her. We talked music for 2 hours. . . . Dear dear! How I enjoyed her singing! (2 September 1876)

And she herself could play the piano again to Hastings' eldest, Willie Hughes' violin. 'I've no right to complain now I may play and sing!'

(10 September). Her voice had lost much of its power but was still hauntingly sweet and true.

Not only was Jeanie enjoying a rebirth of her musical self, her intense political self also came back to life. In May 1876 Imperial Ottoman Turkey had put down a Bulgarian uprising against Muslim rule, massacring 12,000 people. This and subsequent acts of repression were to be known to European history as 'the Bulgarian Atrocities'. The moment that Jeanie was back in the London world, she engaged fiercely with international affairs, sounding out Tom Hughes and Stansfeld on the crisis. On 16 September Jeanie wrote to Walter that she was delighted that 'the women are memorializing the Queen about Turkey – I'm going to send my name, and to get a lot of signatures too'. Two days later she wrote to him, 'I devour all about the Turkish affairs for I am really burning with anger against our Government for disgracing us in the eyes of all the world. . . . I have sent for the womans [sic] petition to the Queen to sign and get signatures'. Next day she sent off the petition for Walter himself to get signatures at a country house he was visiting, including signatures from the women servants there. Knowing his temptation to inaction, she had already stamped and addressed it for him to post.

Approaching ever nearer was the spectre of 'the poor Thorn', her mother-in-law, returning to live with them yet again. Jeanie could not bear the certain prospect of the old lady's chattering to all their visitors about Hastings' bankruptcy and Jeanie's consequent poverty that prevented her, old Mrs. Senior, 'from being able to keep her own carriage, etc. etc.'. Jeanie faced Nassau with an ultimatum: she could only tolerate living in London if she did not always have to ask his mother for money and "hear Gran S. say that she could not afford this and that because poor Jeanie etc.". Otherwise, she 'must ask him to go to the country – I don't care where – as I don't intend to be worried to death' (14 September 1876).

There were, however, two pieces of great good news to buoy her up. Her Nell, who had married from Elm House the previous December, was now pregnant – 'Oh! I shall love my first grandchild' (10 September) and her precious friend, Caroline Stephen,

> is coming to live at 48 Cheyne Walk! . . . – The first thing she said was, "it is so delightful to be dropped down between F.P. Cobbe and you!"; . . . It will make a great difference in my life to have her there, because whenever I am fretted with people or things . . . the sight of her brings me to my right mind; . . . With Carry at 48 I think I may be able to take patiently, and not to care about, poor old Gran's irritating allusions to "poor Jeanie's loss of fortune" and her consequent impoverishment. I know how you'll rejoice for me.
> (18 September 1876)

From the time that she moved into Cheyne Walk, Caroline Stephen set aside a room for weekly Quaker Meetings there.[24]

On 20 September Mrs. Hughes arrived from Colwell, looking exhausted. Unusually for her, she then suffered a complete physical collapse and for the next month Jeanie concentrated on nursing her mother. 'I neglected everything and every one but her', giving her mother her own bedroom while she slept in her sitting room. Only when her mother had turned the corner and was herself again did Jeanie resume letter-writing. On 22 October she confessed to Walter a set-to between herself and Fanny Hughes about her brother Tom. Conservative Fanny Hughes blamed Tom's commitment to Co-operation for all his stress, anxiety and depression and went on to criticize Tom for coming home so thoughtful and careworn that she had to hurry him off to his study 'to get his grave face out of the way'.

> I tried to suggest that all men in professions, politicians, lawyers, doctors, parsons, if they were conscientious and of feeling hearts were often grave and sad after the fight of the day and that Tom's seriousness was not because he was interested in Co-operation etc. . . . I said that ever since the time of our Lord those who worked for others had been men of sorrows – She said "they did no good either" – and I said we shall know that in the day when the secrets of all hearts are opened.
>
> No wonder he is depressed if she tells him that all his work, all his hopes and patience, [have] been of no use, and no good to any one!!

It was a sad end to the unbounded joy that she had felt at sixteen, on hearing of Tom's engagement to her dearest friend.

Jeanie was feeling so much stronger that she was now seriously looking forward to tackling public work again and Tom strengthened this animating hope by telling her that the philanthropist and Liberal MP, William Rathbone,[25] champion of one of her many causes, the National Association for providing Trained District Nurses for the poor, had been speaking enthusiastically about her work and mourning her retirement: 'If you feel quite well again a strong effort must be made to get you re-appointed when our side comes in and no one will work more heartily for that end than Wm. R. who has much influence with Liberals on all such questions.' She wrote to Sarah Forbes next day: 'I really believe that I shall get strong again in a year or so. If so, I shall try to get back to my old work, if the liberals are in then, not only for the love of it but also for the pay.'[26]

The tenth of December 1876 was Jeanie's forty-eighth birthday; the following weeks was so filled with visitors wanting to see her at 98 Cheyne Walk, that her doctor became alarmed at the risk of exhaustion and ordered her to go away for Christmas with Hastings, his four children and Walter, back to her mother at Colwell Bay. As Jeanie reported to Sarah Forbes: 'Mrs. Senior went to her daughter and Nassau remained at home alone which is his idea of perfect happiness.'[27]

Walter worried over his mother's apparent withdrawnness and depression that Christmas at Colwell Cottage hung with berries and evergreens. She tried to explain:

> I am always at Christmas time living more with ghosts than with those in the flesh. It does not make me unhappy at all. Indeed I can't be unhappy about the blessed dead; but living with them gives a certain inward quietness which outwardly looks like dullness or depression. (7 January 1877)

It was the most explicit allusion she ever made to the pull of her beloved dead.

She gave herself a shake and concentrated once more on the needs of the living. She had written a New Year letter to Stansfeld, telling him that she could 'wish him no blessing so great as what he must already have, in having given up all earthly ambition in order to work for a cause which he thinks he is called to work for, in the name of Truth and Justice' (4 January 1877). He responded to her ardour on his behalf by saying that the necessity to concentrate on the subjects of prostitution and syphilis, in the campaign to repeal the Contagious Diseases Acts, did not, in all honesty, feel like a blessing:

> I fear I have not quite the 'joy within' that you suppose, but that is my fault; certainly however I can say that I have not the least regret. But the subject as you know, and as I have said to you, is oppressive; it is a burden and a cross. It is not given to every one to 'bear with joy.' . . .
>
> I shall fancy you, if the weather gets fine and not so cold, out in that donkey chair – shall I be right; and I should not object to a walk by its side – should you? (1 January 1877)

Yet again Jeanie had to tell Walter that she would write him two kinds of letter – once a week to his chambers, she would 'write quite freely, without having to remember that all the family will see what I say, that is paralysing' and also, once a week to Cheyne Walk, 'a public one, in the same style as those to your father' (6 January 1877). Her latest problem was her incorrigible eighty year-old mother who had just volunteered to manage a coal and clothing club for the local poor. Jeanie was divided between crossness and awe:

I never did know such an old person with so fresh a soul. If anyone came to her in an enthusiasm about ascending Mont Blanc, and told her that some good to the world in general would accrue if she personally inspected some establishment on the top ridge, for inducing people to save money or give up alcohol or smoking, I verily believe that she'd have her box packed and start next day for Chamonix! (6 January 1877)

While the Isle of Wight rain poured down interminably, day after depressing day, Jeanie reflected on her cool relationship with her sister-in-law, Minnie. She had felt so bitter for so long about Minnie's hard worldliness and self-interest, culminating in a dispute over Walter's rightful inheritance of the autographed letters written by famous men to his grandfather, Nassau William Senior. Now Jeanie felt impelled to attempt a healing settlement by bringing the whole issue out into the open. She sent her draft letter to Minnie to be checked by Walter first:

I can't stand, any longer, that there should be the cloud of those letters between her and me. In the past I did so much for her and shielded her at my own cost [had it been for Minnie that Jeanie had lied to save her good name?] and I can't bear that we should be on our present terms. I pray and pray, and feel how wrong it is to despise her, and feel this bitterness. It would be wrong if felt towards anyone and towards my sister-in-law and such an old friend it is dreadful, and a constant pain to me and a hindrance in getting nearer to what God would have me to be . . . . for dislike is like devils.
   . . . I know that any way the old Adam i.e. my old Danish blood, will assert itself sometimes, however it is settled. I shall have occasional gusts of rage at the past; but when the thing is settled, I shall have strength to pray better; for then her fault will be cleared away; and if I am still wicked that will be my own sin, and I can wrestle with that and God will help me to conquer it in time, I know. (9 January 1877)

On 13 January Jeanie received the needed letter from Minnie, assuring her that her sister-in-law would do 'the right thing'.

I am so glad, for now I can really feel cordial towards her, and forget other matters in the past in which she has failed to show justice and affection . . . I feel quite lightened and very thankful. I wrote her just a line to say how very happy her letter had made me. (13 January 1877)

The boys were reading *Adam Bede* aloud every evening to their grandmother and Jeanie had started on Mrs. Kingsley's *Life* of Charles Kingsley. Kingsley had once been Tom's ally in the cause of Christian Socialism, but Jeanie had become fiercely critical of his later racist, reactionary politics: 'Kingsley took the wrong side in the American [Civil] war and in the Governor Eyre question, and made a very wrong and violent attack on Newman, and was fond of success and Royalty and nearly broke old Maurice's heart, by his alternate fits of neglect and repentant affection.' Her conclusion was that 'a wife should not write her husband's life. It *can't* be truthful. It can only show him at his very best. . . . [But] we don't get so much help out of the lives of the Saints as out of the lives of sinners who are yet ever striving to be saints' (13 January 1877).

As ever, she was full of projects, including projects for other people. Please would Walter visit his old, lonely great-uncle Tom Wilkinson and check on his welfare? Then there was her brother George's eldest son Herbert Hughes, the young squire at Offley Place, much teased by Jeanie for his hunting and his partridge and pheasant shooting – why could he not aim at artificial substitutes, instead of live prey? Suddenly there was a threat that Colwell Common might be enclosed and ploughed over and lost to the community for ever. That had to be lobbied against and the Commons Preservation Act invoked. And the official documents supporting her statements about the success of boarding-out in Glasgow must be sent off *right away* by Walter to the Poor Law Inspector Murray Browne. A new circulating library was to be set up on the Isle of Wight and she must contribute books. Then there was her dear Octavia Hill who had confided in her most touchingly, just before Jeanie had left London, that she was deeply in love with her fellow worker in the cause of social housing, the lawyer Edward Bond. Octavia needed to be encouraged not to renounce private fulfilment for the sake of her dedication to social reform.

Meanwhile the first volume of the *Life of Kingsley* was taking Jeanie back to the first years of her own marriage.

> If only I had set to work then, and given all my youth and energies as well as my sympathies, to that little band of men who were at work under Maurice's direction, how much I might have helped on the good cause!
> . . . But I was just married, and living with the old people [Nassau William Senior and Grandma Senior], and I saw delightful society for the first time, and I was learning to sing, and living in artist Bohemia a part of my time. I did not understand politics, and I did not care about them, . . . And I was such a coward too. I should not have dared to say where my sympathies lay – . . . I just said nothing. I was even ashamed of owning that, whenever I could, I crept off on Sunday afternoon to Lincolns Inn Chapel to hear the prophet preach, . . . I have Maurice to bless for the fact that mere

amusing myself in pleasant society and hearing music, did not
continue to satisfy me. But it took a long time. And the first distinct
rousing that I remember was the conversation of old Miss Carpenter
who did such splendid work at Bristol, among the girls. That made
me feel that I could not amuse myself all my life. . . .

But I look back . . . with deep humiliation and sorrow, that I put
off real working for my Master till all my best years were gone. It
is such a just punishment that now I fain would work, I cannot.
Thank God for giving us the knowledge that we shall all have a
second innings. (19 January 1877)

In her imagined, anthropocentric Heaven we shall not only love each
other's best selves more perfectly, but we shall also be able to work for others
better than we had done before. Ever since childhood she had been a Seeker
but her un-orthodox religious ideas had evolved further over recent years.
Prevented by her illness from attending church, she had been forced to medi-
tate alone throughout 1875 and 1876. Anglican church-going had, in fact,
long been something of a stumbling block to her. One trial was the clergy
and their hell-fire sermons. In contrast, she loved Maurice's preaching,
'telling us not to condemn anyone' (November 1865). Her Christianity
consisted simply in love of others and thereby trying 'to live as Christ would
have us do' (26 March 1866 and 6 May 1868). Under the pressure of the
mad killing competition of the Franco-Prussian War there came the first
reference to her 'rapidly turning Quaker' (13 November 1870). After the
traumatic loss of her eldest brother George in May 1872 she experienced a
real crisis of faith and a furious anger at *all* clerical interposition. Her
younger friend Henrietta Synnot had also lost a brother and had been much
worried – and criticized by others – over the absence of a clergyman at his
deathbed. Jeanie burst out in a letter to her:

It appears to me the most awful blasphemy to think that He who
sent His Son to reveal to the world that He is Father to every creature should not be able to take care of His children, without the
intervention of a mumbling priest! Just as far as a clergyman is a
priest– (I mean is supposed to be needed to help us to approach
God) – so far do I look on him as an invention of the Father of
Lies – I look on a priest as a help only when he comes as a man, to
minister and sympathise as a brother . . . I am often tempted to
belong to no church: and to publicly renounce my adhesion to
every outward form of worship. I can trust God (if I believe in Him
at all) with myself, soul, and body and sins, and weaknesses and I
can trust Him with the souls, bodies, sins and weaknesses of [those
I love]. (16 June 1872)

Jeanie felt so shocked by the popular conception of Church of England teaching on damnation that she felt she must now leave the Anglican Communion altogether, she told Octavia Hill. Octavia persuaded her to think of Maurice's broad church teaching and therefore stay.

In April 1873 there had followed several testimonies to how deeply attracted she felt by Octavia Hill's Quaker friends in Cumbria: 'There is something very attractive to me about the Friends, a curious calmness about the outward man and a peace that emanates from the inward man, that makes itself felt. It is intensely refreshing of mind and body . . . ' In writing to Henrietta Synnot the following March, Jeanie declared her opposition to *all* outward signs and ceremonies: 'But then I am peculiarly averse by conviction from all ritualism and am not at all clear that I shall not join the Quakers. They seem to be about the only people who recognize the direct influence of God on the heart, without any disturbing forms and ceremonies' (1 March 1874). In June 1874 she declared to Henrietta that she simply could not attend the Wandsworth Parish Church of St. Philip's any longer, for the Vicar, 'old Hall' did not join in the General Confession but 'came out very strong in absolving – with signings and blessings'.

In view of all those passages testifying to her increasing attraction to Quakerism, it does seem that, had Jeanie Senior lived, she would most probably have followed her close friend the Quaker convert Caroline Stephen – 'the finest woman I know both intellectually and morally . . . so clever, so just, and so clear-headed, I feel a little pygmy peeping out and catching crumbs of wisdom' (1 February and 1 March 1873). She would very possibly have been first an 'Attender' at Caroline Stephen's Friends' Meetings at her home in Cheyne Walk, and then, like her, a 'Quaker by convincement'. Caroline Stephen would become the inspiriting source of the revival of English Quakerism during the next twenty years and she would most surely have won Jeanie's eager assent to her declaration:

> The perennial justification of Quakerism lies in its energetic assertion that the kingdom of heaven is within us; that we are not made dependent upon any outward organisation for our spiritual welfare. . . . Quakerism is a religion which [requires] truth in word and deed, plain dealing and kindness and self-control, and which [does] not require ceremonial observances or priestly guarantees – a religion in which practice [goes] for more than theory . . .[28]

As regards more earthly matters, Jeanie was cherishing one last, invigorating fantasy. She would buy up some adjoining fields at Colwell and experiment with organic farming:

I should make a bargain with the surrounding cottagers that if they'd let me have their manure and slops, I'd send and remove them. If I gave moules [i.e. earth closets] to a dozen cottages and a zinc tub for slops, it would give the plan a fair chance. Every day I should send round a donkey and cart and barrel to bring away slops and manure and to put fresh earth in the closets, and I believe, and so does Dyer that the crops we should have would more than pay all expenses. At all events it would be very interesting to try, and if I live I <u>will</u> try it. (28 January 1877)

Her last days at Colwell were filled with listening to Corelli sonatas played by Watts and she herself sang to Tennyson. On one of her visits to the Tennysons, the Laureate had said to her: '"I hear you are a great singer" to which I said that I had been'. She also enjoyed the 'art talk' in Watts' studio. It has been suggested by the art historian David Stewart that Watts' painting of the 'Return of Godiva' as a female Pietà, begun and worked on during this period, could well have been inspired by Jeanie Senior, whose pale, spent face and body he was then seeing almost every day:

> Watts's *Godiva* is a painting that was begun in the hardest days of the women's rights moment, when women were most savagely attacked for breaking free of their separate sphere. It was a time when the cost to women of independent action was painfully noted and heroically borne by women whom Watts knew extremely well such as Jane Senior . . . . This painting is a monument to women's heroism . . . Watts had to insure that *Godiva* sacrificing her body for the good of her sisters, would not become *Godiva* giving up her body to the pleasure of men . . . She is nude, yes, but in place of sensuality he gives a trowelled, crusty and unappealing surface of a kind that disgusted his critics. She [like Jane Senior] subjects herself to the full force of British patriarchy, against the weight of the many men and many women who would attack her with the scandal and the ridicule of "That Woman".[29] Watts's painting is a monument to the women brave enough to withstand the pain and collapse he witnessed at close hand.[30]

Jeanie Senior, however, did not consider herself a martyr, exhausted by her ceaseless efforts for others, especially women. On the contrary, she was as eager as she had always been to laugh. How amused she was by revelations of the latest perturbation caused by Julia Cameron, who was now sending back impossible, and very expensive, directions for her Freshwater house on the Isle of Wight, from the considerable distance of Ceylon. 'I <u>never</u> knew such unpractical people as all the family [of Pattle sisters]' (2 February 1877).

36   Watts' *'The Return of Godiva'* begun in the late 1870s. Courtesy Watts Gallery, Compton, Surrey.

And there followed a long, priceless reminiscence from a Freshwater neighbour about Mrs. Cameron taking a letter to post in a commandeered coal cart that Jeanie *had* to share with Walter (4 February 1877).

Despite a few glorious sunny days when she could gather primrose roots and broadleaved ferns and plan with Dyer where to plant poplars and scotch firs to hedge the kitchen garden, the rain and the cold so persisted, imprisoning her indoors, that Jeanie finally asked Hastings and Walter to come to Colwell Bay to get her. On 19 February 1877 they took her back to London.

For one last time her friends flocked to see her. Stansfeld, who had written telling her how often he thought of his 'visit to her on the Island, and especially of the walks by the side of your donkey carriage' (31 January 1877), was now impatient to hear how she really was. He himself was glad to report that he had just managed to win the campaign for the medical education of women that would enable them to train as doctors. 'I <u>think</u> I shall get the Royal Free Hospital for them – and then all will be won and the way smooth.'[31] Jeanie had let him in on the secret of Octavia Hill's unhappy love for Mr. Bond,[32] even lending him her friend's letter, to which he responded:

> I don't know whether I rightly guess at the meaning of her letter; it reads as if she had doubted what she ought to do – whether she ought not, perhaps, to refuse everything for the sake of her work – and that you had rightly advised her to the contrary. But I shall come and get a talk with you and have things made clearer to me than they are now.
>
> What a friend you are! . . .
>
> I don't like "Janey" [as Octavia Hill spelt Jeanie's name]; I like "Jeannie".

Determined to take up her active life again to the full, having now served much more than the prescribed two years' bed rest, Jeanie Senior then courted catastrophe. In Minnie Simpson's words, 'she over-estimated her strength; she did too much; and one evening, on her return from a visit to an old and invalid uncle, [Tom Wilkinson] to whom she had been singing, she was struck down by her old enemy'.[33] The violent internal haemorrhaging had returned; could it be stopped before she bled to death?

Margaret Hughes was summoned from the Isle of Wight to 98 Cheyne Walk to nurse her daughter. And on 12 March Stansfeld wrote:

> My very dear friend, I just called to enquire after you yesterday and soon after I saw, I suppose, the doctor's carriage at your door.
>
> I am so unhappy about you. I cannot bear to think of you suffering. I cannot doubt that it has been brought on by your grief and anger about your poor friend.
>
> How I wish I were not utterly impotent to save you from this pain, or to help you in any way.
>
> I will wait – I must do so – till I may come, till at least my coming can do you no harm.
>
> And when I do come I will bring so much sympathy and affection to you, that if they can do you any the least mental good, you will have them in heaped up and accumulated measure.

Octavia Hill was then visiting her Quaker friends in the Lake District; she sat 'quite stunned' as she listened for the telegram she dreaded. Meanwhile

Anny Thackeray wrote to Walter that she had just seen both Minnie Simpson and Caroline Stephen to try to get the latest news:

> I did not like to ring your bell . . . – I went to the poor old
> Signor [Watts] sitting miserably by his fire. I can't think of your
> anxiety . . . tho' I do do know how the greatest love makes
> separation less and the only real parting is forgetfulness. I can't
> help writing. Please, please write again, if you can.

CHAPTER SEVENTEEN

Afterwards

The death certificate read: 'Cancer of the womb of many years' standing and exhaustion'. Probate estimated her Estate at 'under £20'. Walter's letters to her friends were thankful for her release from pain.

George Eliot wrote back to him: 'The precious inkstand [her keepsake present] is by me at this moment and will be my constant companion till I too die – bringing to me often the inward presence of your beloved mother.' Jenny Lind asked once more 'to see her face before the earth covers her beautiful features'. Stansfeld made a last visit to her: 'I have seen and bid farewell to your beloved mother' and asked if he might be allowed to attend her funeral. Poor Nell, soon to bear her first child without Jeanie to support her, cried: 'I have never felt about anything as I feel about this; . . . Walter I feel so awful. I cannot get over this one bit.'

Margaret Mitchell – she who had been so delighted to tell Jeanie: 'Dorothea is you!' – wrote:

> . . . She was our dearest friend – it is hard to say whether Arthur or I loved her best. My dear dear Jeannie! [sic] She was the loveliest sweetest most noble woman I ever saw and I shall never forget her . . . How you will miss her love and sympathy. She loved you so utterly. . . . [You] were son and daughter both . . . I am so sorry for Harry and Gerard to whom she was the tenderest of Mothers . . . I loved and reverenced your Mother with my whole soul, and my heart is in bitterness for her. . . .

The far-reaching impact of Jeanie Senior's personality reminds one of the ending of *Middlemarch* – 'the effect of her being on those around her was incalculably diffusive'. It was expressed most eloquently of all in Leslie Stephen's condolence letter to Walter:

> Ever since I have known her, I have felt that merely to know such a woman was a great privilege. I have felt myself a better man, more cheerful and hopeful, whenever I have thought of her. She has taught me how strangely the influence of a noble character can affect people beyond its immediate circle. . . . She would never have believed, even if I could have told her, how much good she did, simply by being so good.

37 Jeanie Senior's tombstone reads:
In Memory of Jane Elizabeth, Wife of Nassau John Senior,
And daughter of the late John Hughes, of Donnington Priory, Newbury.
Died on the 24th of March 1877, Aged 48 years.

(Grave no. 72930, diagonally across from the Columbarium, Brookwood Cemetery, Woking).
Photo courtesy of Meg Hobbs, Brookwood Cemetery Society. J.E.S.'s great-grand-daughters have
restored the headstone.

His sister-in-law, Anny Thackeray, wrote also, of course, insisting on still
using the present tense: 'I can only tell you that I love your mother truly with
a grateful heart.'[1] And Octavia Hill wrote to her colleague in housing
reform, Sydney Cockerell:

> She was, among my many friends, one of the noblest [and] purest-
> hearted, . . . with an ardent longing to serve, a burning generosity,
> which put us all to shame. Moreover she loved me, as few do; and
> I her; and, when I think that I can go to her no more, I dare not
> think of what the loss will be. [The] thought that I can never again
> in human words receive any message from her shakes me with
> passionate sobbing'.[2]

Octavia Hill suffered a breakdown for some months following Jeanie's
death.

Many of the grief stricken reproached themselves for their selfishness in focusing on their own personal loss, now that Jeanie Senior was lost to so many even more needy than they. Watts said this in his letter to May Prinsep, 26 March 1877:

> Alas, Alas, I have no words to express how I grieve . . . [But] my personal regrets and loss are nothing beside a loss that is really national, and will affect thousands, perhaps thousands yet unborn [for] if she had lived, her life would have been devoted to the benefit of those who cannot often find such a friend.[3]

Public notices of Jeanie's death included anonymous verses in *The Spectator* and in *Punch*, the latter most probably written by Tom Taylor. There was also an obituary in *The Kensington News*, and one in *The Spectator* written by Caroline Stephen who testified to Jeanie's 'absolutely single minded', motherly devotion to the welfare of others. She emphasized Jeanie Senior's 'gifts . . . of broad, simple, human sympathy and remarkable uprightness and tenacity of mind' and ended: 'It will indeed be a misfortune for the public service if Mr. Stansfeld's example in appointing a woman to this most maternal office is not followed by his successors' (7 April 1877). Most notably of all, *The Times* saluted Jeanie Senior. It was rare indeed for *The Times* to devote a long death notice to a woman during the 19th century, but Tom Taylor persuaded them to publish his appreciation of the historical importance of the public work of 'The Late Mrs. Nassau Senior'.[4]

Despite all those deeply felt tributes, it cannot be denied that Jeanie Senior's life had been, as she knew, in part a failure. She had succeeded in effecting neither the radical, humane reform of pauper girls' education in the huge 'Barrack' Schools nor in establishing, nationwide, the fostering of destitute, abandoned orphans. Moreover she had failed to establish a successful precedent for the employment of women in those areas of the Civil Service with special responsibility for the female half of the poor, let alone the female half of the population.

Jacqueline Hughes has summed up how all Jeanie Senior's recommendations were subsequently rejected by her male colleagues. 'They condemned Mrs. Senior's findings and defended the status quo in succeeding Local Government Board Reports'.[5] The huge 'Barrack Schools' were not all broken down into small cottage 'family units', as she had advocated, for many decades to come, despite at least three sensational disasters – cruelty to pauper infants, a fire that killed 22 children in a 'Barrack' dormitory, and food poisoning that attacked 141 children in one District School.[6] But still the 'Monster School' system was not abolished. In 1896 The State Children's Association was founded to try 'to obtain individual treatment for children under the Guardianship of the State'. But twenty years after Jeanie Senior's death, history repeated itself when Henrietta Barnett's *Report* of 1897 on all state-supported children, which attacked the very same abuses that Jeanie had attacked, 'let loose avalanches of angry remonstrance . . . I was accused of falsehood, exaggerations, [and disloyalty]'.[7] Children would not be taken out of Workhouses until 1915.

Boarding-out fared no better. The annual *Local Government Board Reports* 1874–1876 ignored all Jeanie Senior's arguments and evidence, and attacked fostering – mostly through unsupported assertion.[8] And the male Inspectors were against recruitment of professional women in social work and the Civil Service

> almost to a man . . . Poor Law was not . . . the area for women to work in . . . [Women] were too sensitive and easily imposed on, . . . It would also interfere with their domestic duties.' . . . [Jeanie Senior] had antagonized them utterly and their reports for the following years showed them . . . united in opposition to almost all her ideas.[9]

Had Jeanie Senior antagonized the Inspectorate, because, in Joanna Hill's words, she had 'refused to kow-tow'? Or would no amount of kow-towing have persuaded them that their institutions needed drastic reform? Was it her fault that she had no immediate woman successor, or was it the fault of the male 'closed shop' of the Civil Service? However one weighs the answers, the *de facto* failure remains. Two years after Jeanie Senior's death, Florence Nightingale gave her judgment:

> Her premature death was a national and irreparable loss. If she could but have held on a few years longer, she would have had successors and the Poor Law Board would as soon have been without Lady Inspectors for girls' Institutions as we should have had Male Matrons. Now that is all over.[10]

Or, as Stansfeld reminisced years later 'unfortunately she broke down and died'.[11]

But that is to place the whole responsibility of Jeanie Senior's failures upon *her* physical collapse. Her appointment, however, had resulted from the meeting of three trajectories – Octavia Hill, Jeanie Senior and James Stansfeld. Had it not been for Octavia Hill's prior commitment to housing reform, *she* would have been the first woman civil servant – but her health also might have collapsed under the strain. It was Stansfeld's determined feminist commitment, not to mention the emancipatory historical moment of the early 1870s, when British women were insisting on entering University education and some at least of the professions, that led him, failing Octavia Hill, immediately to appoint her friend, Mrs. Nassau Senior, in January 1873. Had not Stansfeld then lost his place in Government when the Tories defeated the Liberals in the General Election of February 1874, Jeanie's collapse the following October would have been followed by Stansfeld's immediate replacement of her by another woman appointee, as Jeanie herself had requested, and by the implementation of the reforms that she had advocated, both in her *Report* and in her resignation Memorandum. Was it then her collapse that killed Stansfeld's hitherto very successful experiment in appointing her, or was it the adverse Tory political climate that doomed the experiment? And how far was it the stress of that demanding appointment, accompanied as it was by huge feminist expectations – and by even greater masculinist hostility – that helped to kill her?

The question is thus not simply: Should Jeanie Senior have accepted this pioneering appointment, knowing she was seriously ill? I have tried to show that she had no choice, being the person she was, but to do as she did. The question is rather the hypothetical one of whether a different, physically stronger, woman might not have had more effective medium term success, simply by staying in her Whitehall office long enough to outlive the Tory administration? And that we shall never know. But we can be sure that no other woman would have thrown herself into her year's work of Inspection like one possessed, as she did, and then written and defended 'Mrs. Senior's *Report*', which was uniquely hers.

However one judges Jeanie Senior's degree of responsibility for the areas of failure in her public work, it is undeniable that she also had some very significant areas of success. Far from being, like George Eliot's Dorothea, a 'foundress of nothing', Jeanie Senior was the foundress of more than one considerable something. She was a pioneer of efficient social housing finance. She was a pioneer of women's social work in its earliest stage of voluntary rent-collecting in grim, overcrowded London 'courts'. She was the co-foundress of the British Red Cross as it upheld the Geneva Convention in a huge relief effort for the sick and wounded of both combatant nations during the Franco-Prussian War. Her 1874 *Report* was not only a significant piece of empirical sociology, but also a landmark in educational reform. So many of her sentences still ring out today as a *credo* we repudiate at our peril: '[The] amount of positive scholastic knowledge which [children] acquire, is not so important as the amount of intelligence which can be developed', . . . 'Playing with energy would be a step towards working with energy', . . . 'I am sure that joy is an immense educational power. A hearty laugh is a great help to growth and health'. And 'All children ought by some means to be made bright, self dependent, and capable of innocent enjoyment'. Such child-centred affirmations won over much contemporary public opinion – they reached and had influence in New York and Canada and even as far away as Western Australia. In Britain, as Jacqueline Hughes has noted, it took a little longer. Even Jeanie Senior's apparently lost cause, 'boarding-out', or Fostering and Adoption, *did* triumph in the long term although that too meant waiting for the first half of the 20th century and beyond.[12] Already at the end of the 19th century, no less a child-rescuer than Dr. Barnardo himself acknowledged Jeanie Senior's vital, initial role: 'Boarding-out is an idea only of the last twenty years or so, and really owes its intro-duction in England to the indefatigable labours of the late Mrs. Nassau Senior.'[13] She herself, of course, had been the devoted adopter of Hastings' four children, not to mention Nell, so she knew it could work.

Finally, in this summary of her effective, practical achievements, there was Jeanie Senior's most immediate social legacy – the successful establishment throughout London of the new voluntary organization MABYS – The Metropolitan Association for Befriending Young Servants – based on Bristol ladies' pioneering 'Preventive Mission'. From the membership lists of its subscribers, local committees and General Council, one learns that the 'lady volunteers' included Jews, Roman Catholics, Unitarians and free thinkers, who did manage to work productively together with Anglicans, despite all Mrs.Townsend's forebodings, for decades after Jeanie Senior's death. Jeanie Senior's plan of action for the Association, originally spelt out in the Memorandum appended to her letter of resignation from the Local Government Board, 3 November 1874, was cited by the MABYS President, Rev. Brooke Lambert, in his annual reports[14] and included the provision of girls' Sunday leisure centres, safe lodgings when unemployed, a right to help in sickness, employment registries, penny savings banks, and even clothes for these poorest of working girls. Her old friend Anny Thackeray lent her support by giving copies of her lively essay on the work of the MABYS, 'Upstairs and Downstairs' (1886), to be sold in its aid –

> '[A] boy puts his head in at the door. "Got any work for me?" says he.
>
> "No, no," cry all the girls together. "This isn't for boys; this is for females," and the head disappears'.[15]

Just ten years after Jeanie's death, Free Registry Offices for the girls had been set up in Bethnal Green, Camberwell, Chelsea, City and Shoreditch, Fulham and Hammersmith, Greenwich and Deptford, Hackney, Holborn, Islington, Kensington and Notting Hill, Kilburn and Hampstead, Lambeth, Marylebone, St. Pancras, Poplar, Richmond, St. Saviour's, Southwark, Stepney, Strand, Wandsworth and Clapham, Westminster, West Norwood, Whitechapel and Woolwich. It is quite a roll-call. There were also four training Schools to give the girls a recognized qualification, and thirteen 'safe' lodging houses or Homes.

An anonymous article "Toilers in London; or Inquiries concerning Female labour in the Metropolis', in *The British Weekly*, 1889, included two chapters on 'Slaveys' where the MABYS was singled out for praise:

> By a 'slavey' we mean a child-servant, a Maria, Jane or Susan, who drudges from morning till night in some house where only one servant is kept . . . How many slaveys there are in London at present it is impossible to say; but the MABYS has under its care at least 8,000. . . .This Association is worked upon such excellent principles that scarcely any other agency would be needed for slaveys if only it were in communication with Board Schools as well as with the pauper schools of the metropolis. . . .We have spoken at length about the MABYS because it is the Slaveys' Association par excellence.[16]

By 1893 Edith Sellers could report that the Association now had thirty-two free registries, seven training homes, a convalescent home and thirteen servants' lodging houses.[17]

Perhaps the most astonishing tribute of all to the organization would come from the African-American leader W. E. B. Dubois, in his chapter 'Ideals of Betterment' [for coloured girls] in *The Philadelphia Negro* (New York, 1899):

> The [London] MABYS . . . has organized an employment bureau where . . . young servant girls may be engaged, and at this office the protection of the girl is insured by obliging the mistress to sign a form of agreement stating the number in her family, work required, wages paid, privileges granted, etc. The detailed workings of this bureau and its friendly connection with the girls after their places are secured are set forth fully in [Charles Booth's *Life and Labour of the People*, vol. 8, pp. 215].

Dubois strongly advocated the establishment of a MABYS for the coloured working class girls of Philadelphia. Remembering Jeanie's lifelong anti-racism, she would have been cheered by this particular testimony and outreach from across the Atlantic.

The twenty-five years following her death were the most dispiriting and frustrating period in the history of the British Woman's Movement. Every proposed measure to achieve woman's suffrage continued to be defeated in Parliament, while the press practised a news black-out on the issue. During those bleak years 'Mrs. Nassau Senior' was cited by the struggling feminists time and again as a great pioneer. Her photograph was sent to the Chicago Exhibition of 1893, as part of the collection of eminent British women because, to the feminists coming after her, she was *the* outstanding example of the positive effect of the employment of women in a position of responsibility. She had realized Sara Josepha Hale's vision of women as 'the great civilizers in so far as they help humanity to become more humane'.

Conclusion

Jeanie Senior's story is more than a balance sheet of success and failure in public life. 'People are not followed and loved as [she] was followed and loved because of what they have done, but because of what they are.'[1] What Jeanie *was*, as with every human being, was the unique result of the continuous interaction between the inborn potential she brought with her into the world and the impact upon her of the experiences she underwent. In her case the result was extraordinary.

She had been born gifted with intense emotional vitality and exceptional intelligence as well as with musical talent and a wonderful singing voice; she was also physically strong and lovely to look at. In addition to that head start, she was the cherished only daughter and only sister in a well-to-do, affectionate, large, lively family in the beautiful Berkshire countryside. Most significant of all, however, in my view, was the positive mitochondrial inheritance in her personality, the genetic endowment from her dearly loved mother Margaret Hughes, née Wilkinson and from that mother's beloved mother, Jane Wilkinson, née Hutton, after whom Jeanie had been named. She had their tireless capacity for radiating energetic fellow-feeling. And it was that power of profound sympathy which made so many others love and follow her.

Life then inflicted one appalling personal blow after another on her. She kept her sanity, however, sustained first by the imperative need of others, especially her mother and her son, that she should not break down, and secondly by her need to believe in a Blakeian vision of Heaven. Since there clearly is no justice on earth – for the poor, the sick, the bereaved – the infinitely loving Father of Jeanie's imagination granted compensation for human suffering in an afterlife. 'If there is not another and a better life, God is not just and good. . . . [If] there is no immortality, there is no God. As man conceives his heaven, so he conceives his God.'[2] The heaven that Jeanie Senior conceived – though at times the depth of her grief for her dead made her doubt whether she did really believe – was rapturous eternal reunion with her irreplaceable ones – who would then know and love each other still better than before.[3]

The Times' obituary asserted that Jeanie Senior's 'gift of song . . . employed in public, would have placed her in the foremost rank of vocalists'. She was a truly great singer but, because of the restrictive proprieties of her time, she had to forfeit any chance of an audience commensurate with her musicianship. Jeanie Senior could have sung the great alto solos in Bach's *St. Matthew Passion* and *B Minor Mass* at the Crystal Palace, not to mention the alto solos in Handel's *Messiah* or *Julius Caesar* at the great Handel Festivals, or Gluck's *Orpheo* or Leonora in Beethoven's *Fidelio* at Covent Garden. Instead, she was confined to performing short pieces in private, wealthy drawing-rooms or else, which she liked more, to small, music-starved groups of some of the poorest people in London. What must it have been like to have had so few opportunities and, above all, so little time, for that great body of music within her to be 'given voice'?

Jeanie Senior did break through some of the gender and caste barriers of her day. She finally joined the ranks of the much-caricatured 'Strong-minded Women' after she made her many significant interventions in the public world, winning widespread admiration and gratitude. But she had also to endure intimidation and harassment from male officialdom and even slanderous vilification in the national press. The worst pillorying had been in *The Times* where she was sneered at as a lady scandal-monger, and in Tuffnell's *Observations* which accused her of downright lying. Such a public ordeal required all the grit and strength of nerve she could summon in order to keep her bedridden head held high as she answered her detractors. She had needed every ounce of her Wilkinson Viking blood as she struggled to be 'a Brown', championing the underdogs in her 'Poor Law female infantry'.

Was Jeanie Senior a heroine? The publication of the *Oxford Dictionary of National Biography* in 2004 has provoked much debate about what we mean by 'heroes'. The consensus has been that for us heroism 'incorporates not only courage but . . . innovation, dignity, stoicism, . . . and selflessness'.[4] The editor of *Time* (early October 2004) gives a similar list of requirements: 'an utter dedication of self, determination and a persistence in the face of whatever odds . . . [Somebody] who demonstrates talent, persistence, drive and bravery far beyond that of the average person.'[5] Jeanie Senior would qualify on every one of those criteria. She was not an 'Angel', in or out of the House, but she *was* a heroine.

Why then has her life of heroic kindness been forgotten? She died before she could become one of the acknowledged active leaders of the Women's Movement. It would be over a hundred years before the essential biographical materials were made available. And 'History' has not cared what happened to girls at the very bottom of Britain's social heap. Hence, with very few exceptions, 20th century historians have overlooked 'The Friend of the Workhouse Girl' who did care. She had to be content, in Octavia Hill's prescient words of September 1874, to be one of 'the out-of-sight piers driven deep into the marsh'. But if there was a gendered aspect to her absence from 'History', there was also a gendered, or rather a gender-transgressing, aspect to her heroism in her defiance of the assumptions that then confined 'gentlewomen' to the private world of the home. And, in Julia

Kristeva's view, a woman is a 'genius to the extent that [she is] able to challenge the socio-historical conditions of [her] identity'.[6]

Not, however, that the socio-historical conditions in Jeanie Senior's
private world were any sinecure. Far from being a place of rest and recuperation after her day's efforts at Workhouse visiting, rent-collecting, giving
singing-lessons, administering Red Cross relief, or 'going on a Girl-hunt' as
a Government Inspector, her life at Elm House was almost continuously
fraught with tension; her 'home work' was, if anything, even harder than her
work outside the home. For at Elm House too she was an 'Army of One'.
Onlookers used to marvel at how she always seemed able to keep the peace,
giving everyone of the eleven or twelve people there, not counting the
servants whom she also mothered, individual attention and his or her own
space.[7] But she herself was forced to recognize her limitations and failures.
Her 'Come to us!' approach had finally over-reached itself when she invited
her sick old mother-in-law into Elm House. She was quite unable to prevent
outbreaks of war between the two resident grandmothers or between either
one of them and her husband. She found herself constantly worn and torn
between her duty to keep her husband as contented as possible, as well as the
querulous old ladies happy, and her duty of care to her son and to her
widowed brother with his four motherless 'bairns' whom she had adopted.
It was not Jeanie but her own mother, Margaret Hughes, who finally rescued
the impossible situation by moving herself and Emmy and Hastings' boys
away to Colwell – where her dying, bedridden daughter might also find
refuge.

As for Nassau, 'your poor old Father', 'your discontented old Dad' – he
lived off Jeanie's strength, depending upon her utterly. She pitied his dependence – when not driven distracted by his demands. Nassau's is indeed a sad
story. First the spoilt and then the disinherited son of an overbearing father,
all he had ever wanted was a life of quiet, gentlemanly comfort, preferably
in a mild climate, unbothered by any question of working to earn a living.
Many other fellows managed that and no one questioned *them*. Instead, he
found himself married to a critic on the hearth who constantly challenged
him to do something to help his fellow-creatures. And that critic had brothers, not to mention countless bores of reformer friends, with all of whom he
felt he was being unfavourably compared. Who knows what bitter jealousy
Nassau suffered alone in his 'study'? It was enough to irritate a saint. Who
could be surprised, or even dare to criticize, when a man in such a situation
fled the lot of them to smoke in peace? It was not his fault if eighteen year-
old Jeanie Hughes had imagined him to be what he was not.

But the impact of Nassau's Nassau-ness upon his wife had also been
pitiable. Denied both passion and companionship by her precipitate misalliance, Jeanie Senior had had to endure the tyranny exercised by the weak for
thirty years. Not only did she have to be wife and mother to this problem

child, she had also to take on the role of husband. Instead of his protecting her, she had to shield him as much as possible from the world's disdain, while keeping him in that state to which he had always been accustomed – even earning the money herself to do so. Her life with him was one long repeated disappointment until at last she had to give up hope. And when she was in the final stage of her terminal illness, it was not her husband, but her brother and her son, who would lift and carry her into and out of trains.

It is one of the ironies of her story that Jeanie was known, both in her own time and afterwards, as 'Mrs. Nassau Senior'. Hence she was often mistakenly associated with the famous Nassau *William* Senior, the architect of the implacable 1834 Poor Law and deterrent workhouse system, whereas in fact, of course, she became one its most effective critics. However, her radical social intervention was in part the very consequence of her less than fulfilling marriage to that other Nassau Senior, Nassau *John*. Had her husband been the emotional centre of her life, she would not have needed to look outside her marriage for meaning. Had he been what she had first dreamed he would be, a radical reforming barrister like her brother Thomas Hughes, how eagerly would she have dedicated all her ardent energy to supporting his life-work. But because her husband turned out to have no life-work, it was she who went out to fight dragons – ironically, under his name.[8] Fortunately for her and for the world, Nassau's very inertia – 'your father's one idea is to save himself a little present trouble' – prevented him from rousing himself to oppose her energetic ventures, whether she was co-founding the British Red Cross or entering the corridors of Whitehall.

Given the inner void of her marriage, Jeanie Senior's emotional lifelines were her deep friendships, especially with women, and her relation to her son. Her letters are unquenchably vital – exuberant, depressed, anxious, affirming, self-mocking, self-questioning, indignant, tender, reproachful, compassionate and funny by turn. Wonderfully open in their simplicity and directness, they are the fitting correlative of her eager life spirit. It is unusual for a 19th century public figure – or indeed any public figure – to leave such an unmasked record of his or her inner life behind them. It is even more unusual for an unhappily married woman, lonely at her core, to have such a need to write confidential letters to her son that finally she did so in secret, writing a 'public' letter home as a cover and then sending a simultaneous private letter to him at his work. Judge her who feels fit to judge.

Did Walter Senior survive all that love from his mother? He grew up perfectly 'normal', married, had children and rubbed along very kindly and comfortably in the world without ever setting it on fire.[9] But it is not only some fundamental theories of 'Freudianism' that are challenged by the life of Jeanie Senior; moral relativism and reductionism are also put in question. The very possibility of human goodness defined as unselfish kindness, in other words, 'altruism', is doubted today – altruism being considered merely the form that some people's egoism takes.[10] It is unfortunate that that particular form of egoism should be quite so rare. Whenever Jeanie Senior was faced by alternative ideas or life-paths, she would always adopt what seemed to her to be the kinder one, impelled less by her own (strongly felt) wants than by her keen awareness of others' needs.

For all that she was known as 'Mrs. Nassau Senior', within herself she always remained Jeanie Hughes, her 'naïve core' alive and well. She was the same passionate person at forty, when she 'would have given [her] ears' not to have had to go to dinner at Minnie Simpson's, that she had been at sixteen when she 'would have given [her] ears' not to be going away from Donnington to Europe. In politics, her 'blood boiled' time after time, from when she first learned about penal exile to Siberia under the Tsar, until her rage at Governor Eyre, or Bismarck, or the massacre of the Communards and finally the Bulgarian Atrocities. Her refusal to believe in a Christianity that included the doctrine of Hell stayed with her from childhood until death. Her unbounded joy over the beauty of sky and countryside, sunshine and sea, also stayed with her, never failing to revive her, as did her rapture in music.

For it would be wrong to stress all the bereavements, failures, frustration, emotional and physical pain that she endured and not do justice to her resilience, her quite exceptional capacity for enjoying life. Just weeks before her death, her last letters to Walter ring with laughter over irrepressible Julia Margaret Cameron; they recount her singing to cheer up a depressed-as-usual Tennyson and they share her last fantasy – her plan to collect her neighbours' night-soil to help prove that organic farming works. An 'enthusiast by nature', all her life she was an eager fantasist and a great hero-worshipper – whether of lifeboat men or the Captain of the London Fire Brigade, or the gynaecologist James Simpson, or Garibaldi, 'that noble old fellow', or Mario the great tenor or F. D. Maurice 'the beloved Prophet', or the violinist Joachim, the very God of her idolatry, or Rossel, the Communard martyr, or, or, or, . . . Watts, Mérimée and Tennyson, however, she did not hero-worship, for she knew their all-too-human flaws. And James Stansfeld did not allow her to worship him, for they needed equality and emotional intimacy instead.

Walter Senior was well aware that his mother had been an extraordinary human being and after her death he kept all her letters and filed every piece of correspondence relating to her public work. He destroyed nothing, choosing to preserve her every word.

He must have hoped that one day those words would bring her back to life again.

Appendix I

What happened to the others in the story?

1. *Nassau John Senior*: In 1883 Nassau's mother, old Mrs. Senior, died at 98 Cheyne Walk, aged 93. Her estate was valued at £3,019 4s 10d which she left to Nassau. Nassau settled in St. Helier, Jersey, where he died 29 August 1891, aged 69, leaving £1,231 17s 9d to Walter. His death certificate read 'No profession'. His sister, Minnie Simpson, lived to 1909, having written her vivid memories of Jeanie in 1898.

2. *Walter Senior*: Walter set up a living memorial to his mother in the form of an 'Association for Placing Orphans in Private Families'. It was supported by Stansfeld (as President), Marianne Thornton, Octavia Hill, George Eliot, the Tennysons and Florence Nightingale, inter alia. It only ceased with his death. When his uncle Tom Wilkinson died in February 1878, leaving £35,000, Walter inherited £6,000. In 1888 he married Mabel Barbara Hammersley, daughter of Jeanie's friend Dulcibella Hammersley, née Eden, and niece of her old friend Frederick Eden. Walter's occupation on the marriage certificate was 'Gentleman'. Walter had contracted TB, so it was not until 1896 that they had a baby daughter, whom they called Jennie. She died aged two weeks and five days and was buried next to Jeanie in Brookwood Cemetery, Woking. In 1901 his son Oliver Nassau was born. Walter lived to see his two granddaughters, the elder of whom, Pamela Milne, remembers him as the most *gentle* man she has ever known. The birth of his second granddaughter, Anne Collier, was greeted rapturously by Mary Hughes (see below) as "Another little Jeanie! . . . May she be as full of great impelling devotion as her kind grandfather's mother". Jeanie Senior has twenty-one living descendants, including three great-great-great grandsons and ten great-great-great granddaughters. Walter died in 1933, aged 83.

3. *Margaret Hughes*: In May 1878, a year after Jeanie's death, her mother sold Colwell Cottage and moved with Emmy to 21 Park Walk, Chelsea. Three years later, in May 1881, aged nearly 85, she emigrated to the wilderness settlement of Rugby, Tennessee, in order to support her son Thomas Hughes' fledgling utopian community there and to permit

Emmy to be closer to her beloved father Hastings, now re-establishing his sherry-import business in New York. Her first home was just a hut but soon it was transformed into 'Uffington House', named after her first married home in the Vale of the White Horse. After many vicissitudes, including travel by Atlantic steamer, railroad and wagon trail, outbreaks of typhoid fever in the settlement, fires, crop failures, and colossal money losses for Tom through the ill-fated agricultural community, Margaret Hughes died in Rugby in 1887, aged 90. Positive and practical to the end, Margaret Hughes was nevertheless haunted by her five dead adult children. 'My life has been one of such sore trial in losing those whom I best loved, that I could not have borne my misery, but that I tried to forget myself in thinking of their supreme happiness' (Margaret Hughes to Walter, 18 June 1883). The Rugby settlement was never deserted and has now, a registered charity, been transformed by devoted staff and volunteers, into a working memorial and tribute to the ideals of Thomas Hughes and his family, including Jeanie Senior.

See http://www.historicrugby.org/

And email: rugbytn@highland.net

4. *Jesse Dyer*: The indispensable, immensely capable gardener and handyman Dyer had promised Jeanie before she died that he would never abandon her old mother. 'I gave my word to Mrs. Senior that I would never leave her.' Therefore, aged 47, together with his wife Bessie and their two children, he too crossed the Atlantic with Margaret Hughes and stayed working for her in Tennessee until her death six years later. He saw his son prosper in the United States in ways that would have been impossible in Victorian Britain. Arthur Dyer inherited his father's exceptional practical, problem-solving intelligence and, after working in Pittsburgh, went to the Edison Works, later General Electric N.Y., where he, together with another ex Rugby settler Charles Jefferson, patented a process known as Micanite and managed the Mica Insulator Corporation. His father lived to 84, dying in 1916 in New York where his mother Bessie also died, aged 81, in 1919.

5. *Thomas Hughes*: Tom continued to battle for his and Jeanie's idealistic vision of Co-operation and social justice. He visited his mother and the colony of Rugby each year 1883–1887, but finally in 1891 had to face the collapse of the settlement and of his investment in it. None of his sons or nephews had joined the colony in Tennessee, preferring the farming opportunities in Texas. In 1882 he was made a County Court judge and settled in Chester, dying, aged 71, in 1896. Of his nine surviving children none had a family but the youngest, George ('Plump'), who had settled in America. And it was only his daughters, Lilian Carter

(1868–1912) and Mary ('May') Hughes (1860–1941) who would live out his altruistic social ethic. Lilian worked with her clergyman husband in his parish of Whitechapel; they were drowned together on the *Titanic*. 'Comrade' Mary Hughes spent all her energy as a rescuer and champion of East London's destitute, unemployed and homeless, becoming a Labour Councillor for Stepney and a Quaker. (Gandhi asked to see her when he visited London in 1931.) (See *Oxford DNB* for both Thomas and Mary Hughes.) The Tom Brown's Schooldays Museum at Uffington, Berks., UK, is another memorial to the practical social idealism of Thomas Hughes and his family, including Jeanie Senior.
      See http://www.tombrown.btinternet.co.uk/museum/

6. *John Hughes*: Jeanie's music-loving but unmusical clerical brother lived all his life in Longcot, Berkshire, where he was vicar from 1852 until his death in 1895. After his wife died in 1882 he was looked after by his niece, Mary Hughes, to whom he left the major part of his estate.

7. *Hastings Hughes*: Two years after Jeanie's death, Hastings moved to New York to try to re-establish himself financially in the sherry business. The year 1881 found him in Rugby, Tennessee, administering the infant colony on behalf of his brother Tom but without Tom's sanguine belief in its prospects. In February 1887 he married Jeanie's former protégée Sarah Forbes, twenty years younger than himself. She was a Quaker by convincement, the daughter of Jeanie's old friend, the rail magnate and leading Abolitionist John Murray Forbes, whereby, as Leslie Stephen commented in 1890, Hastings became 'a well-off man – a result which he could never have achieved for himself!' Hastings died in 1907, aged 73, having out-lived his three eldest children.

      Hastings' four children by Emily Clark:
Willie Hughes (1859–1902). Willie emigrated to Texas in September 1878, 'roughing it' with great determination as he worked without pay on a sheep ranch to 'learn the ropes', sleeping on the bare ground in a tent. Eventually he became a successful breeder of sheep, goats and horses until his 'Hughes Ranch had 'stabilized' at *c.* 7,000 acres by 1897. (See Garland Perry, *An American Saga: William George Hughes, 1859–1902*.) He was killed in a railroad accident in 1902 when transporting a consignment of livestock. He had three children, the first of whom he called 'Jeanie'.
Gerard Hughes (1861–1894). Gerard left his informal art apprenticeship to G. F. Watts and joined Willie and Harry in Texas early in 1882; after a year's trial the three brothers formed a business partnership. It is not clear where Gerard worked or lived after Willie's marriage in 1888, but in 1894, while visiting his father's new family near Boston, he acci-

dentally drowned off the coast of Massachusetts.

Harry Hughes (1862–1896). The brilliant, lovable Harry was the real casualty of his father's bankruptcy followed by Jeanie's premature death. Although he had won a Queen's scholarship to Westminster, he was taken away from the school – a decision one cannot imagine that Jeanie would have countenanced. He had hoped to go to medical school – his family nickname was 'Doctor', and would seem to have been studying on his own at night after working, probably in a London office, during the day, until he suffered eye strain. He joined Willie on the Texas ranch in 1880 and became his right-hand man, specializing in the sheep-breeding venture. After his father's re-marriage he moved to Massachusetts and was singled out as very promising by his new step-grandfather, John Forbes, and eventually given a post in the family business. In June 1896 he was returning from a business or journalistic voyage to Asia and South Africa, when his ship, the *Drummond Castle*, collided at night with a reef off the coast of France. It went down in four minutes with the loss of 243 lives.

Emily ('Emmy') Hughes (1864–*c.* 1939) – 'a very stoic little person who kept her chin up, no matter how hard the going' as remembered by her niece Jeanie Hughes in John De Bruyn's memoir *Around the World in Search of Emily Hughes* (Rugby: Tennessee). After her grandmother's death she moved to her father's new home in Milton, Massachusetts and studied nursing in Boston Lying-in-Hospital. In 1902 she married Ainslie Marshall, a former Rugby colonist, and her only child Harry was born in 1904. She ran a model dairy in Milton, Massacusetts until 1917 when they left America, first for Barbados and then for Cornwall. In 1930 Emily and her husband joined their son to farm in Kenya, where Emily died – probably in 1939.

Hastings' two children by Sarah Forbes:

Walter Scott Hughes (1888–1953), engineer. He married twice and had four children.

Dorothea Murray Hughes (1891–1952), nurse and author of *Jane Elizabeth Senior: A Memoir*. 1915. A Quaker after World War I, she became a rescue worker in Poland, where she funded a nursing training school; in 1920. During the years 1923–4 she worked in Salonika with Greek refugees expelled from Turkey (see J. N. Loch, *A Fringe of Blue*). In 1929 she married a planter, David Simmons, of Castle Daly, Jamaica, where she set up a co-operative farm, a college and a nursery school, working tirelessly for the poor. She had no children.

8. (Sir) *James Stansfeld* MP (1820–1898). Stansfeld continued to battle for the Repeal of the Contagious Diseases Acts. He was not against the treatment and cure of venereal disease, but against the compulsory regis-

tration and examination of arrested 'suspect' women – and only women. In his speech to the Commons, moving 'That this House disapproves of the compulsory examination of women under the Contagious Diseases Acts' in April 1883, he said: 'What I have done I have done for conviction and for duty's sake, . . . nor will I cease until I have proved the hygienic failure and imposture of these Acts; but no man knows, or ever can or will know, what to me has been the suffering, the burden and the cost' (Hammond, *James Stansfeld*, p. 230). The Bill repealing the Acts was passed at one o'clock in the morning. Stansfeld then greeted Josephine Butler with the news, 'the tears trickling down his face as he grasped both her hands' (Jane Jordan, *Josephine Butler*, London: John Murray, 2001, p. 215).

Appendix II

The Times, 29 March 1877.

THE LATE MRS. NASSAU SENIOR. – A wider circle than commonly sorrows for the death of a friend has to lament the premature passing away of one who, beyond her claims on private regret, by public service of an unusual kind seems to deserve brief commemoration in our columns. Jane Elizabeth, sister of Thomas Hughes, QC, and daughter-in-law of the late Nassau William Senior, with singular attractiveness and a gift of song which, employed in public, would have placed her in the foremost rank of vocalists, united an untiring benevolence, and a large charity of thought and act which, besides making her the soul of all good works in which she privately engaged, led her at length to public employment – the first woman, as far as we know, who ever filled a salaried office in a most important central department of Government. To say nothing of Miss Nightingale, there have been and are many women rendering valuable service in practical philanthropic work, as the late Mrs. Chisholm, the great promoter and organizer of female emigration to Australia, whose death we were grieved to record a few days ago; Miss Rye, who is still labouring in her vocation of providing homes in Canada for destitute children; Miss Octavia Hill, who has done and is doing such admirable work in improving poor and neglected quarters of the metropolis; and many others;, not to mention the female members of School Boards in London and elsewhere. But these are either unpaid or unofficial labourers or toilers in local as distinguished from central fields of action. Mrs. Senior was the first woman who ever obtained a high salaried official appointment among men, and on the same terms, in one of the most difficult departments of the State, the Local Government Board. She had long before this been active in her private sphere as a visitor of workhouses and an active promoter of the education and the improvement of the poor, and several of her communications on the boarding out of pauper orphans have appeared in these columns. From the time that Mr. Stansfeld assumed the Presidency of the Local Government Board he had felt the want in the service of the Department of feminine knowledge and insight in relation to the female departments of our workhouses and pauper schools. In the course of conversation on this desideratum with Miss Octavia Hill, the name of Mrs. Senior was first brought before him by that lady as that of one eminently qualified by her abilities, character, and private work, for this difficult and delicate employment. He was then personally a stranger to Mrs. Senior. After seeing her and talking the matter over with her, he, in January 1873, gave her an appointment as Assistant-Inspector, at first, by her own wish, temporary, to inquire and report to the Board a woman's view as to the effect on girls of the education in pauper schools. Mrs. Senior made her report in January 1874, after continuous inquiry during the year. The recollection of the warm controversy excited by that report will still be in the minds of many of our readers. It aroused, as was to have been expected, vehement dissent among those connected with these schools, and one experienced and much-respected Inspector in particular who had been prominent in forming and fostering them. This is not the place or the occasion to recur to that dispute. Whatever warmth may have been imported into the controversy, Mrs. Senior's official superiors were satisfied, to use the words of Mr. Lambert, "that Mrs. Senior had discharged her duties in a most conscientious and exemplary manner, though her position was one of extreme difficulty". He adds his conviction that by her labours, short as they were, she effected many and lasting improvements in the management and treatment of girls in pauper schools. But the best proof of the high opinion formed by the President of the Board of the way in which Mrs. Senior had discharged her temporary duty is to be found in the warrant of the 18th of February; 1874, appointing her Inspector of Workhouses and of Workhouse (or separate) and District Pauper Schools, with the duty of inquiring into their female departments and treatment of infants. She was directed to inquire more especially into the condition, management and employment of adult female inmates, the discharge of their duties by the female staff of officers and nurses, the present condition, health, and cleanliness, training and instruction of female children, supervision over the provisions for hiring girls out to service and visiting them in their places; to report defects and suggest improvements to the Board, with the needful powers of entry, inspection and inquiry. The letter enclosing the warrant expressed the Board's general approval of the report Mrs. Senior had already laid before them, and congratulated her on the prospect of new opportunities of usefulness opened out to her by the adoption of plans for the better classification and organization of schools in the metropolis. Mrs. Senior entered at once upon her duties under this comprehensive warrant, but in November 1874, she was unhappily struck down by the illness which has now carried her to the grave. She then reluctantly resigned the appointment of Inspector, which she had received at the beginning of the year. Her letter of resignation enclosed a memorandum of a scheme of work which she had hoped the Board would sanction, and which she hoped might be useful to any one who might succeed her. This was a plan for the appointment of central and local committees of ladies to watch over young servant girls under 18 years of age; to provide places where such girls not having friends could pass their Sundays out safely and pleasantly and proper lodgings for them in the intervals of one situation and another; for help in sickness, penny banks &c. with an outline of the duties of the central and local committees. Her mind was engaged on these subjects while she could work at all, and through her long and lingering illness they were never absent from her thoughts. No successor has been appointed to Mrs. Senior, and it would not be easy to find one; but it is to be hoped that the intention of Mr. Stansfeld is only in abeyance, and that some other woman may yet be intrusted with the duty which Mrs. Senior was forced to drop from her failing hand. Of the loss by Mrs. Senior's death to her family, and a larger and more notable circle of friends than falls to the lot of most, even of the most accomplished and attractive women, it is impossible here to speak. It is by virtue of her peculiar public work that this brief tribute to her beloved memory can claim a place in these columns.

Appendix III

The Reception of Mrs. Senior's *Report*, and Tufnell's *Observations*.

- Anny Thackeray, 'Maïds of All Work and Blue Books', *The Cornhill Magazine*, vol. xxx, no. 177, September 1874.
- Frances Power Cobbe in *The Echo*, 18 September 1874.
- Anon., 'Pauper Girls' in *The Saturday Review*, 26 September 1874.
- 'Caecilius' in *The Press and St. James's Chronicle*, 3 October 1874.
- Anon. (by Tom Taylor?), 'A Blue-Book with a rose tinge', *Punch*, 10 October 1874.
- Anon., 'Girls and Pauper Schools', *The Queen, the Ladies' Newspaper*, October 1874.
- Anon. (by Caroline Stephen), 'A Woman's Blue Book', *The Spectator*, 10 October 1874.
- Anon., 'Children of the State', *The Civil Service Review*, 10, 17 and 24 October 1874.
- Anon. *The Argus*, Adelaide, Australia, 13 October 1874.
- Anon. 'The Education and After-life of Pauper Girls', *The Manchester Guardian*, 23 October 1874.
- Anon., but in fact Dr. Brudenell Carter, who had already cleared it with J.E.S. in September, long article on 'The Girls at Pauper Schools' followed by a long, positive editorial leader, *The Times*, 4 November 1874.
- Anon., articles in *The Morning Post*, 2, 6 and 18 November 1874.
- Menella Smedley, 'Workhouse Schools', *Macmillan's Magazine*, November 1874.
- Anon. (Harriet Martineau?), *Daily News*, November 1874.
- Anon. *The Scotsman*, 17 November 1874.
- Anon, (by Joanna Hill), 'The Training of Pauper Girls', *The Birmingham Daily Post*, 20 November 1874.
- Henrietta Synnot, 'Little Paupers', *The Contemporary Review*, November 1874.
- *Women and Work*, 7 November 1874.
- *The Woman's Suffrage Journal*, Autumn 1874.
- Frances Power Cobbe (on J.E.S.'s resignation), *The Echo*, 2 December 1874.
- Anon., 'A Lady Poor-law Inspector' (on J.E.S.'s resignation), *The Times*, 5 December 1874.

- Anon., 'Public Charities', *The New York Times*, 5 December 1874.
- Anon., *The Investor's Guardian*, 5 December 1874.
- Anon., 'Pauper Schools and Pauper Children' *Capital and Labour*, 9 December 1874.
- C. Edmund Maurice (Octavia Hill's brother-in-law), 'Mrs. Senior's Report', *The Contemporary Review*, 9 November/ December 1874.
- Anon. leader in *The Times*, 'District Schools and Boarding-Out' (pro Tufnell's *Observations*), 26 January 1875.
- Anon. (Frances Power Cobbe?), 'District Schools and Boarding Out' (against Tufnell's *Observations*), *The Echo*, 28 January 1875.
- Anon. (Tom Taylor?), 'Tufnell (Mr.) V. Senior (Mrs.)' in *Punch*, February 1875.
- Anon., 'The Education of Pauper Girls', *The Eastern Post*, 6 February 1875.
- Anon., 'Street Arabs and Destitute Children', *The Western News*, February 1875.
- Anon., 'Boarding Out and Destitute Children in England', *Australian Register*, 24 February 1875.
- Anon., 'English Schools for Pauper Girls', *Australian Register*, 30 March 1875.
- Anon. (Frances Power Cobbe?), 'What of the Children?, *The Echo*, 16 April 1875.
- Anon. (Caroline Stephen?), 'Pauper Children', *The Spectator*, 24 April 1875.
- Charles Lewes, George Eliot's adoptive son, 'Mrs. Senior's Report. etc.', *The Edinburgh Review*, 142, July 1875.
- Edward Bond, friend and suitor of Octavia Hill, 'The Education of Pauper Girls', *The Academy*, 24 July 1875.
- Anon. (Caroline Stephen?), *The Spectator*, 9 October 1875.
- Anon., 'Boarding Out Pauper and Orphan Children, *The Daily Globe*, Toronto, 9 November 1875.

Appendix IV

Published References to 'Mrs. Nassau Senior', 1877–2007

1877	Tom Taylor, Obituary The Late Mrs Nassau Senior in *The Times* (anon.) (29 March)
1877	Caroline Stephen, Obituary in *The Spectator*. (7 April)
1877– c. 1900	Chairman's addresses in *Annual Reports for the Metropolitan Association for Befriending Young Servants*, held in the British Library and the Public Record Office, Kew.
1879	'Prosper Mérimée à-propos de Lettres Inédites', *Revue des Deux Mondes*, pp. 722 et seq.
1879	National Society for Women's Suffrage, *Opinions of Women on Women's Suffrage*, pp. 60–61, describes her as 'Inspector of the Female Departments of Workhouses and Workhouse Schools; appointed 1873'. Quotes her letter to the Secretary, Helen Blackburn, 10 April 1875 in support of suffrage.
1880	(2nd ed. 1895), ed. Helen Blackburn, *A Handbook for Women Engaged in Social and Political Work*. Section 15, p. 40. 'Appointed by Govt. Depts', lists Mrs. Nassau Senior as the first appointment of a woman under the Local Government Board. Section 44, p. 99, 'For the Care of Girls' notes the influence of her Report on the founding of The Girls' Friendly Society, known as GFS, p. 100; the section on the Metropolitan Association for Befriending Young Servants, known as MABYS says: 'Founded in 1874 by Mrs. Nassau Senior'. Chapter xiv, Section 48, 'Obituary of Women who have been Leaders and Pioneers in the Present Reign', lists her death in 1877 after that of Harriet Martineau and before Caroline Chisholm and Mary Carpenter. She is also mentioned (apropos of the founding of MABYS) in the diagram of 'Women's Progress in the British Isles, 1848–1895'.
1881	Anny Thackeray, 'Upstairs and Downstairs', in *The Cornhill Magazine*, reprinted in *From the Porch*, 1913, p. 244 et seq., begins with reminder of Mrs. Senior's critical inspector's report on workhouse schools.

1881 (September)	*The Nineteenth Century and After* 'Women as Civil Servants'.
1883/4	Annie Fields [Mrs. James T. Fields], *How to Help the Poor* (Houghton Mifflin, Boston). Part IV, 'What a Visitor May Do for Children and Young Persons':– "[The] report of Mrs Nassau Senior in England a few years ago, describing the lack of power in girls trained in institutions to stand up and take their place in the world, first drew attention to this great topic. Above all, such girls need friends."
c. 1890	Dr. Barnardo, *Something attempted – something done* refers to the introduction of fostering or 'Boarding-out' in England being owed 'to the indefatigable labours of the late Mrs. Nassau Senior'.
1893	Helen Blackburn, *Collection of portraits of eminent British women as exhibited at Chicago in 1893*. 'Jane Nassau Senior' is included to represent the late 19th century, together with Barbara Bodichon, Josephine Butler, Julia Margaret Cameron, F. P. Cobbe, George Eliot, and Ellen Terry, inter alia; the Collection was presented to The Women's Hall of the University of Bristol in 1894; it is now lost but its catalogue is held in the Blackburn Papers of Girton College Library, Cambridge.
1893	Angela Burdett-Coutts, *Woman's Mission: A Series of Congress Papers on the Philanthropic Work of Women* by eminent writers; part of the Royal British Commission's contribution to the Chicago Exhibition of 1893. Hesba Stretton, 'Women's Work for Children', p. 9: 'The Boarding-Out of Workhouse Children is almost wholly in the hands of women; . . . The Orphan Association, founded in memory of Mrs. Nassau Senior, is conducted on the boarding-out system. She was the first female Inspector of Workhouses appointed by the English Government, and did incalculable service to her country by calling attention to the miserable condition of children in workhouse schools. . . .' Edith Sellers, 'Women's Work for the Welfare of Girls', pp. 35–38: '"workhouse" girls had been sent out into the world at fourteen . . . and then left to sink or float as best they could. Mrs. Senior speedily put an end to this arrangement'. Then details the work of MABYS. Miss E. S. Lidgett, 'Women as Guardians of the Poor', pp. 254–5: 'In the year 1872 a most important step was taken by the Rt. Hon. J. Stansfeld, MP, . . . when he requested the late Mrs. Nassau Senior etc.' And see Miss Gaskell, Appendix on MABYS, pp. 384–5.

1893   Louisa Twining, *Recollections of Life and Work*, pp. 210–13:
            'No more happy selection of a pioneer in this important work
            could surely have been made, or have produced more satisfac-
            tory results, her devoted labours being only too soon ended by
            her lamented death . . . Refers to 'all the beneficial results that
            have followed in twenty years from her all too short beginning,
            and to the "Memorandum of a scheme of work" which she
            sent in with her resignation, and which she hoped might be
            useful to any one who succeeded her.'

1894   Frances Power Cobbe, *Life*, p. 279; '[Pauper children] were
            joyless, spiritless little creatures, without "mothering" (as
            blessed Mrs. Senior said).'

1895   W. T. Stead, ed., *The Review of Reviews*, vol. xi, January–June
            1895, pp. 505 et seq., interview with James Stansfeld, 'the
            tribune of womanhood'. 'By the appointment of Mrs. Senior
            as a Poor Law Inspector, he made the first breach in the male
            ring . . . The initiative so boldly taken by Mr. Stansfeld . . . has
            never been adequately followed up. . . . [So] far no attempt has
            been made to redistribute the offices with anything like the
            proportion to the relative number of men and women under
            surveillance . . . Hanging in [his] hall there is an illuminated
            address [on the appointment of Mrs. Nassau Senior] signed by
            the foremost women of our time, which recognizes . . . the
            services which he has rendered to their sex.'

1896   Georgiana Hill, *Women in English Life from Mediaeval to
            Modern Times*, vol. 11, 'Women and Public Work', p. 312:
            'The most important of these [paid] appointments was that of
            Inspector of Workhouse Schools. The late Mrs. Nassau Senior
            was chosen for this office, in 1873, by Mr. James Stansfeld . . .
            The MABYS was subsequently founded by Mrs. Senior . . .'

1896   Watts' 1858 portrait of her shown at Watts Exhibition, New
            Gallery, London.

1897   Leslie Stephen's entry on the political economist, Nassau
            William Senior, in the *Dictionary of National Biography*,
            ends, unusually, with a postscript section on Mrs. Nassau
            Senior.

1897   *A [Diamond] Jubilee Calendar for the Women of the British
            Empire*, Landmarks IV 'Special Achievement and Associated
            Endeavour for Public Service'; Mrs. Nassau Senior's 1874
            Report, as Poor Law Inspector resulted directly in the forma-
            tion of Metropolitan Association for Befriending Young
            Servants, and less directly in the formation of the Girls'
            Friendly Society.

1897	W. Chance, *Children Under the Poor Law: their education, training and after-care, together with Appendix – A Criticism of the [1896] Report of the Departmental Committee of the Local Government Board on Metropolitan Poor Law Schools.* Praises J.E.S.'s Report as 'everything that a Report should be' (pp. 35–6), but sides with Tufnell's 'Observations' re boarding-out and does not appear to know J.E.S's 'Reply to Tufnell'. Claims, p. 91, that 'most of her suggestions are now carried out' – but omits to mention her basic recommendation that the huge schools be broken up into family-units within 'cottage homes', which had not been acted on.

1898 Edwin A. Pratt, *Pioneer Women in Victoria's Reign, being Short Histories of Great Movements*, pp. 228 et seq. under 'Associations for Girls': Mrs. Nassau Senior had 'a voice which might have won for her a high position on the lyric stage . . . a rare degree of beauty [and] a charm of manner that won all hearts . . . The amount of work she did in pursuit of her mission seems almost appalling.' He sums up her Report and quotes her insistence that the girls want 'mothering'.

1898 M. C. M. Simpson, *Many Memories of Many People*. Her chapter 'Three Distinguished Ladies', after praising Mrs. Grote and Jenny Lind, ends with Jeanie Senior. It is ironic that it should have been Minnie, who had caused Jeanie so much pain and irritation over so many years, and who herself had little or no sympathy with her sister-in-law's earnest values and political idealism, who should, nevertheless, have written such a lively and admiring, though not always accurate, sketch.

1898 Thomas Mackay, *A History of the English Poor Law; Vol. 111: 1834 – present* (London: P.S. King and Sons), ch. xix, 'The education of pauper children', acknowledges that Mrs. Senior's Report 'attracted much attention' but is against boarding-out.

1901 Frederick Boase, *Modern English Biography*. (Of people who had died 1857–1900). Factual entry on 'Jane Elizabeth Senior'. After detailing her public work, mentions Association for placing orphans in private families founded in memory of her in 1877. Refers to obituaries in *Spectator*, 31 March 1877, and 7 April, as well as *The Times*, 29 March 1877.

1900? Walter Money, FSA, 'Recollections of the Hughes Family' in local Newbury periodical.

1901 Frederick Douglas How, *Noble Women of Our Time*. Characteristic collective biography intended for Sunday reading or as girls' Sunday School prize; uses much anonymous contemporary anecdote in chapter on 'Mrs. Nassau Senior'. Unfortunately the hagiographical approach is self-defeating, leaving Jeanie Senior with no complexity of character, let alone any faults to love her by.

1904   Mrs. Hughes (of Uffington) *Letters and Recollections of Sir Walter Scott* (London, 1904); Hastings Hughes, 'Introductory Sketch of Mrs. Hughes', includes references to his sister's intellectual and musical inheritance from her paternal grandmother.

1905   Mrs. Russell Barrington, *G. F. Watts, Reminiscences.* 'Inscribed with grateful affection to the memory of Janie [sic] Senior'. 'I have always viewed our friendship with Watts as a legacy from this beautiful friend, of a nature so large, so generous and tender-hearted'; Jeanie had written to her April 1876, "What a comfort it is to me that you will be near Watts, to urge him to his noblest work and to stave off too many distractions (or should I say attractions)!" p. 7.

1907   Anny Thackeray Ritchie, *Cornhill Magazine* (June), 'In My Lady's Chamber'. Beautiful elegiac evocation beginning with allusion to talking over with Caroline Stephen in Cambridge *c.* 1905, their 'remembrance of things past, and of one example of efforts which had succeeded, [a life] which to the end kept to [its] high level . . . [They] came to the mention of one name among others – that of Mrs. Nassau Senior. . . .' Then goes on to depict the life at Elm House. Republished in 1908 Anny Thackeray Ritchie, *Blackstick Papers.*

1909   *Report of the Royal Commission on the Poor Laws and Relief of Distress.* 'Mrs. Nassau Senior's adverse report on ['barrack' Poor Law Schools] in 1873 . . . gave a great impetus to boarding-out, cottage and scattered homes.'

1911   Tom Percival, *Poor Law Children* (London: Shaw and Sons), pp. 29–30: 'Mrs. Senior recommended the breaking up of the large schools . . . [her report gave] a set back to the system from which it has never recovered.' Good on later 1896–8 controversy re District Schools, pp. 30–32.

1912   Mary Watts, *Life of Watts,* 3 vols.

1913   C. E. Maurice (ed.), *Life of Octavia Hill,* includes many, but not all, O.H. letters to Mrs Nassau Senior.

1913   Anny Thackeray Ritchie, 'In My Lady's Chamber', republished in *From the Porch* (London: Smith, Elder).

1915   Dorothea Hughes, *A Memoir of Jane Elizabeth Senior.* Printed in Boston, USA.

1918   Henrietta Barnett, *Life of Canon Barnett.* Reminiscences of J.E.S. in girls' literacy class.

1928   Ray Strachey, *The Cause: A Short History of the Women's Movement in Great Britain.*

1932   J. L. and Barbara Hammond, *James Stansfeld, A Victorian Champion of Sex Equality*, prepared for the Stansfeld Trustees, Fawcett Library, p.viii: 'What he believed he believed with the whole force of his nature.' . . . 'The third notable event of Stansfeld's administration [of the Local Government Board] was his appointment of a woman Inspector, Mrs. Nassau Senior, daughter-in-law of the economist. Mrs. Senior needed all the encouragement that he could give her in an unfriendly environment . . . [Her Report] encouraged the boarding-out system, and in this way Stansfeld helped to forward a policy which was not adopted as a permanent part of the Poor Law system until 1889' (pp. 112–14).

1934   Winifred Holtby, *Women and a Changing Civilisation*, 'In 1873 Mrs Nassau Senior became a poor-law inspector'.

1938   Hilda Martindale, *Women: Servants of the State, 1870–1938. A History of Women in the Civil Service*, p. 30: '[The] whole question of the care of the children of the State was exercising the minds of progressive philanthropists. That this might be a subject in which a woman official would be of service could hardly be denied . . . in 1873 Mr. James Stansfeld a "Victorian champion of sex equality" . . . took the daring step of appointing a woman inspector. . . . Mrs Nassau Senior . . . produced a thorough and courageous report. . . . [The] Report, which was followed by a great controversy, fell into unsympathetic hands, [unacknowledged quote from the Hammonds, above] but undoubtedly it influenced the trend of public opinion and much of the subsequent progress in dealing with the children of the State may be attributed to it . . . [Mrs Nassau Senior] goes down in history as a graceful and accomplished woman, generally loved for simplicity and sweetness of character [i.e. unacknowledged quotation from Leslie Stephen's *DNB* entry on Nassau William Senior]. She was, however, something more; this first woman civil servant of the higher grades, had vision and courage to a marked degree.'

1952   Mack and Armytage, *Thomas Hughes, The Life of the Author of Tom Brown's Schooldays*, p. 85, 'Tom's sister Jane or Jeannie [sic] Senior was the most interesting of his brothers and sisters, having inherited a good deal of her father's talent and her [paternal] grandmother's energy. . . .'

1959   Jean Heywood *Children in Care* (2nd ed. 1965) (International Library of Sociology and Social Reconstruction; London,

Routledge and Kegan Paul), ch. 5, 'The Poor Law Care of Children, pp. 72–3: '[J.E.S's] conclusion sounded the death knell of the large institutional traditions and began a gradual move away from the administratively convenient device of the barrack home to the family system we have today.'

1962   Kathleen Heasman, *Evangelicals in Action, An Appraisal of their social work in the Victorian Era*, pp. 99 and 120.

1967   Alec and Elizabeth Ross, 'Case Studies of Women in 19th C. Social Administration, 2. Mrs. Nassau Senior and Miss M. H. Mason', *Journal of Social and Economic Administration*, vol. 1, no. 4,. pp. 48 et seq. An important article.

1973   Ivy Pinchbeck and Margart Hewitt, *Children in English Society, Vol. 11, 18thC.–1948* (London: Routledge and Kegan Paul), ch. xvii, 'The release of children from pauperism', pp. 517–19.

1980   F. K. Prochaska, *Women and Philanthropy in 19th Century England*.

1981   Jacqueline Hughes, *Mrs. Nassau Senior, The First Local Govt. Board Inspector*, M.Ed. Dissertation, University of Bristol. An important, informative historical evaluation.

1983   Meta Zimmeck, entry on Jeannie [sic] Senior in *Europa Biographical Dictionary of British Women*.

1987   Patricia Hollis, *Ladies Elect, Women in English Local Government 1865–1914*.

1987   Philippa Levine, *Victorian Feminism 1850–1900* in 'the early one-off appointment of Jane Senior to a workhouse inspectorship'.

1988   Julia Parker, *Women and Welfare: Ten Victorian Women in Public Social Service*. J.E.S. is not one of the ten but she is mentioned.

1993   Felix Driver, *Power and Pauperism, the workhouse system, 1834–1884* (Cambridge University Press), p. 69: 'Jane Senior's arrival was to prove a landmark in the development of official policy towards workhouse children.' 'Her advocacy of cottage homes on the Mettray system was backed by Doyle' – p. 101.

1995   Alastair Laing, *In Trust for the Nation: Paintings from National Trust Houses*, p. 44, G. F. Watts OM, RA, 'Jane Elizabeth ('Jeanie') Hughes, Mrs. Nassau Senior (1828–1877)', "it was their joint concern to do good – he through his art, she by practical action – combined with her physical attractiveness, that drew [Watts] to her" (full-length illustration of Watts' portrait, at Wightwick Manor, p. 45).

1999   Kathryn Morrison, *The Workhouse: A Study of Poor-Law Buildings in England, Royal Commission on the Historical Monuments of England*. Swindon, English Heritage. Chapter 8: 'Poor-law buildings for children', p. 143: 'The idea that pauper children would benefit from the cottage-home system was mooted in 1874 by Mrs. Nassau Senior, the first woman poor-law inspector who recommended "schools of a more home-like character . . . each house containing not more than 20–30 children of all ages."'

2000   Sotheby's sale of Nassau Senior papers, followed by press
(December)   coverage of export ban on the George Eliot letters to Jeanie Senior.

2001   Kate Murphy, *Firsts – The Livewire Book of British Women Achievers*.

2003   Barbara Hardy, 'Art into Life, life into Art: *Middlemarch* and George Eliot's letters, with special reference to Jane Senior', in *George Eliot–George Henry Lewes Studies*, nos. 44–45. September 2003, pp. 75–96.

2004   Barbara Bryant, *G. F. Watts, Portraits: Fame and Beauty in Victorian Society*, (National Portrait Gallery, London) p. 104.

2004   Entry on Jeanie Senior in *Oxford Dictionary of National Biography*.

2004   Veronica Franklin Gould, *G. F. Watts, The Last Great Victorian* (Yale University Press). Jeanie 'had been the love of his life' (p. 133).

2004   Stephen P. Walker (Professor of Accounting, Cardiff Business School), 'Philanthropic Women and Accountancy: Octavia Hill and the exercise of quiet power and sympathy'.

2006   Barbara Hardy, *George Eliot: A Critic's Biography* (London: Continuum), ch. 4, 'Acquaintances and Friends', pp. 118–31.

2007   Graham Senior-Milne, genealogical website: <www.peerage.org>. – 'The descent of Hughes' includes rich illustrative material concerning the Hughes and Senior families.

Notes

Introduction

1 Anonymous tribute from Jeanie Senior's former paying guest and singing pupil, Jessie Hazelhurst, quoted in Frederick Douglas How, *Noble Women of Our Time* (London: Isbister and Co., 1901), p. 160.

2 Excerpt from anonymous tribute quoted by Walter Money, F.S.A. in his 'Recollections of the Hughes Family' in *Newbury Annals*, 1877.

3 Extract from 'Jane Elizabeth Senior *In Memoriam*', a poem almost certainly written by Tom Taylor for *Punch*, April 1877.

4 How, *Noble Women*, p. 160.

5 *Ibid.*, p. 161.

6 Virginia Woolf, 'Speech of January 21, 1931' in Mitchell A. Leaska, ed. *The Pargiters, The Novel-Essay Portion of The Years* (London: Hogarth Press, 1978), pp. xxx–xxxi.

Chapter One: Tom Brown's Sister – Jeanie Hughes

Abbreviation throughout the Notes to this and subsequent chapters:
J.E.S. = Jeanie Senior, née Hughes.

1 Cf. John Hughes' anonymous ballad 'The Magic Lay of the One-horse Chay' on a couple whose clothes had been stolen while bathing naked near Brighton, in *Blackwood's Magazine*, October 1824. And see entry on John Hughes in the *DNB*, 1891, vol. xxxviii.

2 Scott to Southey, June 1824, quoted in Lockhart' s *Life of Sir Walter Scott*.

3 Introduction to Horace Hutchinson, ed. *Letters and Recollections of Sir Walter Scott by Mrs. Hughes (of Uffington)*, (London: Smith and Elder, 1904), p. 3.

4 See Thomas Hughes, 'Early Memories for the Children, '1899, re-edited by Henry Shelley as 'Fragments of Autobiography', *Cornhill Magazine*, 1925, pp. 283–4 and 287–9.

5 Milne Collier Papers.

6 Margaret Hughes's undated mss. note to her eldest son George Hughes, written before 1870. Milne Collier Papers.

7 Letter to [Octavius] Wilkinson, 12 July 1841, Milne Collier Papers.

8 The complete letter was originally published in *The Letters of Charles Dickens*, 1880; reprinted with commentary in W. J. Carlton, 'A five year-old critic of *Nicholas Nickleby*', *The Dickensian*, 1959, vol. lv, pp. 89–93.

9 Thomas Hughes, 'Early Memories', see note 4 above, pp. 282–3.

10 J. E.S., undated mss. fragment, 'Old Servants', Milne Collier Papers.

11 Cf. Maria Charlesworth, *The Female Visitor to the Poor* (1846) and *Ministering Children* (1854) as well as many later productions of The Religious Tract Society, anthologized in Leonard De Vries, *Litttle Wide-Awake, Victorian Children's Books and Periodicals* (London: Arthur Barker Ltd., 1967).

12 J.E.S., undated autobiographical fragment, *c.* 1869, 'New Ground', quoted in Dorothea M. Hughes, *Memoir of Jane Elizabeth Senior* (Boston: Press of Geo. H. Ellis Co., 1916), pp. 110–12.

13 *Ibid.*

14 *Ibid.*

15 J. B. Cramer, 1771–1858, student of Clementi; his pianoforte studies were used by Beethoven for his nephew.

16 Dorothea Hughes, *Memoir*, p. 4 .

17 *Ibid.*, p. 49.

18 Milne Collier Papers.

19 J.E.S.'s letter to her son Walter, 2 February 1866.

20 Dorothea Hughes, *Memoir*, pp. 56–7.

21 *Ibid.*, p. 62.

22 For the long courtship of Fanny Ford by Tom Hughes, see Edward Mack and W. H. G. Armytage, *Thomas Hughes* (London: Ernest Benn, 1952), ch. 3 'Courts and Courting, 1842–1848'.

23 Milne Collier Papers.

Chapter Two: Being 'Mrs. Nassau Senior', 1848–1853

All quotations not annotated are from J.E.S.'s letters to her son Walter.

1   *The Subjection of Women*, 1869, ch. 2. And see Walter Houghton, *The Victorian Frame of Mind, 1830–1870* (New Haven and London: Yale University Press, 1957), pp. 348–53, 'Woman'.

2   *Moral Heroism or the Trials of the Great and Good*, 1846. For Clara Lucas Balfour see *Oxford DNB*, 2004, and Sybil Oldfield, *Collective Biography of Women in Britain, 1550–1900* (London and New York: Mansell, 1999), p. 60.

3   Oldfield, *Collective Biography*, pp. 64–6.

4   Richard Whately (1787–1863), Archbishop of Dublin, who supported Catholic emancipation.

5   Henry, Marquis of Lansdowne (1780–1863), cautious Liberal statesman.

6   Louis Adolphe Thiers (1797–1877) French historian and politician.

7   Francois Guizot (1787–1874), French historian and politician who had fled to London with Louis-Philippe after the 1848 Revolution.

8   Massimo d' Azeglio (1798–1866), Italian politician, painter and writer, supporter of the *Risorgimento*.

9   Carlo Marochetti (1805–1867), Italian sculptor who had left Paris for London after the 1848 Revolution.

10 M. C. M.Simpson [i.e. Nassau William Senior's daughter, Minnie], *Many Memories of Many People* (London: Edward Arnold, 1898), p. 94.

11 Manuel Garcia (1805–1906], Spanish Jewish singing tutor, brother of Pauline Viardot Garcia – great mezzo-soprano, song composer, and later friend of J.E.S.

12 John Lothrop Motley, *Correspondence*, Vol. 1 (London: John Murray, 1889); letter to his wife, 4 July 1858.

13 Simpson, *Many Memories*, p. 95.

14 For the Seniors' family and business background see S. Leon Levy, *Nassau W. Senior 1790–1864, critical essayist, classical economist and adviser of governments* (Newton Abbot: David and Charles 1970), ch. 2, 'Ancestry' and ch. 5, p. 48.

15 See Norman Longmate, *The Workhouse* (London: Temple Smith 1975), and J. F. C. Harrison, *The Common People* (London: Flamingo/Fontana, 1984), ch. 7, pp. 235–40: 'The New Poor Law was by its very nature a piece of class legislation. . . . [It] was basically an attempt to deal with pauperism [i.e.destitute claimants] rather than poverty'. The 'lesser eligibility' principle, articulated by Nassau William Senior, determined that conditions in a workhouse must be worse than conditions outside – husbands must be separated from wives, parents from children. The inmates must only be fed a minimal, monotonous diet, in exchange for which they must work twelve hours a day without pay. It was hoped by this means to deter the poor from dependence on 'relief'. Senior wrote to de Tocqueville, 18 March 1835: 'The greater part of the Act, founded on [the Report of the Poor Law Commissioners] was . . . written by me; and in fact I am responsible for the effects, good or evil . . . of the whole measure.' Levy, *Nassau W. Senior*, pp. 308–9.

16 *Ibid.*, ch. xi, 'Lord Ashley's Ten Hours Bill', esp. p. 111.

17 *Ibid.*, ch. xiv, 'Ireland in 1843–1846'. It should be noted, however, that Nassau William was a liberal on the subject of Catholic Emancipation and the disestablishment of the Church of England in Ireland.

18 Frederick Denison Maurice (1805–1872), Anglican clergyman and theologian, the spiritual force behind English Christian Socialism as opposed to unchristian socialism and unsocial Christianity. See *Oxford DNB*.

19 See CHAPTER 1 above, pp. 11–12 and Geoffrey Rowell, *Hell and the Victorians* (Oxford, Clarendon Press, 1974), ch. 4, pp. 80–3 and 88.

20 See Edward Mack and W. H. G. Armytage, *Thomas Hughes*, ch. 4: 'New Horizons, 1848–1853'.

21. Quoted by Harrison, *Common People*, p. 237.

22 See Jo Manton, *Mary Carpenter and the Children of the Streets* (London: Heinemann, 1976). On 21 May 1852 Mary Carpenter had been summoned to give evidence to the Select Committee of the House of Commons on the question of Criminal and Destitute Children.

23 Joseph Blanco White (1775–1841), theological writer who first abandoned and then re-embraced Christianity, dying a Unitarian.

24. Levy, *Nassau W. Senior*, p. 31.

25 Shelley's love song, 'Lines to an Indian Air' set by John Barnett – 'I arise from dreams of thee /In the first sleep of night'.

26 Mss. from Hughes Museum, Rugby, Tennessee.

27 Walter Houghton, *Victorian Frame of Mind*, ch. 10, 'Earnestness', pp. 242–3.

28 *Ibid.*, p. 244, quoting *Sermons and Discourses*.

29 Henrietta Garnett, *Anny: A Life of Anne Isabella Thackeray Ritchie* (London: Chatto and Windus, 2004), p. 205.

30 Houghton, *Victorian Frame of Mind*, pp. 249–50.

31 *Middlemarch*, ch. 20.

32. *Ibid.*

Chapter Three: Enter Watts and Mérimée, 1852–1856

Watts' letters to J.E.S. were sold at Sotheby's in December 2000; copies are held in the Milne Collier Papers.

1 Cf. Loraine Fletcher on the wretchedly married writer Charlotte Smith, 1749–1806: 'Work, friends and her children were her life', Introduction to Charlotte Smith's *Emmeline* (Broadview Press: Ontario reprint 2003), p. 33.

2 Simpson, *Many Memories*, p. 97. Mary Stanley, daughter of the Dean of St. Paul's, who headed fifty nurses, recalled: 'It was not the wounded we were called upon to tend, but those who were stricken down with fever, dysentery, and frost-bites, from long exposure in the trenches' (A. P. Stanley, *Memoirs of Edward and Catherine Stanley*, 2nd ed. 1880, Appendix on Mary Stanley, pp. 333–47).

3 George Grote (1794–1871), Benthamite Utilitarian, Historian of Greece and founder of the University of London; his wife Harriet Grote (1792–1878) was a lively-minded *salonnière* and biographer.

4 For Adelaide Sartoris see Ann Blainey, *Fanny and Adelaide, The lives of the the Remarkable Kemble Sisters* (Chicago: Ivan R. Dee, 2001).

5 The artist F. B. Barwell, piquantly, in view of J. E.S.'s later work and influence, was the well-known painter of 'The Adoption'.

6 Quoted in J. G. Millais' *Life and Letters of J. E. Millais* (London: Methuen, 1899), vol. i, p. 247 *et seq.* The philosopher Thomas Spencer Baynes reacted to 'The Rescue' in a letter written May 1855: [The] face and form of that woman on the stairs of the burning house are, if not, as I am disposed to think, beyond all, quite equal to the best that Millais has ever

done, . . . [The] agony is too near, too intense, too awful, for present rejoicing even at the deliverance. And that smile on the young mother's face has struggled up from such depths of speechless pain, and expresses such a sudden ecstasy of utter gratitude and overmastering joy, that it quite unmans me . . . It is the most intense and pathetic utterance of poor human love I have ever met'. (quoted in Millais, *Life*, p. 253)

W. M. Rossetti noted 'an ecstatic joy that floods every pulse of her being – parts her panting lips, and lights her azure eyes like cressets'. (*The Times*, 7 May 1855) In 1898 *The Daily News* commented on the painting, now exhibited afresh: . . . 'In the pose of the mother, as she reaches out those long arms of hers, straight and rigid and parallel, there is an intensity of expression that recalls his Pre-Raphaelite days'.

7 Thoby Prinsep (1792–1878) rich East India Co. servant (see *DNB*) had married Sara (1816–1887) one of the seven legendary, beautiful Pattle sisters. See Carolyn Dakers, *The Holland Park Circle: Artists and Victorian Society* (Newhaven, Conn. and London: Yale University Press, 1999), and Elizabeth French Boyd, *Bloomsbury Heritage, Their Mothers and their Friends* (London: Hamish Hamilton, 1976).

8 Sidney Colvin, entry on G. F. Watts in the *Dictionary of National Biography*, vol. 1901–1910.

9 'A Sketch of the Past' in Jeanne Schulkind, ed. *Virginia Woolf: Moments of Being – Unpublished Autobiographical Writings* (London: Sussex University Press and Chatto and Windus, 1976), p. 86.

10 In G. F. Watts, *The Hall of Fame* (London: The National Gallery, n.d.) he is called 'a portraitist of rare power and insight'.

11 Quoted by Wilfrid Blunt in *England's Michelangelo: A Biography of Geoge Frederick Watts* (London: Columbus Book, 1988), p. 79.

12 Mary Watts, *George Frederic Watts, the Annals of an Artist's Life* (London: Macmillan, 1912), vol.1, p. 161.

13 George Sand, *L'Histoire de Ma Vie*, 1854–5, ch. 10.

14 V. F. Gould, *G. F.Watts, The Last Great Victorian*, publ. for the Paul Mellon Centre for Studies in British Art (New Haven and London: Yale University Press, 2004), pp. 38–45 and p. 133.

15 A. W. Raitt, *Prosper Mérimée* (London: Eyre and Spottiswoode, 1970), p. 364. And see Introduction by Nicholas Jotcham, to *Prosper Mérimée, Carmen and Other Stories* (Oxford: The World's Classics, Oxford University Press, 1989).

16 Frank Bowman, *Prosper Mérimée, Heroism, Pessimism and Irony* (Berkeley and Los Angeles: University of California Publications in Modern Philology, vol. 66, 1962), p. 6.

17 Raitt, *Prosper Mérimée*, p. 269. It should be noted that Raitt confuses twenty-five year old Jeanie with her elderly mother-in-law in the correspondence with Mérimée. It was not the same thing at all.

18 Maxime Du Camp, quoted in Raitt, *Prosper Mérimée*, p. 270.

19 Simpson, *Many Memories*, p. 292.

20 Bowman, *Prosper Mérimée*, p. 7.

21 Mérimée's letter to Edouard Grasset, in M. Parturier, *Correspondance de Mérimée*, vol. i, p. 254, quoted by Bowman, p. 53.

22 Raitt, *Prosper Mérimée*, p. 358

23 Jeanie's old friend and doctor, Dr. de Mussy, now living in Paris, had apparently passed the mss. letters to the editor O. D'Haussonville, with Walter Senior's consent.

24 See 'Prosper Mérimée à-propos de Lettres Inédites', *Revue des Deux Mondes*, 1879, p .722.

25 Nassau William Senior, *Journals*, vol. v, pp. 185–207. Madame Mohl was the English-born *salonnière* whose home at 120 Rue du Bac welcomed a host of interesting English visitors, especially women, including Elizabeth Gaskell, Florence Nightingale, Anny Thackeray, George Eliot and J.E.S. herself. She was particularly close to Minnie Senior, who later published *Letters and Recollections of Julius and Mary Mohl* (London: Kegan Paul, Trench, 1887).

26 In fact none of Jeanie's letters to Mérimée have survived; we do not know whether he himself destroyed them or whether they had been destroyed after his death in the Communards' arson attack on his house, 52 rue de Lille, in 1871.

27 Parturier, *Correspondance*, vol. vii, p. 356. I have translated this and all the following passages from Mérimée's letters.

28 Clearly J.E.S. saw that Ruth was no mere pathetic victim, but rather a woman who grows up through her experience of unmarried motherhood, eventually becoming her community's saviour during a terrifying epidemic. Thus Elizabeth Gaskell's 'fallen woman' turns out to be heroically effective, not passively fatalistic like Mérimée's murdered Carmen. Josephine Butler, the crusader for the human rights of prostitutes, cited her reading of *Ruth* as one of the turning-points in her life.

29 Parturier, *Correspondance*, vol. vii, pp. 440–2.

30 *Ibid.*, pp. 461–2.

31 See Raitt, *Prosper Mérimée*, pp. 309–10.

32 Parturier, *Correspondance*, vol. vii, pp. 486–90.

33 *Ibid.*, pp. 510–13.

34 Passages from Stendhal's 'On Love 'which Mérimée may well have wished Jeanie to ponder occur in his ch. 56 (ii) 'Concerning marriage' and include: 'Where there is no love, women's faithfulness to the marriage bond is probably against nature. – This unnatural condition has been sought after by using the fear of hellfire and religious sentiments; . . .

There is but one way to ensure greater faithfulness among women to the bond of marriage, and that is to allow freedom [of choice] to girls, and divorce for married couples.

In a first marriage a woman invariably throws away the brightest days of youth.'

35 Parturier, *Correspondance*, vol. viii, pp. 20–2.

36 Parturier, *Correspondance*, vol. xi, pp. 123–4.

Chapter Four: Surviving Four Hard Years, 1856–1860

1 Dorothea Hughes, *Memoir*, p. 78.

2 Mack and Armytage, *Thomas Hughes*, pp. 90–1, 100.

3 *Tom Brown' Schooldays*, Part One, ch. 1 'The Brown family'.

4 In the early 1850s George Hughes had married Lady Salusbury's adopted daughter, Annie Seward, the presumptive heiress to Offley Place, near Luton Hoo, the magnificent park and house of Lady Salusbury, where Hester Salusbury, later Mrs. Thrale, had enjoyed living a hundred years before. The formidable, will-brandishing, invalid Lady Salusbury (1793–1867) insisted that George Hughes' family should always live with her, either at Offley, or when wintering at Pau in France, for the rest of her life. George, an easy-going, clever, charming, kindly man, with natural gifts for music and every sport he tried, did not have an independent career, therefore, but merely accompanied his wife in her duties as companion to Lady Salusbury. He came to suffer from an acute sense of inferiority to his younger brother Tom and depression at his own lack of achievement.

5 Thomas Hughes, *Memoir of a Brother* (London: Macmillan and Co. 1873), p. 21.

6 Mack and Armytage, *Thomas Hughes*, p. 88.

7 Isabel Quigly, *The Heirs of Tom Brown: The English School Story* (Oxford: Oxford University Press, 1984), ch. 3, 'The school story as moral tale', pp. 59–62.

8 *Tom Brown's Schooldays*. Part Two, ch. 8.

9 Milne Collier Papers – the original was sold at Sothebys in December 2000.

10 How, *Noble Women*, p. 62.

11 Cf. Dickens' *Dombey and Son* and Philip Collins, *Dickens and Education* (London: Macmillan and Co.1965), ch. 7.

12 For Dr. James Manley Gully, M.D. (1808–1883), see *Oxford DNB*.

13 Simpson, *Many Memories*, p. 100.

Chapter Five: Life at Elm House, 1861–1864 – 'Come to us!'

1 Anny Thackeray Ritchie's essay on Jeanie Senior, 'In My Lady's Chamber', *Cornhill Magazine* June 1907, republished in *Blackstick Papers*, 1908 and in *From the Porch* (London: Smith, Elder, 1913), pp. 261–2.

2 Cf. '[The] preoccupation of countless Victorian employers was to get servants to recognize that their inferior status (or 'humble station in life') was the "clear will of God as laid down in both Testaments"' – Pamela Horn, *The Rise and Fall of the Victorian Servant* (New York: St. Martin's Press), 1975, ch. 1, p. 13.

3 Cf: 'The masses of which Mill spoke and which play an important part in *Hard Times* disappear in [Mrs.Gaskell's] novels'. John Lucas, 'Mrs. Gaskell and Brotherhood' in D. Howard, J. Lucas, and J. Goode, *Tradition and tolerance in nineteenth-century fiction* (London: Routledge and Kegan Paul, 1966).

4 See CHAPTER ONE above, p. 000.

5 A Funeral Sermon was preached for Harry Hughes at Trinity Hall, Cambridge by Leslie Stephen, then still in Holy Orders and its substance was published thirty years later in Stephen's *Forgotten Benefactors*. See Frederic Maitland, *Life and Letters of Leslie Stephen* (London: Duckworth, 1906), pp. 70–71. Stephen always maintained that 'Harry Hughes, who was one of my dearest friends, and who had much of her [i.e. Jeanie Senior's] singular sweetness and simplicity of character . . . did me more good than ever I did to him' (Leslie Stephen's unpublished condolence letter to Walter, 25 March 1877).

6 Annie Thackeray Ritchie, 'In My Lady's Chamber', see note 1 above, p. 262.

7 Quoted in Mack and Armytage, *Thomas Hughes*, p. 135.

8 *Ibid.*, p. 137.

9 Sarah Forbes Hughes, ed., *John Murray Forbes, Letters and Recollections* (Boston: Houghton and Mifflin, 1900), vol. 2, ch .14.

10 Dorothea Hughes, *Memoir* quoting her mother Sarah Forbes Hughes, p. 165.

11 Sarah Forbes Hughes, *John Murray Forbes*, vol. 2, p. 38.

12 *Ibid.*

13 Wilfrid Blunt, *England's Michelangelo*, ch. 10, p. 105.

Chapter Six: Father and Son

1 "My father-in-law when he died left the £300 a year which he had allowed us, to his daughter, and nothing at all to Nassau" (J.E.S. letter to J. M. Forbes, 1 February 1872).

2 Levy, *Nassau W. Senior*, p. 192.

3 Public opinion now backed the great engineer Bazalgette, who was constructing an effective underground sewerage system for London, for it had been established by Dr. John Snow and others that cholera was not airborne but contracted from polluted drinking water. See Stephen Halliday, *The Great Stink of London: Sir Joseph Bazalgette and the Cleansing of the Victorian Capital* (Stroud: Sutton Publishing, 1999), pp. 50, 124–5, 129–32, 140–1.

4 St Leonards – Edward Burtenshaw Sugden, Baron St Leonards (1781–1875), Tory legal expert and MP.

5 Lord Cranworth – Robert Monsey Rolfe, Baron Cranworth (1790–1868), Lord Chancellor in 1865.

6 Sir Alexander Duff Gordon, husband of Lucie Duff Gordon (1821–1869), traveller and translator; they and Lucie's mother, Sarah Austin, were old friends of J.E.S.

7 Shaftesbury – Anthony Ashley Cooper, seventh Earl of Shaftesbury (1801–1885), philanthropic reformer.

8 Pye Henry Chavasse, FRCS, 'Advice to a Mother on the Management of her Children and on the treatment on the moment of some their more pressing illnesses and accidents', 8th ed. 1866 (p. 151). This work, in its 19th edition by the end of the century, is the most vivid contemporary account of the perils of childhood illness in Victorian times and of the doubtful remedies desperately applied.

9 For Southwood Smith see *DNB*.

10 For Octavia Hill see biographical studies by E. Moberly Bell (1942), Gillian Darley (1990) and Nancy Boyd, *Josephine Butler, Octavia Hill and Florence Nightingale: three Victorian women who changed their World* (London: Macmillan 1982).

11 Eleanor Southwood Ouvry, ed. *Extracts from Octavia Hill's 'Letters to Fellow-Workers' 1864–1911* (London: Adelphi Bookshop, 1933), pp. 2–3.

12 Sir William Erle (1793–1880) judge, member of the Trades' Union Commission, 1867.

13 James Booth (1796–1880) barrister, legal writer, secretary to the Board of Trade.

14 Herman Merivale (1806–1874), civil servant, see *DNB*.

15 Sir Edmund Walker Head, Bart. (1805–1868), former Governor-general of Canada.

16 Henry Cole (1808–1882), official who had master-minded London's Great Exhibition in the Crystal Palace; British commissioner at the Paris Exhibition 1867, co-founder of Natural History Museum. See *Oxford DNB*.

17 Chaplain to Queen Victoria and husband of Jeanie's friend Jane Brookfield, Thackeray's former inamorata.

18 Malcolm Shifrin, <http//www.victorianturkishbath.org>, (*Victorian Turkish Bath*), 2007, quoting Dr. Garlike in *The Lancet* and an editorial in the *British Medical Journal*, 1864.

19 See *Echoes from the Clubs: A [weekly] Record of Political Topics and Social Amenities*, vol. 1, May–October, 1867.

20 Howard Staunton, *The Great Schools of England* (London: Strahan and Co., 1869), pp. 321, 325– 66. See also Jonathan Gathorne-Hardy, *The Public School Phenomenon* (London: Penguin Books, 1979), part 4: 'Curriculum, Work, Exams'.

21 Ian D.Suttie, *The Origins of Love and Hate* (London: Kegan Paul, Trench, Trubner and Co., 1935), ch. 5: 'The function and expression of love' and ch. 6: 'The taboo on tenderness'.

22 'Notes on the English Character', 1920, in *Abinger Harvest* (London: Edward Arnold, 1936). And see Rupert Wilkinson, *The Prefects: British leadership and the public school tradition* (Oxford: Oxford University Press, 1964), pp. 116–17, and John Tosh, *Manliness and Masculinities in Nineteenth-Century Britain: Essays on Gender, Family and Empire* (London: Longman, 2005).

23 Michael Mason, *The Making of Victorian Sexuality* (Oxford: Oxford University Press, 1994), chapter on 'Carnal Knowledge'.

Chapter Seven: Politics and Society in the Late 1860s

1 Captain Ford quoted by Bernard Semmel, *The Governor Eyre Controversy* (London: MacGibbon and Kee, 1962), p. 17. And see Catherine Hall, *Civilising Subjects: Metropole and Colony in the English Imagination, 1830–1868* (London: Polity, 2002), p. 23.

2 For Thomas Hughes' support for the Freedman's Aid movement, see Christine Bolt, The *Anti-slavery Movement and Reconstruction: A study in Anglo-American co-operation*, Oxford: published for the Insititute of Race Relations, Oxford University Press, 1969.

3 Hall, *Civilising Subjects*, p. 24.

4 See Hansard for Thomas Hughes' speeches in 1866, 1867 and 1872.

5 Semmel, *Governor Eyre*, p. 125. And see G. Dutton, *The Hero as Murderer: the life of Edward John Eyre* (London: Collins, 1967), chs. 19 and 20.

6 Hastings Hughes had recently bought *The South London Chronicle*, a penny weekly partly financed by local advertising, despite his sister's misgivings, in order to support his brother Tom's attempt to defeat the Tories at the polls in Lambeth. (Tom was narrowly elected.) The only microfilm copy of the *South London Chronicle* available to readers now is held at Southwark Library's Local Studies Collection, 211 Borough High St.

7 Hall, *Civilising Subjects*, p. 25.

8 Henry James (1828–1911), QC, lawyer and statesman; Liberal MP for Taunton 1869–1885. See *DNB*.

9 Semmel, *Governor Eyre*, p. 103.

10 Mack and Armytage, *Thomas Hughes*, pp. 150, 158–161. Hughes' greatest contribution to
working men's rights was his advocacy of the legalisation of trade unions.

11 See J.E.S.' letters 13 June 1867, 5 July 1867, 18 November 1868, 5 December 1869, and
February and April 1873, Milne Collier Papers, for her supportive response to Tom's
attempts to practise his social idealism.

12 Hazlitt, *Life of Napoleon*, 1830, ch. xv.

13 Pat Thane, *Old Age in English History, Past Experiences, Present Issues* (Oxford: Oxford
University Press, 2000), ch. 9, 'The New Poor Law and the Aged Poor'.

14 Thane, *Old Age*, p. 171.

15 Entry on Louisa Twining (1820–1912) in Helen Rappaport, *Encyclopaedia of Women
Social Reformers* (Santa Barbara, California: ABC-CLIO, 2001).

16 *Life of Frances Power Cobbe by Herself* (Boston and New York: Houghton, Mifflin and
Co., 1894), vol. 1, ch. xi, pp. 278–9 and 281. 'That which will really brighten their dreary
lives is, *to be made to talk themselves* . . . Ask about their fathers and mothers, brothers and
sisters, everything connected with their early lives.'

17 Republished in *Essays on the Pursuits of Women* (London: Emily Faithfull, 1863).

18 Hugh Pyper, *Mary Hughes* (London: Quaker Home Service, 1985), pp. 9–10. 19. 'By 1867
the old and infirm formed the largest single group, of the 28,000 occupants of forty London
Workhouses . . . [Women] . . . usually formed a majority . . . [in] the old people's wards and
many came from respectable backgrounds' (Norman Longmate, *The Workhouse* [London:
Temple Smith, 1974], chapters 11 and 12).

19 Jo Manton, *Mary Carpenter and the Children of the Streets*, pp. 172–3.

20 Gillian Darley, *Octavia Hill*, chapter 6. And see illustrated evidence in Octavia Hill
Birthplace Museum, Wisbech, Cambridgeshire.

21 Darley, *Octavia Hill*. And see Octavia Hill's article 'Cottage Property in London' in
Fortnightly Review, November, 1866, later reprinted in Octavia Hill, Homes of the London
Poor, 1875.

22 Moberley Bell, *Octavia Hill*, chapter 7, 'The Tenants'. And see Katherine A. Kendall, *Social
Work Education: Its Origins in Europe* (Alexandria, VA: Council of Social Work Education,
2000), p. 4.

23 Kendall, *Social Work*, p. 8 quoting *Extracts from Octavia Hill's Letters to Fellow-Workers,
1864–1911* (London: Adelphi Bookshop, 1933).

24 *Ibid.*, p. 9 for the list of Octavia Hill's principles for her social workers to follow in their
relations with tenants.

25 Cf. *Inside Housing*, 30 March 2001: 'Jane Nassau Senior [sic] . . . was a forerunner of
today's housing finance professional . . . she kept the accounts for social housing pioneer
Octavia Hill.' And see Stephen P. Walker, 'Philanthropic Women and Accountancy: Octavia
Hill and the exercise of quiet power and sympathy', <http://www.centres.ex.ac.uk/cbh/
hillsw.pdf>.

26 Kendall, *Social Work*, p. 4.

27 Darley, *Octavia Hill*, Preface.

Chapter Eight: Interlude: Music and Friendships

1 See John Reed, 'Schubert's reception history in nineteenth-century England' in Christopher
Gibbs, ed., *Cambridge Companion to Schubert* (Cambridge University Press, 1997), and J.
A. Fuller-Maitland, *English Music in the 19th Century* (New York: E.P. Dutton, 1902), ch.
7.

2 Fuller-Maitland, *English Music*, Book ii, 'The Renaissance (1851–1900)'.

3 George Grove, the Secretary of the Crystal Palace, was in sympathy with Christian Socialism
and dedicated to making high culture available to all classes of society, so it is not surpris-
ing that Tom Hughes should have been appointed to the Crystal Palace Board of Directors.
See Percy M. Young, *George Grove, 1820–1900, A Biography* (Houndmills, Basingstoke:

Macmillan, 1980), pp. 78 and 67. For the 'Monday Pop' chamber concerts, see Percy A. Scholes, *The Mirror of Music 1844–1944* (Oxford: Oxford University Press, 1947), p. 207.

4 For Clara Schumann see Eugenie Schumann, *Memoirs* (London: Heinemann, 1927), pp. 195–6, and Joan Chissell, *Clara Schumann: A Dedicated Spirit – A study of her Life and Work* (London: Hamish Hamilton, 1983). For Joachim see Anny Thackeray Ritchie, *Blackstick Papers* (London: Smith, Elder and Co, 1908), 'Concerning Joseph Joachim', and Andreas Moser, *Joseph Joachim, A Biography 1831–1899* (London: Philip Wellby, 1901).

5 Born Elisabeth Lehmann, sister of Frederick and Rudolf Lehmann and wife of the art collector and iron and steel magnate, Ernst Benzon.

6 Probably Mr. and Mrs. Rudolf Lehmann – he was a fashionable portrait painter and she was born Amelia Chambers, a gifted musician and singer and mother of the singer and song composer Liza Lehmann (1862–1918). Jeanie much preferred Mrs. Rudolf Lehmann to her elder sister Mrs. Frederick Lehmann.

7 Julius Benedict (1804–1885) German composer and conductor of opera and oratorios; composer of *Lilly of Killarney*, 1860.

8 Oratorio composed by Benedict for which Jeanie premiered the contralto role.

9 The judge Sir James William Colvile (1810–1880) member of the judicial committee of the Privy Council (see *DNB*).

10 Anna Maria Hall (Mrs. S. C. Hall), 'From the "Kensington News"', 28 March 1877, in S. C. Hall, *Retrospect of a Long Life, 1815–1883* (London: Bentley and Sons, 1884).

11 Janet Ross, *The Fourth Generation* (London: Constable and Co. 1912), p. 54.

12 'Vado ben spesso' – long thought to have been composed by Salvator Rosa, now attributed, without certainty to the 17th century composer Bononcini.

13 Anny Thackeray Ritchie, 'In my lady's chamber', in *From the Porch*, 1913.

14 See *The Hermann Klein Phono-Vocal method based upon the School of Manuel Garcia – the volume for the Contralto Voice*, written by a pupil of the elderly Garcia, published in 1909 and John Potter's review of Garcia's *Traite* 1841, in *Music and Letters*, 84, 2 May 2003, pp. 294–7.

15 Ritchie, 'In my lady's chamber'.

16 Simpson, *Many Memories*, pp. 95–6.

17 See Blainey, *Fanny and Adelaide*, ch. 6, for the aristocratic Thuns' prejudiced unwillingness to have an opera star in the family and ch. 11 for Adelaide Kemble's ceasing to perform publicly in opera on her marriage.

18 Adelaide Sartoris: '*Molly's Abschied* was sung to perfection by my dear Golden-hair', letter to Georgiana Bloomfield, wife of the British Ambassador in Vienna, 2 April 1867. I am grateful to Ann Blainey for showing me this letter.

19 German romantic writer Wilhelm Hoffmann (1776–1822).

20 Emanuel Oscar Menahem Deutsch (1829–1873), Hebraic scholar, Assistant Librarian in the British Museum, friend of George Eliot (original of Mordechai in *Daniel Deronda*). See *Oxford DNB*.

21 See M. Jeanne Peterson, 'The Victorian Governess: Status Incongruence in Family and Society', in Martha Vicinus, ed., *Suffer and Be Still, Women in the Victorian Age* (Bloomington: Indiana University Press, 1972).

22 Quoted in Dorothea Hughes, *Memoir*, p. 95.

23 Sarah Mytton Maury, *An Englishwoman in America* (1848), p. 7, cited in Jane Robinson, *Pandora's Daughters, The Secret History of Enterprising Women* (London: Constable and Robinson, 2002), pp. xiv–xv.

24 Candida Ann Lacey, ed., *Barbara Leigh Smith Bodichon and the Langham Place Group* (New York and London: Routledge and Kegan Paul, 1987). The essay 'Women and Work' 'was greeted with a howl of ridicule', notably in *The Saturday Review* – see Hester Burton, *Barbara Bodichon* (London: John Murray, 1949), pp. 100–1.

25 Milne Collier Papers.

26 1 February 1872, quoted in Dorothea Hughes, *Memoir*, p. 93.

27 *Ibid*.

28 *Consuelo* (1842), allegedly inspired by the singer Pauline Viardot-Garcia (1821–1910), the sister of Garcia, and a legendary mezzo-soprano, talented pianist and composer of songs. *Consuelo*, it has also been suggested, however, might have been inspired by Adelaide Sartoris, née Kemble (see Blainey, *Fanny and Adelaide*).

29 *Armgart*, verse drama written in 1870 during a break in the composition of *Middlemarch* and also perhaps partly inspired by Pauline Viardot-Garcia. The fictional heroine Armgart was famous for her Gluck's *Orpheus*, whose arias Jeanie sang to George Eliot. Armgart becomes, like Jeanie, a professional voice teacher.

30 Rebecca A. Pope, 'The diva doesn't die: George Eliot's *Armgart*' in Leslie C. Dunn and Nancy M. Jones, eds., *Embodied Voices – representing female vocality in western culture*, Cambridge: Cambridge University Press, 1994).

31 *Ibid*.

32 The opening words of Schubert's 'To Music' – 'Thou blessed art, in how many grey hours when life's fierce blows were encircling me, have you . . . transported me to a better world.'

33 William Rathbone Greg, 1809–1881, former mill-owner, essayist, Comptroller of the Stationery Office, 1864–1877. See *Oxford DNB* for his private life.

34 Sir Edward Strachey, third Baronet, 1812–1901. See *DNB*. His second son, St. Loe Strachey, would marry Nassau's niece, i.e. Minnie's only child Aimée.

35 Tom Taylor was barrister, civil servant, art critic and a Professor of English Language and Literature at University College, London as well as the writer or co-writer of eighty plays and, eventually, the editor of *Punch*. See Winton Tolles, *Tom Taylor and the Victorian Drama* (New York: Columbia University Press, 1940).

36 Sir Arthur Mitchell 1826–1909, reformist Scottish commissioner in lunacy 1870–95 and Scottish antiquary. See *DNB* and *Oxford DNB*.

37 See Ann Blainey, *Fanny and Adelaide*, ch. 11.

38 Anny Thackeray Ritchie, 'Mrs. Kemble and Mrs. Sartoris, in *Chapters from some Memoirs* (London: Macmillan, 1894).

39 Blainey, *Fanny and Adelaide*, p. 279.

40 See Anny Thackeray Ritchie, Preface to a Preface, Adelaide Sartoris' *A Week in a French Country House* (London: Smith Elder, 1902), p. xiii.

41 Henrietta Garnett, *Anny*, p. 65 and *passim*. And see Leslie Stephen *The Mausoleum Book*, ed. Alan Bell (Oxford: Clarendon Press, 1977), pp. 12–13.

42 Hester Ritchie, *Letters of Anne Thackeray Ritchie* (London: John Murray, 1924), pp. 125–6.

43 Milne Collier Papers.

44 The complete letter is now held in the National Museum of Photography, Bradford, UK.

45 See John Lehmann, *Ancestors and Friends* (London: Eyre and Spottiswoode, 1962), pp. 210–211. And see Fred Kaplan, *Dickens, a biography* (London: Hodder and Stoughton, 1988), pp. 428, 498–500 and Lucinda Hawksley, *Katey: The lives and loves of Dickens's artistic daughter* (New York: Doubleday, 2006).

46 Kate Collins would become a professional painter during her second marriage, to the artist Perugini.

47 W. Graham Robertson, *Time Was*, p. 95, quoted in Colin Ford, *Julia Margaret Cameron, 19th Century Photographer of Genius* (London: National Portrait Gallery, 2003), p. 55.

48 For Marie Spartali see Teresa Newman and Ray Watkinson, *Ford Madox Brown and the Pre-Raphaelite Circle* (London: Chatto and Windus, 1991), pp. 148–54 and David B. Elliott, *A Pre-Raphaelite Marriage* (London: Antique Collectors' Club, 2006).

49 See Deborah Cherry on Julia Margaret Cameron and Marie Spartali's collaborative 'performance art' in her *Painting Women: Victorian women artists* (London: Routledge, 1993), pp. 197–9 and her *Beyond the Frame: Feminism and Visual Culture, Britain*

1850–1900 (London: Routledge, 2000), pp. 67–9. *The Times'* obituary of 8 March 1927 would refer to Marie Stillman's 'intelligence, charm, sense of humour and spirit'.

50 E. M. Forster, *Marianne Thornton 1797–1887, A Domestic Biography* (London: Edward Arnold, 1956), p. 227.

51 In Noel Annan's exaggerated, patronizing words: 'She was fat, she was ugly, she was excruciatingly dull.' *Leslie Stephen the Godless Victorian* (London: Weidenfeld and Nicolson, 1984), p. 129.

52 'First Steps', 28 April 1866, for which she was paid £3.10.0; she wanted to earn money to pay for projected European travel to see deaconesses' and other nursing training in Paris and Ghent.

53 *Emile*, Book iv, 1760 (London: Dent Everyman), p. 184.

Chapter Nine: George Eliot's Dorothea?

1 George Eliot, *The Mill on the Floss*, Book Five, ch. 4.

2 In 2000 a batch of letters to Jane Senior from George Eliot (with two from George Henry Lewes, and two from George Eliot to Jane Senior's son) were auctioned at Sotheby's. In March 2001 a stay of export in respect of these letters was granted by the Department of Culture, Media and Sport, under the Waverley criteria [which specify historical, national, aesthetic and scholarly value]. Later that year they were bought by the British Library. (Barbara Hardy, 'Art into Life, Life into Art: *Middlemarch* and George Eliot's Letters, with special reference to Jane Senior', in *George Eliot – George Henry Lewes Studies*, nos. 44–45, September 2003, p. 81.) And see B. Hardy, *George Eliot: A critic's biography* (London: Continuum, 2006), pp. 118–30.

3 See Beryl Gray, *George Eliot and Music* (Basingstoke: Macmillan, 1989) and Delia da Sousa Correa, *George Eliot, Music and Victorian Culture* (London: Palgrave Macmillan, 2003).

4 Gordon S. Haight, ed., *The George Eliot Letters* (New Haven: Yale University Press, 1955), iv, p. 422.

5 26 May 1869. Haight, *Letters*, v. 41.

6 Hitherto unpublished letter; mss. in British Library.

7 *Ibid*.

8 *Ibid*.

9 Charlotte Solly Speir Manning, 1803–1871, second wife of the judge James Manning and the first Mistress of Girton College, Cambridge, now just opened temporarily at Hitchin, Hertfordshire.

10 Emily Davies, 1830–1921, 'equality feminist' and educational reformer; successful, pioneering campaigner for university education for women at Girton.

11 Had she been alienated by recent rumours of lesbianism among leading feminists? See note 15.

12 'Woman in France: Madame de Sable', *Westminster Review*, lxii, Oct. 1854, republished in Thomas Pinney, ed., *The Essays of George Eliot* (London: Routledge and Kegan Paul, 1963), p. 81. 'And see George Eliot's 'Margaret Fuller and Mary Wollstonecraft' in *The Leader*, vi (13 October 1855), 988–9, also republished in Pinney: '[We] want freedom and culture for woman, because subjection and ignorance have debased her'.

13 Gillian Beer, *George Eliot* (Brighton: Harvester Press, 1986), p. 87.

14 Haight, *Letters*, iv, 399. George Eliot was writing in support of Emily Davies' and Barbara Bodichon's plans to establish the first women's university college in Britain – Girton, Cambridge.

15 Possibly Bessie Parkes or Barbara Bodichon had told her of the scandalous rumours of lesbianism between Matilda Hays (of *The English Woman's Journal*,) and Lady Monson, or between Charlotte Cushman and Harriet Hosmer in Italy – see Pauline Tear, *Nineteen Langham Place: A rallying-point to help women* (University of Sussex MA Dissertation, 1982).

16 Haight, *Letters*, v, 57–58.

17 Hitherto unpublished letter; mss. in British Library.

18 *Ibid.*

19 Haight, *Letters*, viii, 469.

20 Hitherto unpublished letter; mss. in British Library.

21 *Ibid.*

22 Haight, *Letters*, v, 82–83.

23 Haight, *Letters*, vi, 98. And see Bernard Paris, 'George Eliot's Religion of Humanity' in George Creeger, ed., *George Eliot* (New Jersey: Prentice-Hall, 1970), p. 13, and Barbara Hardy, *George Eliot*, pp. 124–5.

24 Hitherto unpublished letter; mss. in British Library.

25 See Jerome Beaty, *Middlemarch from Notebook to Novel: A Study of George Eliot's Creative Method* (Urbana: University of Illinois Press, 1960); David Caroll, ed., *Middlemarch* (Oxford: Clarendon Press), 1986; Rosemary Ashton, *George Eliot, A Life*, ch. 12, 'Writing Middlemarch 1869–1871' (London: Hamish Hamilton, 1996).

26 *Middlemarch*, ch. 74.

27 Cf. Gillian Beer, *George Eliot* (Brighton: Harvester Press, 1986), ch. 6, '*Middlemarch* and 'The Woman Question'. And Jenny Uglow, *George Eliot* (London: Pantheon and Virago, 1987), ch. 12 'Middlemarch'.

28 See Derek Oldfield, 'The Language of the novel: the character of Dorothea' in *Middlemarch: Critical Approaches to the Novel*, ed. Barbara Hardy (London: Athlone Press) 1967, reprinted in Arnold Kettle, ed., *The Nineteenth Century Novel* (London: Heinemann and Open University Press, 1972), pp. 235 and 239.

29 *Middlemarch*, ch. 72.

30 John Barton, quoted by Melvyn Bragg in *The Adventure of English* (London: Hodder and Stoughton, 2003), ch. 12, 'Shakespeare's English', p. 150.

31 See CHAPTER ONE above.

32 Haight, *Letters*, vi. 46.

33 Letter, March 21st, 1877, in C. E. Maurice, *Life of Octavia Hill in her Letters* (London: Macmillan, 1913), p. 349.

34 Report of the Ninth Co-operative Congress, April 1877, in Mack and Armytage, *Thomas Hughes*, p. 218.

35 Barbara Hardy, *George Eliot*, p. 128.

36 'George Eliot' in *Hours in a Library*, vol. iii (London: Smith, Elder and Co., 1909), p. 217.

37 Haight, *Letters*, v. 372.

38 *George Eliot, A Life* (London: Hamish Hamilton, 1996), ch. 13, p. 331.

39 Milne Collier Papers.

40 Haight, *Letters*, ix, 5–6.

41 *Ibid.*

42 Jeanie Senior's last recorded comment on *Middlemarch* was in the winter of 1874–5 after young Sarah Forbes confessed that she 'could not stand *Middlemarch*, . . . [it was so] heavy and dismal. When I openly expressed these views she smiled and said, "Ah but [it is] so true to life, Sarah"' (Dorothea Hughes, *Memoir*, p. 168).

43 Duncan Nimmo, "Mark Pattison, Edward Casaubon, Isaac Casaubon and George Eliot" in *Proceedings of the Leeds Philosophical and Literary Society*, October 1979, vol. xvii, part iv.

44 Mrs. Oliphant, letter, 20 February 1879, in Mrs. Harry Coghill, ed., *The Autobiography and Letters of Mrs. M. O. W. Oliphant* (Edinburgh: William Blackwood and Sons 1899), p. 277.

Chapter Ten: War on Two Fronts

1 Ernst Leopold Schlesinger Benzon, *c.* 1810–1873, wealthy brother-in-law of Friedrich and

Rudolf Lehmann; a munificent, cultured host and music-lover.

2 Walter Senior was one of the first students at Oxford to read for a degree in the new School of Law and Modern History. He would specialize in Jurisprudence, History of English Law, Roman Law and International Law.

3 Albert Vickers (1838–1919) was, at thirty-two, already the astute, autocratic commercial director of the firm. In the early 1870s Vickers specialized in the production of railway castings and shipyard components, only turning to armaments manufacture in 1888. By 1914 Vickers was 'one of the largest private enterprise arsenals in the world'. Clive Trebilcock, *The Vickers Brothers: Armaments and Enterprise 1854–1914* (London: Europa Publications Ltd., 1977), ch. 2.

4 Bernhard Menne, *Krupp or the Lords of Essen* (London: William Hodge and Co. 1937), Part 11, p. 87.

5 See John G. Stoessinger, *Why Nations Go To War* (New York: St. Martin's Press, 1974), part 7, pp. 223 and 227: '[On] the brink of war . . . [each national leader] confidently expects victory after a brief and triumphant campaign . . . Thus on the eve of each war, at least one nation misperceives another's power.'

6 H. A. L.Fisher, *A History of Europe* (London: Edward Arnold, 1936), ch. 19, p. 987.

7 See Michael Howard, *The Franco-Prussian War* (London: Rupert Hart-Davis, 1961), and David Ascoli, *A Day of Battle: Mars-la-Tour 16 August 1870* (London: Harrap, 1987).

8 For Robert James Lindsay (after 1858 Loyd-Lindsay), Baron Wantage (1832–1901), see *DNB*.

9 Caroline Moorehead, *Dunant's Dream: War, Switzerland and the History of the Red Cross* (London: HarperCollins, 1998), ch. 2, p. 45.

10 *The Illustrated Times*, 13 August 1870, p. 98.

11 Quoted in Ray Strachey, *The Cause*, Appendix, p. 396 and p. 407; first published 1928; republished (London: Virago, 1978).

12 The first 'Notes on the National Society for Aid to Sick and Wounded in war' – Wantage Papers, British Red Cross Archives, Grosvenor Crescent, London.

13 *Ibid.*

14 *Ibid.*

15 Mrs. Loyd-Lindsay to her mother in S. Chomet, *Helena – A Princess reclaimed* (London: Begell House Inc., 1999), p. 94.

16 Lt. Col. Loyd-Lindsay's final report July 25, 1871, Wantage Papers, British Red Cross Archives.

17 2 August 1870, in Cecil Woodham-Smith, *Florence Nightingale* (London: Penguin Books, 1955), p. 377.

18 Milne Collier Papers. Princess Christian's most important function as Patron was fundraising among the élite. See Chomet, *Helena*, p. 96. It is clear from Jeanie Senior's correspondence that it was she, not the Princess, who most regularly presided over the Ladies' Committee (*pace* Moorehead, *Dunant's Dream*, p. 70).

19 For Pauline Viardot see April Fitzlyon, *The Price of Genius: the life of Pauline Viardot* (1964) and Angus Calder, *Gods, Mongrels and Demons: 101 Brief but Essential Lives* (London: Bloomsbury, 2003), pp. 370–373.

20 Howard, *Franco-Prussian War*, pp. 379–80.

21 Florence Nightingale Papers, MS 9004, Wellcome Library for the History and Understanding of Medicine.

22 *Ibid.*

23 Milne Collier Papers.

24 *Ibid.*

25 Ascoli, *A Day of Battle*, p. 60, and see Gerhard Ritter, *Staatskunst und Kriegshandwerk; das Problem des Militarismus in Deutschland* (Munich: 1954), vol. 1, quoted in Howard, *Franco-Prussian War*, p. 456. Cf. George Sand, September 1870: 'We shall have to pity the

German nation for its victories because this is the dawn of its degeneration', *George Sand–Gustave Flaubert Letters* (London: Duckworth, 1922).

26 See Alastair Horne, *The Fall of Paris: The Siege and the Commune 1870–71* (London: Macmillan, 1965; Pan books 2002).

27 Horne, *Fall of Paris*, p. 291.

28 Florence Nightingale had recently sent Jeanie £20 from a poor Negro congregation in the island of Barbados in the West Indies to be forwarded to Nina Inglefield because 'There is nobody like her for spending with real efficient judgment on the sufferer' (Florence Nightingale Papers, MS 9005, Wellcome Library for the History and Understanding of Medicine).

29 'The moment that practical action, by practical English men and women is subordinated to *any foreign bureaucratic elements*, that moment its efficiency will cease.

The Johannites [i.e. Johannes Deaconnesses in Germany] are essentially an aristocratic or princely *Bureau*. But I do not speak of them alone. *All* Prussian authority is a Bureau.

English people can have no idea (who have not lived in Prussian Institutions) what this *means* in every detail of life. What it means to be without the free Parliamentary element where every body, especially every Public Office may be called to give account . . . what it means to be without the free Public press or Public opinion element which would make any thing like the *normal* treatment of Prussian wounded perfectly impossible among us . . .

There is a strong bureaucratic element in the French too of course yes, even or principally (do not think me censorious) among the *Soeurs de Charité* . . . 5 April 1871.' (Milne Collier Papers)

30 See M. C. Simpson, ed., *Conversations of Nassau William Senior with Thiers*, etc. (London: Hurst and Blackett, 1878).

31 'The Communards certainly were socialists – even many of the Jacobins among them – in that vague and yet not unimportant sense in which most people who say they are socialists are so.' John Plamenatz, *The Revolutionary Movement in France 1815–1871* (London: Longmans Green, 1952), p. 157.

32 Louis-Nathaniel Rossel, 1844–1871, 'a student at the *Ecole Polytechnique* who became Minister of War under the Commune and who was without doubt one of the strangest and most attractive figures of the revolution'. Edith Thomas, *The Women Incendiaries* (London: Secker and Warburg, 1969), p. 119.

Chapter Eleven: The First Woman Civil Servant

1 Aria from Handel's opera *Theodora*.

2 Henrietta Barnett, *Life of Canon Barnett* (London: John Murray, 1918), vol. 1, 'Letters, 1872', pp. 42–3.

3 See *The History of Offley Place* [Hertfordshire] by H. L. Hughes, wife of George's eldest son Herbert, privately printed, 1916, and biographies of Hester Thrale, née Salusbury, who had spent much of her youth there. For George Hughes see CHAPTER 4, note 4, above.

4 July 1, 1872. Haight, *Letters*, v, 285–6.

5 Milne Collier Papers.

6 *The Times*' report was a reprinting of what had originally been published in the *Clapham Observer and Tooting and Balham Times*.

7 Florence Davenport Hill (*c.* 1829–1919), one of the three daughters of the radical champion of women's rights, Matthew Davenport Hill, former Recorder of Birmingham. She was a leading woman suffragist in Bristol. See Elizabeth Crawford, *Biographical Dictionary of British Woman Suffrage Movement, 1866–1928* (London: Routledge, 1987).

8 Col. Grant, JP, was on the Bath Board of Guardians and a friend of Matthew Davenport Hill.

9 C. E. Maurice, *Life of Octavia Hill in Letters*, p. 250.

10 Sir Charles Trevelyan (1807–1886). See *DNB*.

11 See CHAPTER 8 above.

12 C. E. Maurice, *Octavia Hill*, p. 278.

13 William Henry Ashurst, 1792–1855, founder of Friends of Italy, 1851 and the People's International League, 1852. For both Ashurst and his daughters see *Oxford DNB*.

14 See J. L. Hammond and Barbara Hammond, *James Stansfeld – A Victorian Champion of Sex Equality* (London: Longmans Green, 1932), pp. 54–75.

15 Quoted in Hammond, *James Stansfeld*, p. 41.

16 *Ibid.*, pp. 115–17.

17 *Ibid.*, p. 112, quoting Stansfeld in *Review of Reviews*, 15 January 1895.

Chapter Twelve: The Government Inspector Goes on a Girl Hunt

Unless otherwise stated, all letters to and from J.E.S. are held in the Milne Collier Papers.

1 W. T. Stead, 'Character Sketch' [of Stansfeld] in *The Review of Reviews*, vol. xi, 15 June, 1895.

2 Harriet Martineau (1802–1876), writer, feminist advocate of women's education and employment rights, supporter of the work of Florence Nightingale and Josephine Butler. See Gaby Weiner, 'Harriet Martineau: A Reassessment' in Dale Spender, ed., *Feminist Theorists* (London: Women's Press, 1983).

3 Isabella M. Tod (1836–1896), suffragist and pioneer advocate of girls' and women's education in Northern Ireland. Supporter of Josephine Butler and of Temperance.

4 Kate Amberley (1841?–1872) feminist suffragist daughter of Lord Stanley, daughter-in law of Lord John Russell, mother of Bertrand Russell.

5 Amelia E. Arnold, feminist wife of feminist Radical writer Arthur Arnold, editor of *The Echo*. She campaigned for women's suffrage and married women's property rights. See *Oxford DNB* entry on Sir (Robert) Arthur Arnold, 1833–1902.

6 Ernestine Rose (1810–1892) rebel Jewish daughter of a Polish rabbi, she became a Utopian Owenite socialist who toured the United States, lecturing on women's rights, free thought and the abolition of slavery.

7 Elizabeth Whitehead Malleson (1828–1916) Unitarian progressive teacher, co-founder of College for Working Women (1864) which later became co-educational in 1874 (see CHAPTER 15 below). A suffragist, she also supported Josephine Butler' Repeal campaign.

8 Emilie Ashurst Venturi (1819/20–1883) divorced sister of Stansfeld's wife Catherine; fierce supporter of Josephine Butler and editor of *The Shield*, 1871–1883.

9 Josephine Butler (1828–1906), charismatic leader of the campaign to repeal the Contagious Diseases Acts.

10 Florence Nightingale (1820–1910), founder of the modern nursing profession.

11 Mary Carpenter (1807–1877), educational reformer, champion of street children.

12 Elizabeth Wolstenholme (1833–1918), teacher and radical feminist.

13 Lucy Wilson, feminist educationist and supporter of Josephine Butler.

14 Clementia Taylor (1810–1908), worker for the enfranchisement and emancipation of women, friend of George Eliot and Mill.

15 See Barbara Stephen, *Emily Davies and Girton College* (London: Constable, 1927).

16 Patricia Hollis, *Women in Public: Documents of The Women's Movement 1850–1900* (London: George Allen and Unwin, 1979), p. 102.

17 Caroline Stephen, *The Spectator*, 7 April 1877. The 'committee' consisted of Henrietta Synnot, Miss Thornton, Caroline Stephen, Sara Stephen, Octavia Hill – when possible – and later Menella Smedley, see note 30 below.

18 For Louisa Twining, see CHAPTER 7 above, pp. 000.

19 Louisa Twining, *Recollections of Life and Work* (London: Edward Arnold, 1893), p. 212.

20 Anna Jameson (1794–1860), *Sisters of Charity, 1855, and The Communion of Labour: Social Employments of Women*, 1856. Her 'version of the communion of labour subverted

the Ruskinian idea of complementarity between the public man and the private woman. E. Janes Yeo, ed., *Radical Femininity* (Manchester: Manchester University Press, 1998), p. 129.

21 Gordon Haight, *Letters of George Eliot*, v, 372.

22 The daughter of Clytemnestra and Agamemnon, sacrificed by her father in order to make the winds blow favourably for the Greek fleet.

23 *Pioneer Women of Victoria's Reign* (London: George Newnes, 1897), p. 229.

24 M. C. M. Simpson, *Many Memories*, p. 98.

25 *Appendix G* to Mrs. Senior's Report, 1874, quoted in Menella Smedley, *Boarding-Out and Pauper Schools for Girls* (1875), p. 391. J.E.S. took the opportunity to beg the authorities: 'Could not each child simply have a continuous record filed in one place under her name?' The registers are now held in the London Metropolitan Archives, Northampton Rd., London.

26 In Part ii of her later *Letter Relating to Pauper Schools*, being a *Reply* to the *Observations of Mr. Tufnell*, April 1875, J. E.S. listed every inquirer and agent on her staff:

These ladies were chosen on account of their large experience, gained in constant work among the poor, and for their practical knowledge of all that concerns the education of the lower classes. In cases where, on account of the distance or locality, the ladies themselves could not make enquiries, agents, supplied with forms to be filled up and who were in close communication with Miss Synnot and myself, were employed. The names of the inquirers and agents were as follows:

Miss Synnot	Mr. R. Pym
Miss M.B.Smedley	Miss Preston
Mrs. Synnot	Miss K. Preston.
Miss Thornton	Mrs. Arnold
Mrs. Farrer	Miss Lloyd
Miss H. Wedgwood	Miss Forster
Miss Gassiot	Miss Wilson

Five Agents

Mrs. Pearson (for many years matron of a certified industrial school).

Mrs. Stone (widow of a tradesman; had practical acquaintance with "general servants", and extensive knowledge of the poor).

Miss Stone (daughter of the above).

Mrs. Logan (for 22 years a valued upper servant, had much experience of under servants, and also of the poor).

Miss Grounds (mistress of a certificated school in Battersea, attended by children of the middle class.)

27 Sara Stephen (1816–1895), daughter of Henry John Stephen and cousin of Caroline Stephen; active with F. P. Cobbe and Miss Elliott in Bristol, later donor and co-founder of MABYS, see CHAPTER 15 below.

28 Dr. Frederick Mouat (1816–1897), former *de facto* Principal of Calcutta Medical College, being successively Professor of Chemistry, Medical Jurisprudence and Clinical Medicine in the 1840s. A 'whirlwind of a man' – Mary Bennett, *Who was Dr. Jackson?* (London: BACSA, 2002), p. 21.

29 Arthur, later Sir Arthur Mitchell (1826–1909), Scottish commissioner in lunacy, 1870–1895; see *DNB* – it was his wife who would write to Jeanie 'Dorothea is you!' later that year.

30 Menella Bute Smedley (1820–1877), the poor, unmarried daughter of a clergyman (died 1837); she had to help support her mother and her widowed sister's children as a writer of verse for children and as a novelist. Her novel *Twice Lost*, 1866, is still interesting as a counter version of *Jane Eyre* in which the Rochester figure is now the villain. She was Jeanie Senior's paid mainstay in the 'tracing operation' concerning girls who had left the workhouse schools the year before and soon became Jeanie's devoted admirer and friend, later editing her *Report* and participating in the ensuing controversy – see CHAPTER FIFTEEN.

31 Emma Cons (1838–1912), social housing manager, founder of 'coffee taverns' and the Old Vic; later first woman London County Councillor. See the *DNB* '*Missing Persons*' volume ed. C. S. Nicholls), (Oxford: Oxford University Press, 1993).

32 Maria Rye (1829–1903) feminist organizer of the employment of women; child rescuer; founder of the female Middle Class Emigration Society in 1861 and the Emigration Scheme for Destitute Girls in 1869 – later the Church of England 'Waifs and Strays Society'. She would be investigated and attacked by the Poor Law Inspector, Andrew Doyle, in 1874 and her work temporarily suspended before being reinstated.

33 Caroline Stephen, *The Spectator*, 7 April 1877.

34 Marie Pape-Carpentier (1815–1878), humane, practical, child-centred educationist who pioneered the education of the infant children of the poor and working mothers in France. A progressive, sympathetic to free-thinkers and Fourierists, she was praised by George Sand and Victor Hugo and was the first woman to lecture at the Sorbonne. But in October 1874 she was attacked by clericalists for not giving enough place to religion in her infants' curriculum and dismissed – only to be reinstated some months later. (The attack on her in France would coincide almost exactly with the later attack on J.E.S. in Britain.) See Jean-Noel Luc, *L'Invention du jeune enfant au xix siecle* (Paris: Belin, 1997), pp. 196–200; and C. Cosnier, *Marie Pape-Carpantier* (Paris: L'Harmattan, 1993).

Chapter Thirteen: Mrs. Senior's *Report*

1 *Third Annual Report* [1873–1874] *of the Local Government Board*, No. 22, pp. 311–12. Unless otherwise stated, all subsequent quotations in this chapter are from this *Report*, pp. 311–94, available from The British Library, Boston Spa. (Third Rep., 1873–74 . . . [C.1071] XXV.1 mf 80.199–206).

2 Jacqueline Hughes, *Mrs Nassau Senior, The First Local Government Board Inspector*'. M.Ed. Dissertation, University of Bristol, 1981, p. 25.

3 The *OED* gives the first use of 'mothering' to mean motherly care and supervision in 1868 in the American journal *Scribner's Magazine*; J.E.S.'s was its first usage in Britain.

4 See note 43 on Mme. Pape-Carpentier in CHAPTER 12.

5 Jacqueline Hughes, *Mrs Nassau Senior*, p. 22.

6 See Iona and Peter Opie, *The Lore and Language of Schoolchildren* (Oxford: Oxford University Press, 1959), and *Children's Games in Street and Playground* (Oxford: Oxford University Press, 1969), for how deprived 19th century workhouse children were of their oral culture.

7 'You are afraid to see him spending his early years doing nothing. What! Is it nothing to be happy, nothing to run and jump all day? He will never be so busy again all his life long.' Jean-Jacques Rousseau, *Emile or Education*, first published 1763 (London: Everyman, Dent, 1963), Book Two, p. 71.

8 Contrast Rousseau's 'Let us lay it down as an incontrovertible rule that the first impulses of nature are always right; there is no original sin in the human heart; the how and why of the entrance of every vice can be traced'. *Emile*, Book Two, p. 56 (for which the book was burnt by the Archbishop of Paris) with St. Augustine's ' Hear me, O God! . . . Who can recall to me the sins I committed as a baby? For in your sight no man is free from sin, not even a child who has lived only one day on earth', *Confessions*, Book1, section 7.

9 The Lock Hospitals incarcerated girls and women suspected of prostitution for several months after having been found infected with VD during a compulsory examination under the CD Acts; they would be released only when pronounced 'clean'.

10 *Report*, Appendix K, 'School Gardening'.

11 *The Saturday Review* had attacked Bessie Parkes for her 'indelicacy' in advocating lessons on physiology for girls in *The Englishwoman's Journal* in 1858.

12 See Report no. 21 on Westminster Schools, in Menella Smedley, *Boarding-Out and Pauper Schools . . . a reprint of the principal Reports on pauper education in the Blue Book for 1873–4*, p. 310.

13 See Thompson and Yeo, *The Unknown Mayhew, Selections from The Morning Chronicle 1849–1850* (London: Merlin Press, 1971).

14 See Beatrice Webb, *My Apprenticeship* (London: Longmans Green, 1926).

15 See CHAPTER 15 below for the founding of the Metropolitan Association for Befriending Young Servants [MABYS].

16 Eighty years later, May Hobbs, who eventually unionized London office cleaners, wrote about being reclaimed from foster carers by her 'natural parents' as soon as she left school at 14 and started earning:

'Shortly after I left school, Lil, my real mother, decided she wanted me back. I had to go because, as the law said, she was my natural mother. . . . .

In their home I was treated as an unpaid servant, a real skivvy. . . .

I went next to work at a sweet factory down the Nile. That was a terrible dump but the pay was quite good at £9 a week However . . . I had to hand over all my pay packet to my mother each week, and out of it she allowed me 6d a day. (*Born to Struggle* [London: Quartet Books, 1973], pp. 29–30).

17 *Appendix H*, 'Scheme for Supervision of Girls in Place' pp. 392–3.

18 'Significantly enough, the first government investigation led by a woman – Mrs. Senior's 1874 report on the conditions of workhouse schools for girls – criticized the institutions for training the young girls so poorly that they turned out to be bad servants'. Janet Horowitz Murray, *Strong-Minded Women and other lost voices from nineteenth century England* (London: Penguin, 1984), p. 48.

19 'In a letter to de Tocqueville dated 18 March 1835, [Nassau William] Senior declared 'The Report of the Poor Law Commissioners, or at least 3/4ths of it, was written by me, and all that was not written by me was re-written by me. The greater part of the Act, founded on it was also written by me; and in fact I am responsible for the effects, good or evil . . . ', Levy, *Nassau W. Senior*, pp. 308–9.

20 Dorothea Hughes, *Memoir*, p. 148.

Chapter Fourteen: Reception of the *Report*

The correspondence with J.E.S. quoted in this chapter, if not otherwise stated, is held in the Milne Collier Papers, Volume III, *Education of Pauper Children*.

1 Quoted in Dorothy Hughes, *Memoir*, pp. 149–52.

2 Treasury papers, National Archives, Kew, ref. T1/ 7371/ 1571; these documents were found thanks to the pertinacity of the archivist Ann Morton.

3 See *DNB* for Sir John Lambert.

4 For Sclater-Booth, Stansfeld's successor as President of the Local Government Board, see *DNB*.

5 For this and the subsequent quotation, Haight, *Letters of George Eliot*, vol. vi, pp. 46–7.

6 Letter dated 16 July 1874, Haight, *Letters*, vol. vi, p. 70.

7 For example, Sir Charles Trevelyan, Col. Freemantle, Joanna and Florence Hill, Miss Preusser of Windermere, etc.

8 See letter from William Rathbone, MP, 1 July 1874.

9 See Edwin Pratt, *A Woman's Work for Women: L.M.H* (London: G. Newnes, 1898). Miss Louisa Maria Hubbard, 1838(?)–1906, was an unsung leader of 19th century British feminism who concentrated on widening the sphere of women's employment as teachers, teacher-trainers, deaconesses, social administrators, inter alia her *Englishwoman's Yearbook*, which she financed, set out to convince impoverished gentlewomen of the dignity of paid work.

10 J.E.S.'s letter to Louisa Hubbard, 22 May 1874, is held in the Women's Library, Old Castle St, London.

11 C. E. Maurice, *Life of Octavia Hill*, pp. 307–8.

12 'Little Maids of All Work and Blue Books', *The Cornhill Magazine*, September 1874.

13 10 October 1874, most probably written by Jeanie's friend Tom Taylor, editor of *Punch*.

14 17 November, written by her friend Dr. Mitchell?

15 Joanna Hill was the sister of Florence Davenport Hill and had hosted Jeanie Senior's inspection visit to Birmingham.

16 See Appendix II for full list of titles, authors and dates of articles and notices of the *Report*.

17 Simpson, *Many Memories*, p. 99.

18 The letter continues:

'The post of School mistress would be well suited for a lady, but of course she must be a certificated teacher – . . . Then there is a delightful post in all the larger school, Head workmistress. Her duties are to cut out or superintend the cutting out, of all the wearing apparel, to understand sewing machines, and patching and darning etc. . . . This would give a woman the chance of getting great influence over the girls. For instance in the evening there are generally 2 hours for needle work for the elder girls before going to bed. Think what an opportunity for good, if the work mistress knew and cared how to utilise it! Reading aloud, teaching poetry etc. –

Most ladies would not like it I fancy but *I* should not at all object to being the "training cook" in one of the big schools . . . A woman of ordinary household experience, and a couple of courses at the School of Cookery would be able to fill such a post splendidly . . . *I* would not mind the post. But then I don't care what I do' (Letter held in The Women's Library, Old Castle St., London).

19 'Seventeen favourable letters and three long articles appeared in favour of boarding out [in *The Times*]. Eight letters and two articles were printed in opposition during the months from November 1874–February 1875.' (Jacqueline Hughes, *Mrs. Nassau Senior*, p. 44, note 152.) Jeanie Senior's respected authority on infant education in France, the pioneering Mme. Pape-Carpentier, whom she had recently consulted in Paris, was also under attack at this very same time and relieved of all her official positions 'en plein climat d'Ordre moral' on 12 October 1874. She was accused by a journalist in *L'Univers* of not having given enough emphasis to the religious education of infants. There was an outcry in her defence and she was re-instituted in January 1875; but 'ces gens-la m'ont tuée' was her comment at her attempted denigration by clerical and reactionary social forces. See Jean-Noel Luc, *L'invention du jeune enfant*, p. 197.

20 *The Times*, 28 November 1874. The deputation, which frequently cited Mrs. Senior's Report, was introduced by Lord Delawarr and included Sir Charles Trevelyan, Mr. W. Forsyth, MP, Mr. Francis Peek (member of the London School Board and Chairman of the National Committee for Promoting the Boarding Out of Pauper Children), Colonel Burdett, Colonel Freemantle, Mr. George Moore, the Rev. S.S. Warren, Mr. W. T. Manning (Coroner to the Queen's Household), Miss Louisa Boucherett, Miss M. J. Catlin, Mr. James Henderson (Inspector of Factories), Mr. Tallack (Secretary of the Howard Society) and Mr. Lightly Simpson. Its failure to convert Sclater-Booth was followed by further bitter letters in *The Times*, including two from another of Jeanie Senior's old foes from autumn 1872, the Rev. Sykes, chaplain of the North Surrey District School at Anerley. (For the autocratic power of a workhouse chaplain, 'determined to maintain his influence over what he regarded as his school', see Frank Crompton, *Workhouse Children* (Stroud: Sutton Publishing, 1997), pp. 109–11.)

21 Haight, *Letters*, vol. vi, 90.

22 Letter dated 22 December 1874 in Twining, *Recollections*, pp. 212–13.

23 For Jeanie Senior's resignation letter see Miscellaneous Government Office Correspondence, Local Government Board. National Archives, Kew, ref: MH 19, / 86/78004.

24 National Archives document MH 32/91 (quoted in part in Jane Senior, *Letter relating to Pauper Schools*, March 1875, pp. 21–2). – I am grateful to the archivist Ann Morton for finding these tucked-away documents. It is strange that Jeanie Senior's whole, handwritten

eighty-three page *Report* should also be filed in that same 'Miscellaneous', un-indexed volume.

25 See Hilda Martindale, *Women Servants of the State 1870–1938 – A History of Women in the Civil Service* (London: George Allen and Unwin, 1938), chapter six, 'The Marriage Bar'.

26 Extract from *Cassandra*, reprinted in Ray Strachey, *The Cause* (London: Virago, 1978, p. 416). This and the following letter from Florence Nightingale were sold at Sotheby's, London, in December 2000; copies in Milne Collier Papers.

27 See CHAPTER 5.

28 Dorothea Hughes, *Memoir*, pp. 166 and 169.

29 *Ibid.*, p. 167.

30 *Ibid.*, pp. 168–9.

Chapter Fifteen: Birth of a New Woman, 1875–1876

All letters to J.E.S. quoted here are held in the Milne Collier Papers.

1 For Menella Smedley see CHAPTER 12, note 30.

2 Milne Collier Papers, vol. 3, 'Education of Pauper Children', p. 132.

3 Hitherto unpublished letter; mss. in British Library.

4 See J. L. and Barbara Hammond, *Stansfeld*, ch. 14 and Glen Petrie, *A Singular Iniquity* (London: Macmillan, 1971), pp. 146–9, for the savage attacks on Stansfeld in the *Pall Mall Gazette*, *The Saturday Review* and *The Times* for joining in 'an hysterical crusade' in October 1874.

5 Jane Senior, '*Reply*' – *Letter Relating to Pauper Schools*, March 1875 p. 18.

6 See J.E.S's letter to the Clerk of the Thame Poor Law Guardians in her '*Reply*' to '*Observations*', p. 10.

7 See CHAPTER 12, note 26 for the annotated list of assistants, published in her '*Reply*' to Tuffnell.

8 Her '*Reply*' is obtainable from The British Library Document Supply Centre, Boston Spa.

9 For Lina Becker see *Oxford DNB* and Crawford, *Women's Suffrage Movement*.

10 For Kate Amberley see *Oxford DNB*.

11 Elizabeth Malleson, 1828–1916, feminist educationist, suffragist, anti-CD laws activist and later co-founder of the Rural Nursing Association to provide qualified midwives for poor country women. See Crawford, *Women's Suffrage Movement*. Tom Hughes was also a supporter of the Working Women's College .

12 'It was that episode, the shame I felt as a man and an Englishman that first turned my thoughts to the position created in England for our mothers, sisters and wives that made me resolve that all schemes of education, of political reform, should include them as equals'. Hammond, *Stansfeld*, pp. 286–7.

13 Hansard, 7 April, 1875, cols 447–453.

14 Hansard, 7 April, 1875, cols 454, 460 and 462.

15 Contrast J.E.S' earlier letter to Louisa Hubbard in June, 1874, quoted in CHAPTER 14, pp. 12–13 above.

16 Letter, dated 10 April 1875, quoted in *Opinions of Women on Women's Suffrage*, issued by the Central Committee of the National Society for Women's Suffrage, 1879, held in '*Women's Suffrage Publications*', in the Blackburn Collection, Girton College Library, Cambridge. Jeanie Senior's letter is published there second to last, after quotations from Mary Carpenter, Anna Jameson, Harriet Martineau and the mathematician Mary Somerville in Part VI – 'Passages from writings or speeches of eminent women no longer living'.

17 In her pamphlet 'Our Policy: An Address to Women concerning Suffrage, published by the Society in 1874/5, Frances Power Cobbe had earlier declared:
    'Mr. Stansfeld's generous appointment of Mrs. Nassau Senior to report to the Government

on the conditions of pauper girls in London, and that lady's admirable performance of her task, will, I trust, lead ere long to the regular employment by the State of Female Inspectors of workhouses, schools and asylums of all kinds wherein either women or children find refuge. . . .[One] woman who does good work at this . . . steadily and thoroughly, does at the same time more for the cause of woman suffrage than one who clamours for it most vehemently, but does nothing to prove the fitness of her sex for any public function. [Indiana University Electronic Text Resource for their Victorian Women Writers Project]

18 See Garnett, *Anny*, pp. 177–8.

19 For Spencer Wells, 1818–1897, gynaecological surgeon, see *Oxford DNB*. He had pioneered the operation of ovariotomy as a life-saving procedure, but had decided that J.E.S.'s uterine cancer was inoperable. All he could prescribe was rest and more rest.

20 Stansfeld had recently made an unsuccessful attempt in the Commons to get the CD Acts repealed – "Must we make statutory Government provisions to enable [our young soldiers] to be safely vicious?" Hansard, 23 June 1875.

21 Adelaide Sartoris had lost her eldest son Greville in a riding accident, in October 1873. (Algy Sartoris had married the young daughter of the President of the USA, Ulysses Grant, in May 1874.)

22 Leslie Stephen, letter to Walter, 25 March 1877.

23 Original mss. held in Rare Book Manuscript and Special Collections Library, Duke University, USA.

Chapter Sixteen: A Bonny Fighter

1 Mack and Armytage, *Thomas Hughes*, pp. 214–16, and 224–5.

2 In fact Margaret Hughes would transplant herself in her eighties to die in the American wilderness of Rugby, Tennessee, out of loyalty to Tom – see Appendix I.

3 See CHAPTER 7 above, note 6.

4 Letter to Henrietta Synnot, May, 1874; see CHAPTER 14 above, and M. Heath-Stubbs' *Friendship's Highway, History of the G.F.S. 1875–1925* (London: 1926), p. 5.

5 Lady Knightley of Fawsley, mss. diary entry for 1 June 1877, Northants. County Record Office, K2897, quoted in Brian Harrison, 'For Church, Queen and Family: the Girls' Friendly Society 1874–1920', in *Past and Present*, no. 61, p. 113.

6 *Ibid.*, p. 109.

7 *Ibid.*, p. 111.

8 Mrs. Townsend was inclined to obsessiveness concerning the virginity of the members of the GFS. See controversy over the GFS Clause Three in Agnes L. Money, ed., *History of the Girls' Friendly Society*, 1911, p. 19 and Harrison, 'For Church, Queen and Family', p. 118.

9 *The Times*, 20 April 1876. For Lord Abedare see *Oxford New DNB*.

10 Letter to *The Daily News*, 17 April 1876.

11 Letter to *The Times*, 20 April 1876.

12 Letter to *The Times*, 22 April 1876.

13 Some London MABYS girls' homes were still open in the 1930s and the charity only ceased to be registered in 2002.

14 Dorothea Hughes, *Memoir*, p. 172.

15 Hester Fuller, *Letters of Anne Thackeray Ritchie*, p. 172.

16 J.E.S's mss. letter dated 30 June, 1876, is held in the George Eliot Collection, Beinecke Library, Yale.

17 Haight, *Letters*, vol. vi, pp. 269–71.

18 *George Frederick Watts, vol. 1 – The Annals of an Artist's Life* (London: Macmillan, 1912), p. 296.

19 Michael Diamond, *Victorian Sensation* (London: Anthem Press, 2003), p. 179.

20 Diamond, *Victorian Sensation*, p. 179 and *DNB* entry on Gully.

21 Jessie White Mario, the army nurse and dedicated follower of Garibaldi. See *Oxford DNB*.

22 Miranda Hill had founded the Kyrle Society for the Diffusion of Beauty in London's poorest districts. See Moberley Bell, *Octavia Hill*, pp. 150–3.

23 Dorothea Hughes, *Memoir*, p. 174.

24 See Jane Marcus on Caroline Stephen, 'The niece of a nun' in *Virginia Woolf: A Feminist Slant* (University of Nebraska Press, 1984).

25 See *DNB* entry on William Rathbone.

26 Dorothea Hughes, *Memoir*, p. 175.

27 *Ibid.*, p. 177.

28 Caroline Stephen, *Quaker Strongholds* (London: Friends' Book Centre, 1890), chapter 2, 'The Inner Light'.

29 A reference to Charles Rickard's friend's condemnation of J.E.S. for taking up a public role – see CHAPTER 17, below, 'Afterwards', note 3.

30 *Bulletin of the Midwest Victorian Studies Association,* Summer 1999, p. 7.

31 For the Medical Education of Women Bill, see Manton, *Life of Elizabeth Garrett Anderson,* Margaret Todd, *Life of Sophia Jex-Blake,* and Hammond, *Stansfeld,* p. 288: "We all owe more to you than any one" – Elizabeth Garrett Anderson.

32 Octavia Hill loved Edward Bond whose possessive mother had no intention of letting him go – see Moberley Bell and Gillian Darley.

33 Simpson, 'Three Distinguished Ladies' in *Many Memories,* p. 99.

Chapter Seventeen: Afterwards

1 This, and all the other condolence messages quoted above, come from the mss. collection headed in Walter's hand 'Various letters to me March 1877', Milne Collier Papers.

2 Darley, *Octavia Hill,* ch. 12, pp. 187–8.

3 Photocopy held in Watts Gallery, Compton. The following day Watts wrote to his patron Charles Rickards:

> I have lost a friend who could never be replaced even if I had a long life before me, one in whom I had unbounded confidence, never shaken in the course of friendship – very rare during 26 years, Mrs. Nassau Senior, whom I dare say you remember talking about with me, who was called by a friend of yours "That Woman". I think when you read the biography of "That Woman", for it is one that will be written, that very few canonized saints so well deserve glorification. For all that makes human nature admirable, lovable and estimable, she had very few equals indeed, and I am certain no superior; it is not too much to say that children yet unborn will have cause to rue this comparatively early death (Watts Gallery, Compton).

4 Reprinted in Appendix III.

5 J. Hughes, *Mrs. Nassau Senior,* p. 37.

6 Henrietta Barnett, *Life of Canon Barnett,* vol. ii, ch. 48, pp. 291–2.

7 Barnett, *Life,* p. 295; and see her article in *The Nineteenth Century,* January 1897, 'The Verdict on the Barrack Schools'.

8 J. Hughes, *Mrs. Nassau Senior,* pp. 37–9.

9 *Ibid.*, p. 39.

10 Letter to Mrs. Verney, 3 May, 1879, Wellcome Library for the History of Medicine, Nightingale Papers, MS 9007/222. In this letter Florence Nightingale says she will break her iron rule of never joining any Memorial Subscription list and agree to Miss Thornton's entreaty that she publicly sign the Memorandum to Mrs. Nassau Senior.

11 *Review of Reviews,* 15 June 1895, quoted in Hammond, *James Stansfeld,* p. 113.

12 J. Hughes, *Mrs. Nassau Senior,* pp. 48–9.

13 Dr Barnardo, *Something attempted – something done, c.* 1890. The book is a compilation of passages from his notebooks, so it is not certain precisely when he wrote that tribute to Jeanie Senior.

14 See *Oxford DNB* on Brooke Lambert. The MABYS Annual Reports are held in The British Library.

15 Republished in Lady Ritchie, *From the Porch* (London: Smith, Elder, 1913), pp. 244–55. The MABYS was only removed from the Charity Register in October 2003. As late as 1951 and 1967 its governing document read:

Objects: Clear income for benefit of girls who are in need and for whom provision is not made out of public funds (1) who have been; in care of the former County Council of London; or (2) who are or have been in the care of the council of any London borough situate in the Inner London Educational Area.

See <http://www.charity-commission.gov.uk/registeredcharities/showcharity.asp?rem> No. 227555. (I am grateful to Graham Senior-Milne for this reference.) The MABYS still awaits its researcher.

16 <http://www.victorianlondon.org/publications3/newtoilers.htm>.

17 Edith Sellers, 'Women's Work for the Welfare of Girls' in A. Burdett- Coutt's *Women's Mission* [papers for the Royal British Commisssion, Chicago Exhibition, 1893.] (London: Sampson Low, Marston and Co. 1893), pp. 35–8.

Conclusion

1 Dame Kathleen Courtney at the funeral of Maude Royden. See Sybil Oldfield, 'The Political Preacher Maude Royden' in *Women Against the Iron Fist, Alternatives to Militarism* (Oxford, UK and Cambridge, MA: Basil Blackwell, 1989).

2 Ludwig Feuerbach, *The Essence of Christianity*. translated into English by George Eliot in 1854, ch. xviii, 'The Christian heaven and Personal Immortality'.

3 Cf. Colleen McDannell and Bernhard: 'It is the anthropocentric view of heaven that has been the most widely articulated perspective [in the history of Christianity]'. See *Heaven, A History* (New Haven and London: Yale University Press, 2001), pp. xiii–xiv, and plate 47, Blake 'The Meeting of a Family in Heaven', 1808.

4 *Oxford DNB Newsletter*, No. 10. November 2004, p. 6.

5 Jim Ledbetter, quoted in *The Independent on Sunday*, 3 October 2004, p. 7.

6 'Is there a feminine genius?' in *Critical Inquiry, 30* (Spring 2004).

7 See How, *Noble Women of Our Time*, 1901.

8 Although she signed her *Report,* and her letters to *The Times* 'Jane E. Senior', her contemporaries always referred to her as 'Mrs. Nassau Senior'.

9 See Appendix I.

10 For a recent discussion of this perennial argument see the review of Robert Frank's 'What Price the Moral High Ground?' in *The Times Literary Supplement*, 3 December 2004, p. 32: 'The aid worker in Africa feels a sympathy for her charges so acute that she suffers their pain and relieving their distress becomes a way of relieving her own.'

Bibliography and Further Reading

Primary Source Materials

Jeanie Senior's son, Walter Senior, 1850–1933, made it his task to preserve all his mother's papers. Not only her letters to him but also important family letters to her, her school diary and youthful travel journal and all her other unpublished writings. He kept bound folders of letters to her from 'Public Persons', 'People connected with Philanthropy', 'People connected with Literature', 'Musical people', 'Artistic People' and 'Private Persons'. He also kept a huge bound file on her official work for pauper children, including reviews from contemporary newspapers, magazines and important correspondence with scores of her contemporaries, including both allies and opponents. All this mostly manuscript material was preserved and handed down intact through the generations. Where any originals had been sold, copies were made available for my research. The rich visual materials include Victorian family photograph albums, and sketches by Jeanie Senior herself. These primary sources are what are referred to as the 'Milne Collier Papers' and are still in private hands.

For Hughes and Senior family history see: <www.peerage.org>.

Secondary materials

Full bibliographic references to all works referred to are included in the endnotes and do not need duplication.

Select Further Reading

General works

Banks, Olive, 1985, *Biographical Dictionary of British Feminists, Vol. One: 1800–1930*. New York University Press and Brighton.

Bauer, Carol and Ritt, Lawrence, eds. 1979, *Free and Ennobled – Source Readings in the Development of Victorian Feminism*. Oxford: Pergamon Press.

Blain, Clements and Grundy, 1990, *Feminist Companion to Literature in English*. London: Batsford.

Burstyn, Joan, 1980, *Victorian Education and the Ideal of Womanhood*. London: Croom Helm.

Butler, Josephine, ed. *1869: Woman's Work and Woman's Culture*. London: Macmillan.

Ellis, Roger, 1997, *Who's Who in British History: Victorian Britain 1851–1901*. London: Shepheard-Walwyn.

Ewan, Innes, Reynolds, eds. 2006, *Biographical Dictionary of Scottish Women*. Edinburgh University Press.

Europa Biographical Dictionary of British Women, 1983. London: Europa Publications Ltd.

Holcombe, Lee, 1973, *Victorian Ladies at Work. Middle Class Working Women in England and Wales 1850–1914*. Newton Abbot: David and Charles.

Hollis, Patricia, 1986. *Ladies Elect: Women in English Local Government 1865–1914*. Oxford University Press.

Hollis, Patricia, 1979, *Women in Public: The Women's Movement 1850–1900*. London: George Allen and Unwin.

Hoppen, K. Theodore, 1998, *The Mid-Victorian Generation, 1846–1886*. Oxford University Press.

Kane, Penny, 1995, *Victorian Families in Fact and Fiction*. London and Houndmills, Basingstoke: Macmillan.

Leighton, Angela and Reynolds, Margaret, 1995, *Victorian Women Poets*. Oxford: Blackwell.

Levine, Philippa, 1990, *Feminist Lives in Victorian England, Private Roles and Public Commitment*. Oxford: Basil Blackwell.

Levine, Philippa, 1987, *Victorian Feminism, 1850–1900*. London: Hutchinson.

Murray, Janet Horowitz, 1984, *Strong-minded Women and other Lost Voices from Nineteenth century England*. Harmondsworth, Middlesex: Penguin.

Nunn, Pamela Gerrish, 1987, *Victorian Women Artists*. London: Women's Press.

Oldfield, Sybil, 1999: *Collective Biography of Women in Britain 1550–1900: A Select Annotated Bibliography*. London and New York: Mansell.

Prochaska, Frank, 1980. *Women and Philanthropy in Nineteenth Century England*, Oxford: Clarendon Press.

Rappaport, Helen, 2001: *Encyclopaedia of Women Social Reformers*. Santa Barbara: ABC-CLIO.

Rendall, Jane, ed. 1987, *Equal or Different. Women's Politics, 1800–1914*. Oxford: Blackwell.

Spender, Dale, 1983: *Feminist Theorists*. London: Women's Press.

Thane, Pat, *Old Age in English History, past experiences, present issues*. Oxford University Press.

Thane, Pat, ed. 2005, *The Long History of Old Age*. London: Thames and Hudson.

Uglow, Jenny, 1982–2006, *Macmillan Dictionary of Women's Biography*. London and Basingstoke: Macmillan.

Vicinus, Martha, 1985, *Independent Women: Work and Community for Single Women 1850–1920*. London: Virago.

Vicinus, Martha, 1977, *A Widening Sphere: Changing Roles of Victorian Women*. Indiana University Press.

Wohl, Anthony S. ed. 1978, *The Victorian Family, structure and stresses*. London: Croom Helm.

Worzala, Diana Mary Chase, 1982, *The Langham Place Circle: The beginnings of the organized women's movement in England 1854–70*. Unpublished Ph.D. thesis, University of Wisconsin-Madison.

Yeo, Eileen Janes, ed. 1998, *Radical Femininity*. Manchester: Manchester University Press.

Monographs

Crawford, Elizabeth, 2002: *Enterprising Women, The Garretts and their Circle*. London: Francis Boutle Publishers. [For Elizabeth Garrett Anderson]

Debenham, Helen, 'The Cornhill Magazine and the Literary Formation of Anne Thackeray Ritchie', in *Victorian Periodicals Review* 33.1 (Spring 2000), 81–91.

Englander, David, 1998, *Poverty and Poor Law Reform in Britain from Chadwick to Booth, 1834–1914*. London: Longmans.

Forster, Margaret, 1984: *Significant Sisters*. London: Secker and Warburg. [For Josephine Butler]

Higginbotham, Peter, 2007, *The History of the Workhouse in Britain*: www. workhouses.org.uk

Hirsch, Pam, *Barbara Bodichon, Feminist, Artist and Rebel*. London: Chatto and Windus.

Jordan, June, 2001, *Josephine Butler*. London: John Murray.

Kent, Raymond, 1981, *History of British Empirical Sociology*. Aldershot: Gower.

Lesser, Margaret, 1984, *Clarkey, A Portrait in Letters of Mary Clarke Mohl 1793–1883*. Oxford University Press.

Manton, Jo, 1965, *Elizabeth Garrett Anderson, England's first woman physician*. London: Methuen.

Oldfield, Sybil, 1984: *Spinsters of This Parish: the life and times of Mary Sheepshanks and F. M. Mayor*. London: Virago Press.

Thomas, Clara, 1967, *Love and Work Enough. The Life of Anna Jameson*. Toronto and London.

Uglow, Jenny, 1993, *Elizabeth Gaskell – A Habit of Stories*. London: Faber and Faber.

Wagner, Gillian, 1979, *Barnardo*. London: Weidenfeld and Nicolson.

Woodham-Smith, Cecil, 1951, *Florence Nightingale, 1820–1910*. London: Penguin Books.

Index